The Rise of the
Soviet Empire

The Rise of the

SOVIET EMPIRE

A Study of Soviet Foreign Policy

JAN LIBRACH

FREDERICK A. PRAEGER, *Publishers*
New York • Washington

BOOKS THAT MATTER

Published in the United States of America in 1964 by
Frederick A. Praeger, Inc., *Publishers*
111 Fourth Avenue, New York 3, N. Y.

All rights reserved
© 1964 by Frederick A. Praeger, Inc.
Library of Congress Catalog Card Number: 64-16682

This book is No. 146 in the series of
Praeger Publications in Russian History and World Communism

AUTHOR'S NOTE

This study deals primarily with Soviet foreign policy in action. I mean by this that problems of ideology are discussed only as they affect actual Soviet moves and attitudes with regard to other nations or states. For ideology cannot become policy until it finds expression in action. This process can be one either of commission or omission, but it cannot result from a mere proclamation of principles. Swiss neutrality, for example, is both a principle and a policy—it originates political acts (such as the manning of frontiers in case of war between neighboring states, or abstention from membership in the United Nations). The Soviet leaders' profession of faith in the ultimate victory of Communism would be nothing but a boast or an interesting psychological attitude were it not for their ceaseless efforts to bring new nations under Communist rule. "Peaceful coexistence" may or may not be a policy of peace, depending on its implementations.

For nearly five decades, the West has been puzzled about the true nature of Soviet foreign policy, more often than not because Moscow intentionally compounds this confusion. Thus the lines separating temporary expedients from long-range aims, propaganda from policy, have become blurred. The main difficulty to the outside world lies in telling apart reality from appearance, differentiating between what Soviet Russia says from what she actually does. It is hoped that this study will make some contribution to an understanding of this problem.

There are some limitations inherent in a work that is devoted to foreign policy only and has to omit a closer examination of Soviet internal developments. The limitations also result from the wide scope of a subject that touches upon the fate of many nations in the four corners of the world. On the other hand, a broad survey of Soviet action in foreign relations creates a certain perspective and makes it easier to observe the recurring patterns of behavior as well as the persistence of general aims. In the citation of documentary sources, an effort was made to quote from Soviet English-language

v

publications and from other primary documents in English, whenever available; however, Russian, Serbo-Croat, Polish, French, German, and Spanish sources have been cited when necessary.

In the preparation of this book I have been encouraged and assisted by a number of friends and associates. My gratitude goes to all of them—diplomats, writers, experts, and librarians. I wish to mention in particular my late friend Janusz Ilinski, who for years urged me to undertake this work. I am especially indebted to Fira Ilinska for her constant interest in this study, and to Colonel Jan Kowalewski, former Polish military attaché in Moscow, for important information on conditions in Central Asia.

A small part of the material in this study, though mostly rewritten, was published in a chapter I contributed to the *Handbook on Communism*. I wish to thank its editors, Professor J. M. Bochenski, O.P., and Professor Gerhart Niemeyer, as well as the publishers, Frederick A. Praeger, for their kind permission to use it here. Lastly, my gratitude goes to Mrs. Jean Steinberg, whose experience and understanding have been invaluable to me in the organization of the material and the editing of the text.

JAN LIBRACH

April, 1964
New York

CONTENTS

vii

The Rise of the
Soviet Empire

INTRODUCTION

Under no political system has theory been assigned so important a place as under Communism. Nowhere else do doctrinal differences lead to political strife of such magnitude, including open violence. In the name of the correct interpretation of Marxism-Leninism, Trotsky was banished and later assassinated; Zinoviev, Kamenev, and Rykov were tried and executed; Molotov, Kaganovich, Malenkov, and Bulganin were consigned to political oblivion. To the Communist, Marxism is first and foremost a body of scientific theory. Therein lie its dogmatic preeminence and practical value. According to Lenin, "Marx's views . . . in their totality constitute . . . modern scientific Socialism."[1] Stalin stated that "Marxism is the science of the laws of development of nature and society."[2] Mao Tse-tung, insisting on the "universal truth of Marxism-Leninism,"[3] maintains that it was "scientifically formulated"[4] by Marx, Engels, Lenin, and Stalin, and verified in practice. The coupling of the terms Marxism and Leninism owes much to Lenin's decisive role in the Revolution, but also to the exaltation of his ideas by Stalin as "the theory and tactics of the proletarian revolution in general and . . . of the dictatorship of the proletariat in particular."[5] With Lenin's interpretations and additions, the doctrine became the Communists' true guide in revolutionary action, statecraft, and policies. Stalin's heirs continued to proclaim the scientific accuracy of the Marx-Engels-Lenin doctrine. They professed to believe "that history ran on the rails according to an infallible plan."[6] As Premier, Malenkov declared that "the Communist Party and the Soviet Government know where and how to lead the people, because they are guided by the scientific theory of social development—Marxism-Leninism."[7] According to Khrushchev, "Marx, Engels, and Lenin . . . created the theory of scientific Communism."[8] The July, 1961, program of the Soviet Communist Party states that "Marxism-Leninism discovered the objective laws of social development," and that "the Party, taking guidance from

3

the theory of Marx-Engels-Lenin accomplished the tasks scientifically formulated in its programs."[9]

But what sort of science is Marxism-Leninism, if Lenin himself
held that "there can be no 'impartial' social science in a society
based on class struggle"?[10] To the Western mind, the idea of a
partisan science, social or otherwise, is patently absurd. Furthermore, by comparing Lenin's statement to some of the allegations
of the new Party Program, one discovers that during the "transition
from capitalism to Socialism,"[11] or even during the "gradual development of Socialism into Communism," Marxism-Leninism is not
yet a science. The implication is that it will become a science
under Communism, for only then will the class struggle have
ceased. However, it is not our objective to demonstrate the obvious
fact that Marxism, or Marxism-Leninism, is neither a science nor
a scientific method, but to find out why the Communists insist that
it is. Lenin's contradiction shows us the way. The claim that Marxism is a scientific and therefore an unshakable theory springs from
political necessity. The Czars, like other absolute monarchs, invoked
a divine right. In a democracy, the mandate to rule is bestowed in
periodic popular elections. What can replace such a delegation of
rights under a regime that refuses to be voted out of power and,
in fact, dares not to hold free elections? The axiom that Marx had
revealed the absolute truth about the development of human societies well fitted Lenin's political intolerance as well as his understanding that Communist ideas could only be imposed by force and
maintained by a small power group. Whether Lenin really thought,
as some imply, that Communism eventually would be freely accepted by the people is a purely speculative assumption. Even in
exile, at the time of Czarist persecutions, he perverted the majority
rule among Russian Marxists by eliminating those who opposed
him, if only on points of tactics. At the secret congress of Russian
Socialists held in Brussels and London in 1903, Lenin garbled the
preparations and proceedings and claimed a majority of two in
order to assume the name of "Bolsheviks" (from the Russian word
meaning "majority"[12]) for his tiny faction. The pretense was so
flimsy that even then some other criterion seemed necessary to explain who should lead the pre-Revolutionary party, and why. The
necessity became imperative after the Revolution, when the Bolsheviks found themselves in a minority in a freely elected Constituent
Assembly, which was dispersed by force on orders of Lenin on
January 18, 1918. Thus the answer to the tantalizing question of
political legitimacy was found in revolutionary practice: The right-

ful leader, the one who correctly interprets the doctrine revealed by Marx, carried forward by Engels, and developed by Lenin, is the man in power; he leads his party and the country along the only right path, since there can be only one correct interpretation of the revelation, and this correct interpretation is the sole passport to authority outside naked force, the only substitute for the legitimacy of leadership and government. Whoever dares to challenge the Party line in theory or practice must therefore be eliminated as a false prophet who wants to lead the people to destruction.

In principle, the same mechanism functions in the satellite Communist parties, which Moscow wants to dominate. Since Stalin's death, they have undergone many purges to bring their leadership in line with the changes in the Soviet Union. It has not always been possible to impose full Soviet discipline on the parties outside the Communist camp. But within the bloc there have been, in nearly half a century, only two open revolts—the Yugoslav and the Albanian—and only one major dispute—with China. The Yugoslav League of Communists and the Albanian Labor Party could oppose Moscow and survive primarily for geographical reasons; neither country borders on the Soviet Union and both have access to the outside world. The revolts in East Germany (1953) and in Poland and Hungary (1956) belong in an altogether different category, since they did not originate within the Communist hierarchy but were of a popular and national character. Despite these upheavals, the Communist bloc has shown a remarkable stability, which it owes to the same mechanism of power as in the Soviet Union: Each dependent country and its Communist Party can have only one political "boss," and he must follow the only true prophet, the man in control of the CPSU and the Soviet Government. Any other arrangement or situation is temporary and subject to tactical adjustments, to be discarded if and when the Kremlin can impose its will.

With the exception of Yugoslavia such was still the situation in February, 1956, when Khrushchev denounced Stalin and first formulated his interpretation of "peaceful coexistence." But the principle of the undisputed leadership of the Party remained valid both in Russia and in the whole Communist world. It meant that the Soviet CP was the sole leader of the other Communist parties, just as the Soviet Government was the leader of all other Communist governments. Since 1956, however, grave complications have upset this simple construction. While Khrushchev successfully fought off rival claims of individuals or groups within the Soviet Union, out-side its borders Moscow's supreme doctrinal and political authority was challenged in various ways. Soviet Russia crushed the Hungarian insurrection by force of arms. But in order to maintain a Communist government in Poland without a dangerous showdown, a tacit compromise had to be struck with the Polish people, allowing a measure of individual freedom (at least in the beginning) unheard of under Communism. Even before matters came to a head in Hungary and Poland, Palmiro Togliatti, leader of the Italian Communist Party, suggested that Communism could no longer be directed from one center and therefore should become many-centered. The idea of "polycentrism" has never been accepted by the Kremlin, yet it had to be taken into account in the face of the greatest challenge to its leadership—the contest for primacy that developed between Moscow and Peking after 1959. Neither the Soviet Union nor China favored polycentrism, but both had to court the various Communist parties in competing for their backing. Therefore, a "polycentric" situation did in fact prevail while Russians and Chinese jockeyed for position in negotiations that were supposed to bring about a compromise solution. For Moscow the situation was seriously complicated by the growing difficulties of an extended economy. Out of Khrushchev's own concept arose the demand for a better life and pressure for liberalization, which, particularly among intellectuals, seemed at times to challenge the very foundations of the Party's power.

Thus, in the 1960's, the Kremlin was faced with two crucial issues: (1) was it possible to rule the Soviet State without the police methods of the Stalin era; and (2) could a polycentric association of Communist states continue the drive for world domination?

ONE

THEORY
AND PRACTICE

1. COMMUNIST DOCTRINE AND SOVIET FOREIGN POLICY

In applying Communist doctrine to foreign relations, Soviet policy for nearly four decades adhered to the following tenets:

a. The Bolshevik Revolution in Russia will be followed by a world revolution—an ineluctable historical development predicted by Marx and Engels and acted upon by Lenin and his successors.

b. Soviet Russia and the "capitalist" countries cannot exist side by side indefinitely. Although war between them is inevitable, it should and can be delayed until such time when Communist forces will be assured of victory.

It was only after Stalin's death that a considerable shift of emphasis became apparent in the interpretation of these quasi-dogmatic beliefs. Gradually, although intermittently, the Soviet state substituted a more flexible posture, coming under the general definition of "peaceful coexistence," for its aggressive attitude. There was nothing new in that idea—or the slogan itself. Stalin had also used it, and it had formed an important premise of Lenin's tactical approach to international relations. But in the last years of Stalin's life, Soviet peace propaganda abroad seemed to have lost momentum. Moreover, the development of nuclear weapons made a revision of the doctrine and tactics governing foreign policy indispensable.

When Malenkov became Stalin's first formal successor, some Western observers believed that perhaps he would bring about a degree of cooperation with the non-Communist world. The assumption was based on his proclaimed policy of giving more scope to light industry, presumably at the expense of an all-out armaments drive. This would have meant a respite for the hard-pressed population of the Soviet Union, and possibly would have promoted a long-expected atmosphere of good will in foreign policy. But it is doubtful whether Malenkov would have gone beyond the motions of "peaceful coexistence," a policy that came to be associated with Bulganin and Khrushchev. Possibly such a change in attitude had already been contemplated before Stalin's death, perhaps in conjunction with a temporary softening of the industrial policy. But in the Bulganin-Khrushchev period, and later under Khrushchev's individal leadership, Soviet heavy industry continued to work full speed for armaments and ballistic projects impossible to dissociate from an arms race with the West. The new attitude in international relations, so emphatically proclaimed from the Kremlin, was therefore, at best, a policy of "coexistence from strength." Nevertheless, some Soviet foreign-policy ideas, in particular the doctrinal belief that war is inevitable under "monopoly capitalism," have been partly revised. It is important to assess the scope and the practical significance of these changes.

Revolution, according to Marx, is the inevitable consequence of change in the conditions of production, leading to class struggle. This he held to be a continuous process until the ultimate goal—the destruction of capitalism and formation of a classless Communist society—was achieved. Bourgeois society was built on the ruins of feudalism. The bourgeoisie, in turn, by improving the means of production, created the conditions for the expansion of the proletariat. The proletariat, thus increased in numbers, became "the modern working class" and gave birth to political parties striving to overthrow bourgeois society. "The epoch of the bourgeoisie," Marx and Engels wrote in the Manifesto of the Communist Party, "has simplified the class antagonism. Society as a whole is splitting into two great hostile camps . . . bourgeoisie and proletariat."[1] And the Manifesto went on to explain that the Communists represented the common interest of the proletariat. Their aim, the "conquest of political power by the proletariat,"[2] can be achieved "only by the forcible overthrow of the existing social conditions."[3] Owing to the cosmopolitan conditions of production and consumption, and the exploitation of a world market, there could be no geographic or national limits to this revolution. The authors of the Manifesto also thought that national differences were rapidly disappearing, and stated (one of their greatest blunders) that "the working men have no country." It was therefore Marx's firm belief that the revolution had to expand from country to country, and that its victory would not be assured "until the proletariat has conquered state power and the association of proletarians has become preponderant in all the dominant countries of the world."[4]

It was therefore logical that the Bolsheviks' seizure of power in

Russia brought an entirely new element into the relations among nations. Not since the French Revolution had a government openly proclaimed its intention to reject the accepted rules of international conduct. Three aims constituted virtually inseparable components of the Communist program:

a. The formation of the Soviets of Workers', Soldiers', Peasants', and other Deputies, constituting "a new form, or rather a new type of state,"[5] embodying the dictatorship of the proletariat, and abolishing private property in agriculture and industry.

b. The immediate conclusion of peace among all the belligerents.

c. The launching of a world proletarian revolution.

On November 8, 1917, the day after the seizure of power, Lenin read to the second session of the All-Russian Congress of Soviets the "Decree on Peace" together with a "Report on the Peace Question." The Decree on Peace was a public declaration addressed to all participants of World War I. It proposed the immediate conclusion of a general armistice, announced the Soviet "determination to sign immediately conditions of peace terminating this war," and declared that the Soviet Government intended to abolish secret diplomacy as well as to repudiate and publish the Czar's secret treaties. The Decree further appealed to the workers of Great Britain, France, and Germany to help bring to a successful conclusion the cause of peace, and at the same time the cause of the emancipation of the toiling and exploited masses of the population from all forms of slavery and all forms of exploitation.

But the Bolsheviks did not regard peace as an end in itself. They had nothing but contempt for "social pacifists," i.e. socialists who wanted peace for its own sake. In 1917, Lenin had written: "We are not pacifists, . . . We have always declared it to be absurd for the revolutionary proletariat to renounce revolutionary wars that may prove necessary in the interests of socialism."[6] As early as November, 1914, Lenin had called on the workers "to turn the imperialist war into a civil war."[7] In 1917, he firmly believed in the imminence of workers' uprisings in the Western countries, particularly in Germany, and therefore viewed a sudden ending of hostilities and immediate negotiations for a "just and democratic peace without annexations and indemnities" as the best means of nurturing world revolution.

Another of the early official acts of the Soviet Government was to proclaim the right of all nations and peoples to fashion their own destiny. The "Declaration of the Rights of Peoples," published on November 15, 1917, stated that all the peoples living in territories

of the former Czarist empire were now equal and sovereign; they
had the right to secede from Russia and to set up independent
states.

Yet the Soviet Government did not believe that the principle of
self-determination embraced the free decision of a national or
ethnic majority regarding future allegiances and forms of government. What the Bolsheviks really meant was the substitution of
the will of the "proletariat" for that of the people. However, when
workers and peasants in most of the non-Russian territories made it
clear that they shared the general desire to secede from Russia, a
further dialectical interpretation substituted the will of the Party
for that of the "proletariat." Lenin provided a striking example of
this sort of "doublethink" in his work on "The Socialist Revolution
and the Rights of Nations to Self-Determination." He wrote:

> The right of nations to self-determination means only the right to
> independence in a political sense, the right to free, political secession
> from the oppressing nation. Concretely, this political, democratic de-
> mand implies complete freedom to carry on agitation in favor of
> secession, and freedom to settle the question of secession by means of
> a referendum of the nation that desires to secede. Consequently,
> this demand is by no means identical with the demand for secession,
> for the partition and for the formation of small states. It is merely
> the logical expression of the struggle against national oppression in
> any form.[8]

Shortly before the Bolshevik Revolution, the All-Russian Conference of the Russian Social Democratic Labor (later Communist) Party had made the following statement in its "Resolution
on the National Question":

> The question of the right of nations freely to secede must not be
> confused with the question of whether it would be expedient for any
> given nation to secede at any given moment. This latter question
> must be settled by the Party of the proletariat in each particular case
> independently, from the point of view of the interests of the social
> development as a whole and the class struggle of the proletariat for
> socialism.[9]

The double maneuver of proclaiming the sovereign rights of peoples in principle and denying them in fact was invariably pursued
in the years after the Revolution.

It is now possible to isolate the basic elements of Lenin's policy
leading to the Peace Treaty of Brest-Litovsk with the Central
Powers:

Seizure of power and cessation of hostilities were for Lenin an inseparable, in fact an almost simultaneous, operation. The Russian Army was disintegrating and the masses clamored for peace. Believing that uprisings in Germany (and possibly in other Western countries) were imminent, Lenin was convinced that any sort of peace, at any price, would lead to an early world revolution. To further this aim he was ready temporarily to lose the non-Russian provinces of the former empire. But he could not immediately impose his will on the Central Committee. Just as the German Imperial Government tried to organize satellite regimes in East-Central Europe, so did the Soviet representatives at Brest-Litovsk refuse to pay heed to the desire for independence of other nations. Joffe and Trotsky, who headed the Soviet delegation, demonstrated that they took "peace without annexations" to mean the widest possible restoration of the Czarist borders. On learning that Poland, the Baltic states, and the Ukraine had already expressed the desire to sever political ties with Communist Russia, one of the members of the Soviet delegation, the historian Pokrovsky, said: "It was impossible to speak of peace without annexations when about eighteen governments (administrative regions) were torn from the Russian Empire."[10] Trotsky wrote to Lenin:

It is impossible to sign their peace. . . . They have already agreed with fictitious governments of Poland, Lithuania, Courland [Latvia], and others concerning territorial concessions and military and customs treaties. In view of "self-determination," these provinces, according to the German interpretation, are already independent states.[11]

Trotsky, therefore, wished to confront the Central Powers with a policy of "neither war nor peace." It was only after a further advance of German troops into Russia that the Soviet Government agreed to accept all the German conditions and signed the Treaty of Brest-Litovsk on March 3, 1918. By this treaty, together with an additional agreement signed in Berlin on August 27, 1918, the Soviet Government recognized the secession of Poland, the Ukraine, Finland, and the Baltic states, as well as the cession of the Caucasian territories of Ardahan, Kars, and Batum to Turkey. This appeared to be a major political and territorial disaster, the like of which Russia had not experienced since its liberation from Tatar domination more than four centuries earlier. Yet there is little doubt that the Peace of Brest-Litovsk saved the Bolshevik regime. A German advance on Petrograd and Moscow would have meant the end of Lenin's government. Russia, troubled with civil war, widespread internal disorder, and the weakness of the Bolshevik forces, would have been able to offer no serious military opposition. All things considered, Lenin believed that the sacrifice would not be in vain, for on the existence of the Soviet state rested the Communists' only hope to carry out Marx's prediction of a world proletarian revolution. But Lenin shared Marx's belief that "final victory of Socialism in a single country is impossible."[12] Consequently, he proclaimed that the new Soviet state was the base for world revolution: "History has given us, the Russian toiling and exploited classes, the honorable role of the vanguard of the international Socialist revolution. . . . The Russians commenced, the Germans, the French, and the English will finish, and Socialism will be victorious."[13]

The conviction that Communism would prevail throughout the world was also held by Stalin, both before and after he embarked on his battle with Trotsky over "socialism in one country." Their antagonism was primarily an expression of the struggle for power, and it has rightly been pointed out that Stalin no more gave up world revolution than Trotsky rejected the chance of building Communism in Russia. Stalin himself held that the Soviets had only one alternative—either to pursue "a revolutionary policy, uniting around the working class of the U.S.S.R. the proletarians and oppressed of all countries," or to renounce revolutionary policy and slide back "from our Socialist country into a 'good' bourgeois republic."[14] Stalin viewed such an extremity with abhorrence, an attitude shared by Malenkov, Molotov, Beria, Kaganovich, Mikoyan, Bulganin, Khrushchev and others. In one of a number of statements on the subject, Khrushchev said: "We are convinced that sooner or later capitalism will perish, just as feudalism perished earlier. The Socialist nations are advancing toward Communism. All the world will come to Communism. History does not ask whether you want it or not."[15]

It is not necessary to dwell upon the fallacies of Communist semantics, on the antiquated significance Khrushchev attaches to the word "capitalism," or on the purely dialectic differentiation between the Communist brand of "Socialism" and "Communism" itself. For our purpose, it is sufficient to demonstrate that the axiom that Communism will eventually rule over the whole world has been held to without interruption from Lenin to Khrushchev.

Although Stalin's death gave the Kremlin the much-needed opportunity for a major tactical shift in foreign policy, it is striking how little it affected the fundamental approach of Soviet Communism to the outside world. On November 6, 1955, Deputy Premier Lazar Kaganovich said at the official celebration of the Bolshevik Revolution: "Revolutionary ideas know no frontiers. . . . The great ideas of Marx, Engels, Lenin, and Stalin . . . have been and will be victorious. If the nineteenth century was a century of capitalism, the twentieth century is a century of the triumph of Socialism and Communism."[16]

Stalin's posthumous demotion at the Twentieth Party Congress, in February, 1956, did not alter the Soviet leadership's confidence that Communism would continue to expand and ultimately be victorious in all countries. In his Secret Speech to the Congress on February 24 and 25, Khrushchev repudiated almost everything Stalin had done, but not his foreign policy. The only exception was to censure Stalin for his quarrel with Tito, evidently regarded by Khrushchev as an internal Communist matter that "could . . . have been solved through Party discussions among comrades."[17]

Although the changes that have occurred in the Soviet attitudes toward other countries do not affect basic doctrinal beliefs, they are concerned with the ultimate tactical question: How, and when, can the world victory of Communism be achieved? It was at the Twentieth Party Congress that Khrushchev came out with an interpretation of "peaceful coexistence" that has become the main theme of Soviet foreign policy. Directly contradicting what Lenin has written and said, the major speakers at the Congress maintained that "peaceful coexistence of the Socialist and capitalist world systems" (Bulganin), or of "states with differing social systems" (Khrushchev) was a Leninist theory or principle. So did Stalin before them. But in at least one important instance, Stalin had truthfully explained what Lenin really meant:

> We must not forget Lenin's statement that as regards our work of construction, very much depends upon whether we succeed in postponing war with the capitalist world, which is inevitable, but which can be postponed either until the moment when the proletarian revolutions have fully matured, or lastly, until the moment when the capitalists come to blows over the division of the colonies.
>
> Therefore, the maintenance of peaceful relations with the capitalist countries is an obligatory task for us.
>
> Our relations with the capitalist countries are based on the assumption that the coexistence of two opposite systems is possible.[18]

As for Lenin himself, he repeatedly asserted that the two systems must clash violently before one of them will triumph:

> The existence of the Soviet Republic side by side with imperialist states for a long time is unthinkable. One or the other must triumph in the end. And before that end supervenes, a series of frightful collisions between the Soviet Republic and the bourgeois states will be inevitable.[19]

Far from believing in peaceful coexistence in the literal sense, Lenin thought that wars would become impossible only after the "bourgeois" states were annihilated: "Only after we overthrow, completely defeat, and expropriate the bourgeoisie in the entire world, and not only in one country, will wars become impossible."[20]

There is, however, only a seeming contradiction between Lenin and his latter-day disciples. The Bolsheviks never accepted the traditional meaning of the terms "peace" and "war" as two opposites describing the condition of men fighting and of men working the plough. According to the definition he took over from Clausewitz, Lenin considered that "war is simply the continuation of politics by other [i.e., violent] means."[21] In other words, these two manifestations of politics are closely linked, and the difference between them is one of method only. From the Communist point of view, revolution is the central aim of all political action, and it can, under various circumstances, be pursued by both methods, i.e., both in time of peace and during, or by means of, war. When, in 1918, Trotsky coined the phrase "neither war nor peace," he revealed a specific state of mind and correctly expressed the Communist maxim of continuous warfare in international relations. Although Lenin, for important practical reasons, then opposed him, Trotsky later wrote that the formula "actually served as a bridge to Lenin's stand."[22] Lenin believed with Marx that class struggle must give birth to civil wars. The victory of Communism in one country, or several countries, would result in wars with other countries, which "will remain for some time either bourgeois or prebourgeois."[23] But Communism could not progress without interruptions, retreats, or even temporary defeats. Accordingly, Lenin demanded from revolutionary leaders "the ability to make all the necessary compromises, to 'tack,' to make agreements, zigzags, retreats, and so on,"[24] when necessary even "to crawl in the mud."[25] For Lenin contended that "to accept battle at a time when it is obviously advantageous to the enemy and not to us is a crime."[26] In foreign relations, this prescription was followed by the Soviet Government both in the passive and active sense: Soviet Russia submitted to Germany in 1918, and thereafter consistently avoided conflict with any country it believed to be stronger or temporarily in a strong political position, whether it was Japan, Poland, Turkey, Finland, or any other neighbor, however small. On the other hand, Soviet Russia never lost an opportunity to threaten or attack a neighboring country that found itself in difficulties. The question of physical and political opportunity is thus an essential qualification of Lenin's view that wars with the "capitalist" states are inevitable, while he understood coexistence merely as the need for breathing spells until such opportunities arose.

In addition to other considerations, one must also take into account the practical impact of atomic weapons on Soviet political thought. The tremendous effect of the American atom bombs dropped at Hiroshima and Nagasaki upset the Russian idea of the balance of world power in the postwar period. From that moment, both the continuation of wartime collaboration with the Western powers and the forcing of the pace of Communist expansion appeared to the Kremlin fraught with danger. Hence a far-reaching change in Soviet methods; public denunciation of alleged Western "imperialist" aims, frantic espionage efforts to obtain the secrets of nuclear production, and a subtle probing of the political and geographic limits of American involvement in Europe and Asia. Even after the explosion of the first Soviet hydrogen device (August 12, 1953), Russian behavior suggested an embarrassed awareness of Western superiority in this all-important domain. On March 13, 1954, Premier Malenkov declared that with the modern weapons, a new world war would mean "the destruction of world civilization."[27] He was, it is true, quickly corrected by Khrushchev, who, on April 26, 1954, explained that the destruction would be only one-sided, as an "imperialist attempt to precipitate a new war . . . will inevitably end in the collapse of the whole capitalist system."[28] Despite some vacillation, this view, on the whole, prevailed. In October, 1961, at the Twenty-second Party Congress, Khrushchev said that should "imperialist maniacs" threaten the Socialist achievements of nations, "the beginning of war would become the end of the antipopular imperialist system."[29]

Whatever the propaganda stance, the Soviet Government does not seem inclined to risk a military showdown by provoking a nuclear war. Even after the long series of nuclear tests in the autumn of 1961, and the loud boasting of atomic superiority, the Kremlin continued to show its preference for the Cold War (which it publicly denounced), i.e., a war that is "neither war nor peace," as best suited to the Communist technique of dialectical propaganda and secret subversion, a policy that Moscow expects to yield slower but certain results, with relatively little risk involved.

2. *PEACEFUL COEXISTENCE*

Khrushchev's most notable contribution to Communist doctrine is the exegesis of the Marxist-Leninist premise that while "imperialist" states exist wars are inevitable, contained in his report to the Twentieth Party Congress of February 14, 1956. In it, the First Secretary stated that the belief in the triumph of Communism "by no means implies that the victory will be reached by armed intervention . . . in the internal affairs of the capitalist countries." It is true, Khrushchev said, that "we recognize the necessity for the revolutionary transformation of capitalist society into Socialist society." But, he added, there are different forms of revolution:

> For a number of capitalist countries, the overthrow of the bourgeois dictatorship by force . . . is inevitable. . . . Leninism teaches us that the ruling classes will not relinquish power of their own free will. However, the greater or lesser acuteness in the struggle, the use or not of force . . . depends not so much on the proletariat as on the extent of the resistance put up by the exploiters.[1]

Let us now go back to the sequence laid down in Marxist-Leninist theory: Changes in the conditions of production lead to class struggle; class struggle gives birth to civil wars; Communist victory in one or several countries will result in wars with non-Communist countries; such violent clashes are unavoidable as long as "bourgeois" or "imperialist" states exist side by side with the Soviet Republic. However, the occurrence of these wars must and can be regulated by the ability of the revolutionary leaders to compromise, retreat, and tack, in order to provide the Communist forces with indispensable respite in their struggle for world power.

Here Lenin's advice ends, and Khrushchev steps in with his interpretation of the original idea: Peaceful coexistence is the only alternative to the "most devastating war in history." Since Lenin's time, changes have occurred; "there is no fatal inevitability of war,"[2] therefore the transition to Communist society will not necessarily take place by violent means. It can be a peaceful transition,

19

as long as those who are opposed to Communism resign themselves to it and agree not to resist.

Since the Twentieth Congress, Khrushchev's doctrine of coexistence has been reasserted and expounded repeatedly. Later statements usually refer to two documents—the "Declaration" adopted at meetings of representatives of Communist parties held in Moscow in November, 1957, the "Statement"* of November, 1960. A third text, the "Peace Manifesto,"† also adopted at the November, 1957, Moscow meeting, soon receded into the background. But it did play a role in the history of the doctrine, and together with the Declaration endorsed the main elements of peaceful coexistence, as presented by Khrushchev in 1956 and 1957:

1. The transition from bourgeois society to Communist regimes can be a peaceful one, without civil wars, perhaps even by utilizing classic parliamentary means.

2. War between countries with different social systems is not inevitable. The "Socialist" countries "have no desire to interfere in the internal affairs of other countries" as Communism cannot be enforced from outside but will be the result of the internal struggle of the working class. And the aim of the Communists is to build a society that will ensure "universal well-being, the blossoming of all nations and eternal peace between them."[3]

This benign presentation of Communist aims is characteristic of the Peace Manifesto; the Declaration, however, contained the ominous corollary to the alleged peaceful transition to Communism, first mentioned by Khrushchev in his Twentieth Party Congress speech:

In the event of the ruling classes resorting to violence against the people, the possibility of nonpeaceful transition to Socialism should be borne in mind. Leninism teaches, and experience confirms, that the ruling classes never relinquish power voluntarily. . . . The forms of the class struggle will depend not so much on the proletariat as on the resistance put up by the reactionary circles.[4]

---

* The Statement is discussed in the chapter on the dispute with China, p. 319.

† The Peace Manifesto was signed by sixty-four Communist parties and was in the form of an appeal to the "reason and hearts . . . of all people of good will throughout the world." Only twelve parties of countries under Communist rule signed the "Declaration," a much harsher policy document, probably considered binding by the signatories. The Yugoslav League of Communists refused to adhere.

Had it not been for events beyond Khrushchev's control, this reservation might have remained a rare departure from an otherwise propagandistic exposition of the purpose of peaceful coexistence. As it happened, Khrushchev's interpretation ran into difficulties inside the Communist camp. It was criticized by the "dogmatists," who apparently wished to uphold Lenin's theory that war with the capitalist countries *is* inevitable. It came under attack in China; the defense of the doctrine also caused fresh attacks against the "revisionists," although they could have been expected to favor certain implications of Khrushchev's ideas. These frictions resulted in new explanations and additions to which we owe a clearer understanding of what Khrushchev means by peaceful coexistence.

The various manifestations of dissent did not come to the surface immediately after the Twentieth Congress. In January–February, 1959, the Twenty-first Congress of the CPSU upheld Khrushchev's position. It unanimously adopted his report stating that "the conclusion drawn by the Twentieth Congress that war is not fatally inevitable has been justified."[5] But it seems that those in the Communist camp who were dissatisfied with the results of Khrushchev's foreign policy could not be ignored, the more so as a long period of haggling and negotiating with the Western powers, begun with the first ultimatum on Berlin in November, 1958, ended without tangible gains when the Soviet Premier wrecked the Paris Summit conference in May, 1960.

There are indications that both before and after that date, Khrushchev came under considerable pressure and felt the need to explain that by stating that war was not inevitable he did not intend to forsake the universal aims of the revolution. In a speech delivered in June, 1960, in Bucharest, at the Third Congress of the Romanian Workers (Communist) Party, the Soviet Premier once again proclaimed his belief in the victory of Communism. He announced that the working class would bury capitalism and form a new Communist society. But at the same time, Khrushchev said that some of Lenin's ideas on imperialism were conceived when the mighty Soviet Union did not exist and when there were no other Socialist states. Therefore, Communists should not mechanically repeat what Lenin said of imperialism many decades ago and insist that imperialist wars are unavoidable as long as Socialism has not vanquished the whole world. Khrushchev went on to say that Communists must not be like children learning to form words out of letters, but should think for themselves and analyze the current situation on the basis of Marxism-Leninism in order to draw conclusions for the benefit of the common cause of Communism. And the conclusion should be that, in the present circumstances, war is not inevitable.[6]

This was not much of an explanation, particularly not in the face of criticism that peaceful coexistence played into the hands of the "capitalists." But it is important to note that Khrushchev explicitly affirmed the need and claimed for himself the right to refresh, interpret, and even expand the sacrosanct doctrine; it meant that under the guise of Marxism-Leninism, he was able to say whatever served the purpose of current Soviet policy.

Shortly after this speech, in July, 1960, *Kommunist*, the theoretical bimonthly journal of the Soviet Party, came forward with more substantial information on the nature of Khrushchev's ideas. In order to assuage Chinese and dogmatist criticism, *Kommunist* began to attack simultaneously the "revisionists" and the "capitalists." "The revisionists," it said, "understand peaceful coexistence as the renunciation of the struggle against imperialism, as a capitulation. . . . Capitalists and revisionists want the Soviet Union to ensure the capitalist countries against class warfare and revolution." All this is wrong, since "the peaceful coexistence of countries with different social systems and the bourgeois theory of a peaceful coexistence of antagonistic classes have nothing in common."[7]

How does this tally with the theory of a peaceful transition to Communism? *Kommunist* repeated the assertion that a bloodless acquisition of power was possible in a number of countries. But at the same time, it stated that both the Twentieth Congress and the Declaration of November, 1957, "did not at all proclaim the peaceful way as the only possible one." On the contrary, "in a number of capitalist countries where the military and political apparatus is strong, one has to be ready to repulse the attempts to subdue the people's will by force, which may lead to most severe forms of class warfare." *Kommunist* also declared that the working class should master all forms and means of struggle and use them, as is taught by materialist dialectics, according to the specific conditions prevailing in each capitalist country.

It would be superfluous to discuss *Kommunist*'s contention that such directives of the leading theoretical journal of the Soviet Communist Party concern only the internal situation of each free country individually. But for the present, let us simply take stock by stating that the original formulation in Khrushchev's speech at the Twentieth Congress in 1956, as well as the explanations contained in the Declaration of twelve Communist parties in 1957, and in

Kommunist's interpretation in 1960, provide the theory of peaceful coexistence with an escape clause: According to these texts, the transmission of state power would be violent if a Communist regime were not accepted without resistance.

In a report to a meeting of the leading ideological organizations of the Party on January 6, 1961,* Khrushchev made another doctrinal contribution—this time to the theory of war. It began with the historically unfounded Marxist allegation that "wars came into being after society broke up in classes." There followed a division of contemporary wars into three kinds: world wars, local wars, and wars of national liberation. "Communists," Khrushchev said, "are the most resolute opponents of world wars, as they are of wars between states in general. Only imperialists need such wars." Next Khrushchev spoke of local wars. Here the Communist position was stated more vaguely. Such wars, he explained, existed in the past and may recur in the future. As an example he mentioned the Suez war of 1956, which, he said, was stopped by the Soviet Union.† Khrushchev then denounced Western preparations for small "brushwood wars." Twisting the defensive idea—the avoidance of nuclear war—underlying such preparations, he said: "Certain imperialist groups fear that a world war might end in complete failure for capitalism, and therefore bank on local wars." But local wars may develop into a thermonuclear war, and therefore, Khrushchev said, "we must . . . fight against both world and local wars."

Finally he came to "wars of national liberation." The examples mentioned were Vietnam, Algeria, and Cuba. The differences between these situations were omitted: "These wars," he said, "began as uprisings of colonial peoples against their oppressors and developed into guerrilla wars." Only in the case of Cuba did Khrushchev add that it was an uprising against an internal tyrannical regime "backed by United States imperialism." The Soviet attitude was defined as follows:

> Can such wars recur? Yes, they can. Can such uprisings recur? Yes, they can. But they are wars in the nature of popular uprisings. Can

* Khrushchev spoke to a meeting of party organizations of the Higher Party School, the Academy of Social Sciences, and the Institute of Marxism-Leninism. The importance of this report was also stressed by its publication in *Kommunist* (January, 1961, No. 1).

† Of the stand taken by the United Nations and the United States, not a word: "We refused to shut our eyes. . . . We intervened and frustrated . . . aggression."

conditions in other countries reach a point where the people's patience is stretched to the limit and they take up arms? Yes, they can.
. . . These uprisings must not be identified with wars between states, with local wars, because the insurgent peoples were fighting for their right to self-determination, for their social and independent national development; these uprisings are directed against decayed reactionary regimes, against the colonialists. The Communists support such just wars fully and without reservations and march in the vanguard of the peoples fighting for liberation.

As can be seen, the distinction drawn here between "local wars" and "wars of national liberation" is far from clear. So is the difference, if any, between wars against "colonialists" and "decayed reactionary regimes." Thus, Khrushchev's theory on wars boils down to the following practical stand:

1. Communists (i.e., the Soviet Government) are opposed to world wars, as they are against "wars between states in general," because "wars between imperialist countries are not the most probable."

2. Communists should stand up against local wars, for "a small scale imperialist war . . . may develop into a thermonuclear war."

3. Communists support "wars of national liberation," ambiguously linked to uprisings and guerrilla wars. They may be said to be waged against "colonialists," or against "decayed reactionary regimes"—whatever the situation demands. Such wars are "just," and —in Khrushchev's own words—should be supported "fully and without reservations," which can only mean to include military assistance.

This, therefore, is a second escape clause from peaceful coexistence: The Soviet Government reserves the right to support by any means, even by force of arms, the wars of national liberation, or "just wars," as well as the right to decide which wars are "just."[8]

It remains to demonstrate that the two escape clauses—(a) in internal relations of non-Communist countries, and (b) between Communist and non-Communist states—are part of the same major premise of political strategy, embodied in the doctrine of peaceful coexistence. This premise is the belief, genuine or not, that Communism will be victorious in the whole world. In the first case, victory in a number of countries could be bloodless if there is no resistance to Communism. Where a strong resistance would have to be overcome, the "most severe forms of class struggle"[9] will be necessary, which can only mean civil war. In the second case, Soviet Russia rejects world wars and local wars, but supports "wars of national liberation" against "colonialists" or "decayed reactionary regimes." In most cases, such wars would also be civil wars. In terms of practical policy it follows that in both cases the doctrine of peaceful coexistence with states having different social systems is conditioned by Soviet reservations to take up arms in support of civil wars.*

The convenient blending of the two escape clauses into one is confirmed by the formulation of the 1961 Party Program. In this tedious, repetitive, 50,000-word document, no place was found for Khrushchev's three kinds of war. The theory was condensed into a few lines:

> The Communist Party of the Soviet Union and the Soviet people as a whole will continue to oppose all wars of conquest, including wars between capitalist countries and local wars aimed at strangling people's emancipating movements, and consider it their duty to support the sacred struggle of the oppressed peoples and their just wars of liberation.[10]

Even a perfunctory glance at this text shows that the division into world wars, local wars, and wars of national liberation has disappeared. There is also no trace of the distinction between wars against "colonialists" or "decayed reactionary regimes." We now learn that there are only two kinds of wars: wars of liberation, which the Soviet Union supports, and wars of conquest, which it opposes.†

Now the entire line of thought falls into a pattern: All means of imposing Communism by military force come under the general designation of "wars of liberation," or simply of "liberation."

All efforts to repulse forced communization are branded as a "suppression of the will of the people," an "encroachment by capitalist reaction," an "export of counterrevolution," wars of conquest, or at least as Cold War, according to circumstances. In the Party Program we read:

> Together with the other Marxist-Leninist parties, the Communist Party of the Soviet Union regards it as its international duty to call on all the peoples of all countries to rally, muster all their internal forces, take vigorous action, and drawing on the might of the world

---

* In this context it is well to remember Lenin's definition that "civil wars are also wars," as well as that "every kind of war is a continuation of politics by other means." ("Military Program of the Proletarian Revolution," *Sochineniya*, XXIII, 67.)

† Cf. Dispute with China, p. 320.

Socialist system, forestall or firmly repel imperialist interference in the affairs of the people of any country risen in revolt and thereby prevent imperialist export of counterrevolution.[11]

Translated into plain language, this means that Soviet Russia and the other Communist governments will try to prevent organized defense against Communism on an international scale. No outside help is to reach a country fighting a Communist-incited civil war, or against an imposed regime, as in Hungary or Tibet. Defense against Communism is to be paralyzed by propaganda, political pressure, and intimidation. Everything will be done to isolate the victim and reduce his resistance to a civil war that the Communist governments will support from the outside.

The analysis of pertinent Soviet documents thus leads to the conclusion that Khrushchev's "peaceful coexistence" actually means the opposite of its logical sense. With the visionary insight of the artist, George Orwell warned in the novel 1984 that "war is peace" would become the slogan of the Communist Party of the future.[12]

This is, so to speak, the mainstream, the basic strategic concept, of the coexistence doctrine. It would be idle to speculate to what extent the guarded disclosure of its true nature satisfied those among the Communist leaders who unjustly suspected Khrushchev of being an appeaser of "capitalism." But this controversy has shown that the doctrine of peaceful coexistence, apart from its significance in global political strategy, provides the Communist leadership with several useful sidelines. The doctrine's propaganda content—aimed at the general public on both sides of the Iron Curtain—is self-evident and therefore heavily played on: "Either peaceful coexistence or the most destructive war in history,"[13] Khrushchev said at the Twentieth Party Congress (a threat often repeated since). "Coexistence signifies the repudiation of war as means of solving controversial issues,"[14] we read in an article he wrote for *Pravda* and *Foreign Affairs* in 1959. In its new Program, the Soviet Communist Party proclaims that its chief aim in foreign policy is "to deliver mankind from a world war of extermination."[15]

The message these same documents and declarations convey to those who understand the inner meaning of the Party jargon is the reverse of the general propaganda line. The central goal of Khrushchev's peaceful coexistence is cloaked behind disguised language. Such is not always the case with the subsidiary benefits the doctrine is expected to yield. On the lower levels, the militant Party member, the fellow traveler, and the Communist-front worker have to be reassured that fundamental revolutionary aims have not been abandoned. They also have to be provided with frequent guidelines on how to behave within the framework of the doctrine, as well as with some tactical pointers that, in various circumstances and places, can be transmitted only through media of mass communications. Such guidelines sometimes are presented quite candidly, without concern for the resulting contradictions.

By way of reassurance, the Party member and Communist-front worker must know that peaceful coexistence does not mean compromise with the non-Communist world. They are told time and again that "under the banner of Marxism-Leninism . . . there is the guarantee for new victories of the world Communist movement, the full guarantee for the triumph of Communism."[16]

Next come the general guidelines. The Party member should know that peaceful coexistence does not mean conciliation of the Socialist and bourgeois ideologies. "On the contrary, it implies intensification of the struggle of the working class, of all Communist parties, for the triumph of Socialist ideas."[17] Therefore, the Party Program defines peaceful coexistence as "a specific form of class struggle," *Pravda* calls it "a higher form,"[18] and Maurice Thorez, the First Secretary of the French Communist Party, "the highest form of class struggle."[19] In some instances, peaceful coexistence is represented as "a policy of mobilizing the masses."[20] An often-recurring slogan holds: "There can be no peaceful coexistence between ideologies."

Finally, let us turn to the tactical indications. Here are a few examples: Peaceful coexistence "affords more favorable opportunities for the struggle of the working class in the capitalist countries." (1961 Program); Peaceful coexistence "facilitates the activities of the Communist parties and other progressive organizations of the working class in the capitalist countries, makes it easier for the peoples to combat aggressive war blocs and foreign military bases, and contributes to the success of the national liberation movement." (Khrushchev, Report of January 6, 1961); "The working class . . . can defeat the reactionary, anti-popular forces, win a solid majority in parliament, transform it from a tool serving the class interests of the bourgeoisie into an instrument serving the working people, launch a broad struggle outside parliament, smash the resistance of the reactionary forces, and provide the necessary condition for a peaceful socialist revolution." (1961 Program).

Sometimes even more candid revelations of method and tactics come from Communist leaders in the satellite countries and their press organs. In a report to the Central Committee of the Polish Communist Party, Wladyslaw Gomulka said on January 22, 1961, that Communists should follow "a courageous policy of united fronts and cooperation with the Social Democrats both on the national and international plane." The policy of peaceful coexistence, Gomulka declared in the same speech, "obstructs the anti-Communist campaign, which is based on the lie of a threatening Communist aggression. In this way arise conditions favoring the fruitful work of Communists within various social strata."[21]

There was nothing original in the appeal to form united fronts. It adhered to a long-standing Communist tradition of "united" or "popular" front tactics. But Gomulka's call is interesting because the democratic Polish Socialist Party (PPS) had played a prominent role in free Poland and was destroyed through an enforced "merger" with the Communists in 1947.* Gomulka's thinly veiled formulas for Communist infiltration should also be looked at in the context of an article in *Trybuna Ludu*, the official organ of the Polish Communist Party:

> It is obvious that the enforcement of the idea of peaceful coexistence on the imperialists is not completed and shall not be completed as long as imperialism does not disappear from the surface of the earth. . . . But the new element of the present situation is the fact that by a knowledgeable, elastic, and creative policy of the Socialist states—Comrade Khrushchev often insisted on these features —it is possible to isolate, neutralize the Cold War circles, and force peaceful coexistence upon them.[22]

The idea of enforcing peaceful coexistence by Communists on non-Communists is the bedrock of the doctrine. It applies both to internal and international relations, and there is no doubt that this is how Lenin himself understood the method. It is striking that ever since the Twentieth Congress, most statements and declarations describe peaceful coexistence of states with different social systems as a "Leninist principle," "put forward by Lenin," "inherited from Lenin," but no relevant quotation from Lenin is offered in that context. The explanation is simply that Lenin cannot be quoted to prove that by peaceful coexistence he meant peace. He meant compulsion and violence, and he can be so quoted. Those who advocated evolution, peaceful transformation of society, who "dissociated [themselves] from *violent* revolution" were renegades in

---

* A number of leaders and adherents of the PPS uphold its traditions in exile.

Lenin's eyes, traitors whom he accused of "desertion to the side of *liberal* labor politics, i.e., to the side of the bourgeoisie."[23]

But great realist and tactician that he was, Lenin understood better than the other Bolsheviks the practical responsibilities of power, "the objective inevitability created in an utterly ruined country."[24] He had the strength and the ability to impose his policy on the Party and to sign a peace with Germany which he called "incredible . . . humiliating, and predatory,"[25] but which he considered as a temporary necessity, like the Treaty of Tilsit signed by Prussia in 1807. In 1921, Lenin temporarily abandoned some of the Communist economic principles in favor of state capitalism, leased Soviet enterprises to foreign, i.e., "capitalist" firms, and made agreements with them on "concessions." He thus submitted to the inevitability of coexisting, but for tactical reasons only, to prepare a further advance, a revenge or to use foreign capital to strengthen the revolutionary capabilities of the Soviet economy. This was Lenin's true idea of coexistence, his "theory of respite"[26] best expressed in the context of the Brest-Litovsk Peace, when he said "I want to yield space . . . in order to gain time."[27] In essence, therefore, there is no discrepancy between what Lenin thought and what Khrushchev wants to do. The new formulation can be summarized in the assertion that "revolutions are quite feasible without war," and that Communists "prefer to achieve the transfer of power from the bourgeoisie to the proletariat by peaceful means, without civil war."[28]

But Marx and Engels wrote in the *Communist Manifesto* that "only by forcible overthrow of all existing social conditions"[29] can the Communists' aims be attained. Lenin held that "the substitution of the proletarian state for the bourgeois state is impossible without a violent revolution," and that "only stern battles, precisely civil wars, can free mankind from the yoke of capitalism."[30]

Is this, then, Khrushchev's departure from doctrine? We read in the CP Program:

> But whatever the form in which the transition from capitalism to Socialism is effected, that transition can come about only through revolution. However varied the forms of a new people's state power in the period of Socialist construction, their essence will be the same—the dictatorship of the proletariat.[31]

We have shown that Lenin vehemently objected to the idea of a peaceful revolution, while Khrushchev accepts it. On the other hand, both maintain the absolute necessity of the dictatorship of the proletariat, of which no new interpretation is offered, and of which Lenin said that: "The fundamental symptom of this concept [is] revolutionary *violence*."[32]* The margin of difference between Lenin's and Khrushchev's ideas of peaceful coexistence may now be measured with some precision. Khrushchev says that violence is not necessarily indispensable in the seizure of power. But he does not deviate from Lenin's teaching that once the Communists take over, the transformation of society can only take the form of a dictatorship of the proletariat, i.e., of revolutionary violence. Khrushchev's innovation therefore is only a matter of timing: Violence may not be necessary to seize power, but it must be used once power has been seized.

---

* It should be noted that the 1961 Program of the CPSU contends that the dictatorship of the proletariat is no longer necessary in the Soviet Union, which has "brought about the complete and final victory of Socialism—the first stage of Communism." Therefore, the program states, the dictatorship of the proletariat "has fulfilled its historic mission and has ceased to be indispensable from the point of view of internal development." We are confronted here with several fictions. Contrary to the first fiction, there never was in the Soviet state, nor in any other state under Communist rule, any dictatorship of the proletariat, only the dictatorship of a power group pretending to rule in the name of the proletariat and its "vanguard"—the Communist Party. The second fiction is that under Communism there is a difference between the stages of "Socialism" and "Communism." The only existing differences are simply in the degrees of industrialization, collectivization of agriculture, and police pressure on the population. A further fiction is that the Soviet Union, alone among the Communist-ruled countries, has achieved "the final victory of Socialism," while other states under Communism are still "building Socialism." Yet, the Soviet Union, as before, is ruled by a single totalitarian party. If the concept about the end of the dictatorship of the proletariat has any practical meaning, it is to be seen in the increasing control of the Party apparatus over the apparatus of the state. It is thus related to another fiction, the "withering away of the state" once a "Communist society" has been built and external conditions allow for it. Whatever Marx and Engels may have thought, in our time these are nothing but variations on dialectical themes for the benefit of Soviet propaganda, both internal and external. As it is, however, even if the Soviet point of view were to be accepted at face value, the 1961 program concept would have no bearing on the coexistence theory, since the dictatorship of the proletariat is supposed to lose its value after "the final victory of Socialism," that is after a country has been under Communist rule for a number of years. Before that, in the period of "Socialist construction," as the same program clearly states, the essence of the new power remains the dictatorship of the proletariat—i.e., according to Lenin, revolutionary violence.

TWO

DIPLOMACY AND OTHER METHODS

3. THE COMMUNIST INTERNATIONALS—COMINTERN AND COMINFORM

Before Soviet diplomacy could successfully act on a wider scene, it had to win a long struggle for recognition of the new regime. This involved a paradox, for the Bolsheviks attempted to establish normal relations with the very same bourgeois governments they intended to overthrow. Lenin's government could not stay in power for long isolated from the rest of the world. On the other hand, it was unable to refrain from proclaiming its revolutionary aims without risking the loss of its identity as well as the hoped-for support of the workers of other countries. This contradiction led to the unique ambivalence of Soviet policy, which finds expression in the deceptive separation of Communist Internationals from the Soviet state and in a remarkable degree of double-think and double-talk, the very essence of Soviet action abroad.

Although a complete program of the Communist International is not supposed to have been adopted before its Sixth World Congress, in 1928, it was Lenin himself who set forth the aims of the Third International (Comintern) and laid down the methods by which they were to be carried out. In the opening and closing speeches at the First World Congress of the Communist International (1919), in the Twenty-one Conditions of Affiliation (Second Congress—1920) of which he was the author, and in his other writings on the subject during the same period, Lenin made it clear that:

a. The ultimate goal of the Third International was to assure "the victory of the world Communist revolution."[1]

b. The method of achieving this victory was "civil war [which] has become a fact, not only in Russia, but also in the most developed capitalist countries of Europe."[2]

c. "The necessary practical form that will enable the proletariat to achieve its domination . . . is the Soviet system with the dictatorship of the proletariat."[3]

The Third International, formed in Moscow in March, 1919, by delegates from thirty countries, was officially dissolved on May 15, 1943. In the second half of September, 1947, at a meeting of delegates of nine European Communist parties* held in southwest Poland, a new International came into being, under the name of Communist Information Bureau (Cominform). It was again dissolved on April 17, 1956.

It would be illogical to assume that during a span of thirty-seven years, the roof organization of Communist parties has remained unchanged. Yet it is most doubtful that the two dissolutions symbolized the true character of the transformations. The years 1919 and 1947, when the successive organizations of the Communist International were formally constituted, marked the beginning of sweeping political offensives aimed at the subversion of "bourgeois" society. On the other hand, in 1943 as well as in 1956, when the dissolutions were announced, the Soviet Union had decided on a change of tactics, best evidenced in the deceptive slogans of peaceful collaboration and competition. But the actual behavior of Communist parties fails to support the Soviet contention that between 1943 and 1947, the coordinating apparatus linking international Communism with Moscow had ceased to function. It is too early to conclude what form the international collaboration of Communist parties assumed after the dissolution of the Cominform in 1956. This move was obviously part of the new line Moscow intended to follow after Khrushchev's momentous revelations at the Twentieth Congress. It seems, however, that this new plan was thrown out of kilter by the events in Poland (June–October, 1956), and in particular by the Hungarian Revolution (October–December, 1956). However, a clear indication of Soviet and Communist intentions may be found in the official statement on the dissolution of the Cominform: "The individual parties and groups of parties . . . will find new useful methods of establishing links with each other."[4]

Pravda of April 18, 1956, also stressed that "the Communist parties are drawn together by the far-reaching community of their interests . . . the unity of goals and the interests of the working classes in the different countries of the world."

The question whether the Communist Internationals were really disbanded as and when officially proclaimed should also be considered in the light of Lenin's instruction that "legal work must

* Soviet, Polish, Hungarian, Romanian, Czechoslovak, Bulgarian, Yugoslav, French, and Italian Communist parties.

be combined with *illegal* work."[5] The same idea is emphasized in Paragraph 3 of the Conditions of Affiliation to the Comintern, adopted at the Second Congress in 1920: "The Communists . . . must *everywhere* create a duplicate illegal apparatus, which, at the decisive moment, could help the party to perform its duty to the revolution."[6]

There was never any serious doubt as to the intimate relation between the Communist International and the Soviet Government. Lenin, the first Chairman of the Soviet of the People's Commissars, was the initiator, founder, and great animator of the Communist International. Its tasks were firmly embedded in his doctrine: "The first International laid the foundations of the proletarian, international struggle for Socialism. The Second International . . . prepared for a broad, mass . . . movement in a number of countries. The Third International gathered the fruits of the work of the Second International . . . and has begun to effect the dictatorship of the proletariat."[7]

Lenin was convinced, moreover, that all over the world, "the best representatives of the revolutionary workers . . . are in favor of the Soviet power."[8] There was in his view complete identity between the government set up in Russia by the Bolshevik Revolution and the power that the Third International aimed at enforcing in all the other countries where the Communist revolution might succeed in the future.

After Lenin's death, his successor-to-be solemnly pledged himself to follow in his footsteps. Stalin wrote: "Departing from us, Comrade Lenin adjured us to remain faithful to the principles of the Communist International. We vow to you, Comrade Lenin, that we will not spare our lives, to strengthen and extend the union of the toilers of the whole world—the Communist International."[9]

For nearly two decades the undisputed master of the Soviet Union, in turn First Secretary of the Communist Party, Prime Minister, and Supreme Commander of the Soviet Armies, Stalin remained faithful to his pledge: "Comrade Stalin took a leading part in the working-out of the program of the Communist International. There is not a single important decision of the Communist International . . . which is not permeated with Stalin's ability . . . to strike a crushing blow at the enemy."[10]

It is further obvious that from the point of view of the Soviet Government, the Third International serves a double purpose: carrying revolution into all the other countries of the world aimed at the "foundation of the international Soviet Republic,"[11] as well as the defense of the Soviet Union by all the Communist parties abroad and by all "true revolutionaries" individually:

> In view of the fact that the U.S.S.R. is the only fatherland of the international proletariat [the latter] must on its part facilitate the success of the work of Socialist construction in the U.S.S.R. and defend her against the attacks of the capitalist powers by all means in its power.[12]

> At present the only determining criterion of revolutionary proletarian internationalism is: Are you for or against the U.S.S.R., the Fatherland of the world proletariat?[13]

Better than any documents, however, the constant support given by the Communist parties outside Russia to the oscillations of Soviet policies between 1919 and 1956 proves that international Communism in that period was a well-knit entity. During these thirty-seven years, all Communist parties recognized by Moscow slavishly copied the alternating tactics of Soviet foreign policy, from open offensive actions abroad (as in 1919 and 1947) to the cunning subtleties of the united fronts (1928) and popular fronts (1935), and the latest tack, peaceful coexistence, which was taken after Stalin's death but seems to have been contemplated as early as 1952.

There were seven World Congresses of the Third International, all held in Moscow: 1919, 1920, 1921, 1922, 1924, 1928, and 1935. The first four took place while Moscow still entertained high hopes for a quick Communist victory in Central and Western Europe. In fact, however, the Polish victory in the battle of Warsaw (August, 1920) put a stop for twenty-four years to the advance of the Communist system west of the Soviet-Polish border, as it was agreed to at Riga (March 18, 1921). Although the Bolshevik leaders may not have realized it at the time, no new Soviet regimes could be formed in Europe unless they were forcibly put into power by the Red Army.

But viewed from Moscow, the Communist tide still seemed to be swelling. At its Second Congress (July 17–August 7, 1920), which closed only a few days before the defeat of the Red Army at the gates of Warsaw, the Comintern adopted a series of documents of an undiluted revolutionary character. They were the Statutes of the Third International,[14] the Thesis, and in particular the Twenty-one Conditions of Affiliation.[15]

Between the Second and Third Congresses, important setbacks

occurred: the battle of Warsaw, the defection of the majority of the Italian Socialist Party, and the defeat of an attempted *Putsch* in Germany. After the Third and Fourth Congresses (July, 1921, and November, 1922), it was possible to detect the first subterfuges, the first retreats from the direct methods of War Communism. At the Third Congress, Lenin spoke of the changing meaning of the term "masses"—and of the character of the struggle; at the Fourth Congress, he made a much-subdued report on the first five years of the Revolution and on the prospects of world revolution.

The Fifth Congress (July, 1924) convened after both the death of Lenin and the turning of the tide of Communist revolutionary efforts in Germany. The double crisis was met by acknowledging a period of relative stabilization, to be used for reorganizing the Communist parties outside the U.S.S.R. The former trend was reversed. It was a further retreat from the masses and a "Bolshevization" of the Communist parties.

The Sixth Congress (September, 1928) adopted the most complete set of rules, aims, and principles, the "Program of the Third International" and the "Constitution and Rules of the Communist International."[16] Except for elaborations in the field of tactics (united front), these documents show that as far as the goal of world revolution was concerned, nothing had changed since Lenin's days and the First Congress in 1919.

The next seven years, until the meeting of the World Congress in 1935, were from the Communist point of view a period of frustration. The rising menace of Hitler's Germany induced the Soviet Government to adopt a line of collaboration with the "bourgeois" countries and the League of Nations. The resolutions of the Seventh and last official World Congress of the Third International registered the new position of the Soviet Union. They demanded a wide "antifacist front" of states and favored the formation of "popular fronts" in the capitalist countries; the Socialist parties in Western Europe were the main target of these tactics.

This first period of "coexistence"—roughly from 1932 to 1939—ended with the signing of the Molotov-Ribbentrop Pact on August 23, 1939. Without exception, the official Communist parties applauded the predatory Nazi-Soviet collaboration and branded as "imperialist war" the British and French assistance to Poland in carrying out their treaties of alliance.

After the German attack on Soviet Russia (June 22, 1941), the Communist parties again aligned themselves with the new Soviet position. The "patriotic war" had begun. Overnight, the British and French parties also became patriotic and stridently anti-Nazi.

Although the term itself was not used at that time, this was in fact the beginning of a second period of "coexistence" with the capitalist Western democracies. One of its highlights was the much-advertised dissolution of the Comintern on May 15, 1943. Its purpose was explained by Stalin with disarming simplicity: "It exposed the lie of the Hitlerites to the effect that Moscow allegedly intends to intervene in the life of other nations and to bolshevize them. . . . It exposes the calumny . . . that Communist Parties in various countries are allegedly acting not in the interest of their people but on orders from outside."[17]

The official dissolution of the Comintern was part of the Soviet diplomatic campaign for the realization of far-reaching war aims. Coming as it did on the eve of the conferences in Moscow (October–November, 1943) and Tehran (November–December, 1943), it was meant to lend Soviet Russia an air of respectability; even leading Allied statesmen were, or pretended to be, taken in by its significance.

The end of this second period of coexistence and the beginning of the Cold War were brought about, or at least precipitated, by Western resistance to forcible Soviet expansion. To counter the effects of the Truman Doctrine, the Marshall Plan, and the decline of Communist influence in Western Europe, Moscow formed the Communist Information Bureau. The harm done to the Communist cause by the bare-faced proclamations of the Comintern period was not forgotten. Zhdanov's declaration of war on the "imperialist and antidemocratic camp" led by the United States in alliance with Great Britain and France was mitigated by pacifist professions and an appeal "to resist the threat of new wars and imperialist expansion." But the grand design of world revolution, though less ostentatious, was still unmistakable:

> The antifascist forces comprise the second camp. This camp is based on the U.S.S.R. and the new democracies. It also includes countries which have broken with imperialism . . . such as Romania, Hungary, and Finland. . . . The anti-imperialist camp is backed by the labor and democratic movement and by the fraternal Communist Parties in all countries, by the fighters for national liberation in the colonies and dependencies, by all progressive and democratic forces in every country.[18]

It is debatable whether the Cominform was the real successor of the Comintern or merely the visible arm of a more formidable but hidden international Communist organization. Its composition seemed to suggest a narrower, and mainly European, task, possibly with particular emphasis on France and Italy. In spite of massive votes for the Communist parties, their hopes in these countries receded with the success of the Marshall Plan. The expulsion of the Yugoslav Communist Party from the Cominform (June 20, 1948), although a grave political setback, seems at first to have had a minor effect compared with Communist failure to influence the fate of the great nations of Western Europe.

What was visible on the surface of the Cominform activity soon merged into the vast pacifist propaganda campaign launched by Moscow early in 1947, a campaign coupled with violent denunciations of the United States and Great Britain as "warmongers." In retrospect, it seemed to have foreshadowed Soviet and Communist *actions directes*, such as the Berlin Blockade and the Korean aggression. In a resolution adopted in 1949, the Cominform stated: "The entire policy of the Anglo-American imperialist bloc is subordinated to the preparations for another war. . . . This policy is served by the enslaving Marshall Plan and its direct sequels, Western Union and the North-Atlantic military bloc, which are aimed at all peace-loving peoples"[19]

The dissolution of the Cominform was the logical consequence of the "coexistence" line adopted again after Stalin's death, and dramatized by the Belgrade Declaration (May, 1955) which was tantamount to a "treaty of peace" between the Communist parties and governments of Soviet Russia and Yugoslavia. Sparked by Khrushchev's condemnation of Stalin at the Twentieth Congress, a new plan seemed to emerge, alluded to by Chinese and Yugoslav press comments. It may have been the idea of a loose "Marxist," rather than Communist, community grouping socialist, leftist, neutralist and fellow-traveler parties, organizations, and, possibly, individuals. To Tito, such a new "international" might have meant a "third force." To Moscow, it would have been a new tactical step on the old road of Communist expansion. Whatever it may have been, any such design has been shattered, for the time being at least, by the Soviet armed intervention in Hungary, and the revulsion against Russia and Communism produced in the civilized world.

After the 1956 setbacks in Hungary and Poland, the Kremlin had to find new forms of keeping its grip on the "fraternal" Communist parties. Since 1957, the visible functions of the Internationals seem to have gradually shifted to meetings of Communist

parties' representatives. The attendance at such meetings grew
from sixty-four in November, 1957, to eighty-one in November,
1960. In the face of the dispute with China, Moscow's reassertion
of authority was slowed down. In 1961, Khrushchev felt it necessary to emphasize that the "Declaration" drawn up by the twelve
ruling Communist parties at the meeting in Moscow in November, 1957, was binding not only on its signatories but also on all the
other Communist parties. In a report to the ideological organizations of the Soviet Communist Party on January 6, 1961, he said
that the Statement adopted at the meeting of the eighty-one parties in November, 1960, was "a militant Marxist-Leninist document
of tremendous international significance. It reaffirms the allegiance
of the Communist parties to the Declaration of 1957." In October,
1961, Khrushchev reverted to the subject in the Report of the
Central Committee to the Twenty-second Party Congress. He
again stressed the significance of the November, 1960, meeting and
said that its "important propositions on the necessity to observe
decisions adopted collectively do not permit any action likely to
undermine Communist unity." Thus, we may conclude, Khrushchev considers that those decisions are as binding on the Communist parties as were Lenin's conditions of affiliation to the
Communist International.

Viewed as an independent phenomenon, Soviet diplomatic action
seems to be a continuation of the aims of Czarist foreign policy
to expand the national domain in all directions, starting from the
original Moscow nucleus. In the context of Communist doctrine,
the work of Soviet diplomacy has become more extensive and sophisticated than that of its Czarist forerunner. From the time of
Ivan Kalita, the "moneybag," an obscure medieval Moscow prince-
ling who collected taxes for the Tatar Khans, until the Bolshevik
Revolution, the success of Russian foreign policy was measured by
territorial acquisition. The Bolsheviks have by no means discarded
this tangible concept. But before 1917, it appeared as a secondary
aim of a proletarian revolution which was not necessarily expected to
start in Russia, and which—according to Lenin and his followers—
was to engulf the whole world. After the success of the November
(October) Revolution, Russia became the "fatherland of the proletariat" as well as the base for world revolution. Was it more important to reaffirm and consolidate Soviet-Russian power over the
land mass of the former empire, or to reach out quickly and carry
the revolution to other countries? The two ideas clashed before

they logically blended. At Brest-Litovsk, Trotsky had already shown how unwilling he was to let go of the non-Russian lands of Czarist Russia; Stalin, both before and after World War II, demonstrated that he never meant to abandon the aims of world revolution.

In 1927, even before Trotsky's ultimate defeat and banishment from Moscow, the international situation had already decided in favor of "Socialism in one country." There were no reasonable prospects for an early Communist revolution in Europe. In Asia, the Comintern suffered a stunning defeat that same year, when the Kuomintang turned against the Communists. Yet, it was after Trotsky was expelled from the Soviet Party that the Sixth Congress of the Communist International worked out its most comprehensive program for world revolution. Only a few months before, the tenth anniversary of the November Revolution marked the official beginning of Stalin's economic program for the Soviet Union. Thus, consolidation of "Socialism in one country" was simultaneous with the long-range preparations for Communist subversion and revolution in other countries.

Seen against this background, Soviet diplomacy reflects two basic aims: the need of coexistence and the drive for expansion of Communist rule. In one case, it assumes the classical role of state diplomacy; in the other, it is merely the other side of the coin of the Communist Internationals. Though never officially admitting responsibility for the Moscow direction of international Communist activities, Soviet diplomacy, as a rule, assists and shields them, as dictated by expediency. Thus, the scope and range of Russian diplomacy has widened. In accordance with the global aims of Communism, it is no longer tied to the land mass of the Eurasian "heartland." While drawing heavily on Russian diplomatic tradition, Communism has transcended the old imperial ambitions. The slogans formerly used to explain or excuse territorial expansion—unification of Russian lands, protection of the Orthodox faith, liberation of the Slav nations, Pan-Slavism, access to warm-water ports—all had logical geographic limits that could not be stretched indefinitely. But Communism, the proposed "union of all proletarians," and the "World Union of Soviet Socialist Republics" have no limits other than the confines of the globe.

4. REVOLUTION AND RESPECTABILITY—
THE WESTERN BORDER

The initial task of Soviet diplomacy was that of finding a way out of a dilemma: Communist Russia had to coexist with the bourgeois states before it could annihilate them. The revolutionary aims proclaimed by Lenin, the repudiation of foreign debts and recognized diplomatic methods, the mass terror that led practically to the extinction of the Russian upper and middle classes made this a particularly difficult assignment. The Bolshevik regime was not a welcome newcomer in the family of nations, although the Central Powers did expect it to weaken the enemy alliance. In all other respects, Lenin's government seemed no more acceptable to the governments of Germany and Austria-Hungary than it was to the Entente.

It was in this situation that Soviet Russia gained its first diplomatic recognition by the peace of Brest-Litovsk. However, this respectability was short-lived. In the nine-month period before the collapse of the German and Austrian imperial governments, the first German Ambassador to Communist Russia, Count von Mirbach, had been murdered, and the first Soviet Ambassador in Berlin, Adolph Joffe, had been shown the door because of his subversive activities. Full diplomatic relations were not restored until 1922, after the signing of the Rapallo Treaty.

The maintenance, and later renewal, of relations with the Entente powers was no less arduous. Although it would have suited Lenin's plans to keep a balance between both sides, the Western Powers could not fail to realize that under the Soviets, Russia had not only left the alliance against Germany and Austria-Hungary, but at times had virtually gone over to the other side. Under these circumstances, Allied military intervention in Russia was not an illogical step. It was later considered to have been a mistake, largely because it failed. And it failed not because of some inherent wickedness, as Communist historiographers claim, but because it was half-hearted, undertaken without an over-all plan and for conflicting purposes. A reactionary, "one and indivisible" Czarist Russia could be neither restored nor maintained. The Allies, however, did not know what they wanted and were unable to agree among themselves. Whatever the reasons, a *de facto* state of war existed between the Western Powers and Soviet Russia in 1918–19. Restoration of normal relations by way of a formal *de jure* recognition of the Soviet Government took five years in the case of Britain and France, and fourteen years in that of the United States.

Soviet diplomacy played its part in the subversion of the free states of the Ukraine, Georgia, Armenia, and Azerbaidzhan. Diplomatic exchanges with these governments were of a limited character: The Red Army invaded the Ukraine only a few months after the recognition of its independence by the Soviets; a second invasion by Soviet troops followed the repudiation by Russia of the Treaty of Brest-Litovsk and the abortive negotiations of the Ukrainians with Foreign Commissar Chicherin; similarly, only nine months elapsed between the recognition by Moscow of the free Georgian Republic and its overthrow by the Red Army.

But the Bolsheviks failed to conquer or subvert Poland, Finland, and the Baltic states. Also, they were unable to penetrate Romania. The decisive events in further developments in this area were Pilsudski's victories in the battles of Warsaw and on the river Niemen, which put an end to Soviet military efforts to establish territorial contact with the German Communists. As a logical consequence of this setback, it was here, along the western border, that, after periods of drastic warfare, the relations between the Soviet Government and a number of non-Communist states were first stabilized.

Before this stabilization, however, Lenin's government and the Third International made strenuous attempts to impose Communist regimes on the neighboring countries. Finland and the three Baltic states were invaded by Red troops in 1918 and were proclaimed as Soviet republics. In all four of these countries, national forces backed by the population resisted fiercely and drove out the Communist regimes. Between February and August, 1920, Soviet Russia made peace treaties with Estonia, Lithuania, and Latvia.

On August 17, 1920, at the very moment when the Russian armies under Tukhachevsky began to retreat from the Vistula River, a Soviet delegation to the peace conference in Minsk offered conditions tantamount to Poland's complete military and political capitulation: Poland was to limit its armed forces to 50,000 men; all arms and military equipment not required by this small force were to be delivered to the Soviets, who in turn would create a "civil militia to be organized among the workers to maintain order and safeguard the security of the population."[1] In a telegram to the British Government, Chicherin did not hesitate to state that such a militia, armed by Communist Russia, would be "a concession" to Poland.[2] Furthermore, the Soviet Government proposed to limit Poland's freedom of relations with all countries other than the Soviet Union and the Soviet Ukraine. The peace treaty was to contain binding directives on Poland's internal life. Had these conditions been accepted, Poland would have become a Soviet satellite a quarter of a century before it actually did. The consequences would have been momentous. Lenin said so explicitly on October 8, 1920: "If Poland had become Soviet . . . the Versailles Treaty would have been shattered, and the entire international system built by the victors would have been destroyed."[3]

As it was, the peace treaties with Latvia, Lithuania, and Estonia were allowed to stand. On October 14, 1920, two days after signing the preliminary peace with Poland, Soviet Russia also made peace with Finland by the Treaty of Tartu. But in 1920, the Bolsheviks were only bowing to necessity. They considered the peace treaties along the western border as a respite; they would hardly have thought that the next opportunity for extending the Communist system farther west would arise only twenty years later. This attitude explains why the work of Soviet diplomacy in Eastern and Central Europe was, for several years, little more than the reflection of the Communist International. Even the major Soviet diplomatic achievement of the twenties—the Treaty of Rapallo with Germany—did not deter Moscow from fomenting a Communist revolution in Germany the following year (1923). Full tranquility was not restored in the region extending from the Finnish Gulf to the Black Sea for several years. Areas bordering on Soviet Russia were like a Wild West frontier, with Communist bands making incursions over the border and Red guards pursuing the escaping refugees. In Poland, a special military frontier defense was created to guard the border regions, which did not become safe until the mid-twenties.

Russia's relations with Finland were marred by a dispute over Eastern Karelia, where about 60 per cent of the population was of Finnish stock. After the Bolshevik Revolution, an even larger percentage would have gladly joined the independent Finnish state.

But in the negotiations for a peace treaty, the Finns were unable to wrest the province from the Russians. All that they obtained for their Karelian kinsmen was a vague promise in Article 10 of the Treaty of Tartu that the autonomous territory of East Karelia should be formed of the Karelian populations in the governments (provinces) of Archangel and Olonets, and enjoy the rights of self-determination.[4] Disappointed and oppressed, the Karelian Finns rose against the Soviet authorities, but were soon subdued. For several years, the Finnish Government repeatedly and vainly tried to alleviate their lot. Russia rejected Finland's demand for an investigation of the Karelian situation by an impartial League of Nations commission. According to Chicherin, this suggestion was "a wholly unprecedented attack on the sovereign rights of the R.F.S.F.R."[5] In a note to the Finnish chargé d'affaires of December 5, 1921, Chicherin denied that there was "a popular rising, as though the population were driven to desperation" in the border region and accused the Finnish Government of having supported and encouraged "raids of bands organized on Finnish territory."[6] In June, 1923, Russia refused to acknowledge the authority of the Permanent Court of International Justice to which the Karelian question had been referred by the Council of the League of Nations. In its official communications, the Soviet Government stated that it would regard "the claim of the so-called League of Nations to intervene in questions concerning the internal situation in Karelia"[7] as a hostile act.

Another grave problem was posed by the conflict with Romania over Bessarabia. The Soviet Government considered it a part of the Ukrainian Soviet Republic, although when the province was reannexed in 1941, it was divided between the Soviet Ukraine and Soviet Moldavia. In January, 1918, in protest against its occupation by Romania, Lenin broke off diplomatic relations with Bucharest. This was preceded by the arrest of the Romanian Minister Constantin Diamandi and the confiscation of the Romanian gold reserve brought to Russia for deposit during the war. A decree of the Soviet Government of January 26, 1918, stated: "The Romanian gold reserve held in Moscow is not to be touched by the Romanian oligarchy. The Soviet Government assumes the responsibility for the safekeeping of this reserve and will hand it over to the Romanian nation."[8]

The gold—314 million gold lei[9]—was never returned, not even after 1945, when, according to the Communists, the Romanian people had become their own masters.

The territorial dispute over Bessarabia further disturbed the relations between the two countries, which were already tense due to frequent border incidents. On April 18, 1918, the Soviet Government protested against the incorporation of the province into Romania, and on November 1, 1920, against its recognition by the Allied powers. The conflict continued to smolder. In 1924, a Soviet-Romanian conference in Vienna failed to find a mutually acceptable solution. Chicherin, in a typical example of Soviet diplomatic language, described the vote of the Bessarabian National Assembly in favor of incorporation into Romania as "an impudent subterfuge on the part of General Mackensen's agents."[10] The Soviet Government made it known that it considered any assistance to Romania in connection with Bessarabia as a hostile act. But when the French Parliament, in March, 1924, ratified the Paris convention on Bessarabia, Chicherin's protest only vaguely threatened to make France coresponsible for Soviet losses in the province. In October, 1924, Moscow gladly accepted French *de jure* recognition and the resumption of diplomatic relations without raising the Bessarabian question; however, this remained a stumbling block in Soviet-Romanian relations.

Despite many obstacles, Russia's western neighbors were seriously striving to establish normal relations with the Soviet regime. They all needed peace, trade, and economic assistance; political instability and talk of war were damaging to their interests. Because the very recent past had convinced them that Soviet declarations of peaceful intentions were of little value, they tried to find security in mutual collaboration. The Soviet Government was opposed to any such moves. Potemkin's *History of Diplomacy** describes the Baltic conferences between Estonia, Latvia, Finland, and Poland as a machination of French diplomacy to form an anti-Soviet front of Baltic countries.[11] In fact, the concept of Baltic cooperation was a purely defensive one. In an agreement signed in Warsaw on March 17, 1922, the four countries promised each other nothing more than friendly concern should any of them become a victim of aggression, and pledged not to participate in compacts directed against any of them.[12] Even during the 1919–20 war, Pilsudski had given ample proof that he did not wish to join any *cordon sanitaire* around Soviet Russia despite his dislike for its regime. The not unreasonable view that the non-Russian nations of the former Czarist em-

---

* A Soviet publication, edited by former Ambassador and Deputy Commissar for Foreign Affairs Vladimir P. Potemkin.

pire should be set free—for their own sake, as well as for the sake of European security—found no practical expression in Polish politics after the failure to rouse the Ukraine in 1920.

But Soviet diplomacy wished to divide the western border states and isolate them from each other and from Western Europe. Moscow also tried to use these smaller countries in a broader diplomatic game of its own. It is instructive to compare the final protocol of the Riga Conference of March 30, 1922, comprising Soviet Russia, Poland, Finland, Latvia, and Estonia, with Chicherin's note to the Polish Foreign Minister of April 24, 1922. In the first document, the Soviet Government agreed with the other signatories "that it would be desirable to coordinate the actions of their representatives [with regard to certain economic questions of general interest to their countries] at the international conference at Genoa."[13] On the very same day (March 30), the Soviet delegation stopped in Berlin en route to Genoa and made far-reaching proposals to the German Government without the knowledge of its Riga partners, and certainly against the spirit, if not the letter, of their mutual agreement. A few weeks later, when the Polish Government, together with other Allied powers, protested against certain aspects of the Rapallo Treaty, Chicherin answered by accusing Poland of violating the 1921 Peace Treaty of Riga.

In addition, the Soviet Government lost no opportunity to blow up the territorial dispute between Lithuania and Poland over Vilno. In the peace treaty with Lithuania, concluded on July 12, 1920, while Russian armies were marching toward the Vistula, the Soviet Union had ceded the town of Vilno and adjacent districts to Lithuania; but on February 17, 1923, in identical notes to Poland and Lithuania, Chicherin protested against these governments' acceptance of League of Nations participation in the settlement of their territorial differences. This, Chicherin thought, was a violation of Article 3 of the Riga Treaty, which stated that the settlement of territorial disputes between Poland and Lithuania, "is a matter which exclusively concerns Poland and Lithuania," and should be settled "by Poland and Lithuania alone."[14] Chicherin therefore declared that bringing in third parties was a violation of the treaty. He considered this a particularly serious offense, since the third party in question was the League of Nations, an international body then held in disdain by Soviet diplomacy. Chicherin's distorted interpretation of Article 3, written into the Riga Treaty expressly to forestall Soviet interference, was coupled with yet another departure from logic. In the same note, Chicherin offered Soviet collaboration to settle the dispute "either alone or jointly with other impartial governments."[15]

The Soviet Government used a similar tactic in its note to Lithuania of March 8, 1924, dealing with the Memel question. Chicherin wrote that the special commission of the "so-called League of Nations" appointed to prepare a decision in this matter referred in its report to the Lithuanian-Polish territorial dispute. Therefore, Chicherin contended, the Lithuanian Government had no right to settle this question with the assistance of third powers "without the consent of the U.S.S.R."[16] This again was a misinterpretation of the Soviet-Lithuanian peace treaty of July 12, 1920.

How could the western border states establish and maintain normal relations with a government perpetually ready to interfere and continuously shifting its political ground and diplomatic or legal arguments? The pressure and the maneuvering of Soviet diplomacy also obstructed closer collaboration of the western border states, although there had been some positive accomplishments—i.e., the Polish-Romanian alliance of March 3, 1921; the Estonian-Latvian alliance of November 1, 1923; good relations among Estonia, Latvia, Finland, and Poland, as well as the three Baltic states. The efforts to organize wider Baltic collaboration foundered on active Soviet hostility, the territorial dispute between Lithuania and Poland, and a lack of interest on the part of Finland, which gravitated toward the Scandinavian orbit. The Warsaw agreement of March 17, 1922, did not enter into force. All that the Baltic Conferences of the early twenties accomplished was a somewhat vague understanding of a common danger and mutual interests, an understanding that was to serve some purpose in later years.

5. RAPALLO

The treaty concluded with Germany at Rapallo has been called the master stroke of early Soviet diplomacy. It aimed at ending the political and economic isolation of Moscow and at disrupting the economic opposition of the Western nations against Soviet expropriations and repudiation of debts. Signed on April 16, 1922, during the Genoa economic conference, the Rapallo Treaty came as a surprise to the Allied camp. It had been prepared in the course of secret Russian-German talks during the preceding months. The two countries were drawn to each other by their political isolation, their opposition to the Versailles Treaty, as well as by prospects of mutual trade. However, not everybody in Berlin was enthusiastic about an alignment of the "have-nots" against the Allies. To overcome any opposition to its plans, Moscow played Germany against its former enemies, while at the same time bringing pressure on the Allies. For example, there was Radek's article in *Pravda* in December, 1921, implying that Soviet Russia might invoke Article 116 of the Versailles Treaty to claim reparations from Germany.[1] A few weeks later, Chicherin accused the Western Powers of trying to use the famine in Russia as an excuse for economic penetration. In March, speaking to a workers' congress, Lenin pretended to see a sinister meaning—he even hinted at a danger of war—in the delayed opening of the Genoa conference occasioned by internal difficulties in Italy. He warned "messieurs the capitalists" that they would gain nothing by procrastination and, in rather hysterical tones, proclaimed that the retreat from Communism was over: "Enough. No more concessions. . . . Tomorrow you will get nothing."[2]

Thus, by putting pressure on the Germans and trying to turn public opinion against the Allies, the Soviet Government prepared to act in two directions. A third policy line, held in reserve, was the agreement reached at the Riga Conference in March with the western neighbors.*

* See p. 47.

At Genoa, the Russians entered into detailed private discussions
with the Allies and kept the Germans in the dark. Then, secretly, in
a surprise move, the Soviet delegation again turned to the Germans: The Rapallo Treaty was completed and signed in one day.[3]

The treaty stipulated that diplomatic and consular relations between the two countries be resumed forthwith; it canceled mutual
claims to war damages and expropriations and provided the most-
favored nation clause in trade and treatment of citizens.[4]

Opinions on whether the Rapallo Treaty was more profitable to
one side or the other vary. In the short run, Soviet Russia certainly
gained some advantages from this diplomatic flanking maneuver.
A few agricultural, industrial, and trading concessions were granted
to German firms, some of which helped the Soviet economy. On
the other hand, German trade credits—and consequently German
exports to Russia—were slow to develop and did not reach significant proportions until 1931, i.e., nearly a decade after the conclusion of the treaty. It is easy to argue that other Western nations
may also have wanted to do business with Russia at the time, despite the objectionable character of Soviet economic methods. But
the fact remains that Soviet-German collaboration after the Rapallo Treaty seriously hampered the Western nations' common
economic action; it strengthened the Russians in their rejection of
responsibility for the financial obligations incurred by the pre-
Soviet regime and helped the Soviet state maintain economic au-
tarchy and political hostility, which receded—to a degree and temporarily—only because of fear of Hitler. Potemkin's *History of
Diplomacy* states that "Rapallo brought to naught Allied efforts to
establish a united capitalist front."[5]

For Germany, the advantages were more dubious. Rapallo did
not bring a dramatic increase in German-Russian trade, which until
1931 did not exceed 3 per cent of Germany's total foreign trade.
The reputation of the Weimar Republic was not enhanced by
undercover military collaboration with the Soviets in circumvention
of the disarmament provisions of the Versailles Treaty. Arms factories were built in Russia with German financial and technical
assistance; the products were shared by both countries. Secret training centers for German pilots, tank crews, and gas warfare were set
up on Soviet soil. This collaboration continued through the early
days of Hitler's rule and helped build the army with which Hitler
conquered Europe.

It is true that Rapallo did break Germany's political isolation
sooner than would have been possible otherwise. But it cast a

shadow of suspicion over German-Western relations even before Hitler came to power. And in the long run, it encouraged German militarism and ill-fated territorial demands. In effect, Rapallo sowed the seed of a policy that later developed into the 1939 Molotov-Ribbentrop Pact and precipitated the outbreak of World War II.

An intermediary conclusion can be drawn at this point. In three instances after the Bolshevik Revolution did Moscow take the initiative for Soviet-German understanding: before Brest-Litovsk in 1917–18, in the case of Rapallo in 1922, and in the Molotov-Ribbentrop Pact in 1939. Thus, the Soviet attitude toward Germany showed a remarkable consistency of purpose, although it would be wrong to think that this purpose was limited to traditional diplomatic collaboration. From the very beginning, Russia's aim was a Soviet Germany. In January, 1918, Maxim M. Litvinov, the future Commissar for Foreign Affairs, declared in an interview with the London *Daily Chronicle:* "It is grossly malicious to represent the Bolsheviks as pro-German or anti-Allies. . . . They would regard it as their highest triumph if they could carry the torch of revolution to Berlin."[6]

In 1919, Chicherin, then People's Commissar for Foreign Affairs, wrote in *Izvestia* that every blow aimed at the Bavarian Soviet Republic (which lasted less than a month—from April 7 to May 1, 1919) "is a blow aimed at us."[7]

In 1920, Lenin said that Germany could free itself from the Versailles Treaty only through collaboration with Soviet Russia.[8] On May 19, 1922, the Executive Committee of the Communist International declared that the Rapallo Treaty was an "alliance with Germany," calling it a fact "of enormous historical importance." It went on to explain what Moscow hoped to achieve:

On the German side the treaty was signed by the present bourgeois Menshevik government, but everybody understands that while the position of the bourgeois Menshevik German government is a temporary thing, the German working class remains. The German working class will one day inevitably conquer power in its own country. Germany will become a Soviet republic. And then, when the German-Russian treaty brings together two great Soviet republics, it will provide such unshakable foundations for real Communist construction that the old and outworn Europe will not be able to withstand it for even a few years.[9]

At that time, these hopes were not merely dreams. The Bolsheviks expected them to materialize in the very near future. Shortly after Rapallo, August Thalheimer, the leader of the German Communist Party, wrote in a message to the German workers: "It is your duty to see that this step is not followed by a step back, but by further steps in the direction of *Anschluss* with Soviet Russia."[10]

6. THE YEAR OF RECOGNITION

The political gains of the Rapallo Treaty were slow to materialize, mainly because of partly spontaneous, partly Moscow-inspired
Communist agitation in Germany the following year. Because of
the catastrophic deterioration of living conditions and a general dis-
content resulting from the French occupation of the Ruhr, the
German Communist Party enjoyed a period of popularity in the
summer of 1923. In August, Cuno's government, which ordered
passive resistance against the French, fell. Cuno was replaced by
Stresemann, who called off the passive resistance and sought to arrive at an understanding with France. This was the signal for the
Kremlin to incite the German Communists to take power by force.
But in October, a badly organized uprising was suppressed in Ham-
burg. In Saxony and Thuringia, the Communist-infiltrated provin-
cial governments were deposed by the army on orders from Berlin.
The German Government obtained proof that the Soviet Embassy
in Berlin was using its diplomatic status to purchase arms for a
revolution that had been openly predicted by the German Communist press. The affair became a public scandal when *Vorwärts*,
the organ of the German Social Democratic Party, revealed details
and reminded its readers of the incident that in 1918 had led to
the expulsion of the first Soviet representative, Adolphe Joffe, from
Berlin. Moscow waxed indignant, and in an official statement published on October 6, 1923, deplored the fact that the German Government had not dissociated itself from the anti-Soviet accusations
of the Socialist newspaper. The statement ended with a reference
to the Rapallo Treaty, to which, it said, the Soviet Government
loyally adhered.[1]

The damage done to Soviet-German relations was considerable
but not permanent, for the Germans still wished to continue the
Rapallo policy. In Moscow, the Communist setbacks in Germany
weakened the influence of the leaders of the Third International
and were used by Stalin to further his own political interests. For

this was also the time of Lenin's mortal illness. He died in January, 1924, the year that Potemkin's *History of Diplomacy* calls "the year of recognition of the U.S.S.R." Neither Russia's meddling in Germany in 1923, nor the conflict over doctrine and Lenin's succession among the Bolshevik leaders seemed to have hobbled Moscow's drive for formal recognition on a wider international scale. Soviet efforts were also favored by the coming to power in Britain and France of the left-of-center governments of Ramsay MacDonald and Édouard Herriot, who wished to establish relations with the Soviet Government for ideological and internal political reasons. Once British recognition was granted, other countries followed. The Soviet regime was recognized *de jure* by England, Italy, and Norway in February, 1924; by Greece and Sweden in March; by Denmark in June; and by France in October.

The British recognition was warmly greeted in Moscow. The Second Congress of the Soviets called it a "historic step,"[2] while Chicherin hailed the "unanimous demand of the [British] working class" and the sagacity of the "best section of English ruling quarters."[3] Litvinov retrospectively praised Lloyd George's attitude on recognition at the Genoa conference. The ground gained by Soviet diplomacy in a few years was indeed considerable. It should be remembered that in 1921, Soviet Russia was the only important maritime state not invited to the Washington Naval Conference.[4] The Soviet Union was also left out of the convention for the neutralization of the Aaland Islands in the Finnish Archipelago, signed in Geneva on October 20, 1921, by the West European powers and all the Baltic coastal states except Lithuania. As late as 1923, no Soviet delegates were invited to participate fully in the Lausanne Conference, which decided on the regime of the Black Sea Straits; they were admitted to only one of the commissions.

The impressive series of foreign recognitions occurred even before Stalin's theory of "Socialism in one country" was first disseminated in December. As later events proved, the theory did not mean that the Kremlin intended to renounce its global revolutionary aims. Nor were the Bolsheviks ready, in 1924, to refrain from spreading the Communist rule to other countries by violent means, as was shown by the abortive coups in Bulgaria and Estonia in September and December, respectively. In October, the publication of the, probably apocryphal, "Zinoviev letter" led to the fall of the MacDonald Government in England. Thus, the inherent contradiction in the external aims of the Moscow regime—between the spreading of world revolution and the need for normal interstate

relations—haunted Soviet diplomatic action. Abroad, the prestige
of the Soviet Union suffered because of these setbacks, but again
the damage was not irreparable; 1924 was the year when, for the first
time, Soviet diplomacy could act on a wider international stage.
For Moscow this was a particularly welcome change, since Soviet
Russia was entering a period of internal strife and economic difficulties that absorbed much of its energy: the struggle for power between Stalin and Trotsky, between Stalin and the "left opposition"
of Zinoviev and Kamenev, followed by Stalin's fight against the
rightist "deviation" represented by Bukharin, Rykov, and Tomski;
the industrial troubles of the First Five-Year Plan (1928–32), the
near civil war of the collectivization of agriculture (1927–33), the
great famines of 1931–33. All these events explain why Soviet diplomacy was mostly used for defensive purposes between the "year of
recognition" and the advent of Hitler in 1933.

7. *LOCARNO*

At the beginning of 1925, Soviet Russia could consider the world situation as relatively satisfactory, although in Moscow it was unfashionable to admit it too openly. Stalin spoke of new complications for which the Soviet Union must be ready.[1] He admitted, however, that there was no need to think in terms of an offensive against anyone. "Our banner," he said, "remains the banner of peace."[2]

Without doubt, the international situation of the Soviet state had improved. No serious trouble could possibly come from the western border states; although relations with England had become strained since the "Zinoviev letter" incident, neither the English nor the French could be suspected of plotting to overthrow the Soviet Government; Germany was slowly regaining its economic strength, its attitude toward Russia had not changed substantially since Rapallo, and its relations with the Western powers remained cool.

The situation in the Far East was even more favorable. Soviet Russia had reasserted its rights in the Chinese Eastern Railway and concluded the important Peking agreement with Japan on January 20, 1925. Japan established diplomatic relations with the Soviet Union and renounced possession of Northern Sakhalin. In a press interview of January 22, Chicherin could therefore say that "the Russian Far East has now entered on a phase of peaceful development and friendly relations with all its neighbors."[3]

However, this favorable picture was somewhat overcast in Europe by the prospect of a treaty that seemed to thwart the policy of Rapallo. Moscow was alarmed over the news of negotiations that ultimately led to the Locarno Agreements. A new situation was developing between Germany and its western neighbors. Germany was to be admitted to the League of Nations, leaving Russia in new isolation. In May, 1925, Soviet apprehension grew, and Chicherin feared that even despite its own wish, the German Government would "find itself in a position which will scarcely make it possible to continue, at least in the same degree as formerly, the relations established between us."[4]

The dangers envisaged by Moscow did not materialize, because Germany did not abandon the Rapallo policy. Other aspects of the Locarno Agreements had some lasting influence on the European situation. The Treaty of Mutual Guarantee, or the Rhine Pact, was the main diplomatic instrument among the agreements initialed in Locarno on October 16, 1925, and signed in London on December 1. Expected by some to strengthen the Versailles Treaty (for many years the object of sharp Soviet criticism), it in fact introduced a new distinction between the validity of Germany's western and eastern frontiers. The western border was guaranteed by Germany itself and the other signatories of the main Locarno Treaty —Belgium, France, Great Britain, and Italy—and therefore accepted as final. But despite French insistence, Germany refused to confirm the validity of its frontiers with Poland and Czechoslovakia; it concluded with them only treaties of arbitration, thereby implying a lack of equality between international obligations in different parts of Europe. There was to be a Europe A and a Europe B,[5] not only in the economic sense, but also from the point of view of international law, security, and political stability. In many quarters it was then assumed that the Locarno Agreements in some way legalized German revisionist propaganda in Eastern Europe. Although the Soviet Union had no common frontier with Germany, there was suspicion in Moscow of a new *Drang nach Osten* encouraged by England, then the villain of Soviet propaganda. In a press interview in Berlin on October 2, 1925, Chicherin voiced the fear "that England can promise Germany great benefits at Poland's expense."[6]

The Locarno treaties were harshly criticized by Stalin, who saw in them "a continuation of Versailles" and the seeds of a new European war. On December 18, 1925, in a speech at the Fourteenth Party Congress, he mentioned in the same breath the losses suffered by Germany as well as by Russia as a result of the Versailles Treaty and charged that the Locarno agreements "would legalize and give juridical sanction to Germany's loss of Silesia, the Danzig Corridor, and Danzig; the Ukraine's loss of Galicia and Western Volhynia; Belorussia's loss of her western territories; Lithuania's loss of Vilna, etc."[7]

It is not unreasonable to point to the thought relationship between this revealing text and Stalin's broad hint to Hitler on March 10, 1939, as he prepared to launch the secret negotiations that led to the Molotov-Ribbentrop Pact. Stalin then accused the West of "egging the Germans on to march further east [to] start war against the Bolsheviks." A comparison of the two texts would indicate that the idea of a new partition of eastern Europe did not spontaneously arise in Moscow in 1939 as a result of Soviet disappointment with the West over "the Munich concessions to the aggressors."[8]

As a consequence of the Locarno Agreements, Soviet diplomacy seemed to have been caught between its dislike of Versailles and the League of Nations on the one hand, and the fear of new German expansion in eastern Europe on the other. In order to preserve the Rapallo policy, Chicherin concentrated on the danger to Russo-German relations stemming from Article 16 of the Covenant of the League of Nations. This article obligated the member states to participate in sanctions against "a violator of the peace." In his Berlin press interview of October 2, Chicherin asked "whether England would not succeed, after the pact was concluded, in forcing an anti-Soviet policy on Germany." He also came out strongly against the League of Nations, which Germany was about to join, stating that the possibility of Soviet participation in it "does not arise in any way. . . . It is a fact that any nation that enters the League of Nations loses its independence, unless of course it is one of the victor states."[9]

Again it is interesting to compare this attitude with the presentation of Locarno in Potemkin's *History of Diplomacy*. Here German diplomacy is accused of betraying its Soviet friends by trying to reach agreement with the "victors." It states that "Germany repeatedly raised the scarecrow of the 'Bolshevik danger,'" and that the Germans lost no opportunity to threaten the Allies that they would "throw themselves into the arms of the Soviet Union." The *History of Diplomacy* seems to deplore the failure to secure a guarantee for all German frontiers and puts the blame on British opposition and Germany's "policy of blackmail."[10] This, most probably, was what the Russians really thought of the Locarno agreements in 1925. They were not concerned—as we may gather from Stalin's speech—with the fate of Poland or Czechoslovakia, but rather with the possible eastward extension of German territorial ambitions and the effects of Germany's membership in the League of Nations. Moreover, internal difficulties made it imperative to maintain peace along the western border. It was a time of increasing tensions among the Bolshevik hierarchy and of the final struggle between Stalin and the "left deviation" or "New Opposition" of Zinoviev and Kamenev. At first, therefore, the Soviet Government tried to prevent the Locarno agreements; it definitely preferred, for itself and for others, the bilateral pacts of neutrality and nonaggression like the one signed with Turkey on December 12, 1925. According to a press interview by Litvinov on December 24, 1925, the Soviet Government was willing to conclude similar treaties with all countries. "This," Litvinov said, "and not the machinations of the League of Nations or pacts like Locarno, will really help to avert war."[11]

Once the Locarno agreements had been signed, Soviet diplomacy pressed Germany for a treaty confirming the policy of Rapallo; Moscow also wanted to make sure that, as a member of the League of Nations, Germany would not participate in military sanctions against the Soviet Union. These ideas were consistent with German intentions. They had already found expression in the Locarno agreements, namely in German reservations to the application of Article 16 of the Covenant of the League of Nations to German-Soviet relations. Soviet-German collaboration was further reasserted in the Treaty of Berlin of April 24, 1926.

8. SECURITY IN EASTERN EUROPE

Internal difficulties and growing tensions in the Far East during the post-Locarno decade again made it imperative for Moscow to avoid disturbances along the western border. But negotiations for a system of treaties in this area dragged on for years, mainly because Russia would not allow the simultaneous signing of security pacts by all its western neighbors. The Soviet Government believed that such a system of synchronized agreements would create a united front with a common policy toward Russia. Since Poland was the largest of its western neighbors, the Soviet Union made considerable efforts to detach it from the other Baltic countries and from Romania. Poland's insistence on collective agreements was met with Soviet complaints and accusations, directed also at England, which had replaced France in the role of alleged mischief-maker in the Baltic area. In April, 1926, Chicherin spoke bitterly of the "desire of the English Government to hinder the prospect of a *rapprochement* between Poland and the U.S.S.R."[1] Litvinov's report to the Central Committee, delivered at the end of April, contained the following passage: "all our efforts to reach a lasting agreement with Poland have up to now been defeated by the Polish Government's anxiety to play the part . . . of the manager of external relations for all the Baltic states."[2]

In fact, Litvinov was accusing Poland of the very thing Russia wanted to do. Attempts to impose the Soviet will on the small nations of the area never abated from 1917 to 1940. In 1926, the positions of both sides were already clear: The Poles feared to make agreements with Soviet Russia that would leave any of the western border states unprotected; the Russians, exaggerating the significance of this stand, contended (as did the Soviet Envoy to France, Rakovsky, in a press interview on October 6, 1926) that a collective treaty of the border states with the Soviet Union "would mean that we ourselves are creating an anti-Soviet coalition."[3] Under the circumstances, negotiations with Poland, Estonia, and Latvia for security or nonaggression pacts made no progress from 1926 to 1931. Only Lithuania agreed to a separate course and concluded a nonaggression pact with the Soviet Union on September 28, 1926. The pact had little effect on Soviet relations with the other border states, particularly since Russia had no common frontier with Lithuania.

When, however, on August 27, 1928, the Kellogg Pact "for the renunciation of war" was signed in Paris, it started a chain reaction that eventually brought about the first multilateral agreement on Russia's western border. The Soviets were not among the fifteen governments originally invited to sign the Kellogg Pact, and it was chiefly for this reason that Moscow initially labeled the pact ineffectual and without binding force. This was largely true, but no one in Europe expected this declaration of peaceful intentions to accomplish anything more than to lessen international tensions. Litvinov also criticized the American project because it was not linked to the Soviet proposals for "total disarmament." Chicherin went further. In a press statement of August 5, 1928, he declared that "the real aims of the initiators of the pact obviously included and include the desire of . . . isolating the U.S.S.R. and fighting against it. The negotiations for the conclusion of the pact clearly are a constituent part of the policy of encircling the U.S.S.R."[4]

The tone changed when, on August 31, 1928, the Soviet Union was invited to join the pact and consented to adhere to it, after a show of bad temper and some reservations. Soon Litvinov was planning to use the pact as a lever for forcing Poland into a separate agreement.[5] On December 29, 1928, he proposed that in their mutual relations the Soviet Union and Poland implement the Kellogg Pact immediately. Warsaw again answered that it would make its acceptance dependent on the participation of Russia's other western neighbors, i.e., the Baltic states, Finland, and Romania.

Litvinov's initiative coincided with the adoption of the First Five-Year Plan and the beginning of collectivization of agriculture, which shook the Soviet state to the core. Furthermore, Soviet-Chinese relations rapidly deteriorated after the spring of 1927. Communist uprisings in China were suppressed, and toward the end of 1928, Russia seemed unable to withstand Chinese pressure in northern Manchuria and along the Chinese Eastern Railway. In view of these difficulties in the east, a manifestation of peaceful intentions along the western border was more important to the Kremlin than tactical maneuverings designed to split the solidarity of the European border states. The Soviet Government, therefore, yielded to Polish insistence. The "Moscow," or "Litvinov," Protocol was signed on February 9, 1929, by the Soviet Union, Poland, Estonia, Latvia, and Romania; Lithuania, Turkey, and Persia signed a few weeks later, and Finland only in 1932. The Soviet Union repeated its claim to Bessarabia.[6]

The effect of this multilateral agreement, although beneficial, was limited (as was the Kellogg Pact itself) to bringing some improvement in the political atmosphere along Russia's western and southern borders. Protracted negotiations for more meaningful diplomatic obligations, i.e., nonaggression pacts, still made little headway. It was not until the end of 1931, when the situation in the Far East became threatening, that the Soviet Government agreed that such pacts cover the whole length of the western border. Significantly, the talks suddenly came to life soon after the Japanese Army began moving into Manchuria in September, 1931, although Moscow implied that its change of attitude was the result of the negotiations for a nonaggression pact with France. On August 27, 1931, Tass issued a statement deriding a document presented to the Commissariat for Foreign Affairs by the Polish Envoy Stanislas Patek. Tass said that Mr. Patek's document merely restated the same conditions that, in 1926–27, had made a nonaggression pact with Poland impossible. Two days later, Litvinov also emphatically denied that any negotiations were being conducted with Poland. But on October 14, 1931, and again on November 22, the Soviet Government asked the Poles to resume negotiations. These led to the conclusion of a nonaggression pact, initialed on January 26, 1932, but not signed until July 25, 1932, because of Poland's insistence that the Soviet Government first conclude similar pacts with the other border states.[7] This condition was only partially met. The Soviet Union signed nonaggression treaties with Finland on January 21, 1932, with Latvia on February 5, and with Estonia on May 4. But Soviet-Romanian negotiations came to naught. It was not until a year later, on concluding the Convention for the Definition of Aggression, that both Soviet Russia and Romania put their signatures on a major diplomatic document. The convention was signed in London on July 3, 1933, by the Soviet Union, Estonia, Latvia, Poland, Romania, Turkey, and Persia. An identical text was signed separately the next day by the Soviet Union and Lithuania. Finland adhered to the Convention on July 22, 1933. The Soviet Government was the initiator of this definition of aggression, which provided, in the Annex to

Article 3, that no act of aggression could be justified by the internal conditions of a state, by its political, economic, or social structure, by alleged defects in its administration, or by its international conduct.[8]

9. HITLER'S IMPACT ON SOVIET POLICY

THE BALTIC GUARANTEE

Relations between Soviet Russia and its western neighbors were never better than at the beginning of 1933, the year Hitler came to power. In view of internal problems, grave economic difficulties, and external danger in the Far East, Russia wished to be free from troubles in the west. Soviet diplomacy worked hard for this goal, particularly after the Japanese invasion of Manchuria in 1931. The conclusion of a series of nonaggression treaties with the western border states in 1932 brought about a period of relaxed tension. Relations with Poland were marked by cultural exchanges, mutual professional visits, and informal political talks. An exchange of visits between Karl Radek, the influential editor of *Izvestia*, and Boguslaw Miedzinski, the editor of the Warsaw *Gazeta Polska* and a prominent supporter of Marshal Pilsudski, were indicative of change in the political climate. Relations with Romania were somewhat improved; those with the Baltic states remained correct. Trade with Germany, particularly German imports, reached sizable proportions. On the eve of Hitler's advent to power, political relations with Germany, though rather stagnant, were also good.

This favorable picture in Central and Eastern Europe was in sharp contrast to the situation in the Far East. After a short military campaign against China in the second half of 1929, the Soviet Union regained its 1927 losses in Northern Manchuria and along the Chinese Eastern Railway. Diplomatic relations with China, broken off by Moscow on July 17, 1929, were not fully restored, but the protocol signed at Khabarovsk on December 22, 1929, provided for a partial resumption of consular relations.

After the autumn of 1931, Soviet positions in the Far East began to be threatened by Japan. Although the Far Eastern Army under Marshal Blücher was more than a match for the Chinese, it could not yet face the might of Japan. Moscow, therefore, tried to gain time and offered to conclude a nonaggression treaty. But Japan was in the ascendancy and would not let the Soviet Government off so cheaply. Feeling unable to meet the challenge, the Soviet Union proposed to sell the Chinese Eastern Railway to Manchukuo, i.e., to Japan. The offer was made on May 2, 1933, and on March 23, 1935, after two years of negotiations, the deal was concluded. Although hailed in Moscow with "deep satisfaction" as "a happy and promising event which should gladden the friends of peace throughout the world,"[1] the agreement meant the loss of all Soviet influence in Manchuria. It was the price of appeasing Japan, at least to the extent of warding off a major conflict. But with the Japanese in control of a satellite state in Manchuria (Manchukuo), and pressing on all lines of contact with the Soviet sphere, the situation remained strained. In the late thirties, the Far Eastern Army evolved into a sort of self-contained military state, which, amid frequent border clashes, on the whole managed to resist Japanese pressure, but took no bolder initiative.

There were good reasons for such restraint. Since 1933, the situation in Europe demanded the undivided attention of the Kremlin. Hitler's appearance on the German scene had brought about a drastic revision of Soviet policy with regard to collective security and, consequently, the League of Nations and the Western democracies. However, in 1933–34, there was a period of transition during which, while showing outward disapproval of Nazi Germany, the Soviets made serious efforts to come to terms with Hitler. On May 5, 1933, Soviet Russia and Nazi Germany extended the validity of the Berlin Treaty of April 24, 1926, stipulating that the relations between the two countries develop on the basis of Rapallo, that they not join in any group of nations united against the other partner, and that they remain neutral in the case of unprovoked aggression against one of them. Gustav Hilger, then a diplomatic official in the German Embassy in Moscow, states that "such persons as Krestinsky, Litvinov, and Molotov went out of their way to assure us that their government had no desire to reorient its foreign policy."[2] The Russians soon discontinued their secret military collaboration with the Reichswehr, presumably because it was too dangerous; but they were still ambiguous in their political strategy. In a speech of December 28, 1933, Molotov criticized the "ideologues of militant national socialism," and yet he spoke wistfully of past friendly relations with Germany. The following day, Litvinov told the Central Executive Committee: "The entire world knows that we can and do maintain good relations with capitalist

states, even if Fascist." Soviet Russia was still open to approaches
by Berlin, although in the same speech the Commissar for Foreign
Affairs drew attention to Hitler's plans as spelled out in *Mein
Kampf*: "by fire and sword to cut a road for expansion to the East,
which was not to stop at the Soviet frontier, and to enslave the
Soviet people."

The novelty of Hitler's policy, and its danger to Russia, lay in
the fact that he would not be content with reconquering "the territories of which it [Germany] had been deprived by the Versailles
Treaty."[3] As usual, there was nothing doctrinaire or ideological in
the way Moscow decided to cope with the danger. Soviet diplomacy moved simultaneously in two opposite directions: a *rapprochement* with the Western powers and the League of Nations,
and an attempt at accommodation with Nazi Germany in the form
of intricate maneuvers involving Poland and the Baltic states. The
Soviet Government asked Poland (in December, 1933) and then
Germany to guarantee or neutralize the Baltic states. "The Soviet
Government wanted these negotiations to be conducted in secret
without informing of them the governments who were directly concerned. The Polish Government opposed the secrecy of the negotiations and made its attitude dependent on that of Riga and
Tallin." At that time, Lithuania was seeking to improve relations
with Poland and less inclined than in previous years to play a one-
sided game with the Soviet Union. Poland, having learned of the
firmly negative reaction of the Baltic states, refused to participate
in the Soviet plan.[4]

In March, 1934, the Russians turned to Germany. Litvinov, in-
terestingly enough, strenuously denied any similarity between this
proposition and that made to Poland. On April 21, 1934, Litvinov
told the German Ambassador:

> We have never at any time proposed to the Polish Government to
> sign any protocol on the Baltic states, but have only proposed a
> joint Soviet-Polish declaration on their determination to protect and
> defend peace in the east of Europe, and to recognize that the two
> states consider as a necessary condition of such peace the integrity
> and complete economic and political independence of the new
> political entities that have been formed out of the former Russian
> empire.[5]

There was some truth in Litvinov's evasions. In both cases, the
Soviet offer was directed at the Baltic states whose freedom of
action would have been limited by a guarantee they did not ask

for. But for the time being Russia needed a partner. In the Kremlin's view, the difference of the two versions of a Baltic guarantee may have been this: Had Poland been forced to accept the Soviet proposition, Estonia, Latvia, and Lithuania would have become the "protected" countries, their independence gradually shrinking in response to Russia's pressure; but acting in concert with Nazi Germany, Russia was probably thinking of including Poland itself in the "protected" area—as was demonstrated five years later by the Molotov-Ribbentrop Pact, although it took a war to implement it. From the beginning, the proposition to Germany had a wider scope. In his communication to the German Ambassador, Litvinov again insisted that the Soviet Government "has demonstrated its ability to maintain the best relations with other states, regardless of their internal regimes." He rejected the German contention that the "regrettable estrangement in Soviet-German relations . . . is due to the Soviet Government's attitude to the National-Socialist regime in Germany." Further, Litvinov took at face value German statements that both governments should maintain friendly contacts "in order to secure agreement on all political and economic questions" and welcomed the possibility of restoring "relations of confidence."[6]

The Soviet Government had, of course, legitimate cause for alarm and for trying to reach agreement with Berlin in the interest of peace. But such were not the Kremlin's intentions. Hence the under-the-counter methods used, the secrecy in approaching first the Poles, then the Germans, and the failure to inform the Baltic states, which were to be the object of the foreign guarantee. Nor can the Soviet diplomatic activities with regard to the Baltic states in 1933–34 be explained by an alleged fear of a German-Polish-Finnish agreement to attack the U.S.S.R.[7] Neither Poland nor Finland contemplated any such design; of this the Soviet Government was well aware, and proved it by its reasonable reaction to the Polish-German declaration of nonaggression of January 26, 1934. During the following years, the Poles held fast to their policy of unalignment with either of their two big neighbors and rejected all German offers directed against Russia, although by accepting them they could have hoped to divert, or at least delay, Hitler's aggression against Poland. But in 1934, no such German offers had yet been made. It would be more logical to speculate that the Russians got wind of the German-Polish negotiations and tried to upset them. But everything in the Soviet behavior indicates that the Baltic-guarantee scheme was more than a tactical maneuver. A

German historian, Georg von Rauch, seems to be near the truth in thinking that by offering Hitler a joint guarantee of the Baltic states, the Russians "may have envisaged a great territorial reapportionment which would assign the Baltic States to the Soviet Union and the Polish Corridor to Germany."[8] This explanation is certainly more in keeping with what really happened in later Soviet-Nazi agreements. But in the spring of 1934, Hitler was not ready for a German-Soviet pact, and he declined to cooperate with Moscow. The threat of Soviet intervention, however vague at the time, brought the three Baltic states closer together. In March, 1934, Lithuania was invited to join the Estonian-Latvian defensive alliance. On September 12, 1934, the three countries signed a Treaty of Good Understanding and Cooperation in Geneva.[9]

The "Eastern Locarno"

There was a close link between the Soviet idea of a Baltic guarantee and the much broader negotiation concerning the East European pact, or "Eastern Locarno," which played an important role in European diplomatic life in the years 1934–35.

The Eastern Locarno project was sponsored jointly by France and Soviet Russia, but there are indications that the idea originated in Moscow. It was based, in a very general way, on the French concepts put forward in 1925 in connection with the Locarno Agreements, and more specifically on a French plan of November, 1932, for the grouping of states in concentric circles. The first Soviet suggestions possibly were made in the autumn of 1933, when Herriot visited Russia, or in September of the same year, during the Assembly of the League of Nations. In October, 1933, Litvinov visited Paris. The official birthday of the plan for an East European security pact was a meeting between French Foreign Minister Louis Barthou and Litvinov in Geneva on May 5, 1934. Litvinov spoke of three interlocking circles of agreements: in Eastern Europe, in the Mediterranean area, and between the great naval powers. Only the first of these projects received serious consideration. Soviet Russia found it particularly convenient to appear as cosponsor in association with France and was not too eager to claim sole parentage. But Soviet diplomacy was active in pushing the project; in June, 1934, Litvinov said that the East European pact "will resemble the Locarno agreements in that the latter guaranteed peace in western Europe, while this pact will perform the same function in the east of Europe."[10]

Despite close French-Soviet diplomatic collaboration in these negotiations, the real aims of the two countries were far from identical. In 1925, at the time of Locarno, the French Government tried in vain to include Eastern Europe in the system of guarantees of the German borders. In 1934, France aimed for substantially the same goal—European stability. But circumstances had changed. Hitler's rule made the quest for security guarantees more urgent, while the treaty obligations with East European states appeared to the French to be increasingly dangerous. Many Frenchmen, as well as other West Europeans, regarded the new Soviet attitude toward collective security and the League of Nations as the proverbial *deus ex machina*. Therefore, exaggerated hopes were attached to Soviet blandishments and alleged intentions.

For the best part of 1934, the French seemed determined to overcome all opposition and obstacles to an Eastern pact. There were many difficulties; the chief one being Hitler's refusal to enter the proposed collective-security system. Poland, determined to maintain a balance in its relations with Russia and Germany, thought that pacts of nonaggression best served that purpose. The Baltic states, although not rejecting the proposed pact outright, feared that it might pave the way for Soviet intervention in their internal affairs. "In the thirties," writes the Latvian diplomat and historian Alfred Bilmanis, "the Bolsheviks tried to entangle the Baltic states in international schemes that would allow them to occupy the states under formulas of indirect aggression and automatic action."[11] The Baltic states, as well as Poland, were suspicious of Soviet motives and would not agree to arrangements of mutual assistance that could be interpreted as a right or a pretext for Russian troops to enter their territories. Not only was this fear well founded historically, but it was tragically confirmed a few years later.

The most interesting aspect of Soviet behavior in these negotiations concerned Nazi Germany. It is striking to find a German diplomatic official then attached to the Moscow Embassy write many years later that "the proposed *Ostpakt*, as the Embassy called it, was only the most ambitious Soviet attempt to establish a *modus vivendi* with National Socialist Germany."[12]

In a press statement on December 7, 1934, Litvinov said that "in particular the U.S.S.R. has never ceased to wish for the best all-round relation with Germany."[13] The following month he declared in Geneva that "the chances of bringing this pact into existence . . . now depend only on Germany."[14] The Soviet leaders used Anthony Eden's visit to Moscow to issue a communiqué dated

March 31, 1935, stating that "it was emphasized in the conversations by Messrs. Stalin, Molotov, and Litvinov that the organization of security in Eastern Europe and the proposed pact of mutual assistance do not aim at the isolation or encirclement of any state."[15] Not until Germany's definite refusal to join the Eastern pact did the Soviet Union fully share the aims of France, who saw in it primarily a means of curbing, or at least balancing, the growing Nazi war potential. Although negotiations for the Eastern pact fizzled out during 1935, Soviet diplomacy did reap some rewards. Russia was able to conclude pacts of mutual assistance with France on May 2, 1935, and with Czechoslovakia on May 16. According to Litvinov, the pacts would "perform in the east of Europe the same functions as does the Locarno Treaty in the western part of Europe."

It was a strange comparison, since the Locarno agreements were actually based on a factor now lacking—German participation. Litvinov must have used the comparison to cover up Russia's frustration, for the real Soviet goal had not been attained. In each of the three attempts to make agreements involving the Baltic states —to guarantee their status together with Poland, in a pact with Nazi Germany, or to include them in the Eastern Locarno—Moscow was preparing the ground for the domination of the independent states situated between Germany and Russia. Five years were to pass before Hitler's complicity made this possible. In the meantime, the Soviet Government developed an alternative policy line— Litvinov became the noisy protagonist of collective security. When, in 1933, Germany and Japan left the League of Nations and the Disarmament Conference, the door was open for the new Soviet role of champion of international cooperation.

10. *THE NEW POLICY*

Few modern diplomatic acts have been more misunderstood, if not willfully misconstrued, than the Polish-German Declaration of nonaggression of January 26, 1934.[1] To the Poles it meant first and foremost that Germany would cease its propaganda for the revision of the Polish-German frontier, which for more than a decade had poisoned the relations between the two countries and undermined the international position of the reborn Polish state. The Polish Government hoped that during the period of the treaty's validity, one of two things would happen: the aggressive mood of the Nazi regime would play itself out or, if not, the Western powers—England and Poland's ally France—would come to understand the universal danger of Hitler's territorial ambitions and rearm. The Poles also hoped that some influential sectors of Western opinion would see the futility of trying to save peace by means of a deal with Hitler at Poland's expense.

For Berlin, the immediate value of the agreement was to demonstrate that, Hitler's *Mein Kampf* notwithstanding, the new German Government would refrain from ventures that endangered the peace. The agreement was signed after a period of grave tensions on the German-Polish border, and as the result of a show of strength on the part of Marshal Pilsudski, who was also secretly sounding out France on the possibility of a preventive military action against the Nazi regime.* Information on this plan may

---

* Until recently, there were no Polish or French documents available to confirm that in the spring of 1933, Pilsudski secretly explored with Paris the possibilities of a common preventive war against Hitler's Germany. But in 1963, Professor Piotr Wandycz of Indiana University published the text of a letter in a Polish periodical in Paris (*Zeszyty Historyczne, Instytut Literacki*, III, 1963) written by Anatol Muhlstein, Minister-Counselor at the Polish Embassy in Paris, to Foreign Minister Joseph Beck, dated April 17, 1933. (The original letter is now in London.) In it, Muhlstein informed Beck of the adverse reaction in French political circles (including Premier Paul-Boncour and Minister of War Daladier) to Polish intentions regarding preventive military operations against Hitler. Senator Joseph Caillaux, a former Prime Minister, told Muhlstein: "Do not make for war. This country will not march."

have reached Berlin and made the German Government all the more inclined to come rapidly to an understanding with the Poles. However, in deciding on peace with Poland at the cost of interrupting the revisionist propaganda against Germany's eastern frontier, Hitler was merely making a choice between means of implementing his territorial ambitions in the east. The Polish Government was aware of this risk, and in the following years frustrated Hitler's hope of enlisting Polish collaboration in Germany's intention to expand in Soviet territory.*

The German-Polish declaration of nonaggression came under considerable fire in the French press, though it was better understood both in French Government quarters and in England. As for the Moscow government, it rightly took the Polish policy of non-engagement with Germany and Russia at face value. When, in the following month, the Polish Foreign Minister visited Moscow, the joint communiqué of February 16, 1934, emphasized that "the conversations between M. Litvinov and M. Beck revealed a community of views in regard to many [international] problems, as well as a firm determination to continue their endeavors for a further improvement in mutual relations." Beck accepted the Soviet proposition to extend the validity of the Soviet-Polish nonaggression treaty of 1932 until December 31, 1945,[2] while Litvinov made a show of good will, declaring at the official reception that "a profound process of *rapprochement* between our two countries coincided to a large extent with the period during which you, Mr. Minister, were in charge of Polish foreign policy."[3]

The Soviet assessment of Polish policy showed considerable in-

---

* Between 1935 and 1939, leading Nazi representatives repeatedly tried to induce the Polish Government to take part in Hitler's plans against the Soviet Union. Beck's Deputy, Under Secretary of State Count Jan Szembek, notes that in January, 1935, during a hunting trip to Poland, Göring almost proposed an anti-Soviet alliance. Later, in an audience with Pilsudski, Göring offered Poland a "zone of influence" in the Ukraine, while Germany would expand in northwestern Russia. But Pilsudski refused to discuss the subject. The theme of a joint "march on Moscow" recurred several times in Göring's and other Nazis' suggestions to Polish officials. The last instance seemed to have been on January 5, 1939, when Hitler told Beck that he would highly value Polish military assistance against Russia. But at the same time, Hitler emphasized that Gdansk (Danzig) must sooner or later become German. After this conversation, Beck informed the Polish Ambassador in Paris that he considered the Polish-German political truce finished and expected war the same year. (Cf. Joseph Beck, *Dernier Rapport*, p. 34; Comte Jean Szembek, *Journal 1933–1939*, pp. 33, 34, 39, 329, 405; Roman Debicki, *Foreign Policy of Poland 1919–39*, pp. 90–92; Bohdan Budurowycz, "Poland and Hitler's Offers of Alliance," *The Polish Review*, III, No. 4 [1958]; Hans Roos, *Polen und Europa*, pp. 145, 209–11.)

sight. Pilsudski and Beck believed that a Polish alliance with either of its big neighbors would upset the balance of power in Europe and endanger the peace. On the other hand, they thought that by being allied with France (and, possibly, later also with England) and geographically separating Germany from Russia, Poland made it difficult for Germany and Russia to attack each other without provoking a general conflagration. This Polish policy was neither illogical nor unrealistic. In the end it proved ineffective, because France and England neglected their military preparations despite Hitler's massive rearmament and also failed to give Poland the financial assistance to modernize its army in time.

The military weakness and the political hesitancy of France and England, which later led to the capitulation in Munich, could not fail to influence subsequent Soviet policy. But in 1934, Moscow could still regard these failings as temporary. In particular, it could then assume that France and England were strong enough or could muster enough strength to prevent a shift in the European balance of power in Hitler's favor. Although not relinquishing the possibility of an understanding with the new German regime, Russia turned to the West. The Soviet Government, now praising the virtues of collective security, was admitted to the League of Nations on September 18, 1934. In an exchange of notes a week earlier (September 10), Russia and Poland confirmed that the treaties they had concluded—primarily the 1932 Nonaggression Pact and the 1933 Convention for the Definition of Aggression—would remain the basis of their mutual relations.

On September 18, 1934, Litvinov for the first time addressed the Assembly of the League of Nations, making good propaganda use of this opportunity. He presented the Soviet Union as an unrelenting champion of peace and asserted that under different circumstances, Moscow would not have agreed to certain articles of the League of Nations' Covenant providing "for the legalization . . . of war." Litvinov mentioned Articles 12 and 15, part of the system of enforcing peace, without which the League's Covenant would not have had more practical significance than the Kellogg Pact. This was characteristic of the Soviets' method of pretending to reject something they particularly wanted, for the value of the League to Russia lay precisely in the fact that it could be turned into a military alliance. As Litvinov declared: "Everybody knows that the exponents of the idea of war, the open promulgators of the refashioning of the map of Europe and of Asia by the sword, are not to be intimidated by paper obstacles."[4]

Russia's new policy was further expressed in the treaties of mutual assistance with France and Czechoslovakia concluded on May 2 and May 16, 1935, respectively. Seventeen years after Brest-Litovsk, Soviet Russia had become a full-fledged member of the League of Nations, occupying one of the five seats reserved to the great powers, an ally of France and Czechoslovakia, with friendly, or at least normal, relations with its western and southern neighbors from Finland to Persia. Recognition by the United States had also been obtained at last, in the exchange of notes of November 16, 1933. Relations with Great Britain were improving, especially after the Moscow visit of Anthony Eden, the Lord Privy Seal. The joint communiqué of March 31, 1935, stated: "Mr. Eden and Messrs. Stalin, Molotov, and Litvinov were confirmed in the opinion that the friendly cooperation of the two countries in the general work for the collective organization of peace and security is of primary importance for the furtherance of international efforts to this end."[5]

Yet, this alignment with the West and with other countries that wished to preserve the territorial *status quo* and avoid a military clash was of short duration. It can be surmised that Russia's determination to use the mechanism of collective security embodied in the Covenant of the League of Nations and to transform its collaboration with France and Britain into an alliance against Germany, and possibly Japan, lasted about two years—from the conclusion of the pacts with France and Czechoslovakia in May, 1935, until the spring of 1937. By then, the Spanish Civil War was nearly a year old, and it had become apparent that the West European powers would not counter the German and Italian intervention by military measures.

It is reasonable to assume that the French and British attitude in the Spanish conflict shortened the period when the Soviet Government appeared to have thrown in its lot with the West. The question arises whether it would have been possible for the West European states effectively to encourage this Soviet policy and, in consequence, permanently to commit Communist Russia to the cause of collective security and peace. Later events have shown that this was not the case, and, furthermore, that such a course would have been contrary to the very nature of the Soviet state and its aims abroad. But this was obscured by French and English inaction, later exploited by Soviet propaganda to explain, if not to excuse, Russia's collusion with Hitler. In the light of subsequent events, it should also be clear that the Molotov-Ribbentrop Pact of 1939, which put an end to the first period of pro-Western Soviet policy, was the crowning of a twenty-year effort, the supreme achievement of the maxim "to utilize each and every contradiction and conflict among the surrounding capitalist groups and governments."[6]

Let us try to separate the objective reasons for Soviet dissatisfaction with the West European powers in the thirties from the fixed rules of Moscow's foreign policy.

On March 16, 1935, Hitler repudiated Part V of the Versailles Treaty and thus unilaterally restored Germany's right to rearm. But even then, France continued to lag in its military preparations, while England virtually condoned Hitler's high-handed action and, on June 18, 1935, concluded a naval agreement with him. The logical consequence of these acts was the retreat of the West European allies before each new demand of the totalitarian powers. Year after year, in Manchuria and Ethiopia, in the Rhineland, Spain, China, and Austria, England and France gave in to Japanese, Italian, and German pressure. By the middle of 1937, the Kremlin must have become convinced that Paris and London would choose to appease rather than oppose, even when their own interests were directly involved.

Under the circumstances, the Soviet Government could not regard its collaboration with the West European powers as adequate insurance against Hitler's territorial ambitions. Faced with a similar threat in 1933, the Polish Government sought to gain time while trying to develop its ties with the West. The Soviet reaction was as different from the Polish one as were its general outlook and political philosophy. The Kremlin did not prefer either England or France to the German National Socialists. According to Communist doctrine, they were all potential enemies and targets for eventual "proletarian revolutions." Whatever the tactical zigzags, everything in Soviet Russia was designed to further the expansion of Communism. Over the years, internal strife and economic weakness, Japanese ambitions in the Far East, and Hitler's threat in Europe had put the Soviets on the defensive. But Moscow was always on the lookout for opportunities to abandon its passive attitude. In the thirties, once the efforts to reach agreement with National Socialist Germany had failed, temporary collaboration with the West became the only alternative. In spite of Litvinov's oratory in Geneva, the Kremlin did not undergo a real change of heart, nor did it develop the desire to stabilize peace by collective security as understood in the West. On the contrary, the Soviets had long-standing designs on the European border states that barred Russia's way to the west. The domination of these countries could best be achieved in times of upheaval and in concert with Germany. Such ambition was the motive of the Bolsheviks at Rapallo. In later years, this grand design had to take the form of a deal with Hitler —hence Moscow's devious maneuvers to gain Nazi cooperation through the Baltic guarantee and the Eastern Locarno and, ulti- mately, Russia's secret negotiations leading to the Molotov-Ribben- trop Pact. The policy became less dangerous for the Soviets once Czechoslovakia was out of the way, since it freed them from the mutual-assistance agreement they had concluded on May 16, 1935. In case of a Franco-German war, failure to live up to a similar com- mitment to France, made in the pact of May 2, 1935, could be ignored, or even be rationalized by France's failure to help Czecho- slovakia. At any rate, the alliance with France would be contingent on the French and English attitudes toward Poland, and could per- haps become a valuable bargaining point in negotiating with Hitler.

It has not been possible as yet to pinpoint when the idea of a new tack in the Kremlin's foreign policy first took shape. One may surmise that it was sometime in the early summer of 1938, i.e., after the disappointing experience in Spain, after the fall of Austria, and when the fate of Czechoslovakia already seemed sealed.* The final decision to prepare a major political move in connection with Ger- many was probably taken in Moscow soon after Munich, in the autumn of 1938. It was alluded to publicly for the first time in Stalin's speech of March 10, 1939. In documents available at this time, the first Soviet diplomatic move in Berlin is recorded on April 17.

---

* In diplomatic circles, Lord Runciman's mission to Czechoslovakia, an- nounced in July, 1938, was generally considered an indication that the Cham- berlain government had decided to give in to Hitler on the question of the Sudeten Germans. According to G. Higler and Alfred G. Meyer (*op. cit.*, 288–89), the first signs of a Soviet desire to ease the tension were noted in the German Embassy in Moscow in the summer of 1938.

11. *SPAIN*

The aims of Soviet policy in Spain, from the establishment of the republic, in 1931, to the end of the Civil War, in 1939, are not entirely clear. It is possible that the Kremlin, fearing the adverse effect a Communist rule in Spain would have in France and England, did not press for the establishment of a Soviet republic. In 1934, Moscow appeared to limit itself to "guiding" the weak left-wing government, not openly dominated by Communists. This was the time of the Comintern's popular-front line, successfully developed in Spain and France in 1935–36. Shortly before the outbreak of the Spanish Civil War, a popular-front government that included Communists took over in France. Moscow hoped for fruitful collaboration with France in Spain, for a test of the spirit of the mutual-assistance treaty, and possibly for the shaping of a wide coalition against Hitler. Disappointment came quickly. The nonintervention policy to which Russia ostensibly adhered meant nonintervention only by France and England. The two Western powers, in effect, rejected a compromising collaboration with the Soviets in Spain, refused to take sides on ideological grounds, and seemed satisfied that Spain's independence and territorial integrity would not be impaired. The Russians soon decided that they were on their own. They then tried to take control of the Spanish army fighting Franco, "and once in possession of the army, they would be in possession of Spain."[1] In fact, they wielded overwhelming influence through a Russian general staff installed at the Spanish War Office, numerous advisers, technicians, and political commissars, and, most important, through the pressure they could bring to bear by either speeding or delaying vital arms, munitions, and food deliveries. On December 21, 1936, Stalin, Molotov, and Voroshilov wrote in a letter to the Spanish Prime Minister Largo Caballero: "We believe that our experience, above all our experience in civil war . . . may have a certain importance for Spain. On that assumption, we agreed to your repeated requests . . . to place a number of our military comrades at your disposal."[2]

The letter also contained "four pieces of friendly advice," all concerned with camouflaging the radical character of the government of Largo Caballero, the "Spanish Lenin,"[3] in order to attract the peasants, the "urban petty and middle bourgeoisie," and the leaders of the Republican Party. "This is necessary," wrote the Soviet leaders, "in order to prevent the enemies of Spain from depicting it as a Communist republic."

Once it became evident that they were on the losing side, the Russians concentrated on prolonging the war as much as possible. In this they succeeded to a considerable extent. They demanded continued resistance "even after the collapse of Catalonia, in January, 1939."[4]

The end of the Spanish Civil War, late in March of 1939, coincided with Stalin's first feelers to Berlin. When Stalin spoke on March 10, the Spanish Government's resistance to Franco could no longer be used as a bargaining point in a deal with Hitler. But collaboration with the West was also rapidly coming to an end. For Moscow, this had always been a second choice. France and England had proved hesitant and weak, even in opposing Germany and Italy in western Europe. How much weaker would they be in eastern Europe? And how much more could be gained in a deal with Hitler?

12. HAND IN HAND WITH HITLER

The Molotov-Ribbentrop Pact of August 23, 1939, was one of the most fateful diplomatic acts of modern history. Ostensibly a nonaggression treaty, it was in fact a *renversement des alliances*, a sudden change of sides in the then existing power alignment. The secret clauses of the pact divided the whole area between the Finnish Gulf and the Black Sea into Soviet and Nazi spheres of influence. It gave Hitler a free hand for aggression against Poland a week later, thus triggering World War II. It was also the first step in a Russo-German quasi alliance that might have led to the division of the whole Eastern Hemisphere into German, Russian, Japanese, and Italian "natural spheres of influence."[1] In November, 1940, the Soviet Government was ready to enter this colossal predatory agreement; the negotiations broke down only because the Russians asked for more than Hitler was ready to give.

It would be entirely wrong to believe that a Machiavellian Soviet Government deceived and waylaid the innocent Nazis. The evidence that Hitler really meant what he wrote in *Mein Kampf* is overwhelming. There can be no doubt that Germany wanted much more than Danzig and a corridor to East Prussia through Polish territory. It is also very likely that Hitler would not have held to the agreement for the division of the Eastern Hemisphere negotiated by Molotov in November, 1940, for longer than the time he needed to subdue England. But in 1939, if not earlier, the two totalitarian powers gravitated toward each other as the result of a natural process generated by their territorial ambitions. The initiative was taken by the Soviet Government, and it must be said that the time was particularly well chosen, for once Hitler understood that Poland would not yield to his demands, he decided on war. Possibly he would have made war anyway. Such was the opinion of Ciano, who after conversations with Ribbentrop wrote that if they were given more than they ask, they would attack just the same, because they are possessed by the demon of destruction.[2] But Poland was the ally of France and England, and Hitler did not want a war on two fronts. The secret Soviet feelers in April, 1939, gave him what he thought to be the means of paralyzing the West European powers while disposing of Poland.

Before Stalin made his first move, in a speech on March 10, 1939, there were signs of things to come, variously interpreted by political observers. Five weeks after the Munich agreements, at the 1938 anniversary of the Bolshevik Revolution, Molotov accused France and England of complicity with Germany and Italy in "defeating" Czechoslovakia: "The four strongest imperialist states in Europe did, without much trouble, defeat little Czechoslovakia. The Fascist and so-called democratic powers of Europe came together at Munich and their victory over Czechoslovakia was complete."[3]

That Molotov put France and England in the same category as the Axis powers, labeling them "imperialist" and "so-called" democratic, could hardly fail to attract notice, although it may have been attributed to anger at having been excluded from the new European "concert" at Munich. Moreover, the speech still contained the familiar invectives against Fascist aggression.

In December, 1938, and in January of the following year, the Soviet-German trade negotiations attracted some attention. They were broken off, however, and the available documentary evidence does not show that either side looked beyond the expansion of mutual trade. When Hitler spoke on January 30, on the anniversary of his coming to power, his usual attack on Soviet Russia was missing. We know now, from Hitler's own statement made at the conference with Germany military commanders on November 23, 1939, that even after the occupation of Prague, he had not yet decided whether to attack Poland or to turn first against the West. His reticence with regard to Russia in the January speech may have been no more than an attempt to reserve for himself future freedom of action; perhaps it was also a reaction against the unsatisfactory conversation Ribbentrop had had a few days earlier in Warsaw with the Polish Foreign Minister. It seems that despite Beck's rejection of the German demands, Hitler still hoped to press the Polish Government into an anti-Comintern pact and make it accede to his demands on Danzig and Pomerania.

On the basis of available documentation, it must be assumed that the first definite indication of a Soviet move toward an understanding with Nazi Germany was Stalin's speech of March 10, 1939.[4] Reporting to the Eighteenth Congress of the Communist

Party, Stalin began by listing the major developments since the previous Congress five years earlier: the wars in Abyssinia, Spain, Manchuria, and China, and the seizure of Austria and parts of Czechoslovakia. Stalin said that "the war . . . has stolen imperceptibly upon the nations . . . and has extended its sphere of action over a vast territory, stretching from Tientsin . . . through Abyssinia to Gibraltar." There followed a denunciation of the "three aggressive states": Japan, who had torn up the Nine-Power Pact, and Germany and Italy, who had repudiated the Versailles Treaty. These three imperialist states, Stalin concluded, had also withdrawn from the League of Nations "in order to have their hands free. . . . The new imperialist war has become a fact."

Stalin went on to denounce the military bloc of Germany, Italy, and Japan formed "against the interests of England, France, and the United States"; at the same time he was concerned lest the "nonaggressive states" make concessions to "the aggressors": "We are witnessing an open redivision of the world and spheres of influence at the expense of the nonaggressive states, without the least attempt at resistance, and even with a certain amount of connivance on the part of the latter."

Why should he suspect connivance? "The chief reason," Stalin said, "is that the majority of the nonaggressive countries have rejected the policy of collective security . . . and have taken a position of nonintervention, a position of neutrality." From this accusation it was only a step to the principal intent of the speech. By pretending to be indignant at the Western press for spreading lies about the weakness of the Soviet Union, Stalin accused it of "egging the Germans to march farther east, promising them easy pickings . . . and telling them: 'Just start war on the Bolsheviks, and everything will be all right.'" He went on to say:

> It looks as if the objective of this suspicious hullabaloo was to incense the Soviet Union against Germany, to poison the atmosphere and to provoke a conflict with Germany without any visible grounds. . . . One may think that the districts of Czechoslovakia were yielded to Germany as the price of an undertaking to launch war on the Soviet Union, but that now the Germans are refusing to meet the bills and are sending them to Hades.

Stalin's message was not lost on Berlin. Ribbentrop spoke to Hitler about it and the German diplomatic missions in Europe were alerted. In a conversation of Stalin, Molotov, and Ribbentrop at the Kremlin on the night of August 23, 1939, after the Soviet-Nazi

Pact had been signed, Molotov "raised his glass to Stalin, remarking that it had been Stalin who—through his speech of March this year, which had been well understood in Germany—had brought about the reversal in political relations."[5] Thus, officially, and in Ribbentrop's presence, the initiative for the Soviet-Nazi collaboration was claimed by Moscow.

But at the time of Stalin's speech, five days before the occupation of Prague, Hitler did not respond. The secret order for the military operations against Poland—*Fall Weiss* (Operation White)— to be started on September 1, was not issued by Field Marshal Keitel until April 3. Even then, no final decision was reached whether or not to wage war in the east first.

On the Soviet side, further moves were foreshadowed by two Tass communiqués (March 22 and April 4) denying press rumors that the Soviet Government had offered to assist Poland and Romania in case of aggression. The first of the two Tass statements spoke of both Poland and Romania,[6] and the second only of Poland[7] and of a possible supply of war materials, which would at the same time be denied to Germany. Both statements were sufficiently eloquent to imply that the Soviet-British conversations were not going well. Yet the Germans still did nothing, with the possible exception of Ribbentrop's instruction to one of his assistants, Peter Kleist, to improve his contacts with the Soviet Embassy. But when Kleist was invited to the Soviet Embassy and the Chargé d'Affaires, Georgi Astakhov, spoke of a possible improvement in political relations, Ribbentrop was "taken aback" and reproached Kleist for having exceeded his instructions. According to Kleist, this conversation took place around April 10 (the exact date is not given).[8]

Also sometime in April, Astakhov broached the same subject at a luncheon with German Vice-Admiral Kurt Assmann and Ambassador Schnurre of the Foreign Office, who was in charge of economic negotiations. Admiral Assmann writes that the Russian diplomat suddenly changed the subject and asked if the trade negotiations could not be used for improving political relations between the two countries.[9] These feelers preceded the first *démarche* recorded in official documents. On April 17, 1939, the Soviet Ambassador in Berlin, Merekalov, called on German State Secretary Baron von Weizsäcker, and in the course of conversation on economic matters, declared:

Ideological differences of opinion had hardly influenced the Russian-Italian relations, and they did not have to prove a stumbling block

with regard to Germany either. . . . There exists no reason why
Russia should not live with us on a normal footing. And from normal, the relations might become better and better.[10]

This text, taken from a memorandum written by Weizsäcker,
marked the beginning of negotiations that, developing slowly, culminated in the Molotov-Ribbentrop Pact. It is recorded in detail in
Nazi-Soviet Relations, a volume based on German documents
seized after the war and published by the U.S. Department of State
in 1948.

Although opinions vary as to when the Kremlin decided to conclude a pact with Hitler—whether it was in March, at the time of
the Stalin speech, or some time later—certain facts are beyond controversy: The Russians took the initiative of a *rapprochement* with
the Nazis and made the first moves in the secret diplomatic negotiations; they also were the first to suggest a nonaggression treaty as
well as a secret arrangement for the partitioning of eastern Europe.
All this went on without the knowledge of England and France,
with whom, from March to August, the Soviet Union pretended to
negotiate for a common front to stop Hitler. A comparison of the
salient factors in the two parallel negotiations gives rare insight into
the Soviet diplomatic method.

There is no record of any German reaction to Merekalov's move
of April 17, 1939. The Soviet Ambassador soon went back to Russia
and faded out of the picture. The man who remained on the scene
was Astakhov, the Chargé d'Affaires. He kept the pot boiling by
taking up the subject with Ambassador Schnurre of the German
Foreign Office. Their conversations took place on May 5 and 17.
On the second occasion, Astakhov explained in detail that the Soviets hoped for a permanent change in relations with Germany. He
also predicted that the Anglo-Soviet negotiations would not have
the result desired by England.

In the meantime, on May 3, Berlin's interest was aroused by the
dismissal of Litvinov as head of the Soviet Foreign Office. He was
replaced by Molotov, who kept the chairmanship of the Ministers'
Council. A telegram from the German Embassy in Moscow states
that the change had caused the greatest surprise, as Litvinov was in
the midst of negotiating with England.

The Russians then proceeded to assure the Allies that Litvinov's
departure had no political significance: Astakhov said it to the
French Ambassador in Berlin; Molotov told it to the British Ambassador in Moscow. During a conversation with the Romanian

Foreign Minister in Bucharest, Soviet Deputy Foreign Minister Potemkin also minimized the significance of the change and specifically denied rumors about an impending Soviet-German understanding. He said that the rumor was being circulated by the "totalitarian powers."[11] But the signs that something was in the air were multiplying. For example, in a speech before the Reichstag on April 28, while repudiating the German-Polish nonaggression agreement, Hitler again refrained from attacking Russia. The German press also remained unusually reticent. Against this background, the dismissal of Litvinov was an important political gesture, and Hitler understood it as such. But the double game continued. On meeting the French Ambassador in Berlin on May 9, Astakhov volunteered the false information that in their conversation of April 17, Merekalov and Weizsäcker had not touched on political matters.[12]

A month had gone by since Ambassador Merekalov made his official bid for Nazi friendship, but there was no German reaction. None came after Litvinov's demotion, and nothing happened during or after Astakhov's conversation with Schnurre on May 17. Therefore, three days later Molotov himself rolled out the big gun and told Ambassador Count von der Schulenburg in the course of a conversation on trade negotiations that "the Soviet Government could only agree to a resumption of the negotiations after the necessary *political bases* for them had been constructed."[13] The cat was out of the bag, or so it seemed to the Germans. They were suspicious, however, and Von der Schulenburg was instructed to "sit tight . . . and wait to see if the Russians will speak more openly."[14] But they did not, and both sides waited for another ten days. On May 30, acting on the basis of new instructions, Weizsäcker proceeded to make more detailed inquiries of Astakhov regarding Molotov's intentions. The gist of the German diplomat's words was that his government's policy in the east was now freer, owing to the increasing tenseness of German-Polish relations. Characteristically, Astakhov did not take up the cue and said that he would have to ask Moscow for instructions. He used the occasion, however, to say that before the German-Polish declaration of nonaggression, Germany "had rejected a Russian offer for an alliance."[15]

This period—from the first half of April to the end of May— might be called the initial phase of the Soviet-Nazi negotiations: The Russians had suggested a change in political relations in several secret conversations; Hitler's government, after some hesitations, took the bait and indicated that, because of the plans about

Poland, they were keenly interested. Now the second phase was about to begin, during which the Russians were able to employ their favorite stratagem: making the other side ask for what they themselves wanted. For the next five to six weeks, German diplomacy was unable to find out how seriously the Soviet Government intended to negotiate with them.

Let us turn to the other Soviet negotiations, those with England and France, which ran parallel to the secret talks with the Nazis. Here the initiative came from the West European powers, taking the form of a suggestion that Russia assist Romania and Poland in case of attack by Hitler. Preliminary diplomatic exchanges during the second part of March had preceded the first Soviet feelers in Berlin. On April 5, Georges Bonnet, the French Foreign Minister, told Surits, the Soviet Ambassador in Paris, that France attached great importance to Soviet assistance to Romania and Poland. On April 9, Bonnet also informed Surits that the French Government was ready to begin military and technical talks with Russia in preparation for an agreement between the two general staffs.[16] Such an agreement had not been negotiated in 1935, when France and the Soviet Union signed a mutual-assistance pact.

The formal negotiations for broadening the anti-Hitler front began in mid-April. Bonnet puts the date at April 14. On that day, Viscount Halifax, the British Foreign Secretary, instructed the Ambassador in Moscow to discuss with Litvinov the question of a Soviet declaration that would commit Russia to assist any of the states along its European border in case of aggression. The British Ambassador spoke with Litvinov on the fifteenth. On April 16, according to Churchill, Litvinov suggested "the creation of a united front of mutual assistance between Great Britain, France, and the U.S.S.R."[17] The next day, the Soviet Ambassador in Berlin made his fateful approach to the German Foreign Office in the conversation with Weizsäcker. That very day Litvinov, in reply to a question by the British Ambassador in Moscow about possible assistance to Romania and Poland, said: "What are Poland and Romania doing? Negotiating with Germany perhaps?"[18] On April 18, the Soviet Union offered a written proposal for a three-cornered mutual-assistance guarantee, in fact a triple alliance; the Russian project included a promise of assistance by each of the three powers to any victim of aggression between the Baltic and the Black Sea.

This day-by-day sequence proves beyond any doubt that in April, 1939, the Soviet Government intentionally embarked on double negotiations, whose aim was the same as that of its diplomatic maneuvers in 1933-35: the control of eastern Europe. That was the price asked of Soviet assistance, and it is doubtful whether in April, 1939, the Russians knew who would be more likely to pay it. They realized that all the countries concerned, from Finland to Romania, were terrified, almost repelled, by the prospect of Soviet troops on their territory, even in the role of allies. To find out if such feelings could be overcome with the aid of the Western powers, it was necessary for Moscow to protract negotiations until the danger of Nazi aggression became imminent. And only on the eve of Hitler's march against Poland would the Soviet Government know how much Hitler was prepared to pay—i.e., what share of eastern Europe he would agree to give up in return for Russian cooperation.

But if there is no documentary proof exactly when the Soviet Government chose Hitler instead of the West, there are strong indications that the decision was reached early in the game. First—the secrecy. At the start of the negotiations, Russia for several years had been politically aligned with the West against the Axis powers; it was a member of the Council of the League of Nations (which Germany, Italy and Japan had left) and an ally of France. Soviet relations with its western neighbors were normal. All the European border states, with the exception of Romania, had concluded non-aggression treaties with the Soviet Union. Under the circumstances, the British and French demand for assistance in case of Nazi aggression was only logical. And although the secrecy of the Soviet advances to Hitler cannot be considered as proof of a definite decision, it certainly points in that direction. Even more significant was the behavior of the Soviet negotiators. In their relations with the Germans, all of them, from Astakhov to Stalin, were considerate, polite, and observant of diplomatic protocol. With the English and the French, Litvinov (while still in his post), Molotov, and Voroshilov were often arrogant, if not insulting. In a rather curious assessment of Molotov's character, Churchill wrote that correspondence with him "was always useless, and, if pushed too far, ended in lies and insults."[19] As far as we know, there was no trace of such behavior in Molotov's relations with the Nazis, which strongly suggests that he possibly expected to come to terms with them from the beginning of the double negotiations. Yet, in view of Poland's resistance to German pressure and the change of heart among Western politicians (particularly in England) after the occupation of Prague, another Munich was most unlikely. On the other hand, Hitler's eventual decision with regard to Poland could have been guessed as early as February, after Ribbentrop's unsuccessful trip to

Warsaw. Possibly, and this is only speculation, Russian intelligence got wind of Hitler's order for Operation White against Poland sometime in April.

For England and France, the negotiations with Russia—from mid-April to the beginning of August—were an uninterrupted series of frustrations. Their positions were different, since France had signed a treaty of mutual assistance with the Soviet Union in 1935. Almost from the beginning, the Russians also tried to induce England to enter into an alliance with them, although they must have realized that in a Continental war only the French could quickly open a front in the west. Russian concentration on England in these negotiations seems to have been prompted by political rather than military considerations. The British Government was more inclined to grant Russia the substance rather than the form of an alliance. Yet a number of concessions, in quick succession, brought the Western powers very near the Russian demands. On May 24, the British Ambassador in Moscow was instructed to say that his government was "now disposed to agree that effective cooperation between the Soviet, French, and British Governments against aggression in Europe might be based on a system of mutual guarantees in general conformity with the principles of the League of Nations."[20] The following day, the British Ambassador handed Deputy Foreign Minister Potemkin the draft of an agreement together with a memorandum pointing out that the proposed guarantees would not be made dependent on the League's technicalities. Had the Soviet negotiators really been eager to form a front against Hitler, they could have had it then and there. Of course, we now know (but the English and French negotiators did not) that on May 20, Molotov had already spoken to the German Ambassador about the necessity for establishing "political bases" of Soviet-Nazi relations. On May 27, Molotov said to the British and French envoys that their latest proposals created the impression that their governments wanted "to continue conversations indefinitely without binding themselves to any concrete engagements."[21] He took exception to the mentioning of the League of Nations and said "that the British and French were prepared to see Moscow being bombed by the aggressor while Bolivia was busy blocking all action in Geneva." Neither the written memorandum nor oral explanations by the envoys could make Molotov budge from this position. In his report, the British Ambassador wrote: "I am sorry to say that quite palpably my words produced not the slightest effect; they seemed not to be heard or understood."[22]

It is important to remember at this stage that while these negotiations with England and France went on in private, the press was informed of them in a general way. The Communists skillfully played on the general desire to halt Hitler. Molotov's speech on May 31, before the Supreme Soviet, was a case in point. He stated Russia's "minimum conditions": (1) an effective pact of mutual assistance with England and France; (2) a guarantee by these three powers to all states of central and eastern Europe, including all of Russia's European neighbors; and (3) a "concrete" agreement implementing the mutual-assistance guarantees, both among the three powers and in favor of all other states mentioned.

A few days later, Molotov handed the Western envoys a counterproposal to their draft agreement. It contained the seeds of further delays in form of demands that the coming into force of a political agreement should be made dependent on the conclusion of military conversations between the three general staffs. Nevertheless, on June 7, Prime Minister Chamberlain declared in the House of Commons that there was general agreement in the Moscow negotiations on the main objective. William Strang (later Lord Strang), a high official of the British Foreign Office, was sent to Moscow to help in the final drafting of a treaty. But in mid-June, the Russians erected a new stumbling block, which became known as the question of "indirect aggression."

This coincided with two other Soviet appeals to public opinion. On June 16, the Soviet press published an official release on a conversation that had taken place the previous day between Molotov and the Western negotiators. A memorandum brought from London by Mr. Strang was discussed. The Soviet press indicated that the results of this conversation were regarded in the "circles of the People's Commissariat of Foreign Affairs as not being entirely favorable." On June 29, *Pravda* ran an article by Andrei Zhdanov, a close collaborator of Stalin, bitterly criticizing the English and French governments for their attitude in the negotiations and blaming them for all the delays. Significantly, Zhdanov was ironic about the Western difficulties with "indirect aggression" and the rights of smaller nations; he asked whether "Lithuania and the Netherlands had agreed to Britain's guarantee to Poland."[23]

In the meantime, the Soviet negotiators made the most of "indirect aggression" to delay the agreement. During the second half of June and all through July, discussions revolved around Russian inquiries as to how they would be helped by the West in various hypothetical situations resulting from aggression on Finland, Estonia, or Latvia. The situation of other states was also brought up, a list of states to be protected was discussed, as well as the question whether these could be put on the list without their knowledge or assured protection without their consent. Undoubtedly this was the real problem calling for solution. The conflicting interests could have been reconciled if, for instance, the Soviet Union had said that it would help the states threatened with Nazi aggression by means other than direct military action: by furnishing arms, ammunition, and foodstuffs. This the Russians were absolutely unwilling to do. At times the discussion became quite acrimonious. In one conversation, Molotov accused the British and French of considering the Russian Government as "naïve and foolish," and he was not satisfied until Potemkin assured him that he had translated the Russian word *duraki* as "imbeciles."[24] On the other hand, the British Government found it impossible to accept the Russian definition of indirect aggression. Early in July, Lord Halifax wrote the British Ambassador in Moscow that "the suggested Soviet definition was quite unacceptable to us, since it could be represented as authorizing almost unlimited interference in the affairs of the Baltic states."[25]

But on July 27, Molotov's tone suddenly changed. He declared that existing differences with England and France did not seem insuperable and demanded that talks between military experts should begin. He wanted the political and military negotiations to run concurrently. This was agreed upon, although a few days later, rather ominously, Russia refused to issue a joint press communiqué with the Western governments. Another meeting between Molotov, Strang, and the two ambassadors was held on August 3. This, in fact, marked the end of political negotiations, although Paris and London believed at the time that it was only a respite, pending the beginning of military talks.

From the West's point of view, the three and a half months of talks yielded very few results; in fact, they yielded none in the most sensitive area, that of Soviet relations with Poland and Romania, which, since the occupation of Prague, were considered the countries most directly threatened by Nazi aggression. The negotiations, which had begun with a Western request that the Soviet Government publicly declare its political solidarity with the anti-Hitlerite forces, became a vast consultation on how the Western powers would help Russia in case of war. The problem of practical Soviet assistance to Poland and Romania was avoided because the Western powers hoped that an alignment of political forces would suffice to avert war, while the aim of the Russian double negotiations was to prove which side would be ready to deliver the area into their hands. Today it seems surprising that London and Paris did not sense that something was indeed wrong, for they must have seen that the Russians were playing a devious game. In an interim report, William Strang predicted that the military talks might bog down over the question of the passage of Soviet troops through Polish territory. He stated that "on the whole, the negotiations have been a humiliating experience."[26]

The Germans, meanwhile, were aware that the British and French were having a bad time with the Russians. On August 7, Schulenburg wrote to Berlin: "We hear that throughout, Herr Molotov sat like a bump on a log. He hardly ever opened his mouth . . . except to say that he was not entirely satisfied." The German Ambassador observed that, in contrast, Molotov was "very communicative and amiable" with him and with Hilger.[27]

Let us return to the Soviet-German talks. We have seen that on May 30, Weizsäcker had had a probing conversation with Astakhov. But the result was disappointing. The Germans were unable to determine from Astakhov's answers, or from a conversation in Moscow with Mikoyan on economic matters, on June 17, whether the Russians meant business, or whether they risked "a peal of Tatar laughter."[28] Perplexed, Ribbentrop decided at the end of June to stop the economic negotiations and to refrain from new advances in the political talks until further notice.

But it would be wrong to assume that this situation developed because Moscow had lost interest. On the contrary, the secret documents give evidence that this was part of a calculated plan. Several times, probably when the Soviet Government thought that German patience was wearing out, the Russians hinted that the deal was still on. Such was the case on June 15, when Dr. Woermann, the under-secretary in charge of political affairs, reported a curious Soviet artifice. Astakhov had called on the Bulgarian Minister in Berlin, whom he knew only slightly. In a long conversation he depicted Soviet foreign policy as vacillating among three possibilities: a pact with England and France; further procrastination; or a *rapprochement* with Germany. He implied that Moscow did not really know what the Germans wanted. "If Germany would say," he told the Bulgarian diplomat, "that she would not attack the Soviet Union or that she would conclude a nonaggression pact with her, the Soviet Union would probably refrain from concluding a treaty with England."[29] Astakhov gave no indication why he told this to the

Bulgarian Minister, who presumed that it was meant to be repeated
to the German Foreign Office. Astakhov could not be quoted or
pinned down for having spoken to an intermediary—but he had
whetted the Germans' appetite. Two weeks later, Schulenburg
asked Molotov for an answer to the weeks-old inquiry about the
meaning of the Soviet suggestion concerning the "political bases"
in Nazi-Soviet relations. Molotov again stressed that "normaliza-
tion of relations was desirable and possible," and that he was "grat-
ified" that in the opinion of the German Government, the Soviet-
German Berlin Treaty of 1926 was still in force. But he answered
questions with new questions and on the whole was so evasive that
Ribbentrop decided to discontinue the political talks.[30] It seems
that during July, contacts were maintained mostly on the economic
plane, with the result that on the twenty-second, the resumption of
Soviet-German trade negotiations was announced officially. This
encouraged the Germans to find out if there would be a follow-up
to Astakhov's overtures to the Bulgarian Minister. Schnurre suggested a *rapprochement* in three stages. But apart from an interesting discussion and Astakhov's promise to ask for instructions, there
was no concrete answer. Time was running out. German military
operations against Poland were set for September 1. Therefore, on
August 3, Ribbentrop himself asked Astakhov to call and told him
of his government's desire to "remold our relations." He also hinted
that Germany wished to agree with Russia on the fate of Poland.
Again Astakhov was unable to reply. The following day, however,
in a long conference with the German Ambassador, Molotov "abandoned his usual reserve and appeared unusually open."[31] But while
repeating that the Soviet Union wished to improve their mutual
relations, he put the blame for their deterioration on the Germans
and asked for proof of the German Government's change of attitude. Another week passed. On August 10, Astakhov came to see
Schnurre and said that "he had *once again* received an express instruction from Moscow to emphasize that the Soviet Government
desired an improvement in relations with Germany." Schnurre told
him that "one question was quite ripe, namely Poland," and that
in the event of a German-Polish conflict, the German Government
was prepared to give the Soviet Government "every assurance desired." Astakhov wanted to find out if the German decision in the
Polish question "could be expected in the next few days and what
the German aims in respect to Poland were." He also said that the
outcome of the negotiations with England was uncertain.[32]

The time for the final showdown had come. The British and

French military missions arrived in Moscow. The Nazis had told the Soviet negotiators what they wanted to hear: that the conflict with Poland was imminent, and they were asked the price of their cooperation. Now events moved quickly. On August 14, on Molotov's instruction, Astakhov called on Schnurre in Berlin and proposed that political talks be held in Moscow. On the fifteenth, in Moscow, Marshal Voroshilov asked the British and French military missions for the right for Soviet troops to pass through Polish and Romanian territory. Soviet military representatives told the Western missions that "without a solution of this question, further discussions are doomed to failure."[33]

All the countries concerned—Finland, Estonia, Latvia, Poland, and Romania—opposed any guarantees that could lead to the presence of Russian troops on their territory. Churchill noted that "Finland and Estonia even asserted that they would consider a guarantee [meaning a Russian guarantee] extended to them without their assent as an act of aggression."[34] On August 18, Léon Noël, the French Ambassador in Warsaw, informed his government that the Poles feared the Soviet troops might enter their territory and then refuse to leave.[35] All the countries concerned, from Finland to Romania, regarded the entry of Soviet troops as a national disaster. A Polish diplomat said in Paris: "We are not going to commit suicide to escape death."

Thus, England and France were unable to give Russia what it wanted. But Hitler was. The Western negotiators were kept in the dark to the very last, and on August 22, it was announced that Ribbentrop would visit Moscow. During the preceding week, the Russians had made it clear to the Germans that they wanted more than a manifestation of a common policy on eastern Europe. They proposed the signing of a nonaggression pact, and simultaneously of a special protocol without which the main pact would not be valid. This was the protocol that provided for the division of eastern Europe between Soviet Russia and Nazi Germany. It seems certain that the Russians drafted it, since Ribbentrop informed Hitler about it while still in Moscow. Although given full power, he cabled Berlin a few hours before signing that in addition to the main pact, "the signing of a secret protocol on delimitation of mutual spheres of influence in the whole eastern area is contemplated, for which I declare myself ready in principle."[36]

On the night of August 23, Stalin and Molotov celebrated with Ribbentrop and drank toasts to "the new era of German-Russian relations." Stalin toasted Hitler: "I know how much the German nation loves the Führer; I should therefore like to drink to his health."[37]

Two days later, when the British and French military missions were taking leave, Marshal Voroshilov said that under the existing circumstances there was no longer any reason for military talks. To the French, however, he said that "nothing in the recent treaty [with the Nazis] made it impossible to observe the Soviet-French Treaty of Mutual Assistance"[38] of 1935. According to a letter the British Ambassador wrote to Lord Halifax, Molotov made a similarly sibylline rejoinder: "Molotov then adopted a manner of almost hearty simplicity and said what a pity it was we could not have helped negotiating to a successful issue by getting the consent of Polish and Rumanian Governments to a passage of troops."[39]

It would be useless to ponder on the deeper significance of these Soviet utterances. But they do suggest that the Russians thought of signing two treaties: one with the Western powers and another with Nazi Germany. Had they succeeded, they could have entered Poland and Romania on the basis of an internationally legal document and still have collaborated with Hitler on the basis of the secret protocol. The fact is that when Molotov spoke these words, the secret protocol was already signed. When, on September 17, the Soviet troops invaded Poland, they pretended to come as friends.

The Kremlin obviously hoped that the secret protocol would remain unknown. In a speech on July 3, 1941, Stalin tried to answer the question: "How was it possible that the Soviet Government agreed to make a pact of nonaggression with such perfidious monsters as Hitler and Ribbentrop?" He explained that a pact of nonaggression is a pact of peace, and therefore the Soviets could not reject the proposal made by Germany in 1939.[40] The myth that it was Hitler who had been the initiator of the pact was also maintained in the official *History of Diplomacy* edited by Potemkin, who personally had taken part in the double negotiations. The introduction to the third volume, published in French in September, 1947, not long before the publication of the State Department's *Nazi-Soviet Relations*, states, contrary to the facts, that the Soviet Government, "faithful to its policy of peace and of economic collaboration with all states, favorably accepted the proposition of the German Government, which was asking for trade credits, soon to be followed by a pact of nonaggression."[41]

Various explanations have been given in justification of the Kremlin's collusion with Hitler, chief among them these two arguments: that Soviet Russia tried to gain time in anticipation of a future war with Nazi Germany, or that it merely continued its "search for security," as it had done earlier in collaborating with the West European powers. Neither of these contentions is borne out by Soviet behavior during the twenty-two months that elapsed between the signing of the Molotov-Ribbentrop Pact and Hitler's attack on Russia. Soviet armies invaded Poland on the seventeenth day of the German-Polish war and attacked the Polish troops in the rear. More than 1.5 million people were deported in 1939–40 from the Polish lands occupied by the Soviet armies, and the territory was annexed by the Soviet Union. Moscow extended vital economic assistance to Germany and backed the Nazis politically against France and Britain. In a memorandum dated May 15, 1941, Dr. Karl Schnurre listed the following Soviet deliveries to Germany: grain, oil seed, petroleum, cotton, manganese ore, phosphates, copper, tin, nickel, platinum, as well as raw rubber in transit from East Asia. He wrote: "The quantities of raw materials now contracted for are being delivered punctually by the Russians, despite the heavy burden this imposes on them."[42]

There is no proof that the Soviet Government anticipated German aggression (although rumors of German war preparations were circulating all over Europe during the preceding spring), despite warnings from many quarters, including Prime Minister Churchill. According to Khrushchev, reports and warnings were sent by the Soviet military attaché in Berlin. In the secret report to the Twentieth Party Congress, Khrushchev said:

> Stalin took no heed of these warnings. . . . Stalin ordered that no credence be given to information of this sort, in order not to provoke the initiation of military operations . . . the necessary steps were not taken to prepare the country properly for defense.[43]

Although Khrushchev's allegations at the Twentieth Congress that Stalin was a military half-wit are quite absurd, the defeats suffered by the Soviet armies in the first weeks of the war, and the many prisoners taken by the Germans, prove that the Soviet leadership had not prepared for the Nazi invasion. With the exception of the southern sector, where the German advance was slower and the fighting heaviest, the Soviet armies sustained tremendous losses during the very first days of the campaign. In the northern sector, twelve to fifteen Soviet divisions were destroyed south of the Dvina between June 22 and 30. In the central sector, the Germans took 289,874 prisoners by July 8; the Russians lost twenty-two infantry divisions, seven armored divisions, six mechanized brigades, and several cavalry divisions.[44]

Communist propaganda also argued that the September, 1939, partition of Poland and the 1940 occupation of the Baltic states were dictated by the need for additional territory in anticipation of German aggression. But no adequate military measures were taken in the occupied lands. The Polish territory annexed by the Soviets after the Molotov-Ribbentrop Pact was overrun by the German armies in forty-eight to seventy-two hours; most of the Baltic states were overrun in a few days. The German invasion began on June 22, 1941. Brest-Litovsk, Vilno, and Kaunas were taken on the twenty-fourth, Lvov (where the advance was slower) on the thirtieth, Minsk and Riga on July 1.

Thus, both the "time" and "space" arguments, as well as the alleged "search for security" are contradicted by facts. Instead, Molotov's negotiations with Hitler and Ribbentrop in November, 1940, prove that in return for a benevolent nonbelligerence, Soviet Russia expected to share in the Nazi spoils. In a longer perspective, the Kremlin hoped for a war of attrition between Germany and the West that eventually would leave Europe open to Communist penetration.

THREE

IMPERIALISM

13. WAR AIMS

Soviet expectations based on the Molotov-Ribbentrop Pact were shattered when Hitler sent his armies against Russia. There are two versions of Molotov's last conversation with the German Ambassador. According to a Schulenburg cable found among German documents, Molotov complained that the Soviet Government "was unable to understand the reasons for Germany's dissatisfaction."[1] A less formal account is given by Grigori Gafencu, then the Romanian Ambassador in Moscow; it has the ring of truth. Molotov said: "It is war. Your aircraft have just bombed some ten open towns. Do you think that we deserved that?"[2] In all fairness, one has to admit that they did not. The Soviet Government had done all it could to please the Nazis. Yet, instead of being in a comfortable, pro-Hitler nonbelligerence, the Soviet Union found itself at war with Germany and a reluctant member of the Allied camp. Within hours, Churchill broadcast the decision of His Majesty's Government "to give whatever help we can to Russia." It is true that he also likened the Nazi regime "to the worst features of Communism," and reminded his listeners that he had been a consistent opponent of Communism. But brushing aside all political differences, he proclaimed that "any man or state who fights on against Nazidom will have our aid."[3] It was a spirited determination, similar to Clemenceau's *"Je fais la guerre"* (I wage war). But it also ushered in an era of political oversimplification that soon boomeranged against the only strategic plan, Churchill's own, that could have saved Europe from the danger of Soviet hegemony. It was right to promise Russia all the necessary help, but it was unreasonable to give it unconditionally all through the war. It was dangerous not to adapt strategic plans to the peculiar character of the new partner and to forget so easily the circumstances that had brought him into the war. The American attitude, while rather cautious initially, became entirely unpolitical as the decisive battles of the war approached. The early British oversimplification was simplified even more by the American dissociation of military strategy from potential political consequences. This misconception was accompanied in some Allied quarters by the hopeful belief that the leopard would change his spots, i.e., that Soviet ambitions would be renounced for the sake of a friendly postwar collaboration with the West. It is indeed a strange paradox that one of the most sophisticated and political minds in America should have accepted the idea that Stalin, if given everything and asked for nothing in return, "won't try to annex anything and will work for a world of security and peace."[4] General Sir Alan Brooke (later Field Marshal Viscount Alanbrooke), the Chief of the British Imperial General Staff, noted in his diary on February 17, 1944: "Our attitude to Russia was of always giving and never bargaining to get something back."[5] As a result of this lack of political forethought, the peace was lost although the war against Hitler was won; Communism was forcibly imposed upon the eastern half of Europe, and Russian soldiers were allowed to camp a hundred miles from the Rhine. The chief stepping stones leading to this situation were: tacit acceptance of Communist Russia as a "democratic" ally; lack of understanding of the political and strategic importance of the nations of east and central Europe; unconditional surrender too rigidly imposed on Hitler's unwilling allies; rejection of Churchill's plans to invade Hitler's "Fortress Europe" from the southeast. Eventually, at the great war conferences of Tehran, Yalta, and Potsdam, practically all Soviet territorial demands in Europe and Asia were granted. Politically, the crowning mistake made by the Western powers was to give in to Russia's concept of "friendly governments," i.e., governments friendly to the Soviet Union; this gave the semblance of international legality to armed interference in the internal affairs of Soviet Russia's neighbors and helped extend Russian power as far as the Elbe.

Soviet diplomacy made the most of these opportunities. Unlike the Allies, the Russians showed considerable political foresight and consistency. In Europe, their first objective was the same as in their partnership with Hitler: to dominate the independent non-Communist states separating Russia from Germany and the rest of Europe. In Asia, the aim was similar: to bring China under Communist rule, thereby opening wider, almost unlimited, possibilities. Except for brief periods of confusion in the first months of the German invasion, Soviet diplomacy all through the war subordinated strategic thinking to political goals. But since these could be attained only after victory in Europe and Asia, there was at first no conflict with the general course pursued by the Allies. The Kremlin delayed its encounter with Japan for obvious military reasons, extracting a high price for the promise of help in the Far East, which was given when it was no longer needed. In Europe, despite initial defeats and great losses in territory, population, and war potential, the Soviet Government only rarely permitted military requirements to supersede political ambitions. Speaking of this period, Stalin said in 1945: "Our government made not a few errors; we experienced at moments a desperate situation in 1941–44, when our Army was retreating."[6] It was, no doubt, during one of these moments that Stalin cabled Churchill on September 3, 1941: "I think the only way is to open a second front this year somewhere in the Balkans or in France."[7] On September 13, he made a suggestion—which Churchill called absurd—for Britain to "land twenty-five to thirty divisions at Archangel or ship them to the southern areas of the U.S.S.R. via Iran for military cooperation with the Soviet troops on Soviet soil."[8]

These seem to have been the rare, if not the only, departures from the firm Russian position of demanding a second front and Western military assistance as far removed as possible from politically sensitive areas of the Soviet Union or eastern Europe. Thus, the British offer to participate in the land defense of the Caucasus was rejected, and the various offers for British and American air assistance in the Caucasus were evaded. One month after demanding that British divisions fight on the Soviet southern front, Stalin ignored Churchill's suggestion that five or six Soviet divisions in Persia be relieved by British troops, for use on the battle front. This was October, 1941, a particularly difficult time for the Soviet armies. Plans for renewed Allied action in Norway, which seemed vitally important to Russia because of the northern convoy route, never materialized. At moments, the Russians seemed to have favored common operations in the far north, but the approval was half-hearted. In one known instance, in 1941, Stalin clearly specified that he expected "one light division or more of Norwegian volunteers,"[9] not British or (later) American troops. If Russia's stand on war operations in Norway is open to interpretation, its view of possible Allied action against Germany in the Balkans was frankly antagonistic. Turkey was a marginal area, both politically and geographically, and Moscow hesitated about backing Britain in inducing Turkey to enter the war. Even as late as the Tehran Conference Stalin refused to say clearly what he wanted. One day he would say that Turkey should be dragged into the war by the scruff of the neck;[10]

on another occasion he called Turkey's participation relatively un-
important. The crux of the matter was that the Soviet Government
wanted a revision of the regime of the Black Sea Straits and a foot
in the Dardanelles, which Stalin did not fail to tell Roosevelt and
Churchill at Tehran. Confronted with Churchill's remark that
"this was an awkward moment for raising the question," since he
wanted Turkey to join the Allies, Stalin replied that "the time
would come later."[11] The general impression is that possible Turkish entry into the war seemed too closely linked with British offers
of Allied operations in southeastern Europe, which Moscow wished
to avoid at all cost.

The British plans for attacking Hitler's *Festung Europa* from the
south or southeast are difficult to pin down even today. They seem
never to have had a code name like other potential war operations
(e.g., "Jupiter" for the campaign in northern Norway). Their projected scope and character must have changed more than once between the autumn of 1942, and January, 1945, when the idea was
abandoned. The practical value of such operations became very
limited after May, 1944, when England and Russia divided southeastern Europe into "spheres of activity," giving the Soviets a dominant position in Romania, Bulgaria, and Hungary; the influence in
Yugoslavia was to be divided 50-50.[12] In November, 1942, however,
soon after the successful Allied landings in Algeria and Morocco,
when Churchill broached the idea of a Balkan front, the war as
well as the postwar situation in Europe could have taken a different
course. But what was it to have been? A localized front in the Balkans? A military action in the northern Balkans, in any part of the
Balkans, in Hungary or Austria? Was the front to extend to Vienna, or was it to be limited to the Istrian Peninsula? All these
geographic possibilities have been mentioned one time or another
in documents and war memoirs. The subject has been widely de-
bated since the war, and Churchill himself entered the controversy
by debunking the Balkan "legend" in the fifth volume of his memoirs. He was incensed by the false interpretation of his intentions,
which showed him as favoring a Balkan operation *instead* of the
invasion of Northern France.

Some light is thrown on this problem by Churchill's memoirs.
He writes:

I was not opposed at this time to a landing in the south of France
. . . in aid of the main invasion across the Channel. Alternatively, I

preferred a right-handed movement from the north of Italy, using the Istrian Peninsula and the Ljubljana Gap, towards Vienna. I was delighted when the President suggested this, and tried . . . to engage him in it. If the Germans resisted, we should attract many of their divisions from the Russian or Channel fronts. If we were not resisted, we should liberate at little cost enormous and invaluable regions.[13]

Churchill thought that the Germans would have resisted an Allied offensive through Yugoslavia. But for how long? With what forces? Once a Channel invasion started, the Germans would have to deploy their forces on three fronts. This, however, is only speculation. What matters in this context is that Churchill's idea was strategically sound. It was also sound politically, for at the time he suggested an offensive through the Ljubljana Gap toward Vienna, Hungary had already secretly offered to come over to the Allied side, Romania was trying to make itself heard in London and Washington, Bulgaria needed little encouragement to throw off the German occupation. Beyond Vienna lay the Silesian Basin, one of the main sources of Hitler's industrial strength, and Poland with its underground army, the greatest in existence, which later bled to death in the heroic but unsupported Warsaw uprising. The regions, as Churchill puts it, were indeed "enormous and invaluable," and the political possibilities unlimited. But with the exception of one instance at Tehran (when Roosevelt spoke of "a possible operation at the head of the Adriatic to make a junction with the Partisans of Tito and then to operate northeast into Rumania in conjunction with the Soviet advance from the region of Odessa"),[14] the Americans opposed such plans, and so of course did the Russians. The American opposition stemmed from a rigid strategic position: to take the shortest road to Berlin. The Russians had other reasons. For them, the prospect of British and American forces showing themselves in southeastern Europe was fraught with great political danger. When Churchill, in November, 1942, brought up the subject for the first time, in connection with plans to exploit an expected victory in Italy, the Soviet armies were fighting on the Don, the Lower Volga and in the Caucasian foothills. Therefore, when the Battle of Stalingrad raged, the Red Army was still 600–700 miles from Warsaw and Bucharest. Should the Western Allies attack through Yugoslavia in a northeastern direction, with enthusiastic Hungarian, Romanian, and Polish support, who would get to east-central Europe first? The plan therefore had to be prevented, and the Russians, maneuvering skillfully, extracted a firm promise that the major assault would be across the English Channel, with a secondary offensive in southern France. Once these decisions were taken at Tehran, the possibility of an extensive Anglo-American operation in central and eastern Europe practically ceased to exist.

A striking example of the Soviet method was furnished after Churchill's generous offer of assistance of June 22, 1941. There was no high-level response from Moscow. Stalin kept complete silence. The Soviet press printed parts of the speech without comment. The Russians let it be known that they wished to send a military mission to London, and that was all. "The silence on the top level was oppressive, and I thought it my duty to break the ice," Churchill wrote in his memoirs.[15] He then sent Stalin a personal message. But almost a month passed before the Soviet dictator answered. Acknowledging Churchill's statement that the Soviet Union and Britain had become fighting allies, he asked for a second front. The tone was set: Britain was always offering to help, one way or another; Russia was always asking for more. Hopkins, during his mission to Moscow in July, 1941, encountered a similar attitude. Roosevelt and Churchill authorized him to say that their governments "were willing to do everything that they possibly could . . . to send material to Russia."[16] Nothing was asked in return, and the deliveries were free of charge. Yet for many months to come, Russia's position was extremely weak. Churchill reflected on it in an afterthought: "For more than one year after Russia was involved in the war she presented herself to our minds as a burden and not as a help."[17] Sometimes the Russians were so insistent that Churchill reminded the Soviet Ambassador that "only four months ago we in this Island did not know whether you were not coming in against us on the German side."[18]

Being supplied unconditionally with matériel, the Soviet Union had no reason to give in on the political front. The first example of this was in Soviet-Polish relations. Hitler's aggression had nullified the Molotov-Ribbentrop Pact. Within a few days, the Polish territory occupied in 1939, and illegally annexed to the Soviet Union, was in German hands. General Sikorski's government-in-exile negotiated the July 30, 1941, agreement with Russia that invalidated the Soviet-German treaties but did not specifically restore the Polish eastern frontier existing prior to the Soviet aggression of September 17, 1939. At best, this agreement was open to conflicting interpretations. After much heartsearching and grave internal conflicts, the Sikorski government signed the agreement, having yielded to British pressure (which should have been exerted on Russia rather than on the Poles). An important factor in the Polish decision was the fate of the more than 1.5 million deportees from the Polish eastern territories kept in inhuman conditions in Soviet concentration and labor camps. The liberation of these innocent citizens of an allied nation should have been a precondition of any British or American help to Russia. Instead, the deportees became hostages, and their release became a Soviet bargaining point in the negotiations. Soon Soviet-Polish relations again deteriorated. The Russians never lived up to the provisions of the July, 1941, agreement, failed to liberate large numbers of Poles still detained in the Soviet Union, and reasserted their claim to territories they occupied in collusion with Hitler in 1939. The Soviet note claiming these territories as already belonging to the Soviet Union was dated January 5, 1942.[19] Five days earlier, at St. James's Palace in London, the Soviet Union had signed the Declaration of the United Nations, thus subscribing to the Atlantic Charter. The Charter states that the signatories "seek no aggrandizement, territorial or other . . . desire to seek no territorial changes that do not accord with the freely expressed wishes of the peoples concerned . . . respect the right of all peoples to choose the form of government under which they will live." Shortly before signing this solemn declaration, the Soviet Government informed British Foreign Secretary Anthony Eden that it wished to annex the Polish eastern territories, the Baltic states, Romanian Bessarabia, and parts of Finland. Romania was to grant Russia military bases. Eden wrote in his report that Stalin had asked for immediate British recognition of the future Soviet frontiers. In particular, the annexation of the Baltic states and of the Finnish territory occupied until 1941 was presented as a condition for the conclusion of the Anglo-Soviet treaty the British Government desired.

At first, both Western powers held that the Soviet territorial demands violated the Atlantic Charter and refused to accept them. But the Soviet Government continued its pressure, and in March, 1942, after a winter of military setbacks, Churchill seemed inclined to give in to these demands. However, Roosevelt and the State Department remained firm in their defense of the Atlantic Charter principles, and the British followed suit. To the Kremlin, however, the matter of securing Allied recognition of the frontier they had acquired with the help of Hitler was of the utmost importance.

The Soviet leaders knew that this was not merely a question of moving three matches on a surface, as Churchill had done in Tehran to demonstrate that the Polish nation was to be shifted west;[20] at stake was the whole line of independent states, from Finland to the Black Sea. By annexing the strategic Finnish area, the Baltic states, and Romanian Bessarabia, by pushing Poland west to the Curzon Line, the Soviet Government hoped to gain much more than merely territories. It sought to undermine the spirit of resistance of these independent nations and thus achieve the territorial link with the German lands which it was denied in 1920. Stalin therefore decided to send Molotov to London and Washington. The main object of the mission was the signing of a Soviet-British treaty of alliance explicitly recognizing the Soviet territorial demands. The mission did not succeed, mostly because of the strong American stand. The British also refused to barter the Polish eastern territories, for, according to Churchill, this would have been contrary to the Anglo-Polish treaty of 1939.[21] General Sikorski, the Polish Premier, played an important part in stiffening Allied opposition. His trip to America and the conversations he had with Roosevelt were particularly effective.* As usual when confronted with strong opposition, the Russians gave in; the treaty Molotov signed with England on May 26, 1942, made no mention of Soviet territorial claims.

Eighteen months later, at the Tehran Conference, Roosevelt and Churchill agreed to all the Russian demands in Europe they had rejected in the spring of 1942. This great victory of Soviet diplomacy was achieved most undramatically, unbeknown to the public, and not alluded to in the official communiqués. The Tehran Conference rightly has been called the turning point of the war, in the sense that it fixed the Allied strategy against Hitler's Germany. But it was also a turning point in the political sense: From that time on, Russia's penetration into the European heartland became a certainty. But this was not generally known at the time, and the Tehran Conference was hailed as a great political success. In later years, after the disastrous consequences became apparent, the Allied diplomacy came under sharp attack. Two main factors gave Soviet diplomacy its historic opportunity. One was the basic mis-

* Count Edward Raczynski, Polish Acting Foreign Minister, who accompanied Sikorski to the U.S., writes in his memoirs: "Despite conflicting auguries up to the last moment, our expedition to America was successful in making the British Government desist from signing the agreement they had contemplated: the Anglo-Soviet treaty of May 26th, 1942, made no reference to frontiers." (*In Allied London* [London, 1962], p. 112.)

judgment of Russia's aims and methods,* the other consisted in decisions on strategy that ignored Clausewitz's famous thesis that war is the continuation of politics by other means.

The full story of the Soviet activities that contributed or exploited these Allied failings cannot yet be written; Russian official archives are inaccessible, and published Allied documents and personal memoirs are still far from complete. But it is nonetheless possible to discern the main lines of Soviet political strategy. It is also possible to define some of the characteristic tactical devices used by Soviet diplomacy. The atmosphere of the personal meetings and of the correspondence between Stalin, Roosevelt, Churchill, and their principal collaborators is particularly revealing. At times it almost seems as if the Russians wished to imply that it was the fault of England and America that Hitler deceived the Kremlin and decided to destroy the Soviet war machine first before concentrating on the West. Here Soviet diplomacy touched on a very sensitive area: the danger that Russia could be totally defeated and the fear lest Stalin again arrive at an understanding with Hitler. The first of these remained a very real danger until the late autumn of 1942. On September 16, 1942, Churchill still feared "the total defeat of Russia or the reduction of this country to a minor military factor."²² After Stalingrad and other German setbacks during the winter of 1942–43, the collapse of Russia became a rather remote possibility, particularly in view of the massive material aid furnished by the Western powers. However, Soviet insistence on a second front was not relaxed. Russian demands in this respect were in themselves understandable. But once the threat posed by the German armies had become less acute, the Russians did not press for a second front just anywhere in Europe, but only for one particular front—in France. They combined this pressure with renewed demands that the Western powers recognize Russian territorial claims in Europe.

Soviet insistence grew in intensity at the time of the Western victories in North Africa, between November, 1942—when the British defeated Rommel at El Alamein—and May, 1943—when Tunis fell

---

* A leading American expert, Ambassador George Kennan, writes of the "inexcusable body of ignorance about the nature of the Russian Communist movement, about the history of its diplomacy." (*Russia and the West*, p. 355.)

Epitomizing the Tehran Conference in retrospect, Churchill stated: "Vast and disastrous changes have fallen upon us in the realm of fact." (*Closing the Ring*, p. 407.)

to the American and British armies. These decisive battles changed the general aspect of the war. Africa was clear of Axis forces. The whole length of the southern Mediterranean coast was now vulnerable to Allied thrusts, and the German and Italians were kept guessing as to the probable invasion point. Yet it was during this period that resistance to Russian territorial claims in Europe somehow evaporated in London and Washington. The methods employed by Soviet diplomacy in no small degree contributed to this result.

When the Harriman-Beaverbrook mission arrived in Moscow in September, 1941—at a time of great danger to the Soviet state—with offers of food and arms, which eventually developed into the gigantic Lend-Lease program, "their reception was bleak and discussions not at all friendly."[23] Recalling Churchill's first personal meeting with Stalin, in August, 1942, Cordell Hull writes of the "intemperate language" used by Stalin toward Churchill.[24] This calculated rudeness, applied in a somewhat different form to Roosevelt, was kept up all through the period of preparation for the all-important meeting of the Big Three at Tehran. In October, 1942, Churchill outlined to Stalin the plans for attacking in North Africa, both in Egypt and from the sea in Morocco and Algeria. In the same cable, he wrote of the forthcoming Allied aid in fighter planes and of the supplies being sent via the dangerous northern convoy route. Stalin's answer, dated October 13, 1942, was: "Your message of October 9 received. Thank you."[25] Messages from Stalin to Roosevelt were as concise: "Your message of October 12 at hand. I am grateful for the information." Or: "I have received your message of October 16. I was delayed in answering because front affairs held my attention. The thing now is to have promised cargoes delivered to the U.S.S.R. as scheduled by you."[26]

It would, of course, be absurd to believe that Stalin did not have enough staff to prepare more explicit replies to the President of the United States. His was a tactical move meant to create the impression that Russia was not being truly helped by the Western powers. When, in December, 1942, Roosevelt asked what had happened to the offer of air assistance in the Caucasus, Stalin cabled that the Anglo-American squadrons with crews were no longer needed in Transcaucasia and that he now wanted aircraft without crews.

Churchill thought that the "Anglo-American victories in North Africa demanded a complete review of Allied strategy." As stated earlier, he thought not only of Italy but of further operations against the southern flank of the "Fortress Europe." The Americans did not accept these plans or suggestions, and the Russians frankly opposed them. The Kremlin congratulated the Western Allies on their successes in Africa, Sicily, and Italy, but it refused to admit that this constituted a second front. In March, 1943, Stalin telegraphed Roosevelt and Churchill that the envisaged invasion of Sicily could by no means replace a second front in France. Apart from the understandable desire to see the American and British land armies fight the Germans on the Continent, the Soviet Government had ulterior motives: It wanted to keep the Allied forces as far away as possible from eastern Europe, and at the same time enjoy the role of the dissatisfied partner deserving of some compensation. Stalin therefore rejected all arguments, even when Churchill explained to him that it would be no help to Russia to throw away a hundred thousand men in a disastrous cross-Channel attack before enough strength was gathered for a successful invasion. In the previously mentioned March, 1943, dispatch to Roosevelt and Churchill, Stalin included "a most emphatic warning, in the interest of the common cause, of the grave danger with which further delay in opening a second front in France is fraught."[27]

Such language was well calculated to raise the specter of a separate peace between Soviet Russia and Nazi Germany. Much has been written on the subject, but no convincing evidence exists that any serious attempts in this direction were made by either side in 1942–43. Some low-level Soviet-German contacts existed in neutral countries, but it is not clear whether they ever went beyond secret-service probings, not unique in time of war. An Order of the Day by Stalin to the Red Army, issued on February 23, 1942, alarmed some Allied quarters. It is doubtful, however, if it proved anything other than that the Soviet dictator was thinking of his relations with the German people after Hitler's defeat. On the other hand, Soviet diplomats, agents, and sympathizers in Western and neutral countries were the source of many rumors that kept alive the fear of a separate Soviet peace. After all, there were two examples from the not too distant past: Lenin's "peace at any price" in 1918, and the Molotov-Ribbentrop Pact of 1939. It was rumored in diplomatic circles that Molotov himself, while in Washington at the end of May, 1942, had hinted to Roosevelt that the Soviet territorial needs in eastern Europe were better understood by Hitler than by the Western Allies. This apparently drew a sharp retort from the President. There is no trace of such an exchange in now-available records, unless an allusion to it could be read into Roosevelt's remark, quoted in the Hopkins papers, that "after all, Mr. Molotov had seen and talked with Hitler more recently than anyone else present."[28] The truth of the matter seems to be that up to the German defeat at Stalingrad, Hitler had hoped that the great battles being fought from Leningrad to the Black Sea would eliminate the Soviet military machine as a serious fighting force. This would have given the Germans control over European Russia. Whether the Soviet regime could have survived the loss of Moscow, Leningrad, and the Caucasus, and yet maintain itself beyond the Urals, is a matter of pure speculation. Since this probably was Hitler's line of thought, it is reasonable to assume that he showed no real interest in a compromise with Stalin. After Stalingrad, the situation was reversed, and Stalin correctly expected to gain more from an alliance with the Western powers than from a new deal with Hitler. In September, 1943, Gromyko, then Soviet Chargé d'Affaires in Washington, informed Cordell Hull that his government had rejected a Japanese offer to bring about a separate peace with Germany.* It also is not at all certain that Hitler, even after Stalingrad, contemplated an accommodation with Russia, but up to the last days of the war, the Nazis had the unfounded hope that the Western powers would turn against the Soviet Union and help them turn back the Communist offensive.† Thus, it seems that the fears of a Russian separate peace were not founded on fact, but only served the Soviet aims by contributing to the feeling in Washington and London that Russia's grievances should be appeased before a second front was opened in France.

The Tehran Conference was preceded by a meeting of the American, English, and Soviet Foreign Ministers in Moscow in October, 1943, and by an extraordinary display of Soviet maneuvering, in which the subject matter of the discussions became so enmeshed

---

* A high-ranking Soviet staff officer who defected to the West asserts that the Japanese made two attempts in Moscow to assist in a Soviet-Nazi reconciliation; both of these were initiated at the highest level—the first in September, 1942, the other in June, 1943. (Ivan Krylov, *Soviet Staff Officer* [London: the Falcon Press, 1951], pp. 200, 241.)

† Goebbels was mystically elated when learning of Roosevelt's death. He thought that this was the turning point, like the death of the Czarina Elisabeth in 1761, which saved Frederick II of Prussia in the Seven Years' War and brought about the "miracle of the House of Brandenburg." (H. R. Trevor-Roper, *The Last Days of Hitler*, pp. 86–88.)

with the question of when and where they would meet that the eventual agreement on the time and place of the conference was made to appear as a major Soviet concession.

Having been made well aware of Soviet dissatisfaction over the second front, Roosevelt first mentioned the project of personally meeting Stalin in the spring of 1942. He was then thinking of a possible summer conference in Alaska. Cordell Hull lists three other unsuccessful attempts by the President to arrange a meeting with Stalin: before the Casablanca Conference in January, 1943; again in May of the same year, when he sent former Ambassador Joseph Davies to Moscow; and in August, 1943, at the time of the Quebec Conference, when he tried to get Stalin to attend a meeting with Churchill and himself at Fairbanks, Alaska.

The general sequence of events can be reconstructed as follows: Roosevelt suggests meeting with Stalin in the spring of 1942; in August, Stalin tells Churchill that he would be willing to attend such a conference in winter. Then begins a game of hide-and-seek. Between December, 1942, and August, 1943, the President makes the three suggestions mentioned above. Stalin evades the issue. On December 6, 1942, before the Casablanca Conference, he cables Roosevelt and Churchill that he cannot leave Russia "even for a single day." In another telegram he informs them that he cannot meet them before next March. He then declares that he does not know what specific subjects Roosevelt and Churchill wish to discuss with him, and asks: "Could we not discuss them by correspondence?"[29] Cordell Hull recalls that in August, 1943, some Soviet newspapers suddenly began to air the idea that a meeting of the three Foreign Ministers would now be timely. On August 9, 1943, the day Churchill arrived in Canada en route to Quebec, a cable from Stalin mentions the opportunity of holding "a meeting of authorized representatives of our states."[30] Roosevelt and Churchill then offer a meeting "at Foreign Office level" as the second-best choice should Stalin be unable to come to Fairbanks. Stalin agrees to the meeting of Foreign Ministers, which in fact means that he agrees to his own suggestion. At the same time he demands that the conference have a more precise character than had been anticipated in Washington and London, and that it make practical decisions at the highest level. This sequence was followed by a brief intermezzo, during which Churchill suggested that the Foreign Ministers meet in England (a midway point). Roosevelt preferred Casablanca, Tunis, or Sicily, but Stalin wanted

Moscow, and although the President informed him that because
of Hull's age and poor health he would not like him to fly so far,
Stalin's will prevailed.

When the Russians suggested a meeting of Foreign Ministers
while still evading a Big Three conference, they obviously knew
that the atmosphere in Washington and London with regard to
their claims in eastern Europe had changed considerably. The subject was widely discussed in diplomatic circles in the early months
of 1943. In March, the Russian ambassadors in Washington and
London told Hopkins and Eden of Russia's intention to annex the
Baltic states, eastern Poland, and parts of Finland. From Hopkins'
note one can assume that neither he nor Eden had reservations
about these Soviet declarations, not even when Litvinov told Hopkins that the territorial decisions should be imposed on Poland by
the Western Allies themselves. Eden, it is true, defended the idea
of a European federation, but he did not oppose Ambassador
Maisky's formula that Poland should have a government "friendly"
to Russia, which could have meant only that Moscow claimed the
right to interfere in Polish internal affairs. Maisky's conversations
with Eden and Hopkins were characteristic examples of many instances when Soviet diplomats or agents found out that the opposition they had met with previously had vanished. Such indeed was
the case. On the eve of the Moscow Conference, Roosevelt told
Cordell Hull that as for the Baltic states and Poland, "he intended
to appeal to him [Stalin] on grounds of high morality."[31] But the
Russians, having had their unpleasant experience with the Soviet-
British treaty of May, 1942, wanted to be sure of their ground before engaging the supreme authority of Stalin himself.

Soviet expectations at the Moscow Conference were not disappointed. The Italian front was not accepted as a second front in
Europe, and Molotov's first request was to obtain confirmation of
the plans to invade France from the Channel in 1944. Once this
was done, the Soviet Foreign Minister occupied his Western col-
leagues with matters that to him were of relatively lesser importance: opposition to Chinese participation in a Four-Nations Declaration; demand that Russia be given part of the Italian fleet,
which had sailed to Malta and surrendered. And they also posed
two prying questions: Would the Western powers agree to exert
pressure on Turkey to enter the war immediately, and would they
induce Sweden to provide air bases against Germany? Both Cordell
Hull and Eden noticed Molotov's and Stalin's amiability, "signs of
an intention to open a new chapter," to prepare for "permanent

friendship with Britain and the United States."[32] This genial atmosphere was not disturbed by the American refusal to entertain the Soviet suggestions on Sweden and Turkey, or even by the delay in dealing with the question of the Italian fleet. There were no notable difficulties in drafting the final text of the press communiqué of October 30, and of the secret protocol of November 3, 1943. Everybody seemed pleased with the outcome of the conference: Churchill, because it smoothed "many points of friction"; Cordell Hull, because China was eventually permitted to sign the Four-Nations Declaration, and because Russia had shown willingness to cooperate in the future United Nations Organization. The American Secretary of State was particularly pleased with Stalin's unsolicited and seemingly unconditional promise to join in the war against Japan after Germany's defeat. Russia also had important reasons to be satisfied. The opening of a second front in France in 1944 had been solemnly promised. As Eden informed Churchill, "the Russians were completely and blindly set on our invasion of northern France. It was the only decision in which they took an absorbing interest."[33] The discussion on the future of Germany showed a trend toward decentralization of that country or even its partition. The Polish question came up only in Eden's request that the Soviet Union re-establish relations with the Polish Government, broken off by Moscow in April. No one came out against Soviet annexational claims in eastern Europe. Molotov emphatically objected to plans for the smaller European nations to set up federations or confederations. Such ideas, he said, smacked of a *cordon sanitaire* around Russia. The Western ministers did not insist. Finally, a discussion on the interpretation of the important Paragraph 6 of the Declaration of the Four Nations on General Security indicated that no one then thought of Soviet designs on countries accessible to the Red Army.[34]

Molotov's request of an immediate interpretation of this paragraph was one more demonstration of careful Soviet preparation for the postwar period. According to Cordell Hull, Molotov wanted to be sure that no obstacles resulted from agreements that one of the three might have with other countries for mutual assistance and the establishment of bases—a clear indication of future Soviet methods in central and eastern Europe.

All through the Moscow Conference, and until November 9, 1943, the Western powers kept up their insistent demand for a Stalin-Roosevelt-Churchill meeting. Such a conference was obviously in the Soviet interest, and there is little doubt that Moscow expected much from it. Although Stalin and Molotov agreed "in principle" to the necessity of such a meeting, it seemed to be impossible to find a date acceptable to the Soviet Generalissimo. The other major difficulty was the site of the meeting. Several places were suggested to the Russians: Cairo, and/or the neighborhood of the Pyramids, Baghdad, Basra, the British Air Force desert training center at Habbaniya in Iraq, Ankara, Asmara (the capital of Italian Eritrea), some port in the eastern Mediterranean. The Russians said that only one place would do—Tehran—and nothing would make them change their mind. In a telegram dated October 14, Roosevelt informed Stalin that the capital of Iran was not convenient for him: "The Congress will be in session. New laws and resolutions must be acted on by me after their receipt and must be returned to the Congress physically before ten days have elapsed."[35] The President explained that the flight to Tehran over the mountains was unpredictable and that planes were often held up for several days. "For Constitutional reasons" he therefore could not take the risk of going there. Ten days later, Roosevelt reminded Stalin that he was ready to travel to within 600 miles of Russian territory and that he was deeply disappointed by Stalin's attitude. In Moscow, Hull and Eden pleaded and insisted. "I got nowhere with this," Hull writes in his memoirs.[36] Making a show of his indifference, Stalin offered to send Molotov in his place. In a conversation with Eden he also said that if the Western powers did not have enough divisions to fight simultaneously in Italy and France," a meeting of the heads of governments would not create them."[37]

Stalin's assertion that he could not absent himself even for a short time was untenable. The Soviet insistence on Tehran was motivated by other considerations. Stalin could go to Tehran almost without leaving the Soviet military area, since northern Persia was then occupied by Russian troops. But the most important motive was his desire to wear down the Western partners by haggling over a matter that in itself was devoid of political significance and thus make them more willing to concede important political points. On November 8, Roosevelt informed Stalin that he had solved the Constitutional difficulty by arranging to fly from Tehran to Tunis and back to Tehran should Congress pass a bill he would want to veto. The President thus gave in to Stalin's wish at the risk of considerable inconvenience to himself. A telegram from Roosevelt to Churchill of November 12 shows that even after accepting what

Stalin wanted, the President was not sure that the meeting would come off: "I have just heard that Uncle J. will come to Tehran. I wired him at once that I had arranged the Constitutional matter here, and therefore could go to Tehran for a short meeting with him, and told him I was very happy. Even then I was in doubt as to whether he would go through with his former offer to go to Tehran."[38]

After all the preparatory maneuvers, it is not surprising that the conference at Tehran (November 28–December 1, 1943) was conspicuous for its lack of serious controversy. Some acrimony was displayed between the Russians and the British, mostly in the process of dissipating the last shadows of Churchill's Balkan plans, a matter in which "the Americans and the Russians would form a united front."[39] Under the circumstances, the defeat of Churchill's rearguard action concerning operations in southeast Europe was a foregone conclusion.* Stalin and his collaborators once more made certain that on the Western side everything would be subordinated to "Overlord," the cross-Channel operation; they were not particularly interested whether or not the difficult assault on the German defenses in France would be well prepared and how much headway it could make. All that mattered to them was to tie down the maximum number of German divisions in the west so as to facilitate their own westward progress. Sir Alan Brooke noted in his diary on November 28, 1943: "I feel that Stalin saw through these strategical misconceptions, but to him they mattered little; his political and military requirements could now best be met by the greatest squandering of British and American lives in France."[40]

At Tehran there was no thorough debate of the pending political problems. Ripe apples simply fell into the Russian basket. Stalin advanced the following territorial claims in various forms:

    a. Hangö and/or Petsamo in Finland
    b. The Baltic states
    c. The Königsberg area
    d. Eastern Poland
    e. Some form of control or bases in the Black Sea Straits

* In October, 1944, during conversations with Churchill in Moscow, Stalin apparently agreed that Allied troops be landed on the eastern Adriatic coast. At that time, Soviet forces already had entered Romania, Yugoslavia, and Hungary, and therefore the problem had taken on a different aspect. The circumstances of Stalin's agreement are, nevertheless, not clear. (Cf. Chester Wilmot, *The Struggle for Europe*, p. 630.)

f. A warm-water port in the Far East

g. Sakhalin and the Kurile Islands

With the exception of the Turkish Straits, on which the Russians did not insist at the time, all the other claims were granted either tacitly or explicitly. The demands were presented without a shred of objective justification, and if questioned, the Russians pushed them through with calculated cynicism and brutality.

Because of an error in translation, Stalin thought that Roosevelt was suggesting an international trusteeship for the Baltic states. He immediately replied that these three states "had by an expression of the will of the people voted to join the Soviet Union and that this question was not therefore one for discussion."[41] (He was referring to the sham elections held in 1940, while the Baltic states were under Red Army occupation.) The Polish question was the subject of several discussions. Stalin introduced Soviet claims to Poland's eastern territories by accusing the Polish government-in-exile of having "joined with Hitler in slanderous propaganda against Russia."[42] This was also the Kremlin's only safe reply to the Polish demand that the murder of several thousand Polish officers whose bodies had been discovered in the Katyn Woods near Smolensk be investigated by the International Committee of the Red Cross.[43] The lands Russia wanted to annex lay east of the demarcation line fixed in the Soviet-German Boundary and Friendship Treaty signed in Moscow by Molotov and Ribbentrop on September 28, 1939, as "the boundary of their respective national interests in the territory of the former Polish State." We read in the Churchill memoirs: "Eden asked if this meant the Ribbentrop-Molotov Line. 'Call it whatever you like,' said Stalin. Molotov remarked that it was generally called the Curzon Line. 'No,' said Eden, 'there are important differences.' Molotov said there were none."[44]

As to the Finns, Stalin thought that they should be taught a lesson. No one wished to remind him that four years earlier, Soviet Russia was shown the door by the League of Nations for its aggression against Finland.

The claim to the Königsberg area was explained by Russia's need for a warm-water seaport. In view of the announced reannexation of the Baltic states, which would give Russia Memel and the Latvian ports, particularly Liepaja (Libau), the argument was without foundation. In this connection we may note one other instance of the peculiar distortion of logic used by the Soviet negotiators. Stalin declared that he would be ready to accept the Curzon Line as the Soviet-Polish frontier if Russia were given parts of East Prussia, including Königsberg. In other words, for being willing to accept eastern Poland (which they coveted), the Soviets would be given a piece of Germany. The brazenness of having the annexation of nearly half of Poland seem a concession, and that of Königsberg a condition for making this concession, was repeated in a telegram from Stalin to Churchill:

> We claim the transfer of the northeastern part of East Prussia, including the ice-free port of Königsberg, to the Soviet Union. . . . Unless this minimum claim of the Soviet Union is met, the Soviet Union's concession in recognizing the Curzon Line becomes entirely pointless, as I told you in Tehran.[45]

In response to the request for a warm-water port in the Far East, Roosevelt offered Russia access to Dairen under international control.

The discussion on the German problem did not lead to a unanimity of views, except that the three heads of governments favored the division of Germany into several parts: Roosevelt into five (or more, if one includes the proposed United Nations trusteeships); Churchill (probably) into two, with the south forming a "Danubian Confederation"; Stalin simply into parts that could not reunite. He was opposed to Churchill's idea of a South German Danubian Confederation, suspecting that Austria, Hungary, and Romania would be invited to participate. Apart from these generalities, the future of Germany was left undecided and was referred to the European Advisory Commission.

The military results of the conference were put down in a secret protocol initialed by Roosevelt, Churchill, and Stalin on December 1. Paragraph 4 stated that "Operation Overlord" would be undertaken in May, 1944, "in conjunction with an operation against southern France." Apart from the general declaration signed by the Big Three on the same date, and sometimes referred to as the Tehran Communiqué, and a declaration on Iran (signed also by the Prime Minister of Iran), no other official documents embody the conclusions of this Conference. The all-important political decisions or attitudes were, it seems, registered only in the notes of the collaborators and interpreters of the three chief participants.

The great achievements of Soviet diplomacy at Tehran were not the result of political sacrifices. Such temporary concessions to the West as Stalin's first war speech of July 3, 1941, when he paid lip service to democratic principles and the right of self-determination, or the dissolution of the Comintern on May 22, 1943, were also logical consequences of the internal Soviet situation. Confronted with the German invasion, the Communist regime appealed to the national feelings of the Great-Russians and waged a "patriotic war." The departures from revolutionary ideology and Communist semantics made a profound impression in Anglo-Saxon countries, raising hopes of enduring collaboration with Soviet Russia. On opening the first session at Tehran, Roosevelt greeted the Soviet leaders as "new members of the family circle."[46]

Despite some of the unpleasant exchanges that took place during the conference, Churchill proposed a toast to "Stalin the Great."[47] In this atmosphere, the true picture of Soviet totalitarianism had become blurred. Future Russian preponderance in eastern Europe was accepted as a matter of course; only a few understood that the then developing doctrine of "friendly governments" meant something more than a politically harmless protection of legitimate Soviet interests. Larger Soviet ambitions went unnoticed. After Hitler's defeat, the Russians were banking on the speedy evacuation of American and British troops from Europe. It would then become possible to install Communist governments in a number of countries, perhaps even in Italy and France. At Tehran, Stalin had told Roosevelt that it was Pétain and not de Gaulle who represented the real France. But this was certainly no longer true then, and Stalin, well informed of the French situation by an active Communist underground, knew it. One must assume that Moscow was preparing for the not too distant future and thought it more expedient to have a Pétain government in France, which could be accused of collaboration with Hitler, rather than the unblemished de Gaulle. In the Far East, the Russians had no use for a strong China allied to the West and therefore played down the Chinese role in the future world organization. But Soviet neutrality with regard to Japan was scrupulously observed, to the point that Molotov refused Roosevelt's invitation to participate in the Cairo Conference, which preceded Tehran, because of the presence of the Chinese. But in the privacy of Tehran, Stalin repeated that Russia would fight Japan after Germany's defeat. The promise did not cost much; although Britain and the United States were waging a desperate war in the Far East, the Soviet clamor for an immediate second front in France was not countered with the logical request of a second Soviet front in the Far East. Apart from trying to push China out of a leading position in the future world organization, the Russians at that stage were not difficult about their collaboration with the international body. Roosevelt's offer that Communist Russia become one of the four members of the highest enforcing agency, one of the "Four Policemen" responsible for world peace, gave the Soviet state formal recognition not only as a great power but also as a moral authority.

Soon after the conference, the American Embassy in Moscow reported an almost "revolutionary change" in the Soviet press, now full of praise for Allied unity and the "historical decisions" at Tehran. The protection of these promising developments and their effective completion while the Red Army was pushing west and southwest became the chief task of Soviet diplomacy in the period between Tehran and the next conference of the three heads of governments, which was held at Yalta in February, 1945. The main obstacle was the perennial Polish problem, the traditional barrier to Russia's domination of east-central Europe and thus to wider Communist penetration of Europe. Although Roosevelt and Churchill had given in to the Soviet territorial demands, they both knew that the overwhelming mass of the population in Poland backed the government-in-exile as the true and legal Polish authority. This was borne out by Polish participation on most Allied fronts, the massive resistance of the Polish people against the Nazi occupation and the creation of a vast underground organization, civilian and military, without precedent in the history of any country. At the head of the underground state was a deputy premier, a member of the London government. The Home Army under the commander-in-chief in London was preparing to renew the open warfare interrupted in October, 1939. The Nazis knew that they were sitting on a volcano, and numerous German troops were needed to preserve lines of communication with the eastern front. Despite the efforts of Soviet propaganda to obscure the issue, it was generally known that no Russians lived in eastern Poland. At least half of the 13 million population was ethnically Polish or pro-Polish. Of the others, many Ukrainians or Belorussians (though by no means all) wanted an independent state; but they also hoped for the liberation of their countrymen in the Soviet Union, and most of them were as opposed to Communism and Russian rule as was the Polish population.

There is a little doubt that Roosevelt and Churchill were not happy about the Tehran arrangement, that they were uncertain of public opinion at home, and that they still hoped to be able to save Poland's independence. To the Poles, the attitude of the Western leaders seemed misguided and their hopes unfounded. Most of them were convinced, and were soon to be proved right, that there was no point in trying to appease the Soviet appetite with territorial and political concessions, that Moscow's real aim was the liquidation of a truly independent Polish state. The government-in-exile therefore rejected the Soviet territorial claims based on the Ribbentrop-Molotov Line (which the Russians preferred to call the Curzon Line). An extraordinary situation developed: Allied armies, in this case the Soviet Army, for the first time entered an Allied country, but instead of liberating it they claimed its territory under a treaty concluded with Hitler. The U.S. Department of State was in favor of leaving territorial decisions to the peace conference; Churchill was uneasy and (in February–March, 1944) leaned toward a complicated temporary arrangement that would defer the final decision about frontiers to the peace conference while allowing the Poles to administer the area west of the Curzon Line. According to a cable sent by Churchill to Stalin, this would make "the occupation by Russia of the Curzon Line a *de facto* reality."[48] Although the Prime Minister also took pains to proclaim publicly that he approved of the Soviet claim to this frontier, and in dispatches to Stalin confirmed his agreement on the intended annexation of Königsberg, relations between Moscow and London became rather tense. The Russians declared that eastern Poland was already a part of the Soviet Union, but at the same time wanted approval of the annexation both by the Western Allies and the Poles. Soviet pressure in the Polish and other matters took the form of sharp criticism and devious maneuvers. On January 17, 1944, *Pravda* revived the separate-peace controversy by accusing "two leading personalities" of having recently met with Ribbentrop in Spain. Again in January, Stalin indignantly cabled Churchill that it had never occurred to him that a decision arrived at by the Big Three at Tehran could be revised in any way. With regard to the Poles, his demands steadily increased, and he tried to influence the composition of the Polish Government. In March, 1944, Churchill let Stalin know that he intended to inform the House of Commons that British attempts to assist in a Soviet-Polish arrangement had broken down, that Britain would continue to recognize the Polish Government as that "of the ally for whom we declared war upon Hitler," that "all questions of territorial change must await the armistice or peace conferences . . . and that in the meantime we can recognize no forcible transference of territory."

In answer, Stalin accused Churchill of making Soviet Russia appear "hostile to Poland, and virtually deny the liberating nature of the war waged by the Soviet Union," a denial tantamount to a confession. He warned that should Churchill make the intended speech in the Commons, this would be considered a "gratuitous insult to the Soviet Union."[49]

In the last week of June, 1944, the Russians launched a strong offensive on the central front, north and south of the Pripet Marshes. They made considerable progress, and by the end of July were rapidly approaching the Vistula. On August 1, the Polish Home Army began its uprising against the Germans in Warsaw, liberating important sectors of the city. The uprising was encouraged by Soviet broadcasts; the insurgents counted on help from the approaching Russian forces. Here, however, the "liberating nature of the war waged by the Soviet Union" was vividly demonstrated. In a conversation with Premier Mikolajczyk, who had come to Moscow on Churchill's and Roosevelt's insistence, Stalin denied that there was an uprising in the Polish capital. Then the Soviet armies stopped a few miles short of the city; for two months they looked on while the Poles fought an uneven battle to its bitter end. On August 5, Stalin cabled Churchill that his information about Warsaw was "greatly exaggerated and unreliable."[50] During August, there were a number of diplomatic exchanges with Moscow aimed at helping the Warsaw fighters. Cordell Hull states that on August 14, the American Government "sought to obtain permission from the Russians for a shuttle mission of American bombers to drop arms to the Poles who were fighting desperately to hold their capital until the Russian forces could arrive. On August 15, the Soviet Government refused our request."[51] On August 20, Roosevelt and Churchill sent a telegram to Stalin beginning with the sentence: "We are thinking of world opinion if anti-Nazis in Warsaw are in effect abandoned." Hull writes that Stalin eventually gave permission for one shuttle flight on September 18. Warsaw capitulated on October 3, 1944, after sixty-three days of fighting, with the Soviet Army under the Russified Pole Marshal Rokossovsky standing across the Vistula. The city was in ruins; the Poles had lost 200,000 soldiers and civilians. Soviet behavior in the struggle of the Polish capital had far-reaching consequences.

The *Survey*, published under the auspices of the London Royal Institute of International Affairs, states: "Despite all later efforts to mend the breach between East and West, the bad blood created in Poland in 1944 proved the beginning of the end. The streets of Warsaw had been sown with dragons' teeth."[52]

In June, 1944, the general character of the war began to change radically. Strong American and British forces successfully stormed German beach defenses in Normandy, won a great battle further inland, and swept into France along a wide front. On August 15 began the successful supporting invasion of southern France. By October, most of France and Belgium was liberated. The Italian campaign had also progressed successfully: Rome had been liberated on June 4, two days before the Normandy landing. Before the winter, the Allies reached the narrow top of the Italian boot, roughly along the Pisa-Ravenna line. During the same period, the Soviet armies attacked Romania from southern Poland, meeting with little resistance. The Romanian Army joined in the fight against the Germans. The Russians entered Bulgaria and Hungary in September and established contact with Tito's Partisans in Yugoslavia. By the end of the year, the Russians were in Bucharest, Sofia, and Belgrade and were besieging the Germans in Budapest. The Bulgarian Army fought on the Russian side. So did part of the Hungarian Army, on orders believed to have been issued by Admiral Horthy before his arrest by the Germans. At the end of August, the Germans crushed a Slovak uprising; as in Warsaw, the Soviet offensive in the area came to a sudden stop, giving the enemy ample time to finish off the insurgents. The events in eastern and southeastern Europe, from the start of the Warsaw uprising in August to the siege of Budapest in the winter, demonstrated what momentous opportunities had been lost when the Allied forces did not advance from Italy in the direction of Vienna. Thus it was the Russians who reaped the benefits, occupying vast regions in which they were most unwelcome. They quickly installed Communist stooges in Bulgaria and Romania; they were enthusiastically greeted by Tito in Yugoslavia (where the British had withdrawn support from the pro-Western Mikhailovitch); and they secretly backed the Communist conspiracy in Greece.

Despite these events, and concurrent with them, the October, 1944, Moscow meeting of Churchill, Eden, Stalin, Molotov, and Harriman confirmed the compromise arrived at in May of the same year for a division of the Balkans into various spheres of influence. In fact, however, the compromise was already superseded by events. Wherever their armies were, the Russians, paying little heed to Western entreaties, subjected the local population to varying degrees of Communist rule.

The October Moscow Conference was also notable for a dramatic discussion of Poland's future. Polish Premier Mikolajczyk and Foreign Minister Tadeusz Romer had been summoned from London. At a plenary session the Poles first heard of the Tehran decision that "the Curzon line does not only correspond with the attitude of the Soviet Government, but it has also the concurrence of all the three great powers." When Mikolajczyk defended Poland's eastern territories, Stalin called him an imperialist. When the Polish Premier tried to find out if the cession of 40 per cent of Polish prewar territory would be coupled with a guarantee of independence for the country, Stalin interrupted: "Who is it that threatens the independence of Poland? Is it perhaps the Soviet Union?"[53]

Also during the Moscow Conference, Stalin accepted American military plans for Soviet participation in the war against Japan. He promised to engage sixty divisions three months after a victory over Germany, provided the United States furnished the necessary supplies—more than a million tons of equipment in addition to the Lend-Lease deliveries for the European front. Another condition, Stalin informed the conference, was that the Soviet Government be given the right to make territorial and other claims in the Far East.

On the whole, the Stalin-Churchill meeting in Moscow produced only superficial results. From the Western point of view, many problems remained unsolved: The situation in eastern and central Europe was highly unsatisfactory; the future of Germany had not been decided; the Soviet promise of participation in the war against Japan needed further clarification. A conference on the world security organization held between August and October at Dumbarton Oaks had shown basic differences of opinion between Russia and the Western powers. Roosevelt and Churchill therefore again thought of a meeting with Stalin, who made the usual difficulties. Even before the October Moscow Conference, he had made a point of showing a lack of interest: "I do not know," he cabled Roosevelt on October 8, "what points Mr. Churchill and Mr. Eden want to discuss in Moscow. Neither of them has said anything to me so far."[54]

Roosevelt suggested that the meeting of the three powers be held either at some Adriatic port or somewhere in Italy. Stalin again did not wish to leave Soviet territory; for reasons of prestige and convenience, he wanted the two Western partners to come to the Soviet Union and demanded that the conference take place on the Black Sea coast. After a short Anglo-American gathering at Malta, the three met at Yalta (February 4–11, 1945). What the Russians aimed at in Yalta can be deduced from their stand in regard to the subjects under discussion. Their immediate goals in Europe were the consolidation of their grip on Poland, the unhampered occupation of the Soviet Zone in Germany, and maximum German reparations. In Asia, the aim was to arrange for such territorial gains and related privileges that would, in effect, give Russia a dominant position in China.

When the Big Three met at the Livadia Palace in Yalta, many of the original Soviet war aims were already within reach. The scope of agreement that Moscow wanted to obtain from the Western Allies had therefore narrowed. The situation stood as follows:

a. Poland was occupied by the Red Army, and the two Western partners had agreed that the Curzon Line should become Russia's western border. There was still some bickering about leaving Lvov and the oil-fields region to Poland; the West still insisted that Poland should have a free and democratic government that would also be "friendly" to Russia. Since he had the country occupied and had obtained Roosevelt's and Churchill's consent to his territorial claims and the "friendly government," Stalin was not inclined to make anything but verbal concessions on a position he considered as settled: that Poland was to be politically and economically dominated by Soviet Russia and administered by the "Lublin Poles," whom Churchill described as "a kind of Quislings."[55] But because the first country to fight Hitler was to be treated as a vanquished foe, Stalin wanted to keep up the pretense of self-government, provided he did not pay for it in territory or political influence.

b. The Soviet armies had entered Germany and hoped to reach Berlin before the Western Allies. A large zone of occupation had been allotted to the Soviet Union by common consent in the Protocol of September 12, 1944. This Eastern zone was the fulfillment of long-standing Soviet aspirations. For all practical purposes it extended the Soviet rule to the Elbe and the Bavarian border. Having sustained great war losses, the Russians felt that material compensation should be quickly and easily obtained. Unless the physical removal of German capital goods and industrial equipment could be agreed upon among the three chief Allies, difficulties and controversy would ensue. Lack of agreement would also limit Soviet reparation claims to the western zone of occupation. Moscow therefore desired a general agreement on German reparations.

c. Soviet claims in the Far East were carefully calculated to result in a hold over China. The most important demands centered on Manchuria, then the only industrially developed region. In addition, Moscow wanted international endorsement of the "independence" of Outer Mongolia, in fact a Soviet satellite. The Russians also sought the annexation of Southern Sakhalin and the Kurile Islands, useful bases for pressuring Japan.

Soviet tactics at the conference were greatly helped by American insistence that agreement be reached on the world peace organization and on a "Declaration on Liberated Europe." For the Russians, the founding of the United Nations was certainly desirable. But in urgency and importance it could not be compared with the tangible gains derived from the occupation of a country or a port, or from the exacting of reparations. The Declaration on Liberated Europe, in which the three powers pledged their help in restoring sovereign rights and self-government as well as freely chosen democratic institutions, was no more binding for Russia than the Atlantic Charter. On the other hand, the formulations of some of the promises of the three powers to assist in establishing "conditions of internal peace" or in the forming of "interim governmental authorities broadly representative of all democratic elements in the population"[56] could serve as a useful cloak for exerting Soviet influence. The Declaration was therefore entirely acceptable to the Kremlin. Both the world peace organization and the Declaration on Europe were used by the Russians as bargaining points and presented as important concessions. Stalin also gave in to Churchill and Roosevelt on the question of French participation in the Allied Council for Germany. The concession was an easy one, since the French zone of occupation was to be carved out of the two other Western zones. Although less than a month before, on December 10, 1944, General de Gaulle had signed a Soviet-French treaty of alliance and mutual assistance in Moscow, Stalin at Yalta continued to speak of him as unfavorably as he had at Tehran. He also said that "France opened the gates to the enemy . . . had not done much fighting in the war,"[57] and generally demonstrated an anti-French bias, which helped him to make French participation in the Allied Control Council for Germany seem like a concession. By grudgingly agree-

ing to Western proposals in matters that to them were secondary
(like French participation in the Allied Council for Germany), or
less urgent (like the peace organization), or even desirable (like
the Declaration on Liberated Europe), the Russians succeeded in
creating an aura of friendly collaboration. It was best illustrated by
Hopkins' note to Roosevelt during the final meeting in Yalta: "Mr.
President—The Russians have given in so much at this Conference
that I don't think we should let them down."[58] In fact, they did not
give an iota on matters that were really important to them: Poland,
German reparations, Far East claims.

When the question of Poland's boundaries came up for discussion, Stalin made an "impassionate speech." According to the
stenographic notes made by the future Secretary of State James
Byrnes, Stalin said that the Curzon Line was "the line of Curzon
and Clemenceau and those Americans who took part in 1918 and
1919 in the conference which then took place. . . . Now some people want that we should be less Russian than Curzon and Clemenceau were. You would drive us into shame. What will be said by
the White Russians and the Ukrainians? They will say that Stalin
and Molotov are far less reliable defenders of Russia than are
Curzon and Clemenceau. I could not take up such a position and
return to Moscow with an open face." Byrnes also relates that this
was the only instance during the Yalta Conference when Stalin
stood up to speak.[59]

A simple analysis of this declaration (as recorded by Byrnes and
confirmed by Secretary of State Stettinius as well as by the Bohlen
and Matthews minutes of the Yalta documents published by the
Department of State) shows that Stalin did not know, or pretended not to know, who drew the demarcation line he was speaking of and when; that he chose to ignore that it was never meant
as a state frontier, and that it was irrelevant in relation to Lvov. It
is also evident that while pretending to speak in the name of the
Ukrainians and the Belorussians (White Ruthanians), Stalin revealed his true position as an exponent of Russian-Communist
imperialism. He would be ashamed to go back to *Moscow*, not to
Kiev or to Minsk (the capital of Belorussia); he could not be less
Russian than Curzon and Clemenceau, and feared to be considered
an unreliable defender of *Russia*. One might point out other mis-
representations, such as Stalin's assertion that during the last thirty
years the Germans had twice attacked Russia through Poland.
Neither in 1914 nor in 1941 was there a Polish state separating
Russia and Germany, since Poland was then partitioned between

them. There was no German aggression against Russia when Poland was a free and independent state.

The Russians won out completely on the boundary issue, without having the merits of the case discussed at the conference table. The composition of the future Polish government was the subject of more ample debate, although totally unrelated to political reality. For once the indefinable idea of a Polish government "friendly" to Russia was accepted, it carried with it the principle of Soviet interference. The Report published at the end of the conference stated that Russia's western frontier should, by and large, follow the Curzon Line. The section on the political future of Poland described the Communist Lublin Committee as "the Provisional Government now functioning in Poland." This body was to be "reorganized on a broader democratic basis with the inclusion of democratic leaders from Poland itself and from Poles abroad." A commission of three—with Molotov and the two Western ambassadors in Moscow—was to help in the reorganization. The new or transformed governing body would be called the "Polish Provisional Government of National Unity."[60] In reality, it was Molotov who was to decide which Pole was democratic and who could be a member of the government. The pledge of free elections by a government formed under Molotov's guidance was a contradiction in terms.

It has often been argued that since Poland was already occupied by the Red Army, there was nothing else the Western powers could do. This is not a valid argument. The only rational course would have been open opposition to the Soviet claims in Poland. At the time of the Yalta Conference this could no longer influence the course of the war against Germany, and a separate bargain had been made about the Far East. The Russians would have done what they did in Poland anyway. But the Western Allies would have kept a moral and political position of great strength, allowing for future bargaining with Moscow in the interest of Poland's freedom and their own influence in eastern Europe.

A disagreement in principle was recorded at the time with regard to German reparations, although the public was not informed of it until 1947. After considerable debate, the Russians stuck to their stand that Germany should pay reparations in the total amount of $20 billion, of which Russia would receive half. At that stage there was no disagreement about the form of the reparations: physical removal of capital goods and equipment, annual deliveries, and

German labor. But the British felt that it would be wrong to fix a total amount. The sum of $20 billion seemed to them very high, and they feared the political consequences of a permanent impoverishment of the German population. Roosevelt at first hesitated; later he sided with the Russians. Thus, according to the "Protocol of Proceedings" of the conference (which did not appear until 1947), the Soviet and American delegations agreed on the $20 billion total, of which 50 per cent was to go to the Soviet Union. The British delegation, which felt that no specific sum should be set, did not agree to this. The matter was referred to the Moscow Reparation Commission established at this same conference.[61]

The Soviet Far Eastern claims had been prepared well in advance. Because of the expected difficulties in the war against Japan, Russia was aware of its strong bargaining position. It was widely believed that Soviet assistance was indispensable to the successful and speedy conclusion of that campaign. Stalin proceeded carefully. He first announced in a conversation with Secretary Cordell Hull in Moscow in October, 1943, that Russia, apparently unconditionally, would enter the Pacific war after the defeat of Germany.* He repeated the promise in October, 1944, during talks with Churchill and Harriman, in which he also outlined Soviet military plans and requirements. But at that time he hinted that political conditions might be attached. These conditions were communicated to the Americans through diplomatic channels sometime before the Yalta meeting. From the Yalta documents as well as from information contained in the Byrnes and Stettinius memoirs, one can surmise that at Yalta only secondary points gave rise to some discussion. Roosevelt did not want to make Dairen and Port Arthur available to Russia outright, but only as free ports; he also insisted on joint Soviet-Chinese operation of the Chinese-Eastern Railroad, instead of simply restoring former Russian rights. Stalin yielded on Dairen and the railroad, but not on Port Arthur, where a Soviet naval base was to be installed. The grave political significance of the Soviet incursion into Manchuria was not understood until later. It is impossible to say exactly how much of the future developments in the Far East the Russians were then able to foresee and were trying to prepare for. But it is safe to state that they attached the greatest importance to following in the Czarist footsteps in Manchuria, and thought well in advance of using the opportunity presented by the war for expanding Communist rule in the Far East.

---

* Some of Stalin's demands in the Far East apparently were known to Roosevelt at Tehran. Cf. *The Conferences at Cairo and Tehran*, p. 869.

Diplomatic preparations were very thorough; everything was done to avoid arousing Japanese suspicion and to alleviate Western or Chinese distrust. Strenuous efforts were also made by Soviet propaganda to obscure the issue of Communism in China and to make people believe that Chinese Communists were merely "agrarian reformers."[62] In September, 1944, Molotov told an American diplomat that the Russians were not supporting Chinese Communists, who were not Communists at all. And this is what Hopkins said Stalin had told him in May, 1945: "He made [a] categorical statement that he would do everything he could to promote unification of China under the leadership of Chiang Kai-shek . . . this leadership should continue after the war. . . . He specifically stated that no Communist leader was strong enough to unify China."[63]

The Yalta negotiations on the Far East were conducted in strictest secrecy; even Secretary Stettinius knew about them only vaguely. This could easily be explained by the necessity for keeping Japan in the dark about Russia's extensive war preparations, but it put Roosevelt in an awkward position. He promised to obtain Chinese consent to concessions made in their name without their knowledge, but the President died before any talks between him and Chiang Kai-shek could take place. However, the secret agreement signed at Yalta stated that "these claims of the Soviet Union shall be unquestionably fulfilled after Japan has been defeated." Chinese consent was therefore only a matter of form. The agreement granted Russia the use of Dairen as an international free port, the lease of Port Arthur as a Soviet naval base, the joint operation with China of the Chinese-Eastern and South Manchurian Railroads, the preservation of the *status quo* in Outer Mongolia (i.e., its separation from China), and the occupation of Southern Sakhalin and the Kurile Islands. It stated that "former rights of Russia violated by the treacherous attack of Japan in 1904 shall be restored."[64]

The Far Eastern agreement was signed on the last day of the Yalta Conference, when the other issues vital to the Soviet Government had already been conceded. The discussion on the peace organization brought a compromise on the points not settled at Dumbarton Oaks.

The conference confirmed the earlier Tito-Subasic agreement; it was supposed to bring some non-Communists into the executive and legislative structure of Yugoslavia, and it was as futile and short-lived as similar arrangements with regard to Poland.

Yalta, even more so than Tehran, was greeted as a highly successful demonstration of enduring Allied unity. Said Hopkins: "We

really believed in our hearts that this was the dawn of the new day
we had all been praying for. . . ."[65] Byrnes recalls that public opinion in many countries, particularly American opinion, applauded
the outcome of the conference. The Poles almost alone thought
otherwise. In a declaration published on February 13, 1945, the
Polish government-in-exile called the annexation of the eastern territories "a fifth partition of Poland," and correctly predicted that
with Soviet troops in the country, free elections would be impossible.[66] The Soviet press, on the other hand, was full of praise.
Izvestia said that the Yalta Conference was "the greatest political
event of current times."[67]* There was indeed ground for rejoicing
in Moscow. The fulfillment of many aspirations was at hand.

The forcible transformation of the East European countries into
Soviet satellites had begun well before Yalta. In Bulgaria, the entry
of Russian troops in September, 1944, brought violence and terror
in its wake. Communist sources admit that 2,800 executions took
place and 7,000 prison sentences were meted out during the first
six months of Soviet occupation. Free Bulgarians estimate the number of missing persons in the same period at 50,000. In Romania,
the pressure at first was less obvious, although Soviet occupation
forces openly favored the small Communist minority and assumed
a threatening attitude toward other political parties. In Hungary,
the formation of a coalition government was allowed, but the Communists were the true masters of the country. Deportations, abuses,
and violence by Soviet troops and the local and imported Communists were a clear indication of things to come. In Poland, on orders
from the London government-in-exile, Home Army detachments
had gone into action all along the 1939 Polish-Soviet frontier and
fought the Germans together with the advancing Red Army. This
was the last thing the Russians wished to admit, hence Stalin's
false charges at Yalta that the Poles were killing Russian soldiers.
As is so often the case with Soviet accusations, the reverse was true.
Polish Home Army leaders who contacted the advancing Soviet
troops and cooperated with them mysteriously disappeared once
the Germans had evacuated the area. Soon it became known that

* It is interesting to quote the comment of the official *History of the Communist Party of the Soviet Union,* issued under Khrushchev by a group of
professors and members of the Soviet Academy of Science: "The decisions
of the Crimea Conference dealt a blow to the plans of the German imperialists and Anglo-American reactionaries who would have liked to conclude a
separate peace with fascist Germany behind the back of the Soviet Union."
(P. 596.)

they were being arrested and executed by the Russians. Mass arrests followed.

The Western Allies were informed of these events, but hoped that the Yalta agreements and the Declaration of Liberated Europe would change Soviet behavior. As Byrnes puts it, they were soon disappointed, even before Roosevelt's return from Yalta. The Soviet Government quickly made a mockery of joint Allied control in Romania; in February, Deputy Foreign Minister Vishinsky and Marshal Malinovsky installed a Communist government in Bucharest, under threat of armed intervention. In March, the negotiations for the formation of a Polish government came to a standstill. It became apparent that Moscow and the Western Allies had a different interpretation of the Yalta decisions on the "friendly government." Consequently, no Polish representation was invited to participate in the United Nations San Francisco Conference in April. This meeting faced several difficulties, the most important again being the interpretation of a text agreed upon at Yalta. The Russians wanted the veto right of the great powers to apply to all matters, including procedure, which would have made it impossible to discuss a complaint against any one of them.

During March and April, Stalin sent Roosevelt and Churchill increasingly irritating messages. He firmly refused Roosevelt's request to let American aircraft evacuate or bring medical and other assistance to a number of ex-American prisoners of war in Poland and the Soviet Ukraine. Permission to survey this problem in Poland was first granted to, then withdrawn from, the American Military Attaché in Moscow, General Deane. For the Russians this was a touchy question, as ex-prisoners of war were often well informed about local conditions that the Soviet authorities preferred to keep concealed. A much graver dispute arose about contacts with German military commanders who wished to surrender to the Western Allies. Even at this late hour, the Russians were genuinely alarmed that the rapid surrender of German troops in Italy would result in the Western occupation of parts of the Danubian countries. Churchill notes that Molotov handed the British Ambassador an insulting letter on this matter. The last days of Roosevelt's life were marked by particularly unpleasant cables from Stalin charging that the American Government misinterpreted the Yalta agreements on Poland, accusing the Western Allies of secretly negotiating armistice terms with German commanders (so as to enable them to move troops against the Russians), and implying that General

Marshall willfully misinformed the Soviet General Staff about an impending German counteroffensive.[68] According to Byrnes, Roosevelt was greatly offended by Stalin's attitude and the exceedingly objectionable language of at least one of his messages.[69]

Shortly before Roosevelt's death, the Soviet authorities arrested sixteen top leaders of the Underground State in Poland, among them Deputy Premier Jankowski and Commander of the Home Army Okulicki, who, believing Soviet promises that they could take part in negotiations for the formation of a coalition government, had come out into the open.

When Truman assumed the Presidency, he thus had good reasons to be disturbed by the state of relations with Russia. Harriman's views were also gloomy. After having observed Soviet Russia for three years at close quarters as American Ambassador, he thought that Europe was faced with a "barbaric invasion." Harriman told Truman that Russian control of foreign countries would mean the Soviet system with its secret police and the extinction of freedom of speech.[70] Practically every day brought some new confirmation of this appraisal of Soviet methods and intentions. Russian troops occupied Austria, and Stalin was making difficulties for Allied representatives wishing to enter Vienna. Moscow backed Tito in his claims to Trieste and Istria. In May, the tension became so grave that the possibility of an armed clash between Yugoslav troops and Marshal Alexander's forces was not ruled out. Churchill gave orders to have a solid mass of troops in the area. In a cable to Truman, the British Premier on May 12 for the first time spoke of an Iron Curtain descending across Europe: "We do not know what is going on behind."[71]

In the Western capitals there were conflicting theories in explanation of Russia's "strange" behavior. A British Labour MP asked a Polish diplomat how far he thought the Russians would go. The answer was: "If you stop them at Waterloo Station, they will stop there. If you stop them at Victoria Station, they will go as far as Victoria." Such opinions, shared by many informed East Europeans, were then not popular in London and Washington. The reasonable explanation—that the Soviet Government wanted to grab as much of Europe as it could without an open clash with England and the United States—was generally rejected as too simple.

In this situation of uncertainty, President Truman decided to send Harry Hopkins to Moscow once more, a suggestion immediately accepted by Stalin. An understanding with the Western Allies was clearly in the Soviet interest, for the valuable concessions obtained at Yalta could best be implemented in an atmosphere of interallied collaboration and good will.

Hopkins had several long conversations with Stalin, whose tactics were to counter serious American grievances and demands with secondary or imaginary Soviet piques. Stalin's complaints included the invitation of Argentina to the San Francisco Conference, France's participation in the Reparations Commission (which Stalin termed "an insult to the Soviet Union"), and his claim to a part of the German fleet, which had surrendered to the West. But two items brought up by Stalin were of prime importance to Russia: to continue to obtain supplies on the Lend-Lease scale, despite the end of the war in Europe, and to make the Americans accept the fiction that Poland was an independent country.

Hopkins brought up Poland as the main subject to be discussed. But he obscured the plan for fundamental rights in Poland and for the release of some of the arrested resistance leaders by stating that Poland was not important per se, but only as a symbol of American readiness to work with the Soviet Union. Hopkins further weakened his negotiating position by showing how anxious he was to dispose of the Polish problem quickly, lest it "stir up endless trouble" in future meetings. By tolerating Stalin's accusations that England was trying to revive a *cordon sanitaire* against Russia, he gave the impression that America would not necessarily back England in eastern Europe. President Truman had seen Molotov a month earlier in Washington and spoken to him sharply about Russia's negative attitude on the Yalta agreements. Despite all previous mistakes, firm language might have done some good. But if Truman's bluntness made any impression, it was soon dissipated by Hopkins' vagueness.

Stalin evaded all ideological discussion by stating that democratic rights have to be curtailed in time of war. He refused to release any of the arrested Polish leaders; their public trial in Moscow the following month was meant to demonstrate to the Polish people that they could not rely on British or American assistance.

But to show his good will and alleviate American fears that Russia wished to dominate Poland, Stalin hinted that he was inclined to allow some Polish leaders from London to join the Provisional Government. This was the concession the Western governments were waiting for. It soon led to the short-lived participation of a few genuine non-Communists in the Warsaw government. The best known of them, former Premier Stanislav Mikolajczyk, had to flee Poland in 1947.

Hopkins was able to report that Russia would be ready to attack Japan on August 8. Stalin agreed to take up directly with the Chinese the claims granted Russia in the Yalta Protocol on the Far East. However, an additional Soviet demand in the Far East came up: Stalin wished to share in the occupation of Japan; he asked for an agreement about zones of occupation in Japan as well as about "areas of operation" in China and Manchuria.

Hopkins seems to have believed Marshal Zhukov's nomination to the Allied Control Council for Germany was a concession made by Stalin. But the attitude of all three powers in regard to Germany had changed considerably since Tehran and Yalta. One did not speak of partition any more, although in fact the country was provisionally divided into the occupation areas of Soviet and other Allied troops. Soon it was to be divided for many years to come into the zones of occupation agreed to in 1944 and confirmed at Yalta. Despite this division, the Allied Control Council briefly became the *de facto* central government of Germany. In this way, Russia had undisputed possession of its own zone, and in addition, through the Control Council, political access to Western Germany.

Objectively, the only real concession Stalin made to Hopkins was his agreement to the American proposals on the voting procedure in the Security Council of the United Nations. Thus, according to Hopkins' biographer, the San Francisco Conference had been saved. It is a matter of opinion whether this was a fair return for what was given away. It seems that the Russians had more valid ground for satisfaction. Once again they had traded words, promises, and U.N. procedures for domination of foreign countries, Lend-Lease deliveries, and striking bases for further expansion.[72]

The Stalin-Hopkins talks were the last of the important wartime negotiations in which the Russians won most of their demands. The Potsdam (or Berlin) conference (July 17–August 2, 1945) marked the beginning of a belated resistance (except in regard to Poland) to the ever-mounting Soviet claims. President Truman and his Secretary of State, James Byrnes, were more realistic than their predecessors. While the new British Government of Clement Attlee did not change the policy line, the British representatives now had to cope with the results of wartime diplomacy in Europe and were more firm in dealings with the Russians.

Soviet aims at Potsdam were not limited to a consolidation of the territorial and political gains already secured by warfare and diplomacy. The list of items demonstrating the intention to continue the expansion of Soviet possessions and influence is rather impressive. It included bids for one of the Italian colonies on the African shore of the Mediterranean, for trusteeships in Korea and in unnamed mandates of the League of Nations, for two Turkish provinces in Transcaucasia and bases in the Black Sea Straits, for participation in international administrations of the Ruhr and of Tangiers; it further included attempts to extend the concessions obtained in the Yalta Far Eastern agreement, as well as attempts to gain footholds in Spanish, Italian, Greek, and Levantine affairs. But, for the first time in the summit negotiations, most of the new Soviet demands met with opposition, or at best with evasion. Their claims for outlets on the Mediterranean, in Tripolitania, and on the Black Sea Straits were referred to later negotiations, and eventually failed. Their formal proposal that the Big Three break off relations with Spain and force a change of government in Spain was not accepted. The idea of an international administration of the Ruhr (with Soviet participation) was abandoned. A Soviet suggestion to include an item on Syria and Lebanon in the Protocol did not materialize, and Russia grudgingly agreed to a British demand that both countries begin to withdraw their troops from Iran.

In the important question of German reparations, the Soviet representatives at Potsdam found that the Americans now shared the British view and refused to fix a high total figure. The Western Allies proposed that each of the three powers obtain its claim from removals in its own zone of occupation. The Russians had already begun to take everything movable out of Eastern Germany. Since the Soviet zone was not as industrialized as the other three zones, it was proposed that Russia in addition be given a fixed percentage of capital industrial equipment from the Western zones. From the economic point of view, this was a generous offer. Yet it was not what the Russians expected, and they obviously felt that such an arrangement would limit their freedom of maneuver in West Germany. But they realized they had to accept or get nothing beyond what they themselves could lay their hands on. Byrnes told Molotov that he and Truman were ready to leave for home whether the Conference was a success or not; this was language the Russians both understood and respected. After hard bargaining on the percentage figures, Stalin accepted a package deal offered by Byrnes that also included Poland and the question of admission into the United Nations.

There was also stiff opposition to the Soviet demand that the governments of Finland, Bulgaria, Hungary, and Romania be formally recognized by the Western Allies. Strong counterdemands for a reorganization of the Bulgarian and Romanian governments and Allied supervision of elections had a new flavor and must have been considered as danger signals. Stalin complained to Churchill that "he had been hurt" by an American note on southeast Europe he had received on the opening day of the conference. But the most bitter exchange developed with Churchill, who charged that no one knew what was going on in Bulgaria and Romania and that the British mission in Bucharest "had been penned up with a closeness approaching internment." Here is a characteristic excerpt from the American minutes of the Potsdam meeting:

> Stalin broke in to ask if it were really possible for him [Churchill] to cite such facts that had not been verified. Churchill said that they knew this by their representatives there. Stalin would be very much astonished to read a long catalogue of difficulties encountered by their mission there. An iron fence had come down around them. Stalin broke in to exclaim: All fairy tales! Churchill said that of course they could call each others' statements fairy tales and added that he had complete confidence in his representatives there.[73]

No effort was spared to obtain Western diplomatic recognition for the Communist-run governments in southeast Europe. Stalin again assured Churchill that "in all the countries liberated by the Red Army, the Russian policy was to see a strong, independent sovereign State."[74] He was against Sovietization of any of those countries. But in the final Protocol, the American formula linking the diplomatic recognition of former German satellites to the political conditions prevailing on the spot was retained. Although this merely delayed formal acknowledgment of Soviet domination, the Western opposition at Potsdam was a sign of a slowly changing tide.

A change of attitude was also evident in the conversations between Americans and Russians at Potsdam (but not carried on at the conference table) concerning the Far East. Soviet-Chinese negotiations for a treaty of alliance had started before the Potsdam Conference, and Chinese Foreign Minister Soong was to return to Moscow after Stalin's return from Berlin. An atmosphere of deep suspicion surrounded the negotiations, since it was clear to the Americans that the Russians wanted to get more than had been granted them at Yalta. However, no change in the previous plans for Soviet entry into the war against Japan were made at Potsdam, despite the successful launching of the first experimental atom bomb in New Mexico, and although the Japanese had sent out peace feelers, among them a message from the Emperor transmitted to Stalin by the Japanese Ambassador in Moscow and a demand for Soviet mediation to end the war. It is noteworthy that Stalin displayed no particular interest when Truman informed him of the atom-bomb experiment in New Mexico. He also played down the significance of the Japanese peace feelers. On July 18, after receiving the Emperor's message, he asked President Truman "whether it was worthwhile to answer this communication."[75] Eventually, such diplomatic problems were solved by the entry of Soviet troops into Manchuria two days after the atom bomb fell on Hiroshima. No doubt the Kremlin felt that Far Eastern matters had been successfully handled at Potsdam, despite unfavorable circumstances that could have upset previous arrangements.

14. *THE TAKEOVERS*

The expansion of Soviet rule and Communist regimes to today's geographical limits was achieved in two separate periods in the aftermaths of the two world wars. Owing to this lapse of time, it is difficult to group chronologically the events leading to the incorporation of non-Russian nations into the Soviet state and to Russian domination of the east-central European satellites. However, the unity of purpose is indisputable, for the subjugation of the Ukraine was an indispensable prelude to the domination of nations further west, while the conquest of the Transcaucasian Republics made possible subsequent attempts against Turkey and Iran. In the east, reconquering the Czarist domains in central Asia and the Far East turned out to be a prolonged process that left Soviet Russia little opportunity for advances beyond the Czarist borders. It was not until 1944 that the central Asian state of Tannu Tuva, in fact a protectorate since 1911, was incorporated into the Soviet Union. After World War II, Soviet diplomatic action and military occupation led to the creation of a Communist state in North Korea and paved the way for a Communist regime in China. But these subjects are discussed in other chapters.

Here we are concerned only with the essential facts resulting in the imposition of Soviet or Communist rule (or paramount influence, as in the case of Finland) over organized national bodies, some of which would or would not have chosen to live in some federation with a democratic Russia headed by a man like Kerensky, but all of which categorically rejected any ties with Communist Russia.

THE UKRAINE

A Ukrainian Central Rada (Council) had been formed in Kiev in March 1917, after the first Russian Revolution. It was backed by the Ukrainian National Congress, and in two public statements, or universals (June 23 and November 20, 1917), expressed the aspirations of the Ukrainian masses for national independence. The Central Rada was willing to remain in close association with a Russian federation or confederation, but negotiations to this effect with the Provisional Government proved difficult, and were not concluded when the Bolsheviks took over in Petrograd. The Rada refused to recognize the supremacy of the new regime, and on January 22, 1918, proclaimed full sovereignty and the Ukraine's complete independence. The country's right to separate from Russia had already been officially recognized by the Soviet Government, who on December 17, 1917, in a note to the Central Ukrainian Rada, stated:

We, the Soviet People's Commissars, recognize the Ukrainian National Republic and its right to separate from Russia or to make an agreement with the Russian Republic for federative or other similar mutual relations between them. Everything that touches national rights and the national independence of the Ukrainian people, we, the Soviet of People's Commissars, accept clearly without limitations and unreservedly.[1]

At the same time, the Soviet Government presented the Ukrainian Central Rada with a forty-eight-hour ultimatum. It demanded Ukrainian assistance in Bolshevik military action against White forces in the Don region, and free passage and toleration of Soviet troops in the Ukraine. Rejection of these demands, they said, would compel the Soviet Government to declare war against the Ukraine.

The Central Rada's opposition to the Soviet ultimatum was supported by the overwhelming majority of the delegates to the Third Peasant Congress of the Ukraine, as well as by the All-Ukraine Congress of Soldiers', Workers', and Peasants' Deputies (although originally called by the Bolsheviks). But after the Communists were expelled from Kiev, they formed a rival body—the Central Executive Committee of the Ukraine—in Kharkov. On December 25, 1917, Soviet forces invaded the Ukraine. After fruitless contacts with semiofficial representatives of the Entente, the Ukrainians turned to the Germans and signed a peace treaty with the Central Powers on February 9, 1918.[2] This agreement was endorsed by the Soviet Government in the Treaty of Brest-Litovsk (Article 6).

At the end of April, 1918, the government of the Rada was replaced by a regime subservient to the Germans and headed by a monarchist, General (Hetman) Skoropadsky. Following the defeat of the Central Powers, the Ukrainian Directory, an independent governmental body, was established in Kiev. It was presided over by Vladimir Vinnichenko; Simon Petlura became head of military affairs. Despite a Soviet Ukranian armistice signed in Kiev on June 12, 1918, Soviet Russia in November appointed a "Provisional Workers' and Peasants' Government of the Ukraine" in Kursk, headed by the Bolshevik Grigori Piatakov. Shortly before, Stalin, though himself a Georgian and at the time Commissar for Nationalities of the Russian Soviet Republic, had himself elected to the Central Committee of the Communist Party of the Ukraine. The Moscow-sponsored Communist government had to be brought into the Ukraine by force of arms. Therefore, the Directory's negotiations with Moscow yielded no results, although Chicherin repeated assurances of Russian respect for Ukrainian independence. A new Soviet invasion followed. Kiev fell on February 4, 1919. The situation once more changed in the summer of 1919, when the Communist government of the Ukraine had to withdraw to Russia. Ukrainian, Communist, and White Russian troops fought for control of the country. Kiev changed hands several times, but in the end fell again to the Bolsheviks, despite considerable popular support for the Directory.

In the treaty of April 21, 1920, Poland recognized the Ukrainian Directory.[3] Forces of the Ukrainian National Republic led by Petlura fought on the Polish side in the Soviet-Polish war in 1920. In May, the Russians again left Kiev for a short time. When the war ended with a compromise (Peace of Riga), the Soviet Government established its rule in the Ukraine and the National Ukrainian Government was forced into exile.

A semblance of political independence was maintained by the Soviet Ukrainian Republic until the conclusion of the Treaty of the Union of Soviet Republics (December 29, 1922). After that, and the promulgation of the first constitution of the U.S.S.R. in 1924, foreign powers were able to maintain only consular representation in the Ukraine. The Bolshevik Dmitri Manuilsky appeared at the head of the Soviet Ukrainian delegation to the United Nations in 1945. This delegation, representing the Ukraine in name only, furnishes the Soviet Union with an additional vote.

BELORUSSIA

Belorussian attempts to organize a free state along the principle of self-determination of peoples were as ruthlessly suppressed by the Soviet Government as those of the Ukrainians.

Shortly after the first Russian Revolution, Belorussian organizations set up a National Committee at Minsk, which in July, 1917, took the name of Central Rada of Belorussian Organizations. In October, 1917, this body was transformed into the Great Belorussian Rada and declared itself as the representation of the Belorussian people. In December, 1917, the first All-Belorussian Congress, attended by 1,872 democratically chosen delegates, was held in Minsk.[4] The Congress adopted a resolution providing for the creation of the Belorussian National Republic. But on December 31, 1917, Red Army units appeared, surrounded the building where the Congress sat, and dispersed the delegates. The Congress, however, was able to reconvene the next day and proceeded with the organization of a free republic and with the preparations of its defense against Soviet aggression. But Soviet troops intervened again, and the leaders of the independence movement were arrested.

On February 21, 1918, after Minsk had been cleared of Soviet troops, the executive committee of the All-Belorussian Congress formed the first government of the Belorussian Republic. But the Germans followed on the heels of the Russians. On February 25, Minsk was occupied by the German Army. Belorussian units were disarmed, though Belorussian political activities were tolerated. On March 25, 1918, the Rada of the Belorussian National Republic proclaimed the country's independence. The activities of this governmental body were suppressed again when the Soviet Army retook Minsk on December 10, 1918. A Belorussian Soviet Republic was formed on January 1, 1919. Politically under the Communist rule, it is merely a province of Soviet Russia.

TRANSCAUCASIA

After the revolution of March 1917, the Russian administration began to lose its hold on the Transcaucasian territories. In Georgia, Armenia, and Azerbaidzhan, local revolutionary committees, most of which were sympathetic to the right-wing socialists (Mensheviks), controlled the situation. There was, however, no pronounced movement for secession from Russia until the Bolshevik Revolution, and a "Special Committee for Transcaucasia," nominated by the Provisional Government of Petrograd, established itself at Tiflis. After the November Revolution, the situation radically changed. The local revolutionary committees refused to recognize the authority of the government of the Soviets. National committees came into being. A Federation of Transcaucasia, and

soon afterward the independent republics of Georgia, Armenia, and
Azerbaidzhan, were set up.

a. Georgia. The Georgian National Council was elected by a National Congress on November 22, 1917. After the dissolution of the
Constituent Assembly by the Bolshevik Party in January, 1918, a
parliamentary Assembly of Transcaucasia was formed. The Assembly rejected the provisions of the Treaty of Brest-Litovsk granting
the Caucasian provinces of Batum, Ardahan, and Kars to Turkey
and in April, 1918, proclaimed the independent Transcaucasian
Democratic Federative Republic and its secession from Russia. But
the Federation was short-lived, and as a result of internal dissension, it dissolved on May 26, 1918. On the same day, the Georgian
National Council formed the Georgian Democratic Republic. The
German troops withdrew after the collapse of the Central Powers,
and after the armistice of Mudros (November, 1918), the Turks
evacuated Batum. The town was subsequently occupied by British
forces. It was not until 1920 that the whole of Georgia was free of
foreign troops. But as early as February, 1919, despite the presence
of British troops, general elections took place. The vote unequivo-
cally confirmed the dominant position of the Social Democratic
Party. The Communists obtained less than 1 per cent of the votes,
and did not get even a single seat in the Constituent Assembly.[5]

The Supreme Council of the Allied powers granted Georgia *de
jure* recognition on January 27, 1921.

The Soviet reaction to the proclamation of Georgian independence was in no way consistent with the Declaration of Rights of
Peoples. Through the Supplementary Treaty to the Treaty of Brest-
Litovsk (Article 13), Soviet Russia had recognized Georgia as an
independent state. But after the defeat of the Central Powers, the
Soviet Government made it clear that it still considered Georgia
a part of Russia. At the end of May, 1920, Soviet troops moved into
Georgia from northern Caucasus. They were repulsed, however,
suffering heavy losses inflicted by a small but efficient Georgian
army. A second attempt to occupy Georgia was staged by Soviet
Russia in the early spring of 1920. Communists seized power by an
armed *coup d'état* in Baku (Azerbaidzhan), and Soviet forces invaded Georgia from the east. But again the Red troops were defeated and forced to retreat. A Communist attempt to overthrow
the Georgian Government in Tiflis (May 2, 1920) also failed.

Realistic as always, the Soviet Government negotiated with a
Georgian mission that was already present at Moscow when the

Soviet invasion of Georgia began. A peace treaty was signed on May 7, 1920, by which Soviet Russia solemnly recognized the independence of the Georgian state and bound itself to refrain from any interference in its internal affairs. Article I of the Peace Treaty reads in part: "Russia recognizes without reservations the independence and the sovereignty of the Georgian State, and voluntarily renounces all sovereign rights which belonged to Russia with respect to the Georgian people and territory."[6]

On February 11, 1921, nine months after the signing of the treaty, the Red Army again invaded Georgia without any warning, from five directions. Pretenses at explaining the invasion by local disturbances were dropped later. In a report to the General Committee of the Russian Communist Party dated December 6, 1921, P. Makharadze, Chairman of the Georgian Communist Party wrote: "The arrival of the Red Army and the establishment of Soviet power in Georgia had the outward appearance of a foreign occupation because in the country itself there was nobody who was ready to take part in a rebellion or a revolution."[7]

On February 25, 1921, Soviet troops entered Tiflis; the deposition of the legal government of President N. Jordania was announced. Georgian armed resistance nevertheless continued until the second half of March, when Soviet troops entered Batum. The Georgian Government left the country on March 17, 1921, to continue its struggle in exile.

b. Armenia. In October, 1917, shortly before the Bolshevik Revolution, Lenin wrote: "It is our duty immediately to satisfy the demands of the Ukrainians and the Finns. We must guarantee them, as well as all the other non-Russian nationalities in Russia, full freedom of secession. The same must apply to the *whole* of Armenia; we must undertake to evacuate it."[8]

Yet, when the Armenian National Council proclaimed the country's independence, there was no response from Moscow. Stalin from the very beginning was opposed to the independence of Transcaucasia, and an Armenian office was created in the Soviet Commissariat of Nationalities under his direction. But Communist strength in Armenia was negligible, and this earned the country a two-year respite from serious Soviet pressure.

On January 19, 1920, Armenia was given *de facto* recognition by the Supreme Council of the Allied powers. U.S. recognition was granted on April 23, 1920.

In May, 1920, Communists organized riots in several Armenian towns. They had little popular support and were easily quelled. As a result, peace negotiations with an Armenian mission were instituted in Moscow. Before they were concluded, the Red Army invaded Armenia. A temporary armistice, signed on August 10, 1920, forced the Armenian Government to cede the regions of Zangesur, Karbakg, and Nakhichevan to Communist Azerbaidzhan. On November 18, Armenia in turn concluded an armistice with Turkey. But ten days later, Soviet forces again crossed the Armenian border. Two days thereafter, a Bolshevik Military Revolutionary Committee, headquartered at a frontier village, proclaimed the overthrow of the legal Armenian Government. At the same time, the Turkish Army threatened Erivan. The Armenian Government in its plight signed the treaty of Erivan (December 2, 1920), which was supposed to guarantee Armenia's sovereignty and territorial integrity as an Independent Soviet Socialist Republic. As proved to be the case, the Erivan Treaty was nothing but a face-saving device for complete sovietization of Armenia.

c. Azerbaidzhan. The independence of Azerbaidzhan was proclaimed on May 29, 1918, after the dissolution of the Transcaucasian Federation. On December 7, 1918, the first Azerbaidzhani Parliament was elected in universal suffrage. A short-lived Soviet regime in Baku fell in July for lack of support from the workers. Until 1920, Azerbaidzhan was relatively free from Soviet pressure. On January 2, 1920, Chicherin, the Soviet Commissar for Foreign Affairs, wrote in a note to the Azerbaidzhani Government: "The Government of the R.S.F.S.R. turns to Azerbaidzhan with the proposal immediately to enter into negotiations with the Soviet Government for the conclusion of a military agreement between the Commands of both countries for the purpose of accelerating the defeat of the White Guard armies in the South of Russia."[9]

But Chicherin's note at the same time contained thinly disguised subversive appeals to the "laboring classes," which were not missed by the Azerbaidzhani Government. Although reluctant to take part in the Civil War, it nevertheless resolved to enter into negotiations for the establishment of normal diplomatic relations with the Soviet Government. Further exchanges of notes followed, but Chicherin insisted on military cooperation while putting off the formulation of political clauses.

Meanwhile strong concentrations of Soviet forces were noticed along the northern border of Azerbaidzhan. The Azerbaidzhani Foreign Minister cabled Chicherin on April 15, 1920, requesting an explanation. The telegram also offered to open negotiations. But there was no reply from Moscow. Instead, on April 27, 1920, Soviet troops entered Azerbaidzhan, which was unable to defend itself against overwhelming odds. Before the end of the month, an Azerbaidzhani Soviet Independent Republic was proclaimed in Baku under the protection of Soviet bayonets.

POLAND

By decree of the Council of People's Commissars of August 29, 1918, the Soviet Union abrogated all treaties and agreements of the former Czarist government relating to the partition of Poland.

During the eighteen years between the Peace of Riga (March 18, 1921) and the signing of the Molotov-Ribbentrop Pact, Soviet Russia on the whole maintained normal neighborly relations with Poland. The two countries concluded a number of treaties, conventions, and agreements; among the most important the following should be mentioned:

1. The Protocol (between Estonia, Latvia, Poland, Romania, and the U.S.S.R.) for the immediate entry into force of the Treaty of Paris of August 27, 1928 (Kellogg-Briand Treaty), regarding renunciation of war as an instrument of national policy, signed at Moscow on February 9, 1928.

2. The Pact of Nonaggression between Poland and the U.S.S.R., signed at Moscow on July 25, 1932.

3. The Convention for the Definition of Aggression (between Estonia, Latvia, Poland, Turkey, the U.S.S.R., Persia, and Afghanistan) signed at London on July 3, 1933.

4. The Polish Soviet Protocol extending the Polish-Soviet Pact of Nonaggression (of July 25, 1932) until December 31, 1945, signed at Moscow on May 5, 1934.

5. The exchange of notes between Poland and the U.S.S.R. on the Soviet Union's entry into the League of Nations, datelined Moscow, September 10, 1934.

6. The Joint Polish-Soviet Communiqué on the "inviolability of peaceful relations between the two States," issued on November 26, 1938.

As late as May 31, 1939, in an address to the Supreme Soviet, Molotov said:

As is known, a special communiqué was published in February last confirming the development of good relations between the U.S.S.R. and Poland. A certain general improvement is now noticeable in our relations with Poland. Furthermore, the Trade Agreement concluded in March with Poland may considerably increase the trade turnover between the U.S.S.R. and Poland.[10]

In fulfillment of their obligations to Nazi Germany, the Soviet Government ordered its troops into Poland on the night of September 17, 1939, while the Polish armies were still fighting the invading Germans. In a note read to the Polish Ambassador in Moscow at 3 A.M. on September 17, Potemkin, the Deputy People's Commissar for Foreign Affairs, tried to justify the Soviet aggression by claiming that the Polish Government had disintegrated, and that the Soviet Government "cannot view with indifference the fact that kindred Ukrainian and Belorussian people . . . are left defenseless."[11]

The text of the secret Soviet-German Protocol, which, of course, was not meant for publication, gives the lie to the reasons advanced in the Soviet note. A further proof of Soviet embarrassment at the time of their aggression against Poland is provided by Molotov's conversation with the German Ambassador in Moscow on September 16, 1939, when the Soviet Foreign Secretary said: "The Soviet Government unfortunately saw no possibility of any other motivation, since the Soviet Union had thus far not concerned itself about the plight of its minorities in Poland and had to justify abroad, in some way or other, its present intervention."[12]

Polish armed resistance against the dual Nazi-Soviet invasion continued until the beginning of October, 1939. On September 28, 1939, a further Nazi-Soviet agreement signed by Molotov and Ribbentrop implemented the partition of Poland as provided for by the Secret Protocol of August 23. The Russian-occupied Polish territory was annexed, Soviet citizenship forced on Polish nationals who were conscripted into the Soviet armed forces; the Soviet authorities ordered mass deportations, arrests, and executions. The Polish Government, continuing its struggle in exile, protested in vain. The number of Polish citizens deported to Russia in the period 1939–41 is estimated at 1.5 million, including 230,000 Polish officers and men taken prisoner by Soviet forces in September and October, 1939. The appalling conditions under which these men were detained resulted in a mortality rate of up to 70 per cent. Further arrests and deportations followed the entry of Soviet troops into Poland in 1944. It is estimated that, apart from war casualties, about one million Polish citizens who had been deported to Soviet Russia either disappeared or failed to return.[13]

On July 30, 1941, after Hitler's attack on Russia, the Polish Government seated in London concluded a new agreement with the Soviet Union, which invalidated the Soviet-German pacts of partition of 1939, re-established diplomatic relations, restored freedom to all Polish citizens in Russia, and allowed the Polish Government to form an army on Soviet soil under a Polish commander. A military agreement was also signed by the two governments on August 14, 1941, in Moscow.[14]

But when called on to carry out its promises, the Soviet Government failed to do so: Release of Poles from prisons and camps was sabotaged; Polish citizens of Ukrainian, Belorussian, and Jewish descent, or of any faith other than Roman Catholic, were forcibly treated as Soviet citizens; rations and equipment were denied to the army that was forming. When, in 1942, the Polish Commander, General Anders, left Russia, he could take only about 114,000 officers and men, including civilians, and 10,000 children with him.[15]

On April 20, 1943, the Soviet Government again broke off relations with the Polish Government, using as the pretext the Polish demand that the International Red Cross Committee make an impartial inquiry into the mass graves of several thousand Polish officers discovered in the Katyn Forest, near Smolensk. Moscow was once more reverting to its true policy line. In 1920, in the wake of Tukhachevsky's armies, a Revolutionary Committee composed of Polish Communists (including Feliks Dzierzynski) was established at Bialystok and prepared to take over the government after the fall of Warsaw. During World War II, similar Polish Communist bodies were set up in Russia. One of them, the Committee of National Liberation, proclaimed itself the provisional government of Poland on December 31, 1944, and was recognized by the Soviet Union. Although completely lacking popular support or any mandate from the nation, this government concluded various agreements with Moscow, among them the treaty of alliance of April 21, 1945, and the treaty of August 16, 1945, purporting to legalize the annexation of nearly half of prewar Poland by the Soviet Union.[16] The puppet regime installed by the Red Army abolished the Polish Constitution and set up a Soviet regime on the Russian model.

When, after Stalin's death, the Soviet leadership allowed a limited "thaw" in Russia, the Polish Communists reluctantly followed suit. A discussion in literary circles beginning in 1954 took momentum slowly, without visibly endangering the regime. But there was a deeper undercurrent, which burst into the open with the Poznan rising. On June 28, 1956, following a street demonstration, striking workers attacked government and Party buildings. It was estimated that about 50,000 workers struck and that many thousands participated in the riots. The demonstrators demanded "bread and freedom" and the end of the Communist regime and of the Soviet occupation. The government called out the troops, part of whom fraternized with the workers. Disturbances on a smaller scale continued the following days. According to official sources, 53 persons were killed and around 200 injured. Unofficial estimates were much higher.

The government at first took the line that "imperialist agents" were responsible for the rising. But soon the Communist leadership was forced to grant concessions. A wave of open opposition was threatening to sweep the country, and it was apparent that the regime could not stem it without drastic changes. The situation came to a head on October 19, when the Eighth Plenum of the Central Committee of the Polish United Workers Party elected a new Politburo, dropping seven of its eleven members. Among those ousted was Rokossovsky. Wladyslaw Gomulka, a lifelong Communist, was elected First Secretary. He had spent over three years in prison and had only recently been readmitted to the Party.

These changes in the Polish Communist leadership were dramatized by the arrival of a top Soviet delegation in Warsaw on October 19. The delegation was composed of Khrushchev, Molotov, Kaganovich, Mikoyan, and, according to reports, Zhukov. Their mission apparently was to intimidate the Central Committee and thus influence the composition of the Presidium of the United Workers Party. It was widely assumed, although without real proof, that Gomulka resisted the Soviet pressure, which helped his popularity among the masses. Reports of Soviet tank formations moving toward Warsaw, unverified rumors of an armed clash between Polish and Soviet forces near Szczecin (Stettin), and the appearance of Soviet naval units along Poland's coastline underscored the seriousness of the situation. It would seem that Gomulka was able to ride out the storm by persuading the Kremlin that allowing temporary deviations from Communism in Poland was the only way of keeping a Communist government in power without risking a war.

On November 18, 1956, a Polish delegation went to Moscow, and in a joint statement confirmed the Soviet-Polish alliance and the fact that under its new leadership Poland was still a member of the Soviet camp. A month later, on December 17, a treaty providing for the "temporary stay of Soviet troops in Poland" was signed in Warsaw.[17]

During the following years, the quasi-revolutionary situation began to subside. To many Poles, the Gomulka regime seemed at first to express the changes brought about by the bloodless "October Revolution"; later there were clear signs of a gradual reversion to less lenient methods. However, a number of the individual freedoms won in 1956 remained substantially unimpaired. Many Poles were able to travel abroad, and effective Communist control was limited to the governmental and administrative sphere. The virtual collapse of nationalized agriculture led to higher grain yields and improved the lot of the peasant. But the general economic situation of the country remained precarious. In foreign affairs, Gomulka soon belied his reputation as an alleged "national Communist" by becoming one of the most faithful satellite followers of Khrushchev. On May 10, 1958, during an official visit to Budapest, he went so far as to praise the Soviet armed intervention in Hungary as "correct and indispensable."[18] In the Soviet-Chinese dispute, Gomulka resolutely sided with Moscow, without any indication that he intended to profit from the situation to gain more elbow room, as did the Romanian Communists, for example—although they are considered "Stalinists."

THE BALTIC STATES

After unsuccessful attempts to impose Communist regimes on the three Baltic states in 1918, the Soviet Government recognized their independence, renounced "voluntarily and forever all rights of sovereignty formerly held by Russia,"[19] and concluded peace treaties with each of them in 1920. The Soviet-Nazi conspiracy to suppress the independence of the Baltic states was embodied in the same Secret Protocol of the Molotov-Ribbentrop Pact of August 23, 1939, which prepared the aggression against Poland.

Twenty-two years earlier, *Izvestia* had published an article saying: "Estonia, Latvia, and Lithuania are directly on the road leading from Russia to Western Europe, and are, therefore, a hindrance to our Revolution. . . . This separating wall has to be destroyed."[20]

Events testified to the unaltered purpose of Soviet policy.

a. Lithuania. On February 16, 1919, the Lithuanian National Council unanimously adopted a resolution calling for the re-establishment of an independent Lithuanian state. A provisional constitution was promulgated, and the first government formed in November of the same year. But in December, 1918–January, 1919, Soviet troops invaded the country and proclaimed a Soviet Lithuanian Republic; they were expelled at the end of 1919. On July 12, 1920, the Soviet Union signed the Peace Treaty of Moscow with the Lithuanian Government, recognizing "the sovereignty and independence of the state of Lithuania with all juridical consequences resulting from such recognition, and voluntarily and forever renounces all sovereign rights possessed by Russia over the Lithuanian people and territory."[21]

On September 28, 1926, the two countries concluded a pact of nonaggression whose validity was extended on April 4, 1934 until December, 1945. A Convention for the Definition of Aggression was signed by Soviet Russia and Lithuania in London on July 5, 1933, similar to that concluded two days earlier with Latvia, Estonia, and other neighbors of the Soviet Union.

In the secret German-Soviet Protocol of August 23, 1939, Lithuania was assigned to the German sphere of influence. But the second Molotov-Ribbentrop agreement (September 28, 1939) transferred most Lithuanian territory to the Russian-controlled zone, in exchange for German control of the Polish province of Lublin and parts of the province of Warsaw.[22]

On October 10, 1939, by threatening invasion, the Soviet Government imposed on Lithuania a mutual-assistance treaty providing for Russian garrisons in several strategic places. But this was only a short interlude, for in June, 1940, a Soviet ultimatum requested the dismissal and trial of a member of the Lithuanian Government, the immediate formation of a government "capable of assuring proper fulfillment of the treaty of mutual assistance,"[23] and free entry for new Soviet troops, to be garrisoned in the most important centers of the country. This was, obviously, the end of Lithuanian independence. Soviet troops made their entrance that same day. On July 14, elections were held in accordance with a new electoral law on the Soviet model. Although most of the electorate abstained from voting, fictitious election results were published, showing the usual Communist victory. The president of Lithuania, A. Smetona, left the country on June 15, 1940. On July 1, the new Diet proclaimed Lithuania a Soviet Republic. The "admission" of the new republic was decided upon by the Supreme Soviet of the U.S.S.R. on August 3, 1940.

b. Latvia. The First Latvian National Assembly met in November, 1917, and set up the Provisional National Council. On November 17, 1917, it published a declaration to foreign countries claiming the right of self-determination, and on January 5, 1918, informed the All-Russian Constituent Assembly of Latvia's separation from Russia.

In December, 1918, Soviet troops invaded Latvia, occuping Riga early in January. A Latvian Soviet Government was recognized by the U.S.S.R. The Russian occupation lasted until the spring of 1919, when Latvian troops liberated the capital. On February 1, 1920, an armistice was concluded between Latvia and Soviet Russia, followed by a peace treaty signed at Riga on August 11, 1920. The formula of recognition of Latvian independence was similar to that of the Lithuanian peace treaty.

On February 5, 1932, Soviet Russia concluded a treaty of non-aggression with Latvia; on April 4, 1934, its validity was extended until December 31, 1945.

The treaties and obligations binding Soviet Russia to Latvia were broken by the secret Soviet-German Protocol of August 23, 1939. The sequence of events leading to the suppression of Latvian independence was almost identical with that of Lithuania. Latvia was forced to sign a pact of mutual assistance with Soviet Russia on October 8, 1939. A Soviet ultimatum was handed the Latvian Minister in Moscow on June 16, 1940. While delivering it, Molotov said that "whether or not the ultimatum would be accepted, Red Army troops would be ordered to cross the Latvian border."[24] The following day, the occupation of the country was effected. On June 20, a government of Russia's choice was appointed by A. Vishinsky, Deputy Commissar of Foreign Affairs. After sham elections were held (July 14–15) giving the Communist bloc nearly 98 per cent of the vote, the President of Latvia, Ulmanis, was deposed. On July 19, the People's Diet proclaimed the Latvian Soviet Republic. It was "admitted" to the fold of the Soviet Union on August 5, 1940.

c. Estonia. The Estonian National Council proclaimed the independence of the country on February 24, 1918. But Soviet troops invaded Estonia in November, 1918, and set up a Soviet Estonian Government. In the spring of 1919, the Soviet troops were driven out. A Peace Treaty with Soviet Russia was signed at Tartu on February 2, 1920. A few days before its conclusion, *Izvestia* published the following report: "Comrade Lenin answered a question about the terms of the peace with Estonia. . . . He said that we do not want to shed the blood of workers and Red Army soldiers for the sake of a piece of land, especially since the concession is not forever. . . . The workers . . . will soon overthrow this government and form a Soviet Estonia."[25]

Lenin's declaration did not prevent the Soviet Government from renouncing "voluntarily and forever all rights of sovereignty formerly held by Russia over the Estonian people." As in the case of the other Baltic countries, Soviet Russia signed a treaty of nonaggression with Estonia in 1932, and the Convention on the Definition of Aggression in 1933. A pact of "mutual assistance" was forced on Estonia on September 28, 1939. Providing for Soviet garrisons on Estonian territory, it was the beginning of the end of Estonian independence. A Soviet ultimatum was delivered to the Estonian Minister in Moscow on June 16, 1940 (the same day as to Latvia, and exactly to the same effect). Molotov told the Estonian envoy that, should it not be accepted in the time prescribed (eight and one half hours) "the Red Army units concentrated at the frontier . . . would be ordered to march into Estonia, suppressing all resistance by armed force."[26]

The Red Army completed the occupation of Estonia on June 18, 1940. A puppet Estonian government was nominated and on July 14, the sham elections that were held produced a Communist Parliament. The President, K. Päts, was forced to resign and was deported to Russia. He has not been heard of again. On August 6, 1940, the Supreme Soviet of the U.S.S.R. "admitted" the Soviet Estonian Republic into the Union.

FINLAND

The Russian Provisional Government set up after the March, 1917, Revolution restored to Finland its ancient political rights. But negotiations for a closer definition of the future relations between the two countries had not been concluded when the Bolsheviks came into power. On December 6, 1917, the Finnish Diet proclaimed the independent Republic of Finland, formally recognized by Soviet Russia on January 4, 1918.[27]

But Lenin's government failed to recall its troops from Finland. By the end of January, they had seized key points of the capital and set up a Soviet government, which at one time occupied large parts of southern Finland. They were driven out of the country during the Finnish War of Independence (January–March, 1918). On October 14, 1920, Soviet Russia and Finland concluded the Treaty of Peace of Tartu confirming the recognition of Finland's independence and terminating her former union with Russia.[28]

In the following years, further agreements were signed between the two countries, including:

1. The Treaty of Nonaggression and Pacific Settlement of Disputes, signed at Helsinki, January 21, 1932. (The Preamble to this treaty confirmed the validity of the Briand-Kellogg Pact.)

2. The Convention of Conciliation, signed at Helsinki, April 22, 1932.

3. The Convention for the Definition of Aggression, signed at London, July 3, 1933.

4. The protocol renewing until December 31, 1945, the Treaty of Nonaggression and Pacific Settlement of Disputes (of 1932) signed at Moscow, April 7, 1934.

5. Furthermore, on September 1 and 17, Finland and Soviet Russia exchanged Declarations of Neutrality in the German-Polish war of 1939.

This good-neighbor policy came to an end with the Molotov-Ribbentrop Pact and Poland's defeat in September, 1939. In the following months the Soviet Union asked Finland to sign a mutual-assistance treaty and demanded important territorial concessions, including the lease of the Hanko Peninsula for the establishment of a naval base. The Finns were not opposed to compromise. But Moscow wanted their submission, similarly to that of the three Baltic states. On November 28, 1939, alleging Finnish attacks on Soviet troops, Molotov denounced the treaty of nonaggression, and the following day broke off diplomatic relations. On November 30, Soviet forces crossed the border (without declaration of war) and Helsinki was bombed from the air.

Finland turned to the League of Nations, invoking Articles 11 and 15 of the Covenant. On December 14, the Assembly and the Council of the League of Nations condemned the Soviet aggression and Soviet Russia was expelled from the League.[29]

But Moscow still pretended not to be at war with the "Finnish people." That was the answer Molotov gave the Secretary General of the League of Nations. On December 1, 1939, in a declaration from a frontier village, a puppet Communist government headed by Otto Kuusinen called "the overthrow of the Government of the Finnish White Guards" its primary task. On December 4, Molotov signed a Treaty of Mutual Assistance and Friendship with this "People's Government of the Democratic Republic of Finland," which granted Russia all its territorial demands.[30]

Kuusinen's declaration claimed, against all evidence, that "the masses of the people of Finland meet and welcome the valiant and invincible Red Army with tremendous enthusiasm."[31]

In fact the Finnish people gave a rare demonstration of unity

and courage against overwhelming odds, and during the first
months of the war Soviet troops were repeatedly routed. Early in
March, when negotiations were resumed, Finland was by no means
a defeated nation, although it could not hold out long without outside help. The Soviet decision to conclude peace was no doubt influenced by the threat of French-British armed intervention.

With the peace treaty signed in Moscow on March 12, 1940, the
Soviet Union achieved all its objectives except Finland's subjugation. However, this was only a temporary respite. Between March,
1940, and June, 1941, the Finnish authorities cited 194 Soviet violations of Finnish territory. In November, 1940, during the secret
Soviet-Nazi negotiations, Molotov asked Hitler for a free hand in
Finland. Soviet pressure on Finland was resumed the following
summer, when Moscow asked for either the demilitarization or
joint defense of the Aaland Islands. In October, the Russians began
to press for the transfer of the rich nickel mines of Petsamo.

When, on June 22, 1941, Hitler attacked Russia, Finland was
unable to maintain its neutrality and thus was later grouped among
the nations defeated by the Allies. The armistice agreement of September 19, 1944, and the Peace Treaty of Paris of February 10,
1947,[32] gave the Soviet Union the province of Petsamo and the
Karelian Isthmus, as well as other border regions and the lease of a
naval base of Porkkala-Udd.* Russia received a substantial sum in
reparations, the Finnish Army was limited to 35,000 men, the Air
Force to 60 aircraft, and the Navy to a total tonnage of 10,000.

The present situation of Finland, which has retained a truly
democratic system of government but only limited freedom of action in international affairs, is a reluctant Russian tribute to the
patriotic determination of her people and the realistic policy of
her leaders. This unique position of a small, defenseless country
within Soviet grasp but not forcibly sovietized is, however, primarily the result of Russia's respect for the armed neutrality of
Sweden, which Moscow is unwilling to push into the Western defense system.

CZECHOSLOVAKIA

In contrast to Poland, Hungary, or Romania, pro-Russian feelings prevailed in the Czech lands from the second half of the nineteenth century. After the Bolshevik Revolution, such pro-Russian
tendencies did not disappear altogether. Despite Thomas Masaryk's

---

* Relinquished by the U.S.S.R. on January 26, 1956.

classically democratic and liberal philosophy, both he and his successor, Dr. Eduard Beneš, thought that Czechoslovakia could play
an active part in bringing about a *rapprochement* between Communist Russia and the West. Beneš was an early proponent of the
recognition of Soviet Russia and "succeeded in normalizing commercial relations between his country and Soviet Russia"[33] after the
failure of the Genoa Conference of 1922.

On May 16, 1935, Czechoslovakia signed a pact of mutual assistance with the Soviet Union. Soon after the outbreak of the German-Soviet hostilities, the Soviet Union concluded a new agreement on joint action against Germany with Dr. Beneš' Provisional
Government (established in London). At the end of 1943, Beneš
went to Moscow, where on December 12, the Czechoslovak Ambassador, Zdenek Fierlinger, signed a Treaty of Friendship, Mutual Assistance, and Postwar Collaboration.

While in Moscow, Dr. Beneš, with Klemens Gottwald, the exiled
head of the Czechoslovak Communist Party, also laid down the
principles of the future organization of the Czechoslovak state. It
was implemented in the "Kosiče Program," published on April 5,
1945, which turned out to be the blueprint for the sovietization of
the country.* Fierlinger, completely subservient to Soviet wishes,
became Prime Minister. A National Front, composed of Communists and Socialists and a sprinkling of Liberals and Catholics, became the only legal political group.

As a final demonstration of Czechoslovak compliance with Russian demands, Fierlinger on June 29, 1945, signed a treaty providing for the cession of the Sub-Carpathian Ukraine to the Soviet
Ukrainian Republic, possibly in exchange for Soviet support of the
Czechoslovak claims against Poland in the Teschen area.[34]

All these far-reaching concessions were extended on the strength
of Dr. Beneš' belief that they would meet the Soviet concept of a
"friendly government" and thus assure Czechoslovakia a secure
position. The reward of this policy was continual frustration, and,
finally, total subjugation.

When in the summer of 1944, the Red Army reached the Car-
pathians, an uprising broke out against the Germans in Slovakia.
It was proclaimed on August 29, 1944, by the commander of the
Slovak garrison at Banska Bystrica and backed by the Social Demo-

* "In effect the two most significant features of the program were the
avowed Russian orientation and the instrumentality of the National Committees, which were to function essentially as soviets." (S. H. Harrison Thomson, *Czechoslovakia in European History* [Princeton, N.J., 1953].)

crat and Liberal groups, which, together with the Slovak Communists, had signed in Bratislava on December 24, 1943, a secret
"Christmas agreement" for the restoration of Czechoslovakia in
close collaboration with the Soviet Union. It took several German
divisions two months to crush the insurrection, which began when
the Warsaw rising was already almost a month old. As at the gates of
Warsaw, the Red Army was "delayed" and "watched this national
tragedy quietly. Around 30,000 Slovaks of all political shades were
killed in this uprising . . . and thus the ground became better
prepared for the Soviet occupation."[35]

On May 6, 1945, Patton's advance columns reached a point 8
miles west of Prague. They were ordered back because of the protests of the Soviet command. The liberation of Prague was to be
the privilege of the Soviet Union. In December, 1945, both the
American and the Soviet armies were withdrawn from Czechoslovakia. But even this short period of Soviet occupation, coupled with
the application of the "Kosiče Program," sufficed to put Communists in most of the key positions in the country. They were especially successful in taking over the Department of the Interior and
the police. In the first elections, held on May 26, 1946, the Communists gained 114 seats out of a total of 298. They emerged as
the largest party. Together with the Social Democrats, they gained
the absolute majority in the Prague Parliament. But in Slovakia
they ran second, behind the Social Democrats. After the elections
Gottwald became Prime Minister. It seemed as if all Communist
ambitions had been achieved in a legal manner. But events were
to prove that Czechoslovakia had to be brought in line with the
other satellite states, in which communization was proceeding
more harshly. This bringing in line was achieved by a series of police operations beginning in the autumn of 1947 and culminating
in the *coup d'état* of February 22–25, 1948.

The resignation of twelve non-Communist members of the Gottwald Cabinet served as the pretext for Communist-staged street
demonstrations and a one-hour general strike on February 24, 1947.
The Cabinet members had relinquished their posts in protest
against the rapid communization of the police apparatus. But the
Communists were prepared for a showdown. On February 24, Gottwald declared in a public speech: "Today more than ever, we are
tightening the bonds which unite us to the Soviet Union. The destiny of our popular democracy, the very existence of the nation, and
the liberty of our state are closely linked to our alliance with the
Soviet Union."[36]

Nor did the Soviet Union neglect to demonstrate its support of the coup. Deputy Minister of Foreign Affairs V. A. Zorin was dispatched to the scene to assist the Communist Party. The Soviet press conducted a violent campaign. *Izvestia* wrote: "The 200 million people of the Soviet Union stood behind the heroic fight of the Czechoslovak Communist Party against reactionaries."[37]

The Communist police searched houses and made arbitrary arrests; police and Communist-led mobs occupied the offices and printing shops of other parties and newspapers. On February 25, 1948, the ailing Beneš was persuaded to accept the resignation of the non-Communist ministers and the appointment of a new Gottwald government, which became a willing tool of Moscow. On March 10, 1948, Foreign Minister Jan Masaryk, son of the first president, either committed suicide or was murdered. Beneš resigned on June 7, and died on September 3, 1948, a broken man.

HUNGARY

In March, 1919, in the wake of a lost war, Bela Kun succeeded in establishing a Hungarian Soviet Republic. This seemed like the fulfillment of Lenin's expectations. The Revolution was marching westward. On March 22, 1919, Bela Kun proclaimed: "On this day the proletariat of Hungary has concentrated in its own hands all the power of the State. . . . Hungary will be a Soviet [Socialist] Republic. . . . It declares its complete intellectual and spiritual unity with the Russian Soviet Government and offers an armed alliance with the proletarians of Russia."[38]

Lenin cabled Kun that "the working class of Russia will come to your aid in every possible way." He also assured the Hungarian Communists that "the workers throughout the world . . . will not permit the imperialists of any country whatever to make any attempt against the new Socialist Republic."[39]

But Bela Kun had to flee Hungary four months after taking power, and Soviet Russia did not lift a finger in the defense of his regime. Apparently the time was not ripe. It seems, however, that the collapse of the first Hungarian Soviet Republic made a deep impression on the Russian Communist leaders. Their behavior in October–November, 1956, showed how determined they were not to let Hungarian history repeat itself.

The Molotov-Ribbentrop Pact placed Hungary in the German sphere of influence. Although formally accepting this arrangement, the Soviet Government demonstrated its interest in Hungarian affairs at every opportunity. By favoring Hungarian territorial demands in Romania, they hoped to further their own designs on Bessarabia. In June, 1940, Soviet Russia, having decided to annex Bessarabia, wanted Hungary to provide a pretext for armed intervention. Stalin summoned the Hungarian Minister Kristoffy. The following conversation took place: STALIN: "Has Hungary given up her claims to Transylvania?" KRISTOFFY: "No, she has not." STALIN: Why then don't you attack Romania? Now is the time."[40]

Hungary did not heed this perfidious advice. But when Hitler, in the Second Vienna Award of August 30, 1940, decided to divide Transylvania between Hungary and Romania and guaranteed Romania's new frontiers, a serious misunderstanding developed between Moscow and Berlin. Molotov charged that the Germans had violated the Nazi-Soviet pact.

For a country that had signed the anti-Comintern Pact (February 24, 1939) and the Tripartite Pact (November 20, 1940), declared war on the United States (December 13, 1941), and fought against Russia—however unwillingly—Hungary showed a remarkable degree of resistance to Nazi pressure. Until the country's total occupation by German troops, the successive Hungarian governments (with the possible exception of that headed by Laszlo Bardossy) present an impressive record of overt as well as secret pro-Western activities. Fifty thousand Polish soldiers passed through Hungary on their way to fight with the Polish forces in the West. Many Jews found asylum in Hungary.*

As early as 1941, secret negotiations began between representatives of Hungary and of the Polish Government in London in preparation for Hungary's coming over to the Allied camp. In 1943, Hungarian emissaries were in touch with British and American representatives regarding conditions for an Allied armistice with Hungary. In March, 1944, a U.S. military mission was parachuted into Hungary.

But because of a lack of appropriate political decisions on the part of the Western Allies, none of these efforts yielded tangible results. The Russian troops that entered Hungary fighting against

---

* "We helped more than 50,000 soldiers in the fall of 1939 to get to France and to the free army of General Sikorski." (From the testimony of Monsignor Varga, in Communist Occupation and Takeover of Hungary, Special Report No. 10, Select Committee on Communist Aggression, House of Representatives [Washington, D.C., 1954], p. 8.)

the Germans did not differentiate between enemy soldiers and local population. A preliminary armistice was signed in Moscow on October 1, 1944, by a Hungarian delegation and the Soviet High Command. But the Germans arrested Admiral Horthy and installed the Nazi-like Szalasi regime in Budapest. German armed resistance to the Russian advance in Hungary did not end until April, 1945. Budapest was almost completely destroyed by a siege that lasted more than seven weeks, and the abominable behavior of the Soviet troops brought the Hungarian people to the verge of despair.[41]

Thus a political void was created in Hungary. A group of Communists who had been members of Bela Kun's regime returned with the Soviet armies and gradually took all the important political positions. On December 21, 1944, a Provisional National Assembly was convened in Debrecen. The Communists obtained the nomination of 72 out of a total of 230 deputies. A government under the Prime Ministership of General Bela Miklos was appointed. Although outwardly this was a coalition government, the Communists took over the key positions: police, transportation, and agrarian reform. Terror, abuse, arrests, mass deportations, confiscations, and requisitions were practiced by the Red Army and condoned by the Communist members of the government. The armistice agreement of January 20, 1945, provided for the organization of the Allied Control Commission for Hungary, presided over by the Soviet Marshal Voroshilov. But it soon became apparent that the Commission was run exclusively by the Russians; the American and British sections wielded no practical influence. By the terms of the agreement, Hungary reverted to her 1937 frontiers and had to pay substantial reparations to Soviet Russia, Czechoslovakia, and Yugoslavia.

Although Soviet forces controlled the country, the first postwar elections (November 4, 1945) nonetheless gave the Communists only 17 per cent of the votes cast. The Smallholders' Party won an overwhelming victory, obtaining 57 per cent of the votes cast; it proved the main obstacle to the sovietization of Hungary and consequently became the principal target of Communist pressure. In 1948, it was the turn of the Social Democratic Party, which was forced to merge with the Communist Party. The last opposition party—the People's Democratic Party—was dissolved in 1949. In May, 1949, single-list, Soviet-style elections were held, giving an expected majority to the People's Front. In February, 1949, Cardinal Mindszenty, Primate of Hungary, was condemned to life

imprisonment after a sham trial. He had been arrested in December, 1948, on trumped-up charges and savagely tortured in prison.*
Since 1949, no open opposition to sovietization has been tolerated by the Communist authorities.

On January 31, 1946, the National Assembly declared Hungary a People's Republic. On February 10, 1947, Hungary signed the Peace Treaty of Paris with the Allied powers. Article 22 of this Treaty reads:

> Upon the coming into force of the present Treaty, all Allied forces shall, within a period of ninety days, be withdrawn from Hungary, subject to the right of the Soviet Union to keep on Hungarian territory such armed forces as it may need for the maintenance of the lines of communication of the Soviet Army with the Soviet zone of occupation in Austria.[42]

This clause was invalidated by the Soviet ratification of the State Treaty with Austria (June 11, 1955); but the Treaty of Warsaw (May 14, 1955) substituted a new justification for the presence of Russian troops on Hungarian soil.

The October, 1956, Hungarian revolution was the direct result of Russian exploitation and Communist misrule. On October 23, Hungarian security police fired upon students demonstrating in front of the Bem memorial. Bem was a Polish general who fought for Hungary in 1849. This incident became the signal for widespread street fighting and for the first intervention of Russian troops, supposedly at the request of the Hungarian Government. But the government had changed during the night and the new Premier, Imre Nagy, a former Communist Prime Minister, disclaimed any knowledge of such a request. It was later ascribed to Erno Gero, first secretary of the Communist Party, dismissed on October 25.†

Imre Nagy, who for some time previously had been in disgrace with the Communist Party, yielded to popular pressure for the complete liberation of Hungary from Soviet occupation and the establishment of a democratic regime. He announced the abolition

---

* *New York Times*, December 6, 1956. Cardinal Mindszenty was liberated from prison by Hungarian revolutionaries on October 30, 1956. A few days later he had to seek refuge in the American Legation in Budapest.

† In July, 1957, G. Marosan, Minister of State in Kadar's government, claimed the responsibility for calling in the Soviet troops on October 23–24, 1956. Since at that time he was a member only of the Politburo and did not join the government until November 4, his declaration appears to be no more than a face-saving gesture for the benefit of the Russians.

of the one-party system, the withdrawal from the Warsaw Pact, and proclaimed Hungary's neutrality. He also requested Russia to begin negotiations for the withdrawal of its troops.

On October 30, the Soviet Government published an official statement in which it pledged to abide, in the relations between the nations of "the great commonwealth of socialist nations . . . by the . . . principle of full equality, respect for territorial integrity, state independence and sovereignty, and noninterference in the domestic affairs of each other." The statement went on to say that Russia deeply regretted the development of events in Hungary, leading to bloodshed, and declared, "the Soviet Government has given an instruction to its military command to withdraw the Soviet units from Budapest as soon as this is recognized by the Hungarian Government to be necessary."[43]

But on October 31, fresh Soviet troops were already entering Hungary.* On November 1, Imre Nagy repeatedly protested to the Soviet Ambassador and notified the Secretary General of the United Nations. However, the Russians seemed reassuring and the Soviet Ambassador spoke of a simple regrouping of Soviet troops. On November 3, a joint committee of Soviet and Hungarian military representatives began discussions in the Soviet headquarters in Budapest.

On November 4, Nagy made the following statement over Radio Budapest: "This is Premier Imre Nagy speaking. Today at daybreak, Soviet troops attacked our capital with the obvious intent of overthrowing the legal democratic Hungarian government. Our troops are in combat."[44]

Half an hour later, he spoke for the last time over Radio Budapest: "Imre Nagy, Premier of the national government, appeals to Pal Maleter, Defense Minister, Istvan Kovacs, Chief of the General Staff, and the other members who went to the Soviet Army Headquarters at ten o'clock last night . . . to return at once. . . ."[45]

For more than two years, nothing was heard of these Hungarian delegates.† A massive attack by Soviet armored forces crushed the Hungarian Revolution. Moscow imposed a new Revolutionary

---

* In fact, "Soviet authorities had taken steps as early as 20 October, to make armed intervention in Hungary possible. Evidence exists of troop movements from that date on." (From the Report of the Special Committee of the United Nations on the Problem of Hungary, p. 137.)

† The Hungarian Government announced their execution, as well as that of Imre Nagy, on June 17, 1958.

Workers and Peasants Government, headed by Janos Kadar. Imre Nagy himself at first found refuge in the Yugoslav Embassy. But later he was arrested by Soviet Security Police despite Kadar's official promise of safe conduct and pledge for Nagy's safety given to the Yugoslav Government.

The determination of the Hungarian people to resist against such overwhelming odds can only be ascribed to mass despair. The Soviet Government rejected or ignored all pleas, demands, and resolutions of the United Nations requesting the withdrawal of its troops from Hungary. Russia vetoed a resolution in the Security Council on November 4. In the Assembly, ten resolutions were adopted between November 4 and December 12 dealing with the crushing of the Hungarian uprising by Soviet forces. In its resolution of December 12, the Assembly:

1. Declares that by using its armed force against the Hungarian people, the Government of the Union of Soviet Socialist Republics is violating the political independence of Hungary.
2. Condemns the violation of the Charter of the U.N. by the Government of the Union of Soviet Socialist Republics in depriving Hungary of its liberty and independence and the Hungarian people of the exercise of their fundamental rights.[46]

The Kadar regime followed Russia's example by refusing entry visas to U.N. observers and rejecting Secretary Hammarskjold's offer to visit Budapest himself. On January 10, 1957, by fifty-nine votes to eight, the Assembly of the United Nations established a five-nation Committee to observe the situation in Hungary and take testimonies from Hungarian refugees. In the summer of 1957, the over-all figure of Hungarians who left their country to escape persecution since November, 1956, was assumed to have passed the 200,000 mark.[47]

On May 27, 1957, Kadar's government signed a new agreement with Soviet Russia on the legal status of Soviet troops "temporarily stationed" in Hungary. It followed the pattern of similar accords concluded since the Hungarian Revolution with other satellite governments. Article I states: "The temporary presence of Soviet forces on the territory of the Hungarian People's Republic in no way affects the sovereignty of the Hungarian State; the Soviet forces do not interfere in the internal affairs of the Hungarian People's Republic."[48]

On June 20, 1957, the Special Committee of the United Nations, consisting of representatives of Australia, Ceylon, Denmark, Tunisia, and Uruguay, made public its report on Soviet intervention in Hungary. The Committee unanimously branded Soviet Russia as the perpetrator of a "massive armed intervention by one power on the territory of another," and left no doubt that "what took place in Hungary in October and November, 1956, was a spontaneous national uprising." The Committee charged that Russia had prepared its military intervention in Hungary in advance, even "before the students met to discuss their demands." The Russian forces attacked Hungary despite the "popular nature of the uprising" and although "no clause of the Treaty of Warsaw provides for the intervention by armed forces of the Soviet Union to dictate political developments within any signatory's frontiers."[49]

But the Warsaw Treaty is primarily an instrument of Russian domination of the satellite countries. On May 14, 1957, the second anniversary of the signing of the Warsaw Treaty, *Pravda* wrote: "When counterrevolution tried to seize power in Hungary with the help of international imperialism, the Soviet Union . . . came to the assistance of the Hungarian people. Counterrevolution was defeated. By this fact the indestructible might of the Warsaw Treaty was clearly and convincingly manifested."

ROMANIA

The line dividing the spheres of influence of Soviet Russia and Nazi Germany, agreed upon in the Secret Protocol of the Molotov-Ribbentrop Pact, ran right across the Romanian territory.

Less than a year later, on June 23, 1940, Molotov informed the German Ambassador that Soviet Russia intended to avail herself of the treaty provisions. He said: "The solution of the Bessarabian question brooked no further delay. The Soviet Government was still striving for a peaceful solution, but it was determined to use force, should the Romanian Government decline peaceful agreement. The Soviet claim extended likewise to Bucovina, which had a Ukrainian population."[50]

Three days later, on June 26, the Romanian Government was handed the Russian ultimatum. Hitler recommended submission. In France the Pétain government had just accepted the terms of the German armistice, and no British assistance seemed possible. The Romanians yielded to the Soviet demands, and on June 28,

1940, Russian troops poured into Bessarabia and Northern Buco-vina, perpetrating brutalities, deporting thousands of people to the Soviet Union, thus causing a mass flight to Romania across the new frontier.

In October, 1940, German troops in turn began to enter Ro-mania. In February, 1941, they numbered 680,000. A few months later, the Antonescu government joined Germany in the hostilities against Russia, despite the opposition of Juliu Maniu and Con-stantin (Dinu) Bratianu, leaders of the Peasant and Liberal Par-ties, respectively.

Despite the declaration of a formal state of war with Great Britain (December 7, 1941), Romanian representatives abroad strove for secret contacts with the Allied powers. Such contacts with emissaries of the Polish government in London were never interrupted. As in the case of Hungary, the lack of appropriate political approaches on the Allied side prevented these conversa-tions from yielding practical results. In March, 1944, a secret rep-resentative of King Michael was dispatched to Egypt with full authority to discuss Allied conditions for an armistice with Ro-mania.

On April 3, 1944, Molotov made the following statement: "The Soviet Government declares that it does not pursue the aim of acquiring any part of Romanian territory, or of changing in what-ever manner the existing social order in Romania."

Molotov confirmed this declaration on August 25, stressing that the Soviet Union in no way intended to limit Romania's inde-pendence.[51]

Encouraged by Molotov's declarations and other Allied pro-nouncements, King Michael announced Romania's withdrawal from the war on August 23, 1944. Prime Minister Antonescu was arrested and a pro-Allied government formed. The Nazis retaliated by a three-day long bombardment of Bucharest. The first Soviet troops arrived in the capital on August 28 and, although greeted as friends, behaved in their usual fashion. But even Moscow recog-nized the service rendered to the Allied cause by King Michael by awarding him the Soviet Order of Victory.*

The armistice convention, signed in Moscow on September 12, 1944, returned Bessarabia and Northern Bucovina to Soviet rule

---

* Text in Tufton Beamish, *Must Night Fall?*, p. 134. The citation read: "For a courageous act of decision in reversing Romania's policy, breaking with Hitlerite Germany and making an alliance with the United Nations, at a time when the defeat of Germany was not clearly in sight."

and imposed heavy reparations on Romania. It also provided for Romanian participation in the war against Germany and established an Allied Control Commission under Soviet chairmanship in Romania. All of Transylvania was returned to Romania.

When the Soviet armies occupied Romania, the local Communist element was very small. According to Ana Pauker, there were fewer than 1,000 Communists.

Yet on February 28, 1945, Soviet Deputy Foreign Minister A. Y. Vishinsky handed the King of Romania a two-hour ultimatum demanding the dismissal of the Radescu government. After a display of Russian military might in the streets of Bucharest and additional pressure by Vishinsky and Marshal Malinovsky, a National Democratic Front Government was formed, headed by a Communist stooge, Petru Groza. It soon became evident that the Romanian Constitution was no longer in operation and that there could be no change of government without Moscow's consent. The decisions of the Moscow Conference of Foreign Ministers of December, 1945, adding two opposition members to the Groza government served only to emphasize that the Western powers were in no position seriously to influence the situation. In the first postwar elections (November 19, 1946), under conditions of Communist pressure and intimidation, the number of seats allotted to the opposition parties was determined in advance. The garbled results gave the Communists and groups collaborating with them in the Bloc of Democratic Parties more than four-fifths of the total number of seats in Parliament.[52] During 1947, opposition parties were politically paralyzed or completely liquidated by means of the well-known methods of intimidation, false accusations, and police terror.

On December 30, 1947, the Communist regime forced King Michael to abdicate; he was able to leave the country with his family. A Romanian People's Republic was officially established on April 13, 1948.

The Allied powers and the Soviet-controlled Romanian Government signed the Peace Treaty of Paris on February 10, 1947. Article 21 of the Romanian Treaty of Peace was identical with Article 22 of the Treaty with Hungary. In spite of the ratification of the Peace Treaty with Austria (June 11, 1955), Soviet troops remained on Romanian soil. As in the case of Hungary, their presence was covered by the Treaty of Warsaw. A Soviet-Romanian agreement on the "temporary stationing" of Soviet forces on Romanian soil was signed in Bucharest on April 15, 1957. It closely resembles similar understandings with other satellite governments.

BULGARIA

Russia played an important role in the liberation of Bulgaria from Turkish bondage in the last quarter of the nineteenth century. Remnants of pro-Russian feelings therefore still lingered in Bulgaria between the two world wars, but there was little popular support for Communism. Although the Bulgarian Communist Party had been outlawed in 1934, Molotov nonetheless told the Italian Ambassador on June 25, 1940: "Bulgaria and the Soviet Union were good neighbors. The Soviet-Bulgarian relations were strong and could be strengthened even more. The Bulgarian demands for Dobruja and for access to the Aegean Sea were considered justified by the Soviet Government, which had recognized them and had no objections to their realization."[53]

In the light of the secret Nazi-Soviet documents it is apparent that Molotov's aim was not to satisfy Bulgaria's territorial aspirations, but to incorporate the country into the Soviet sphere of influence. Bulgaria was the subject of the fifth secret protocol, which Molotov suggested in order to clinch the negotiations with Hitler for the division of the world into zones of influence. The text of this proposal reads as follows:

> A fifth protocol between Germany, the Soviet Union and Italy, recognizing that Bulgaria is geographically located inside the security zone of the Black Sea boundaries of the Soviet Union and that it is therefore a political necessity that a mutual assistance pact be concluded between the Soviet Union and Bulgaria, which in no way shall affect the internal regime of Bulgaria, her sovereignty or independence.[54]

The Soviet intentions, of which the Bulgarian Government was not informed, were not then carried out only because the Balkans became a bone of contention between Moscow and Berlin. On March 1, 1941, Bulgaria, unable to resist the pressure from both sides, was forced to accede to the Three-Powers Pact (signed on September 27, 1940 between Germany, Italy, and Japan), and to accept the presence of German soldiers on her soil. In the circumstances, however, it was an unexpected achievement for Bulgaria, which under the terms of the Tripartite Pact had declared war on Great Britain and the United States (December 12, 1941), to be able to avoid fighting against the Soviet Union. Indeed, Bulgaria was the only signatory to the Axis Pact to remain officially neutral in the German-Soviet war.

After March, 1941, Bulgaria was virtually under German occupation. Only in June, 1944, when the German position had begun to deteriorate, could the Bulgarian Government show its real feelings. Stoicho Moshanov, a leading political figure, was sent to Turkey and Egypt to begin negotiations with the Western powers. On August 23, 1944, Prime Minister Bagrianov told Parliament that Bulgaria had officially withdrawn from the war. German occupation troops were to be disarmed and interned. On September 2, 1944, a coalition government took over from Bagrianov. The Communist-led Fatherland Front, however, refused to participate. The reason for this abstention was revealed on September 5, when the Soviet Union declared war on Bulgaria. A demand for an immediate armistice was not accepted by Moscow. On September 8, Soviet troops began to pour into the country. The following day, a detachment of the Military League, in association with the Communists, arrested the Bulgarian Government while its delegates were negotiating with Allied representatives in Cairo. A new coalition government was formed by the Fatherland Front, with Communists occupying the key positions. The Bulgarian Army was put under Red Army command and fought against the Germans in Yugoslavia, Hungary, and Austria. Fatherland Front committees, organized on the model of Russian Soviets, took over the administration. A wave of arrests and assassinations terrorized the population. Parliamentary elections, postponed because of American and British protests, were carried out in November, 1945, under conditions typical of police terror; the Fatherland Front got an absolute majority.

In September, 1946, Bulgaria was proclaimed a people's republic. King Boris had died in August, 1943, under mysterious circumstances, on his return from a visit to Hitler's headquarters.* He was succeeded by his son, Simeon II, then under age. King Boris' brother, Prince Cyril, who became Regent, was executed after a show trial in February, 1945. King Simeon was able to leave the country with the Queen Mother after the proclamation of the people's republic.

* Hitler and Goebbels attributed his death to poisoning. There is strong suspicion that the King was indeed poisoned, on Hitler's orders. (Cf. *The Goebbels Diaries* [New York, 1948], pp. 47, 433, 442. Also: N. P. Nikolaev, *Le règne et la mort de Boris III* [Upsala, 1952].)

FOUR

THE COLD WAR ERA

15. *NEITHER WAR NOR PEACE*

The concept of a global, nonshooting conflict between Soviet Russia and the Western powers is vague in the extreme. Although the term "Cold War" has gained currency, it is as difficult to say when the Cold War began as what it really is. In Western countries, the idea is associated with malevolent Soviet activities against the freedom and independence of nations. In Communist propaganda jargon, Cold War is something the "capitalists" wage against "peaceloving" countries. If by Cold War we mean underhanded Soviet actions against Allied nations, then it was waged against Poland as early as 1941, against China and Greece in 1943, and against Britain soon after. If, on the other hand, we mean the open break in Big Three collaboration, the date should be fixed at some time in 1946–47. The truth of the matter is that a state of political "neither war nor peace" set in at different moments in the various spheres of East-West contacts as the logical consequence of Soviet inability to participate in the life of the international community. The Soviet Union may seem less closed than it was a decade ago, but its relations with the outside world are still regulated and controlled by the state. The Soviet system is still incompatible with democratic freedoms, and this was even truer in 1945. The Soviet Union had suffered great war losses. Conservative estimates put military and civilian casualties at 20 million. One-quarter of the Soviet capital equipment was lost because of military operations.[1] No country had such large numbers of defectors, particularly among Ukrainians, Balts, Tatars, and Kalmuks. One quarter million Cossack troops, together with Turkestani, Caucasian-Mohamedan, Georgian, and Armenian legions, fought against the Russians on the German side. The number of so-called "volunteers," the armed paramilitary organizations recruited by the Germans from among Soviet prisoners of war, deserters, and civilians, is said to have been one million. Vlasov's anti-Soviet Russian army comprised about 50,000 men.² While its great armies stood in the middle of Europe, Soviet Russia felt far more weakened than Great Britain, not to speak of the United States. A long, sustained effort and large capital outlays were needed to make up for the vast material losses. Manpower was in short supply and had to be replaced by prisoners of war, deportees from the dependent countries of eastern Europe, and various sources of slave labor. Soviet political vulnerability made it impossible to accept Western economic aid other than at arm's length. As far as possible, the Soviet Union and its new European satellites had to remain closed to the searching eyes of foreign diplomats, journalists, and social workers.

One factor, more than any other, influenced the Soviet attitude at the close of the war. The Americans had the atom bomb. This made them so powerful that an open conflict could not be risked. As a result of these considerations, a twilight period in East-West relations set in. The Soviet armies pushed forward—west and south-westward in Europe, eastward in Manchuria—but stopped short of open military conflict with Western troops. At diplomatic conferences, Soviet representatives covered up Russia's weakness and made demands for additional concessions. But the new political map of Europe had been drawn at Tehran, Yalta, and Potsdam; nothing more could be added to these Soviet gains. In Asia, however, Stalin tried to gain a foothold on Japanese soil. On August 16, 1945, the day the Japanese Emperor ordered a general cease-fire, Stalin asked Truman to extend the area in which the Japanese armies were to surrender to Soviet forces to the northern half of the Hokkaido Island, a part of Japan proper. "I am most anxious," Stalin cabled, "that the modest [sic] suggestions set forth above should not meet with any objections." Truman answered that all Japanese islands were to surrender to General MacArthur, who, as Supreme Allied Commander, could employ Soviet troops as one of the "Allied token forces" for the temporary occupation of Japan. That was not what the Kremlin had in mind. Their idea undoubtedly was a separate zone of occupation in Japan, however small, that could be turned into a Communist base, similar to the Soviet Zone in East Germany and in North Korea. But there was nothing Stalin could now do to force Truman's hand, the more so as he was also asking that the Kurile Islands be turned over to Soviet forces, in line with previous agreements. But Stalin showed his disappointment by angrily turning down Truman's demand for air-base rights (for military and commercial purposes) on one of the Kurile Islands. This was one of these Western ideas of mixed influence that the Russians regard with the utmost suspicion. Stalin retorted that such demands "are usually laid before a vanquished country or before an allied country that is unable to defend a particular part of its territory."[3]

The matter was smoothed over, but relations were deteriorating. At the first postwar meeting of the Council of Foreign Ministers in London, in September, 1945, a controversy flared up over Eastern Europe. The Foreign Ministers met again in Moscow in December, 1945, in Paris in June, 1946, and in New York in November, 1946. In the meantime, the Big Powers' representatives publicly quarreled over Iran's complaint against Russian interference. The negotiations with the Soviet Government during this period did not change the territorial and political decisions arrived at during the wartime conferences. Despite the tremendous change in the balance of power in America's favor, the peace treaties with Finland, Hungary, Romania, and Italy prepared at the Paris Peace Conference (July–October, 1946), which were signed in February of the next year, followed the division of Europe devised during the war. Italy lost its colonies but retained its sovereignty. Greece remained free. Finland became a buffer between Russia and Sweden. All the other countries of mid-Europe between Finland and Greece were left to Communist rule. In Asia, the Manchurian operation boosted the chances of Communism by supplying Mao Tse-tung with Japanese arms and valuable territorial gains. But at the same time, Russia signed a treaty with Chiang Kai-shek and disclaimed any interest in China's internal affairs. With the exception of China, where Mao became victorious during the next four years, the physical advance of Communist power had come to a halt. In Europe, East-West rivalry froze along the Iron Curtain. Political trench warfare replaced the political war of movement of the earlier period. Now Soviet Russia could no longer launch frontal attacks on the Western positions. It had to develop methods of infiltrating or outflanking the West.

As seen from Moscow, the outlook for a political offensive in Western Europe along the pattern of popular or united fronts seemed particularly propitious. In France, more than 5 million people voted Communist in the first postwar elections of October, 1945. The Communist Party emerged as the largest group in Parliament, and Communists sat in the coalition governments from 1944 to 1947. In the Italian elections of June, 1946, the Communists and Socialists got 9 million votes. In October of the same year, the two parties formed a popular front. Four Communists held cabinet posts in the De Gasperi government formed in July, 1946. The trade unions were under Communist influence. Under the circumstances it was not unreasonable to expect the local Communist parties to gain power in France or Italy, or both, by legal means, as Hitler had come legally to power in Germany. It was even less unreasonable to prepare for a Communist takeover by a combination of electoral strength, trade-union influence, and revolutionary tactics.

Truman Doctrine and Marshall Plan

The period of a limited collaboration with other parties in France and Italy closely following Lenin's advice "to combine illegal forms of struggle with *every* form of legal struggle"[4] ended in 1947. Things had not gone as smoothly as expected, and strong resistance to Communist methods developed both in France and Italy. In January, 1947, the Italian Socialists split over collaboration with the Communists, the right wing later forming its own party. In May of the same year, the Communists lost their seats in the government and, later in the year, organized nationwide strikes and riots. In France, the Communist and Socialist opposition had forced De Gaulle into retirement in January, 1946. But the grass-roots struggle between the Socialists and the Communists contradicted the talk of working-class unity. In May, the Socialist Ramadier forced the Communist ministers out of the government. In June, the Communist Party launched a series of strikes that seemed to foreshadow a violent struggle for power. In November, a general strike ordered by the Communist Party resulted in a split in the major trade-union organization.

These events had a significant counterpart in Eastern Europe. Nicola Petkov, the leader of the Bulgarian opposition, was arrested in June and sentenced to death. He was executed on September 23, 1947. In Hungary, the first half of 1947 saw a terror campaign against the Smallholders' Party. Its Secretary General, Bela Kovacs, was arrested and charged with espionage. In May, Premier Ferenc Nagy and Speaker of the Assembly Msgr. Bela Varga were forced into exile. In Romania, the Peasant Party leader Juliu Maniu was arrested in July and later sentenced to life imprisonment. In Poland, the January, 1947, elections were conducted in an atmosphere of terror, their results falsified. In October, Stanislaw Mikolajczyk, the leader of the parliamentary opposition, escaped arrest and fled the country.

These were the highlights of a series of events that led to the liquidation of legal opposition to Communism in Eastern Europe. Russia's new satellites were firmly tied to Moscow and to each other by a network of political, military, and economic pacts concluded between 1945 and 1948.

It is difficult to say with certainty whether the change in Communist tactics in Western Europe in 1947 was a logical extension of events in the eastern part of the continent or a reaction to the Truman Doctrine and the Marshall Plan. Perhaps the initiative of the United States served to accelerate Communist plans. The Truman Doctrine, proclaimed on March 12, 1947, was of a mixed military and economic character. It was immediately applied in Greece and Turkey, and it also contained a general warning to Soviet Russia that the United States would not tolerate aggressive or subversive acts against other free, independent countries anywhere. Yet it was not illogical that the Marshall Plan (announced in General Marshall's Harvard address of June 5), although limited to economic assistance in Europe, should have seemed more dangerous from the Soviet point of view. The Truman Doctrine, unwelcome though it may have been in Moscow, was a defensive policy, proclaiming nothing more than the containment of Communism. This was elaborately confirmed in George Kennan's famous article in the July, 1947, issue of *Foreign Affairs*. But the Kremlin must have seen the Marshall Plan as an attempt at an American offensive, not only in Western Europe, but well beyond the Iron Curtain into Soviet Russia itself. At the Paris Conference of June–July, 1947, Molotov, although not fighting the Plan openly, professed to see a threat to national sovereignty in the common pool of European needs suggested by Secretary Marshall and supported by Britain and France. In fact, however, the very principle of massive American assistance to Europe went against the grain of Soviet policy: Communism thrived on the economic depression in Western Europe; any American economic assistance in Eastern Europe was bound to revive the issues of political freedoms and national independence. Even if some safe form of American loans to Soviet Russia itself could be devised, it was dangerous to allow direct American aid to Eastern Europe. The Soviet Government therefore rejected the Marshall Plan and forbade its European satellites (and Finland) to participate in it. The Plan was viciously attacked by Soviet propaganda. According to *Izvestia*, the working people in the Marshallized countries of Europe had convinced themselves "that the 'Marshall Plan' means a decline in wages, a growth of unemployment, hunger and poverty."[5] The highbrow *Literaturnaya Gazeta* compared the American administrators of the European Recovery Program in European countries to the *Gauleiters* of Hitler's Germany.

No allusion was made to the fact that American economic assistance was also offered to the Soviet Union, and particularly to Eastern Europe, which became the real victim of Soviet policy on the Marshall Plan. Although precise over-all figures are not available, it can be estimated that by 1947, Russia had obtained—by removals of industrial equipment and other goods from East Germany, Western Poland, Romania, Hungary, and Czechoslovakia —capital value of more than $10 billion. Together with the wholesale removal of machinery from Manchuria, the wealth thus acquired by U.S.S.R. was already considerably higher in 1947 than the $11 billion that Western Europe was to receive under the Marshall Plan during the following three years.

GERMANY

Russia saw a great difference between the peace treaties with the former satellites of Germany and the problem of a peace treaty with Germany itself. The 1947 peace treaties formalized Russia's dominant position in Eastern Europe. That was a closed chapter for Moscow. A peace treaty with Germany, on the other hand, was to maintain an open situation, to create new opportunities for westward Communist expansion. Therefore, Moscow favored a strong central government for the whole of Germany, in which Communists would hold important posts, the international administration of the Ruhr (with Soviet participation), and high reparations from current production. Apart from the material benefits expected from such reparations, the system would allow Soviet interference in economic affairs throughout Germany, perhaps for years to come. These aims ran into various difficulties, and in the end all were defeated. The idea of a strong central government for all of Germany was in conflict with the proposal for a federal system and limited powers for a central government made by the West. Centralization also was a practical impossibility in view of Germany's division into four occupation zones. Because of differences in attitudes and administrative methods, the three Western zones and the Soviet sector were drifting apart and soon reflected the divergent ways of life of the occupying powers. The Western plans for economic unity were no more realistic than the Soviet demand for administrative unity, and they also foundered on the concrete fact of Germany's division. Soviet demands for immediate reparations out of current production were rejected. Both Secretary Bevin and Secretary Marshall pointed out that such reparations would have to be paid by America and England, who were trying to revive the German economy. "We put in," Marshall said, "and the Russians take out."[6] Finally, after the negotiations on Germany had come to a standstill, international control of the Ruhr was instituted, without Soviet participation and despite their angry protestations.

Between November, 1946, when the four powers addressed themselves to the problem of a German peace treaty, and December, 1947, when negotiations ceased, the four foreign ministers and their deputies spent many weeks in fruitless negotiations in New York, London, Moscow, and again in London. With the exception of a decree dissolving the Prussian state, no agreement could be reached on any major aspect of the German problem. There was no escaping the fact that the interests of the two groups were not in accord, and that the Western powers, now aware of the conflict of interests, refused to give in to Soviet persuasion or pressure. After the breakdown of the London Conference in December, 1947, Marshall said: "The situation must be stabilized. Western nations at the least must be firmly established on a basis of governments and freedoms."[7]

Russia did not want the stabilization of Germany or of Western Europe. The Soviet Government was particularly perturbed by the merging of the American and English zones of occupation. On November 6, 1947, at a thirtieth-anniversary celebration of the Bolshevik Revolution, Molotov charged in a speech that the United States of America and Britain had departed from the democratic principles of the Yalta and Potsdam Conferences and had violated the jointly adopted decisions. Because of the creation of the bizone —the merged zones of occupation—the Russians, Molotov said, had lost all possibility of influencing the situation in West Germany. Andrei Zhdanov, a member of the Politburo and the moving spirit of the Cominform, violently denounced the United States, accusing them of imperialism, and asserting that "the crusade against Communism" was leading America toward fascism; he described the Truman Doctrine as "frankly aggressive," and called the Marshall Plan a "trap."[8]

However, verbal displays of dissatisfaction were not enough. Practical decisions had to be made, involving either acceptance of stabilization along the lines of the military occupation in Germany or a westward push against an opposition whose strength remained to be tested. The strikes in France and Italy in June, 1947, the creation of the Cominform in the autumn of the same year, and the tone of the Soviet press would seem to indicate that a general decision had been made in Moscow before the collapse of the four-power negotiations in December, 1947. The weakest Western position was held by the token American, British, and French forces stationed in West Berlin. Unimaginative wartime decisions had left the three Western sectors of Berlin without a free road link to the west.* Soon after the Moscow Conference of Foreign Ministers, the Russians began to interfere with the Berlin lines of communication. After February, 1948, Soviet pressure steadily increased, culminating in the full blockade of Berlin on June 23, 1948. Less than three years after Potsdam, 300,000 soldiers stationed in East Germany laid siege to 6,500 American, British, and French soldiers, and tried to cut off food, water, electric power, and other services indispensable to the 2 million inhabitants of West Berlin. Russia's *action directe* against its wartime allies was an international scandal as well as a grave provocation that in theory could have led to war. The cautious Stalin, who in two decades of autocratic rule had never risked war against a strong opponent, now decided to challenge the Western powers in Berlin, despite U.S. atomic supremacy. The ostensible immediate aim was to force the small Western detachments out of the city. As it was, Stalin's calculation proved correct. Atomic weapons were not used as a means of diplomatic pressure. Suggestions that an American armored column break the blockade did not materialize.† It may be assumed that had this happened, the Russians would have backed down while trying to confuse the situation. After all, in Soviet terminology the blockade was no more than a series of traffic measures "to safeguard the economy of East Germany against the pernicious influence of

* In 1944, Philip E. Mosely, who was political adviser to Ambassador John G. Winant on the European Advisory Commission and his assistant in the Committee on Dismemberment (of Germany), submitted a plan for a corridor connecting Berlin with the prospective Western zones of occupation. There also was a proposed division which would have made of Berlin the meeting place of the American, British and Soviet zones. Cf. Philip E. Mosely, *The Kremlin and World Politics* (New York, 1960), pp. 166, 171. The book provides valuable firsthand material on the negotiations that led to the division of Germany into zones of occupation.

† This was repeatedly advocated by the U.S. Military Governor in Germany, General Lucius D. Clay. (Cf. W. Phillips Davison, *The Berlin Blockade*, p. 126 and *passim*.)

separate Western acts . . . to prevent the Western mark from penetrating into East Germany, including Greater Berlin."[9] This semantic confusion was maintained over the years, and the Soviet Government has never admitted that it blockaded Berlin. On the contrary, an official *Historical Survey* published jointly by the Ministers of Foreign Affairs of the U.S.S.R. and the German Democratic Republic (East Germany) states: "In effect, the Western powers thus themselves blockaded West Berlin."[10] Yet, in the eyes of the world, the Soviet blockade was an established fact. Its immediate failure through an American show of force would have meant a colossal loss of face for the Soviet Union. Still, as far as Russia was concerned, it was well worth the risk, since a forced Western withdrawal from Berlin would have jeopardized the American position in all of West Germany, if not in all of Europe. In addition, or concurrently, the Soviet Government hoped to use the blockade in diplomatic bargaining to delay the formation of a West German state while setting up a Communist state in its own zone of occupation.

Neither of the extremes occurred: The Americans did *not* send an armored column to break through the Russian lines; the Russians did *not* seriously interfere with the airlift. By the turn of the year, the Soviet Government must have realized that the Western powers would not let themselves be pushed out of Berlin. Thus, once again, negotiations had to be instituted. The talks of Stalin and Molotov with Western representatives in Moscow in July and August of 1948, as well as the efforts by neutral governments, had been frustrated by the Russians. But now Moscow had to find a way out. On January 31, 1949, while answering questions from Kingsbury Smith of the International News Service, Stalin hinted that the Soviet Government was ready to negotiate the Berlin situation. Had this hint been ignored, there can be no doubt that it would have been repeated in some form or other. But Stalin's statement was taken up by American diplomacy, and after several months of private talks an agreement was reached. The blockade was lifted on May 12. The joint communiqué of May 5 showed the typical Soviet concern for face-saving locutions. The word "blockade" was never used. The agreement dealt with the mutual lifting of "restrictions" between the Eastern and Western sectors of Berlin. During the ensuing negotiations at the Paris meeting of Foreign Ministers (May 23–June 20, 1949), the Russians were able to maintain their positions in Germany. Berlin reverted to the pre-blockade status. "We tried and failed to get a physical corridor from Helmstedt to Berlin," writes former Secretary of State Dean Acheson, who took part in the conference.[11] This was a major failure of Western diplomacy, the consequences of which are still felt. Yet probably nothing short of an atomic threat could have persuaded the Russians to grant the West free land access to Berlin. And by then it was too late for such threats. Western opinion may have backed atomic diplomacy immediately after the imposition of the blockade, but not after ten months of airlifting. Apart from the communiqué, the conference brought no tangible results for either side, although weeks of discussions among Foreign Ministers somewhat obscured the fact that Soviet policy had sustained a stunning defeat. The siege of Berlin had failed, and Russia's westward offensive was stymied. Moscow had underestimated both Western determination to stay in Berlin and the West's ability to circumvent the blockade. As a matter of fact, it was not easy to foresee that so large a city could be supplied by air for so long. The Soviet failure to understand the human and political factors—i.e., that America and Britain had reached the limits of concessions in Europe, and that the inhabitants of Berlin would display such a strong will to resist—was a far more serious error, the reasons for which lie partly in the Communist's contempt for democratic societies and partly in Russian reluctance to admit to themselves how deeply Soviet rule is abhorred in the subjugated countries.

Did the Soviet leaders realize that their imperialistic policy might boomerang, that it might drive the countries of Western Europe into a defensive alliance, and, most important of all, bring the Americans back to Europe? This is not certain, but even if they had, the temptation to grab that which was near was too strong, and the memory of the sweeping concessions wrung from Roosevelt and Churchill at wartime conferences were a sort of psychological blinder. Once the reaction to Soviet expansion began to solidify, the Kremlin could do no more than conduct a rearguard action in the fields of diplomacy and propaganda. Moscow was unable to delay the formation of a West German government (September 20, 1949), or to prevent England, France, and the Benelux countries from signing the Brussels Defense Treaty (March 17, 1948), out of which, on April 4, 1949, grew the North Atlantic Treaty. For the first time in its history, the United States committed itself in peacetime to armed assistance in case of aggression against any of its treaty partners. The balance of power in Europe was thus restored, and any further forcible expansion of Soviet rule would incur the risk of war with America.

AUSTRIA

What followed was a logical consequence of the defensive nature of the North Atlantic Treaty. For the next twelve years (until the erection of the Berlin wall in August, 1961), the only physical change in the East-West positions in Europe was the voluntary Soviet withdrawal from Austria. The Austrian State Treaty of May 15, 1955, was concluded after a full decade of Soviet evasions and delays. At the wartime conferences, Austria had been granted a privileged position. In the "Declaration on Austria," drawn up at the 1943 Moscow Conference, the Big Three recognized that the *Anschluss* had been imposed on an unwilling population. Austria therefore was to be re-established as a free and independent country. According to the Yalta "Declaration on Liberated Europe," Austria was entitled to the assistance of the three powers in "the earliest establishment through free elections" of a democratic government. At Potsdam, the three powers decided that Austria would not have to pay reparations. But difficulties arose as soon as Soviet troops entered the country. As in East Germany, the Russians began to confiscate capital goods and other property on the pretext that these were German assets. Western protests were of no avail, although the matter of German assets had been agreed upon in 1943, and German property titles acquired under duress were not to be recognized. In July, 1946, Russia announced the confiscation of all German-owned property in Austria's Soviet zone of occupation. At the Council of Foreign Ministers, Molotov refused to discuss a treaty with Austria. It was not until the spring of 1947 that Moscow allowed placing the matter on the agenda. But this was only the beginning of many years of evasive tactics. In his report to the President, after the Treaty was finally signed in 1955, Secretary of State Dulles stated that the Austrian Treaty had been considered at 379 separate sessions of the Foreign Ministers Council and other bodies. Secretary Dulles wrote:

> By the end of 1949, agreement was finally reached on the German assets question. . . . However, one excuse after another was used by Soviet representatives to delay final action on the treaty, and it became apparent that the Soviet Government was basically unwilling to grant Austria its promised freedom. It was unwilling to withdraw its troops from Austria.[12]

This situation continued for another seven years. There was no change in the Soviet attitude, even after Stalin's death. In December, 1953, the U.N. Assembly voted forty-eight to nothing for a Brazilian resolution demanding the conclusion of a treaty with Austria. The Soviet Union and the satellite governments abstained; Moscow denied U.N. competence in the matter and considered the resolution "illegal." Finally, on February 8, 1955, Molotov declared that under certain conditions Soviet troops could be withdrawn from Austria. Soviet intransigence on Austria was largely caused by the need to justify the stationing of Russian troops in Romania and Hungary. The peace treaties with these countries provided the right to keep "such armed forces [on their territories] as may be needed for the maintenance of the lines of communications of the Soviet Army with the Soviet zone of occupation in Austria." Once West Germany was admitted to NATO, a change of policy became possible. There can be little doubt that Molotov's speech on Austria followed the decision to form a counteralliance of Communist-ruled states. The Warsaw Pact, which was signed one day before the Austrian State Treaty, provided a new formal basis for the presence of Russian troops in the participating countries. It should also be noted that in exchange for leaving Lower (or eastern) Austria, the Soviet Government obtained the withdrawal of Allied, and particularly American, troops from a line (Linz-Friedberg-Fürstenberg) not more than 10 miles from the Hungarian frontier. As a neutralized buffer state, Austria served the Soviet policy of keeping Western troops as far away as possible from Communist-held borders. Moreover, a neutral Austria disrupted the continuity of NATO's north-south land communications in central Europe and pushed them westward from the Brenner to the French-Italian frontier. But the most important reason for the shift in Soviet policy was no doubt the need to boost the "coexistence" policy with a "good-will" gesture. The Austrian treaty opened the way to the first postwar summit meeting, held in Geneva in June, 1955.

But military and political considerations did not prevent the Soviet Government from selling its consent to the Austrian treaty for hard cash. Despite the Potsdam promise that Austria was to pay no reparations, Russia sold back to Austria "property rights and interests held or claimed as German assets," as well as equipment and property "held or claimed as war booty."[13] According to Article 22 of the State Treaty, Austria was made to pay $150 million within six years for these rights and for property situated on its own soil. According to the same provision, the Soviet Union further received: a thirty-year "concession to oil fields equivalent to 60 per cent of the extraction of oil in Austria for 1947," together with all property rights to buildings, construction, and equipment belonging to these oil fields; 60 per cent of all exploration areas located in eastern Austria "that are German assets" (which clearly indicates that property rights listed previously were not former German assets); "the right to carry explorations on the exploration areas mentioned in the present paragraph for eight years and to subsequent extraction of oil for a period of twenty-five years"; "oil refineries having a total annual production capacity of 420,000 tons of crude oil"; the assets of the Danube Shipping Company located in Hungary, Romania, and Bulgaria; and "100 per cent of the assets of the Danube Shipping Company located in eastern Austria."

The extortion was made possible by the West's strong desire to restore Austria's freedom and sovereignty, and by the fact that the Austrian Government was prepared to pay heavily for the speedy departure of Soviet troops. It is characteristic of Soviet methods that the compensation to Americans and the citizens of other U.N. member countries resulting from the transfer of Austrian property to Russia had to be provided for separately, "in view of"— as we read in the Austrian *note verbale* to the American Legation in Vienna—"the refusal in principle of the Soviet delegate to permit such an obligation for compensation on the part of Austria to be incorporated in the Treaty."[14]

GREECE

Between 1943 and 1949, the Greek Communist Party three times instigated civil war. Its guerrillas attacked other resistance groups under the German-Italian occupation in 1943–44; after the liberation, the Communists twice attempted to seize power by force. In their second attempt, begun in 1946, they were directly supported by the Communist governments of Albania, Bulgaria, and Yugoslavia. Although there is no absolute proof that the Greek Communists acted on orders from Moscow, one written document—the sensational letter by Markos Vafiades, one-time supreme commander of the Communist guerrillas and head of a "provisional government"—if authentic, provides such proof.* But there is also

* The letter revealed Stalin's and Molotov's role in the Greek Civil War. It was addressed to Nico Zachariades, Secretary General of the Greek Communist Party. The text was first published in the *Giornale d'Italia* of May 12, 1948, then in the London *Greek Bulletin* of June 1, 1948. It also appears as an appendix to F. A. Voigt's *Greek Sedition*. The London Royal Institute of Inter-

ample political evidence pointing in that direction, particularly on the third phase of the civil war (1946–49). A striking example is furnished by Tito's behavior after his quarrel with Stalin in 1948. Barely two weeks after Yugoslavia was expelled from the Cominform, Yugoslav help to Communist guerrillas in Northern Greece ceased abruptly.

After the fall of Crete in June, 1941, the whole country was under German-Italian occupation. Despite a puppet government formed by the occupying powers, Greece remained at war. King George II and the Tsouderos government moved to London. The nation did not accept defeat, and the majority of the people remained strongly opposed to the Hitler-Mussolini Axis. This was the perfect setting for underground resistance, and the Communists, who before the war did not play a prominent part in Greek politics, were the first to grasp the opportunity. In September, 1941, they formed the EAM (National Liberation Front), ostensibly a coalition of several parties, but in fact entirely under Communist control. The following spring, the EAM organized armed guerrilla bands—the ELAS (National People's Liberation Army). Other resistance groups and guerrillas came into existence. The British Middle East Command, trying to coordinate these groups and give them a common tactical purpose, sent some arms. But although ELAS accepted arms, it did not follow Allied advice; its primary interest was the elimination of rival resistance groups. In May, 1943, ELAS attacked the EKKA (National Social Liberation). During the autumn, ELAS eliminated the PAO (Panhellenic Liberation Organization). It finally destroyed or absorbed the EKKA the following spring, but failed in a similar attempt against its strongest rival—the EDES (Greek National Democratic League). In March, 1944, the Communists announced the formation of the Political Committee of National Liberation and provoked serious disturbances in the Greek forces in Egypt. A coalition government was organized by George Papandreou, which the Communists eventually joined in August, 1944. In September, at a meeting in Caserta, the rival ELAS and EDES guerrillas agreed to recognize the authority of the Papandreou government and were placed under the orders of the British Allied Commander General Scobie.

---

national Affairs published it in its *Documents of 1947–48* (pp. 318–20) as the "alleged" Markos letter, dated February 10, 1948. Voigt thought it was undated and probably written in January, 1948. The letter is also referred to in the Royal Institute's *Survey of International Affairs 1947–48* (p. 177n): "There is at present no reason to doubt the truth of the facts recited in this letter."

The landings in Greece began in October, and British troops entered Athens on October 16. As mentioned earlier, Greece became a British responsibility in the deal between Churchill and Stalin. In his war memoirs, Churchill stresses that he had obtained Russian abstention from Greek affairs at the Moscow Conference "at a heavy price."[15] But ELAS did not feel bound by any agreements, whether made in Moscow or Caserta. They had 40,000–50,000 men under arms at the time of liberation (as against EDES' 10,-000–15,000) and occupied a large part of the country on the heels of the departing Germans. The showdown came when the Greek Government decided to disarm all guerrillas. At first the six Communist members of the Papandreou coalition seemed to concur. But at the same time, ELAS concentrated its troops in and around Athens. Suddenly, on November 29, 1944, the six EAM ministers resigned from the government, and the Communist Party called a general strike for December 3; clashes occurred between demonstrators and police. ELAS, defying General Scobie's order to evacuate the Athens and Piraeus area, made a determined effort to seize the capital. Churchill then ordered General Scobie and his 5,000 men to intervene. British reinforcements were brought from Italy. But for several weeks, the situation remained precarious. On Christmas Day, 1944, Churchill made a dramatic flight to Athens. After discussions, King George's return was postponed until a plebiscite could decide on Greece's future regime: Archbishop Damaskinos became Regent; General Plastiras took over from Papandreou as Prime Minister. This phase of the Civil War and the armed British intervention lasted about six weeks. On January 15, 1945, a truce was signed at Varkiza; although a compromise, it was a military and political defeat for the Communists. The horrors of the Civil War had turned the majority of Greeks against them. In the plebiscite of September 1, 1946, 69 per cent of the electorate voted for a monarchy.

Throughout history, civil wars have been attended by atrocities. It has been proved, however, that in Greece the burden of guilt rested heavily on the Communists. On the day the Varkiza truce was signed, Sir Reginald Leeper, the British Ambassador to Greece, in a cable to the Foreign Secretary, said: "Ever since the Germans left (to say nothing of what happened before) the small but well-armed Communist Party has been practicing a reign of terror all over the country. . . . Men, women, children were murdered here in large numbers and thousands of hostages were taken, dragged along the roads and many left to die." The Ambassador further described the fate of a group of 800 hostages, driven northward from Athens, of whom about 200 died within ten days. Sir Reginald wrote: "Greek Communists have not only imitated the Germans in taking hostages. They have, and still are, treating them with the ruthless brutality of the Gestapo."[16]

In the week after the Varkiza agreement was signed, a delegation of the Trade Union Congress (the British labor federation) headed by Lord Citrine arrived in Athens for an on-the-spot investigation. In their official report, the delegation stated that during the German occupation the ELAS had done little fighting against the Germans, but "had fired upon Greek guerrillas when these were actually in combat with the Germans. . . . We were impressed with the universal opinion of [these] British troops that had they not been ordered into action against ELAS there would have been a wholesale massacre in Athens."[17] The trade-union delegation investigated reports of atrocities committed by a terrorist section of the ELAS named OPLA. At Peristeu, a suburb of Athens, the delegation saw bodies being exhumed from trenches. About 250 bodies were laid out for identification, and other trenches were still to be opened: "We questioned relatives on the spot and there seems no reason to doubt that practically all if not the whole of the dead had been the victims of organized murder. All had been executed at close quarters. There was no sign that fighting had taken place and many of the victims had their hands tied behind their back with rope or electric wire."[18] Regent Damaskinos told the delegation that the number of persons murdered was estimated at 10,000. According to a British Government declaration in the House of Commons the following October, the bodies of 8,752 hostages taken by ELAS were found in southern Greece.

A large part of Western opinion strongly disapproved of the British intervention in Greece. This was yet another case of the strange fascination that the extreme left exercised over a large segment of British and American opinion. Churchill bitterly recalls that the vast majority of the American press condemned British policy in Greece. Some British newspapers also censured "what they considered [our] reactionary policy."[19] In the circumstances, the absence of adverse comment in *Pravda* and *Izvestia* impressed Churchill as an indication that Stalin was adhering to their agreement of October, 1944. Yet, one wonders. Even without the Markos letter (of which more later), it seems improbable that the Greek Communist Party would have taken it upon itself to provoke dangerous international complications without Soviet backing. The indirect approach and action by intermediaries have always been favorite Soviet methods. There were many reasons why Moscow preferred not to show its hand in December, 1944. Not until January, 1946, did the Soviet delegate in the Security Council back the protests of the Greek Communists against the presence of British troops. Later that year, Communist guerrillas in the northern border regions of Greece became more aggressive. In the autumn they undertook large-scale action, supported from bases in Yugoslavia, Bulgaria, and Albania. The Civil War was on again.

According to Markos' letter to Zachariades, a "historic message" from Stalin in December, 1944, gave the Greek Communist Party the signal for the attack on Athens. This, he wrote, "had its well-known tragic results leading to Varkiza, results due to the fact that when we appealed for help to Moscow, Comrade Stalin forgot all his promises and spoke of diplomatic commitments." Stalin's behavior as described by Markos seems true to form. The first phase of the Greek Civil War provided Moscow with an important propaganda victory. In view of the Soviet plans in Eastern Europe, it was important that the British be accused of oppressing the Greek people. But after a few weeks of fighting, ELAS began losing ground, and an intervention on their behalf could not possibly make sense to the Soviet Government, particularly when a crucial diplomatic meeting with the West was in the making. The situation changed again after Hitler's defeat. Markos writes that then "Comrade Stalin saw that his hands were free."[20] In December, 1945, Greek Communist leaders met "at the historic congress at Petrich." At this secret meeting, Markos was chosen as military leader of the Greek Democratic Army, with headquarters at Bulkes, Yugoslavia. "On orders from Comrade Stalin to our nothern neighbors, our supplies of arms and amunition began to arrive so that we could march on Athens."[21] In return for the assistance they received, the Greek Communists (still according to Markos) had to agree to a revision of the frontiers of their country in favor of the three northern neighbors.

As a result of a complaint from the Greek Government against Yugoslavia, Bulgaria, and Albania, the Security Council, in December, 1946, appointed a Committee of Investigation. Its findings were unfavorable to the Communists, but Soviet opposition prevented the Council from taking practical steps. In October, 1947, the matter passed to the Assembly, which established the United Nations Special Committee for the Balkans, made up of representatives of the eleven members of the Security Council. But the Soviet and Polish governments refused to participate, while Yugoslavia, Bulgaria, and Albania would not allow the Committee to work inside their borders. The Committee's final report confirmed that the three Communist governments gave the Greek guerrillas sanctuary on their territory and supplied them with arms and equipment, thus threatening the independence and integrity of Greece. The report also established that the guerrillas were abducting large numbers of young girls and children.*[22]

At Christmas, 1947, the Communists announced the formation of a "provisional government." In his letter to Zachariades, General Markos wrote that after postponing Soviet "entry into the struggle," Molotov (then Soviet Foreign Minister) told the Greek Communists in December, 1947: "Establish an official government and announce to the Greek people your determination to continue the struggle for victory and we shall immediately recognize you as the official government of the country." While it was naïve to expect that Russia would join the struggle, a broken promise of official recognition was by no means unusual in the history of Soviet relations with foreign Communists. It was certainly more convenient for Russia to embarrass the Greek and American governments by indirect methods. After the proclamation of the Truman Doctrine, American assistance to Greece was quick and on the whole efficient. By the end of September, Greece had already received aid equivalent to $222 million, of which $159 million were allotted for military purposes. During 1948, the government troops took the offensive. In February, 1949, Markos was replaced as Commander of the Democratic Army. Energetic American assistance to Greece, dissension in the Cominform and among Greek Communists, and the withdrawal of Yugoslav support contributed to the gradual fading away of Communist guerrillas. In May, 1949, a new Greek

* The abduction of children began in the spring of 1948 and was continued in areas invaded by the Democratic Army until the end of the Civil War in the autumn of 1949. By that time, 25,000–30,000 children between the ages of three and fourteen had been seized and sent north. Greek protests in the United Nations led the General Assembly to adopt a resolution on November 27, 1948, recommending the return of the children by the Communist governments and asking the International Committee of the Red Cross to help in their repatriation. But no practical results were achieved. The Polish Government denied harboring any of the children, and the other satellite governments held that the children were refugees from Greek oppression. The only large group known to have come back are the 540 children returned by Yugoslavia in 1952.

Communist "government" tried a political salvage operation by proposing negotiations with Athens. The move was synchronized with a Soviet plan calling for a general amnesty in Greece and free elections supervised by Russia, the United States, and Britain. The three powers were also to control the northern border regions of Greece. The Soviet Union first proposed the plan to the British and American governments, then in the General Assembly. Such arrangements three years earlier might have saved Greece from civil war. In 1949, after the many Communist outrages, and in view of their certain defeat, these proposals were no longer acceptable.

TURKEY

The secret agreements of 1915 providing for Russian annexation of Constantinople and the Black Sea Straits were repudiated by the Provisional Government of Prince Lvov in May, 1917. Lenin actively supported this policy both before and after the Bolshevik Revolution, and the Soviet Government also disclaimed any annexationist aims with regard to Turkey. A Soviet-Kemalist collaboration soon developed in Transcaucasia. In the period between the wars, these good relations found expression in a series of treaties and agreements. Article 5 of the Soviet-Turkish Treaty of Friendship and Cooperation of March 16, 1921, explicitly barred the conclusion by the signatory powers of any agreement that might "diminish the full sovereignty of Turkey, or the security of her capital city of Constantinople."[23]

Other Soviet-Turkish agreements of that period include the Treaty of Friendship with the Soviet Republics of Azerbaidzhan, Armenia, and Georgia, signed at Kars on October 13, 1921; the Agreement of Neutrality, Nonaggression, and Friendship of December 17, 1925; the Maritime Protocol of March 3, 1931; the Convention of Definition of Aggression of July 3, 1933.

Molotov's secret negotiations with Hitler and Ribbentrop clearly demonstrate that Turkey was included in the Soviet "natural sphere of influence." All the Soviet-Turkish agreements were thus to be broken with the assistance of Nazi Germany. But the deal did not come off, and Turkey was saved from the ordeal by the falling apart of the Soviet-Nazi partnership.

But as events proved, Soviet territorial designs on Turkey were only temporarily postponed. They were brought up again, substantially in the same shape, at the end of World War II, as soon as the Soviet Government felt that its military and diplomatic position was sufficiently strong.

On March 19, 1945, Moscow denounced the December 17, 1925, treaty. The Russian terms for the conclusion of a new treaty were communicated to the Turkish Government on June 25, 1945, and included in the Soviet note to Turkey of August 7, 1946. Russia demanded that a new regime for the Straits be established with the sole participation of the Black Sea powers, to the exclusion of all other states, and that Turkey and the Soviet Union jointly organize the defense of the Straits.[24]

In the diplomatic exchanges during the latter part of 1946, Turkey successfully resisted all attempts to limit its sovereignty, or to cede or lease any part of its national territory to Russia. In consequence, no Soviet military base could be established in the vicinity of the Straits. Because opinion had changed considerably since Yalta and Tehran, Turkey, unlike Poland, was backed by the United States and Great Britain.

Turkey's foreign policy of close collaboration with the Western powers continued to be distasteful to Soviet Russia. Moscow angrily protested against Turkey's accession to the North Atlantic Treaty Organization (1951). However, after Stalin's death, a new zigzag was attempted. On May 30, 1953, the Soviet Union told the Turkish Government in a note that it "has no territorial claims on Turkey whatsoever," and declared itself contented with the existing regime of the Straits.[25] This position was outwardly maintained despite the active Turkish role in bringing about the Middle East Treaty Organization.

An explanation of Moscow's relatively conciliatory attitude may be sought in the Soviet drive for penetration of the Middle East by way of the Arab states. The establishment of Soviet influence by means of friendly governments or bases in this region would in effect outflank Turkey and might bring about the renewal of Russian territorial claims.

On April 3, 1956, *Pravda* suggested a Soviet-Turkish treaty of nonaggression and neutrality to replace a similar treaty unilaterally abrogated by Moscow in 1945. A new clash occurred in September, 1957, when Soviet Premier Bulganin, in a letter to Prime Minister Menderes, accused Turkey of playing a role in plans to unleash military action against Syria. Bulganin wrote that the Soviet Union was "profoundly alarmed" at reports of Turkish troop movements on the Syrian border.[26] In October, Marshal Rokossovsky was appointed commander of the Transcaucasian military district. After

Soviet troop movements on the Turkish frontier, Secretary Dulles warned the U.S.S.R. that an attack on Turkey "would not mean a purely defensive operation by the United States, with the Soviet Union a privileged sanctuary from which to attack Turkey."[27] The crisis abated in November, after a bitter debate in the Assembly of the United Nations. The controversy about Syria seemed to have been artificially inflated by Russia as part of its campaign to force a summit meeting on the Middle East.

But a climate of mutual distrust continued. In a speech on October 31, 1959, Khrushchev charged that as a result of Turkey's participation in NATO and CENTO, its territory "has been converted into a military establishment where foreign rockets will be maintained."[28] At the time of the U-2 incident, Turkey, as well as Pakistan and Norway, received a strongly worded Soviet note. "The Soviet Union," the note stated, had the means "to render harmless . . . military bases used for aggressive actions" against it.[29]

IRAN

Lenin's government emphatically condemned the Czarist policy of annexations and interference followed with regard to Persia since the time of Catherine II. In notes to the Persian Government dated January 14, 1918, and June 26, 1919, the Soviets renounced all Russian concessions and privileges in Iran, annulled the Persian debts to Russia, and declared the Anglo-Russian treaty of partition of 1907 null and void. Article 2 of the Soviet-Persian treaty of February 26, 1921, branded as "criminal" the policy of the Russian Czarist government and stated: "The Government of the R.S.F.S.R. unconditionally rejects that criminal policy not only as violating the sovereignty of the Asian states but also as leading to organized brutal violence of European robbers on the living bodies of the peoples of the East."[30]

These Soviet assurances, like so many others, also proved meaningless. Although Soviet troops left Persian soil in 1918, they reappeared in May, 1920, in pursuit of Denikin's forces. Bolshevik detachments occupied Gilan province and used the pretext of a local rebellion in order to proclaim a Persian Soviet Socialist Republic. Protected by Russian troops, this new Soviet "government" maintained itself in Gilan until autumn 1921. In the summer of the same year, Persia's fate seemed to hang in the balance. The last British detachments withdrew in May. New Soviet forces were coming in, and the Gilan government made menacing gestures against Tehran. Yet, in September, 1921, the Russian troops suddenly departed, leaving their Gilan stooges without protection. Local support was insignificant, and the rule of the central Iranian Government was easily re-established as soon as the Soviet occupation ended.

The joint wartime action with Britain in 1941 provided Soviet Russia with a new opportunity for resorting to direct methods. The entrance of British and Soviet troops into Persia was explained by the necessities of war, dangerous German activities, and requirements of Allied transport to Russia. Iran officially became one of the Allied nations by the Tripartite Treaty with Great Britain and Soviet Russia (January 29, 1942). Article 1 confirmed previous British and Soviet undertakings "to respect the territorial integrity, sovereignty, and political independence of Iran." Article 5 stated: "The forces of the Allied Powers shall be withdrawn from Iranian territory not later than six months after all hostilities between the Allied Powers and Germany and her associates have been suspended by the conclusion of an armistice or armistices, or on conclusion of peace between them, whichever date is earlier."[31]

On September 9, 1943, Iran declared war on Germany. But Iranian compliance with Allied demands did not prevent Russia from carrying out a new attempt at forcible sovietization within its zone of occupation. After several years of political indoctrination, faked elections were staged in Persian Azerbaidzhan in autumn 1945. As a result, the Autonomous Republic of Azerbaidzhan was proclaimed at Tabriz on December 12, 1945. A police state on the Soviet model was installed; its government was headed by a known member of the Comintern, J. Pishevari. Simultaneously, a Kurdish People's Republic was proclaimed in the border regions of Persian Azerbaidzhan and Iraq at Mahabad.

The two separatist "governments" concluded a treaty of alliance (April 23, 1946). These events were made possible by the protection of Soviet occupation authorities and troops that indiscriminately backed the Tudeh (Communist) Party and any existing separatist elements and prevented regular Iranian troops from reaching the northern provinces.

In January, 1946, Iran appealed to the Security Council. Russia had demanded that Iran recognize Azerbaidzhani "autonomy" and refused to abide by the treaty of January 29, 1942, providing for the withdrawal of Allied troops on March 2, 1946. The crisis came to a head in the same month, when, the British troops having departed and new Soviet forces having entered Iran, the Tudeh Party staged violent street demonstrations in Tehran. Iran once more appealed to the Security Council and received lukewarm support. Suddenly, the Russians rather surprisingly consented to evacuate all Iranian territory "within one and a half months from Sunday, March 24, 1946."[32]

Thus, Russia once again abandoned the Persian Communists to their own fate. The "autonomous" Azerbaidzhani government outlived the departure of Soviet troops only by a few months. Pishevari sought refuge in Russia. The Kurdish People's Republic also collapsed. On October 22, 1947, the Iranian Parliament refused to ratify an oil agreement with Soviet Russia.

It is still not entirely clear why twice, in 1921 and 1946, Soviet Russia evacuated its troops from occupied Persian provinces in which the formation of Soviet regimes was already well under way. In both cases Western reaction was not sufficiently strong to force a Russian withdrawal. Although the same explanation may not be valid over a span of twenty-five years, there are similarities and parallels in the two situations.

In 1921, the Bolshevik drive for the "liberation of the dependent countries" of the East was still in its infancy. Moscow may therefore have felt that a new case of outright annexation so soon after the crushing of the three Transcaucasian republics would have a damaging effect on the execution of more ambitious plans in Asia.

The reasons of the Soviet retreat from Iran after World War II are also rather obscure. In the spring and summer of 1946, British policy was ostensibly inclined to compromise with Russian demands. The American attitude, although gradually stiffening, had not yet reached the stage of proclaimed opposition to Communist expansion initiated a year later by the Truman Doctrine. The Iranian Government of 1946 was no better equipped to undertake its own defense that that of 1921. The publicity given to the Soviet encroachments by the debate in the Security Council was unwelcome and unpleasant, but not in itself sufficient to make Russia desist from its intention of establishing a "friendly government" in Azerbaidzhan, and possibly in Tehran.

Yet, in December, 1946, Russia did not lift a finger in defense of the Soviet regime in Azerbaidzhan, and the following year meekly accepted Iran's repudiation of a much-desired oil agreement. Barring the existence of some unpublished Soviet-American diplomatic exchanges, these facts seem to indicate a change of Russian plans on a wider political arena, which may have been hampered by the completion of a difficult and politically embarrassing operation in Iran.*

The withdrawal of Russian troops did not immediately open a period of stabilization. Mutual accusations continued, and in 1949, both countries closed their consular offices. But in 1950, a trade agreement was signed and the Soviet Government agreed to return 11 tons of Iranian gold deposited with it in 1943. This deposit was not returned until 1954, after several years of insistent Iranian demands (Soviet-Iranian Agreement on War Debts and Frontier Delimitation, December 2, 1954).

New difficulties arose when Iran joined the Baghdad Pact (October, 1955). The Soviet Government repeatedly protested in Tehran, implying that they disposed of a dangerous political weapon, which could be used against Iran should the international situation allow it.[33] Article 6 of the Soviet-Persian Treaty of February 1921 conceded to Russia the right "to advance its troops into Persia" should any third party try to use Persian territory as a base against Russia. In spite of this threat, Iran flatly rejected all Soviet protests. These seem to have been the correct tactics, since the disagreement over the Baghdad Pact did not prevent the Soviet Government from inviting the Shah and the Empress of Iran to a state visit in Russia (June 25–July 12, 1956). Speaking at an official banquet, Voroshilov assured the Iranian monarch that Soviet Russia had no territorial aspirations. In January, 1959, Russia made a serious effort to detach Iran from its allies. A note warned Tehran not to sign the bilateral agreement then being discussed with the United States. At the same time, Moscow offered to join in efforts to improve Soviet-Iranian relations. A Soviet mission came to Tehran to negotiate a treaty of nonaggression and technical assistance. These negotiations broke off on February 10, 1959. The head of the Soviet delegation, Deputy Foreign Minister V. S. Semyonov, accused the Iranian Government of rejecting the hand of friendship held out by the Soviet Union and of a two-faced policy, which showed that "the government of the Shah is now openly following in the wake of the aggressive American policy . . . and has now openly taken to the road of collaboration with foreign aggressive forces.[34]

On March 2, the Iranian Government stated that it had denounced Articles 5 and 6 of the Soviet-Persian Treaty of February

---

* *The New York Times* of April 25, 1960, published a statement by ex-President Harry S. Truman in which he said that a virtual ultimatum was presented to Stalin in 1946 to the effect that should Soviet troops fail to withdraw from Iran, the U.S. fleet would move up the Persian Gulf.

26, 1921, which gave Soviet troops the right to enter Iranian territory under certain conditions. On March 5, 1959, Iran signed a defense treaty with the United States that includes a promise of American military assistance in case of aggression.

Soviet-Iranian relations improved somewhat in 1960. In July, Khrushchev sent the Shah a personal message suggesting the restoration of neighborly relations. But the following spring, in an interview with Walter Lippmann, Khrushchev spoke of overthrowing Iran's regime. Lippmann wrote: "He will do all he can by propaganda and indirect intervention to bring down the Shah."[35] Virulent Communist radio agitation from Moscow, Tashkent, Baku, Stalinabad, Bucharest, and Peking was conducted in Persian, Azerbaidzhani, Arabic, and in Turcoman idioms. In February, 1962, it was reported that broadcasts from Moscow urged Iranian students to rebel and assassinate the Shah, overthrow the government, and murder its members. After the January, 1962, riots in Tehran, the Iranian Prime Minister officially protested to the Soviet Ambassador against the presence of Soviet Embassy cars among the demonstrators.

THE EASTERN ARAB STATES

A look at the map will show that the Soviet domination of Caucasia is like a hand stretching southward. But to reach the shores of the Mediterranean and the Persian Gulf, the Soviet Union would have to break through the Turkish barrier and overpower Iran, something neither Czarist nor Communist Russia has been able to accomplish. The latest drive in the area south of Batum and Baku began around 1954–55. Directed primarily at the Middle Eastern Arab states, it aims at either bypassing or leapfrogging the traditional Turkish and Iranian obstacles.

Between 1947 and 1954, the Soviet Government displayed little interest in Middle Eastern affairs. The small Communist parties in the Arab countries were given only minor assistance by Moscow, whose main postwar objective was expansion in Europe and the Far East. When Soviet Russia reappeared on the Middle Eastern scene, its methods were more sophisticated and more likely to succeed than any previous Russian or Soviet efforts in that area. The major themes were Arab nationalism and economic assistance.

The task seemed easy enough. The area stretching from Iraq to the Sudan is beset by social, political, and economic problems. Its population is poverty-stricken, intensely nationalistic, and, in varying degree, resentful of the West. Despite their Pan-Arab ideals, the governments in the region are divided by political and economic divergences, not to speak of dynastic, tribal, and personal ambitions. The timing of the Soviet offensive could not have been better; the last British troops were due to leave the Suez Canal zone in June, 1956. Short of military intervention, the Western powers could no longer enforce a regional balance of power and the limited embargo on arms proclaimed on May 25, 1950. Against this background, Soviet policy in the Arab countries could play on a number of unresolved issues: oil royalties, the Suez Canal, the state of latent war with Israel, and the claims of the Kurdish tribes.

The new Soviet drive had been in preparation for some time before the bombshell of the Egyptian-Czechoslovak arms deal exploded September 27, 1955. Within twelve months after the Czechoslovak agreement, a flow of arms from behind the Iron Curtain reached Egypt, Syria, and Yemen. In November, 1956, the value of the arms imports to Egypt and Syria was estimated at nearly $500 million.[36] The Israeli and Franco-British military action against Egypt the following year was in no small degree attributable to Egypt's arms build-up. But it is probable that the Russians expected to provoke an Arab attack on Israel. However, it did not matter to them who started the hostilities. The Suez war gave the Soviet Government a unique opportunity to display its friendship for the Arabs by threatening to defend Egypt by force of arms. It also diverted attention from their suppression of the Hungarian insurrection. In a note to the British Prime Minister, Bulganin wrote on November 5, 1956 (twenty-four hours after Soviet tanks went into action in Budapest): "If rocket weapons had been used against Britain and France, they would probably have called it a barbarous action. . . . We are fully determined to crush the aggressors and restore peace in the East through the use of force."[37] A similar letter was received by the French Prime Minister. On November 10, Tass issued a statement announcing that Soviet volunteers would go to Egypt should England, France, and Israel refuse to withdraw their troops. According to official Egyptian sources, 50,000 Soviet citizens had volunteered, and 250,000 men had been offered by Communist China. But there was no evidence of Soviet military preparations, and it is generally assumed that despite its menacing tone, Soviet Russia would not have acted singly.

The Suez war enhanced Soviet prestige in the Arab countries. The resulting atmosphere favored Russian feelers to establish diplomatic relations, engage in trade, and give economic and technical assistance. Egypt had been the main target since 1954, when the first Soviet offers were made to assist in the gigantic Aswan Dam project. Soviet diplomacy, supported by the satellite governments, moved with skill and speed. In July, 1955, Czechoslovakia concluded a most-favored-nation trade agreement with Nasser. On September 6, Radio Cairo reported the signing of an agreement with the Soviet Union for the exchange of Russian crude oil and Egyptian rice. Then came the famous "arms deal" with Czechoslovakia, announced on September 27. There can be little doubt that this was part of a broader understanding with the Russians, in preparation since spring. A year later, President Nasser said that he was able to buy arms from Russia: "I say Russia, not Czechoslovakia."[38] On October 14, 1955, Egypt concluded a trade agreement with Communist China. In February, 1956, it was agreed to establish a nuclear laboratory in Egypt with Soviet assistance. In March, the British Foreign Office confirmed press reports that Czechoslovak instructors were training Egyptian troops;[39] according to the same sources, Egyptian military personnel were training at Soviet bases in Poland. When Soviet Foreign Minister Shepilov visited Cairo in June, 1956, it was reported that the Soviet Union had offered to shoulder the whole cost of the Aswan Dam construction—$1.2 billion.

The economic results of these efforts were quite spectacular. From 1954 to 1958, Soviet trade with the Middle East increased threefold. Egyptian and Syrian (from 1958 to 1961, the United Arab Republic) imports from the Soviet Union rose from 1.4 per cent in 1954, to 12.3 per cent in the first half of 1959. The corresponding figures for export to the Soviet Union increased from 1.3 per cent to 24.5 per cent. Simultaneously, Egyptian and Syrian trade with other East European countries also rose considerably: imports from 4.2 per cent in 1954 to 13.6 per cent in the first half of 1959; exports for the same period rose from 9.6 per cent to 25 per cent.[40] The most important feature of Egyptian–Communist-bloc trade was the exchange of cotton and rice for arms, crude oil, and industrial equipment.

Not all Middle Eastern Arab countries responded to Soviet blandishments. Saudi Arabia, Jordan, Lebanon, Sudan, and Libya remained on the fringe of the drive, or chose to reject various Soviet offers. Iraq followed the trend only after the overthrow of the monarchy in 1958. Nevertheless, by the first half of 1959, Communist-bloc assistance—mostly in credits—to the United Arab Republic, Iraq, and Yemen amounted to nearly $1.3 billion. The largest recipient was Egypt, with $658 million, of which $315 million was in military assistance.[41]

An important corollary of increased economic and trade relations was the presence of technicians and specialists from the Soviet Union and other Communist-ruled countries. It was estimated that 2,200 were in the United Arab Republic, Yemen, and Iraq in the first half of 1959.

The apogee of Soviet political and economic penetration in the Eastern Arab countries was reached sometime in the spring of 1958. In April, President Nasser paid an official visit to the Soviet Union. The mutual feelings were recorded in a joint communiqué that stressed "profound satisfaction with the development of close and steadily expanding relations."

This was simultaneously the climax of the idyllic relationship and the beginning of its end. It soon became apparent that the concordance of Soviet and Egyptian political interests was superficial. Their opposition to Western influence in the Middle East, to the Eisenhower Doctrine (which Tass called a clear-cut program of colonial plunder)[42] and to the Baghdad Pact was prompted by entirely different motives. Moscow and Cairo had opposite reasons to be elated over the Iraqi *coup d'état* of July, 1958; their shared anger at the Anglo-American military assistance extended to the governments of Jordan and Lebanon could not for long obscure the fact that a three-cornered struggle was developing in the Arab countries: for Communist subversion; for Egyptian domination; and for the independence of the smaller states, backed by the West. The formation of a nationalistic republican regime in Iraq brought the situation into the open; although the new government at first paid lip service to Nasser's friendship, it soon revealed ambitions of its own and refused to acknowledge Egyptian leadership. It was not lost on Nasser that despite all the thunder of Soviet propaganda, American marines and British troops, sent in response to appeals of the Beirut and Amman governments, arrived quickly and unhampered. Nor did he fail to see that in terms of global strategy, the West was also interested in upholding Egypt's independence, whereas in Iraq after the *coup d'état* the Communists seemed to have gained the run of the place and were on their way to taking over the government. For about a year following the downfall of the monarchy, Iraq became the scene of a struggle between pro-Nasser and pro-Communist or openly Communist forces that culminated in a military revolt in Mossul in March, 1959, and riots in Kirkuk in July. While the Mossul affair seemed to be Egyptian- or

Syrian-inspired, Iraqi Prime Minister Abdel Karim al-Kassim frankly accused the Communist Party of being responsible for the Kirkuk riots, which cost seventy-nine lives and many injured. At a press conference on July 29, Kassim disclosed that a plot had been uncovered to provoke similar disturbances in other Iraqi towns and to assassinate a number of prominent citizens. Indeed the Kirkuk revolt seems to have been the nearest thing to an attempted Communist *coup d'état* in the Middle East. It is impossible to say whether the Communist plan to overthrow the government through carefully planned street riots was a local reaction to Kassim's measures or whether Moscow had decided that Iraq was ripe for a "people's democracy." At any rate, the struggle in Iraq affected Nasser's attitude toward Communism, and Khrushchev reacted to Nasser's reversal. In January, 1959, about 100 Egyptian and Syrian Communists were arrested. In March, 1959, Nasser accused the Arab Communists of working for foreign masters and of having concluded a truce with Britain in order to fight Arab nationalism.

The complexity of the situation was clearly revealed by Iraq's withdrawal from the Baghdad Pact in March, 1959—a welcome move from Nasser's viewpoint. That same month, Iraq signed an agreement on economic and technical assistance in Moscow, and in June it renounced American military aid. Until the Kirkuk riots on July 14, both Nasser and Khrushchev could believe that Iraq was moving into the Communist camp, and possibly Khrushchev had some additional information on what would happen should Kassim resist. Khrushchev showed himself particularly sensitive to Nasser's accusations against Syrian and Iraqi Communists. The Soviet Premier also criticized Nasser's attitude toward Iraq and rebuked Nasser for having changed his opinion of the Iraqi revolution since the time when they had "rejoiced together" at the downfall of the monarchy. Indeed, times had changed since July, 1958, when, on learning of the American and British landings in Lebanon, Nasser flew to Moscow for emergency talks. Now Khrushchev was "grieved" by Nasser's attacks on Communism. Nasser retorted by accusing Khrushchev of meddling in Arab affairs. On March 22, he shot a poisoned arrow when he admitted for the first time that Russia had not saved Egypt in the Suez War, since the Soviet offer of help came after the campaign was over.[43]

The round was won by Nasser, for more was involved than propaganda: The Soviet Government did not wish to give up the positions gained in the U.A.R., even if it meant a loss of face. So the

economic assistance continued. But after the Kirkuk riots, both the
Cairo and the Baghdad governments, while remaining at logger-
heads, slowly began to mend their relations with the West. Nasser
had long insisted on "positive neutralism" and tried to find a niche
for himself in alignment with Tito and Nehru. But he sided with
the Soviet Union whenever it suited his aspirations with regard to
the "three circles" (leadership of the Arab world, Islam, and Black
Africa). Premier Kassim also professed neutralism of the "positive"
kind. Syria continued to adhere to this brand of neutralism after its
secession from the U.A.R. in October, 1961. Whatever positive
neutralism may mean, the trade agreements and technical assistance
afforded the Communist governments an active presence in Egypt,
Syria, Iraq, and Yemen. Soviet technicians, instructors, and specialists arrived in large numbers. A Soviet staff of 380 worked at the
construction of the Aswan Dam, Russia being the only country to
assist Egypt in the project by a loan said to amount to $400 million.
It was estimated that in 1961, Egypt purchased about $61 million
worth of military equipment in the Soviet Union and contracted
for considerable quantities of Communist-made arms for the following years.[44] As a result of the 1957 agreements, the Syrian army
was to a large extent Soviet-equipped. After seceding from the
U.A.R., the new Syrian regime lost no time in applying for Soviet
arms on its own; a mission traveled to Moscow in February, 1962.
Iraq continued to purchase arms behind the Iron Curtain and to
accept technical assistance from Communist governments. Soviet
engineers built the first modern harbor of Yemen at Hodeidah on
the Red Sea, while the Chinese were responsible for the construction of a 300-mile highway.

It is true that the four Arab countries discussed here do check or
suppress the visible manifestations of local Communism and accept
Western economic assistance more or less graciously. One can say
that Soviet Russia did not achieve the monopolistic situation in the
Eastern Arab states it had hoped for after the Czechoslovak arms
deal of 1955. Still, the doors remain open to Soviet and other foreign Communist personnel and valuable positions, which could be
of incalculable value at a time of crisis, are maintained. Furthermore, the Soviet Government holds two trump cards: the Israeli
and Kurdish problems.

Since the beginning of its new drive in the Middle East, the
Soviet Union has resolutely sided with the Arabs against Israel, thus
capitalizing on the most emotional of all Arab issues. Despite the

prominent role that many Jews played in the Bolshevik Revolution, Khrushchev's Russia reverted to the anti-Semitic Czarist tradition. Moscow considers Zionism a natural enemy because of its interest in the 2–3 million Soviet Jews. A standard accusation in the Soviet press is that Zionism has organic and permanent ties with "imperialism," with the "aggressive policies" pursued by the United States in the Near and Middle East.[45] The Israeli Government is also charged with being NATO's Trojan horse in Africa. This stand gives Soviet Russia a powerful propaganda lever among the Arabs; it easily could be transformed into a dangerous political weapon.

Considerable potentialities to stir up trouble are also inherent in the Kurdish problem. About 100,000 Kurds live in Soviet Azerbaidzhan, a sufficiently large group to furnish a number of Communist agents. Barely 150 miles separate the Soviet frontier from the central areas of Kurdistan. After the collapse of the short-lived Kurdish People's Republic, Soviet action for a number of years was limited to propaganda, political agitation, and occasional smuggling of arms. The Kurdish problem was taken up more seriously again in 1955, when it was reported that Russia backed Kurdish claims in confidential negotiations with Egypt and Syria.[46] In October, 1958, much publicity was given the return to Iran of Mullah Mustafa Barzani, who had spent eleven years behind the Iron Curtain. The most colorful figure among Kurdish nationalists, he was a prominent member of the Mahabad "government" and is renowned for his ability as a military leader. Whether Mullah Barzani belongs to the category of Asian nationalists who believe that they can use the Russians and then outsmart them is not relevant. His name has been linked with the Soviet Union for nearly twenty years. On his return to Iraq, he was accompanied by Khalid Bakhdash, another prominent Kurd and one of the chief Communist leaders in the Levant. In March, 1959, the Barzani tribe helped Kassim to suppress the pro-Nasser Mossul revolt. In July of the same year, Kurdish-Iraqi troops took part, or were used by the Communists, in the Kirkuk riots. Two years later, in September, 1961, regular Iraqui troops intervened in a confused intertribal struggle in the mountains—against the Barzani, it seems. Fighting subsided during the winter, but in March, 1962, a widespread uprising developed, headed by Mullah Mustafa Barzani. Despite air bombardments and the deployment of relatively large regular forces, the Kurds were reported in April to be in control of the northern tip of Iraq, from Mossul to the Turkish and Iranian borders, long considered a sort of Kurdish Piedmont. In a manifesto that reached Baghdad late in April, Mullah Barzani called for an "autonomous Kurdistan within the Iraqi Republic" and the deposition of the Kassim regime.

In December, the Kurdish guerrillas took the name Revolutionary Army of Kurdistan. After the overthrow of the Kassim government in February, 1963, the new Baas (right-wing Socialist) regime began negotiations with the Kurdish leaders, promising them concessions. Simultaneously, the Baghdad government moved strongly against the Iraqi Communists. The talks with the Kurds collapsed in June, and the Iraqi Army resumed its offensive against the Kurdish-held area. The Soviet position, reflected in the Russian and satellite press, was one of strong support of the Kurds. Moscow evidently was eager to facilitate a Kurdish-Communist collaboration in Iraq. On June 20, 1963, *Pravda* explained that persecution of Communists was only "a first step of the reactionaries in their offensive against all democratic and progressive organizations," and a prelude to "the declaration of war against the Kurds." In August, Tass spoke of the arrival of a special Kurdish envoy in Moscow.

KOREA

The future of Korea formed one of the subjects of the Cairo declaration (December 1, 1943). In it the United States, Great Britain, and China stated that "in due course Korea shall become free and independent." This assurance was confirmed in Paragraph 8 of the Proclamation to the Japanese people issued at Potsdam on July 26, 1945, on behalf of the United States, Great Britain, and China. The Soviet Government, in turn, "associated itself with the Allied declaration of July 26,"[47] when declaring war on Japan on August 8, 1945. It was also at Potsdam that the 38th parallel was indicated as separating the areas of military operations between the American and Russian forces in Korea, as well as for the purpose of accepting the surrender of the Japanese armies in that theater of war.

Soviet troops entered North Korea on August 12, 1945. Under their aegis, "people's committees" composed mostly of Communists took over the administration in the Soviet zone of occupation, which in February, 1946, was made a separate puppet Communist state under the name of Korean People's Democratic Republic.

The most distinctive feature of Soviet activity was the training of a North Korean army, which by 1948 was said to have numbered more than 200,000 men. Once this force was well in hand and equipped with modern weapons, the Soviet Union proposed that both Russian and American troops be withdrawn from Korea. In these circumstances, the Soviet-American negotiations for the creation of a unified government of Korea had to be abortive. They were discontinued in October, 1947, after nearly two years of futile haggling. The Russians strenuously opposed the idea of free elections, not only in their own zone of occupation but also in South Korea, to the point of sabotage, the fomenting of strikes and disorders, and exhortations to boycott the vote.

In spite of the Soviet and Communist opposition, the elections in South Korea held on May 10, 1948, proved a complete success for the anti-Communist parties. It is reasonable to assume that these developments marked the turning point of Soviet policy on South Korea, which from now on could be incorporated into the Communist system only through armed conquest.

The invasion of South Korea began on June 25, 1950. After a two-hour artillery barrage, North Korean forces made a concentrated attack by land, air, and sea. According to a Tass report of June 27, quoting a communiqué of the North Korean command, the Communist troops claimed a 15-kilometer advance south of the 38th parallel on the first day of the invasion, and one of 25 kilometers by the morning of June 26. Seoul, the capital of South Korea, was captured the same day. On the morning of June 26, the Prime Minister of North Korea appealed to his troops to "liberate" the South.[48] Despite the tension obtaining between the two parts of the country for some time before the aggression, South Korean forces, unprepared and badly equipped, were taken by surprise. These incontrovertible facts prove beyond doubt the absurdity of Communist charges that South Korea was the aggressor.

The Soviet Union consistently approved of the North Korean action, refused to support the majority of the U.N. members in demanding an early cease-fire, and called the U.N.-sponsored assistance to South Korea illegal. At a later stage, Soviet Russia approved of the Chinese armed intervention in the Korean War and upheld the North Korean and Chinese allegations that they had been attacked by U.S. forces. The Soviet press hailed the invasion of South Korea from the first days. On June 27, 1950, *Pravda* and *Izvestia* published Tass communiqués speaking of "inhabitants of liberated regions" of South Korea, calling the South Korean forces "enemy forces," and generally giving the Communist invasion the aura of a legal restitution.

In its diplomatic exchanges with the U.N. and the Western powers, the Soviet Union adopted a similar attitude. In reply to a request by the U.S. Embassy in Moscow dated June 27, 1950, that it disapprove of the North Korean invasion and use its influence with the Pyongyang authorities with regard to the resolutions of the Security Council, the Soviet Government "charged both the Republic of Korea and the United States with aggression and declared the Council's action illegal."[49] Similarly, in reply to the Secretary General of the United Nations the Soviet Government stated: "It is perfectly evident that this resolution by the Security Council on the Korean question has no legal force."[50]

The resolutions of the Security Council of June 25, June 27, and July 7, calling for the cessation of hostilities, the withdrawal of North Korean forces to the 38th parallel, and recommending armed assistance to the Republic of Korea under a unified command held by the United States could be adopted only in the absence of the Soviet delegate. He had abstained from taking part in the proceedings of the Council since January, 1950, ostensibly in protest against the refusal to admit Communist China.* This was a major tactical blunder of Russian diplomacy, and the Soviet delegate promptly reoccupied his seat in the Council on August 1, 1950, where he soon demonstrated his sympathy to Communist China and North Korea. Soviet support was further displayed by "the presence of a Russian military mission of 3,500 persons and provision of equipment and advice for the North Korean armed forces."[51] Evidence of Russian and Chinese Communist assistance to the North Korean armies in munitions and trained manpower was also submitted to the Security Council by the Unified Command of the United Nations on September 18, 1950.[52]

After the Chinese intervention in the Korean war (November, 1950), the Soviet delegates to the Assembly and the Security Council defended the Chinese position and renewed the charges of aggression against the United States. On February 1, 1951, the Communist Government of the People's Republic of China was condemned as an aggressor by the Assembly of the United Nations.[53]

* It is often assumed that the Communists were encouraged in their plans to attack South Korea by Secretary of State Acheson's statement of January 12, 1950, placing the Republic of Korea outside the U.S. "defensive perimeter." On the other hand, it seems very likely that the general idea of the aggression was conceived earlier. That the absence of the Soviet delegate after mid-January was also part of the Communist plan with regard to Korea is a very plausible theory, though not yet proved by documentary evidence.

When a third Chinese offensive collapsed in May, 1951, and U.N. troops again entered North Korea, it was Malik, the Soviet delegate to the United Nations, who called for a cease-fire. It was signed two years later, on July 27, 1953.

The aims of the Communist aggression in Korea were not attained. The demarcation line dividing the two parts of the country is nearly the same as before the war. Chinese and Korean Communist armies suffered 2 million casualties. Three million North Koreans "died from war ravages and the inhuman neglects which their rules have imposed."[54] Evidently no written documents are available to prove the Soviet Russian responsibility for the North Korean aggression. But circumstantial evidence of political action and open material support is overwhelming. It is, therefore, safe to conclude that Moscow condoned, and possibly ordered, both the North Korean invasion and the Communist Chinese intervention in the Korean war.

16. SUMMIT DIPLOMACY

A new period of active international collaboration, of peaceful coexistence with the capitalist world, was in the offing during the last year of Stalin's life. In the last essay Stalin signed, he upheld Lenin's theory that war was inevitable as long as capitalism existed, but admitted the possibility of "the temporary preservation of a particular peace."[1] At the Nineteenth Party Congress, in October, 1952, Malenkov spoke of peaceful competition between Communism and capitalism. In the spring of 1953, Russia suddenly reversed its attitude with regard to Turkey, and rescinded its territorial claims. Later the same year, and in the first half of 1954, the Soviet Union and the satellite governments rejoined the International Labour Organisation and Unesco, which they had left a year earlier in protest against the admission of Spain. Many signs indicate that at the beginning of 1955, Stalin's heirs in the Kremlin and their associates in Peking felt ready to launch a new diplomatic offensive based on the coexistence idea. The adverse effects on Soviet interests of the military integration in Western Europe and in the Middle East (NATO and the Baghdad Pact) were not allowed to interfere with the planned campaign, and possibly even confirmed the need for more flexible methods. On February 2, 1955, Malenkov was forced to step down. The policy he had prepared (probably on Stalin's orders) was to be implemented by Bulganin, who took over as Premier; behind him loomed the rotund silhouette of Khrushchev. Molotov's star was also on the wane, but he still was Russia's chief negotiator at the second Geneva Conference (October–November, 1955). At the end of May, with Khrushchev playing a leading role, the Russians made their peace with Tito. But the major opening gambit in Europe was Soviet negotiations with Austria, which rapidly built up to the climax of the first Summit Conference at Geneva in July 1955.

A conference of the heads of the Big Four governments was first suggested by Churchill in a speech in the House of Commons on May 11, 1953. He spoke of a meeting of the leading powers at the highest level, without a rigid agenda and amidst conditions of informality and privacy. Churchill again brought up the subject in Washington in June, 1954, and once more in July, after the Geneva Conference on Indochina. His proposal was in line with the recurrent Soviet predilection for summit meetings; it is therefore possible that it was prompted by some suggestion through diplomatic channels soon after Stalin's death, when hopes of a real change in Soviet policy were raised in the Western capitals. A formal proposal for a heads-of-governments conference was made to the Soviet Union by the three Western powers on May 10, 1955. There followed a relatively short wrangle over the subjects to be discussed, yet it is difficult to escape the impression that once again the Soviet Government agreed to a conference it very much desired, and perhaps had actually suggested. According to the Western note of May 10, the summit meeting was to be followed by a working conference instructed to implement the directives of the heads of governments.

In the speeches by Bulganin and Molotov, as well as in the Soviet proposals made during the two Geneva Conferences, three items stand out as the main Soviet goals: a new attempt to gain a political foothold in West Germany by some form of East-West political intermingling in an "All-German Council"; the dissolution of NATO and the withdrawal of American troops from Europe; prohibition of atomic weapons without international control. It is also evident that there were matters the Soviet Government did not wish to discuss seriously, or even wished to keep from the Conference table: free German elections; the situation in Eastern Europe; the role of international Communism. In a broader view of the Soviet aims at Geneva, one should consider the questions not mentioned in speeches or proposals, but which played an important part, so to say "behind the scenes." Soviet Russia was preparing a diplomatic breakthrough in the Middle East, where its influence appeared to be negligible; an agreement to furnish Communist-bloc arms to Egypt was negotiated in strictest secrecy. Moscow also was playing for time in disarmament negotiations. A hydrogen device had been exploded in the Soviet Union on August 12, 1953; other explosions followed, and we now know that a vast program of nuclear armaments was developed during the following years. Thus, in keeping with its usual practice, the Soviet Government found it all the more desirable to contribute to a "relaxation of tension in international relations" and to encourage the belief that agreement was possible on several crucial points, notably on disarmament.

At the first Geneva Conference (July 18–23, 1955), Prime Minister Bulganin spoke of peaceful coexistence, of a reduction of armed forces, and of the prohibition of atomic weapons under international control, but without spelling out what he meant. He explained engagingly the Soviet propositions for an "all-European system of collective security" that would allow the withdrawal of foreign forces from Europe. He regretted that the conference had not had time to consider China's request for admission to the United Nations, but he did not press the point. Though anxious to maintain an atmosphere of good will, Bulganin refused to discuss East European affairs, as "the regime of the people's democracies has been established in those countries by the people themselves of their own free will." The subject of international Communism raised by President Eisenhower was dismissed by Bulganin with the time-proved formula that interstate relations are divorced from Communist Party activities.[2]

Although Bulganin indicated Soviet preference for a security system "with the participation of both parts of Germany on a basis of equality, until reunification is achieved," the Soviet delegation agreed in the Heads of Governments Directive to the Ministers of Foreign Affairs on "the settlement of the German question and the reunification of Germany by means of free elections." As was soon to be demonstrated, this was only a time-saving device. Otherwise, the Directive was a rather superficial compromise, speaking in general terms of a European security system, which both parties desired, of further disarmament talks within the framework of the United Nations, and of East-West contacts expected to lead to a "progressive elimination of barriers" and "free contacts and exchanges."[3]

There was much praise for the results achieved, which the press liked to attribute to a beneficial "spirit of Geneva." The Supreme Soviet adopted a resolution that the conference had opened a new stage in improving relations between states of different social systems, based on confidence and peaceful coexistence.

The short period between the two Geneva Conferences—from July 23 to October 27, 1955—offers an interesting opportunity to observe the Soviet coexistence policy in action.

The first Geneva Summit meeting had hardly begun when Egypt, on July 19, signed a trade agreement with Czechoslovakia. The first information was only about the usual trade and credit arrangements. Soon, however, more details came to light. On September 27, Egypt's Prime Minister (later President), Colonel Abdel Nasser, announced in a broadcast that the arrangement with Czechoslovakia consisted of an exchange of arms for Egyptian cotton. The three Western powers had hitherto succeeded, on the basis of their declaration of May 25, 1950, in maintaining a balance of power between Israel and the Arab states. Arms from Communist-ruled countries would undoubtedly make a considerable change in this situation. The official Soviet point of view was contained in a Tass statement of October 2. Moscow took up the defense of the Egyptian Government, which, they said, had been subjected to pressure and to "intolerable interference detrimental to the independence of Egypt."[4] The Soviet Government upheld the right of every state to buy arms wherever it chose and declared that it had expressed its views on the subject to the Egyptian and Czechoslovak governments. There is little doubt that Russia deliberately planned to upset the balance of power in the Middle East. The Soviet Ambassador to Egypt told reporters in October that Russia would send "economic missions, scientific missions, meteorological missions, and any other kind of missions you can imagine"[5] to the Middle East. It is not known exactly when the negotiations for the arms deal began. There are reasons to believe that they were initiated by Dmitri Shepilov, the editor of *Pravda*, then a rising star of Soviet diplomacy. He had accompanied Bulganin and Khrushchev on the peace-making journey to Belgrade in May–June, 1955. On June 1 of the following year, Shepilov replaced Molotov as Foreign Minister. The Kremlin attached high hopes to the spectacular agreements with Egypt, which in the autumn of 1955 had all the earmarks of a Soviet diplomatic breakthrough in the area. As it turned out, despite the dramatic events of the Suez campaign, the Arab leaders had the political sophistication to resist Russia's wooing and Communist infiltration. But this development was still in the future. For the time being, the Soviet Government seemed to have gained an ominous political victory at the expense of the West. Yet Moscow continued to play on the theme of peaceful coexistence. During the summer, the Soviet delegation to the U.N. Disarmament Subcommittee was careful not to lay undue stress on the differences in policy that were becoming more evident. Other moves were planned to substantiate the Soviet contention that a new era in East-West relations had begun. On August 12, the Soviet Government announced the decision—"with view of promoting the relaxation of international tension"—to reduce its armed forces by 640,000 men.*[6] Soviet-Japanese peace negotiations began on June 1, and continued all through the year. In August, limited contact (not involving diplomatic recognition) between the United States and the Peking regime was established in Geneva for the repatriation of nationals and "certain other practical matters."[7] But perhaps the most spectacular example of "relaxation of tension" was the invitation to Chancellor Adenauer to visit Moscow; on September 13, an agreement was concluded to establish diplomatic relations between the Soviet Union and the Federal German Republic. But Russia made no concessions on German unification, refused to accept Adenauer as spokesman for all Germans, and, making its attitude even more unequivocal, concluded a treaty with East Germany. Signed on September 20 by Bulganin and East German Prime Minister Otto Grotewohl it stipulated (Article 1) that East Germany was henceforth "free to decide questions concerning its internal and foreign policy, including its relations with the German Federal Republic as well as its relations with other states."[8] On September 19, Russia signed an agreement returning the Porkkala naval base, 6 miles southwest of Helsinki, to Finland. Marshal Zhukov told foreign correspondents that the Soviet Union had decided to liquidate its military bases on foreign soil. It was not known at the time that the Finns would find only ruins and desolation at Porkkala. In view of Russia's dominating position of the southern Baltic shore as far as Stettin, Porkkala was of little use as a military base. Nothing else happened to substantiate Zhukov's announcement, and the Soviet military bases in East Germany, Poland, Hungary, and the other satellites remained unaffected.

President Eisenhower aptly described the second Geneva Conference (October 27–November 16, 1955) as the "acid test" of the alleged progress made at the summit meeting three months earlier. It soon became evident that the foreign ministers were unable to translate the generalities into a specific agreement. The final communiqué of November 16 registered only common disagreement on the three items entrusted to them in the Directive, i.e., (1) European security and Germany, (2) disarmament, (3) development of contacts between East and West.[9] Yet, the proceedings show that both sides genuinely tried to narrow the margin of disagreement that separated them—the West because it believed in a policy of

---

* Secretary Dulles said a few days later that "the military significance of the Soviet reduction [was] not easy to judge. No official information was ever provided as to the size of Soviet armed forces."

stabilization and peace, Russia because its diplomatic and political offensive could best be served by the appearance of an agreement. But no way could be found to bridge the fundamental differences on all points under discussion. On Germany the stumbling block was the question of free elections: the Western powers could not renounce them without repudiating their main article of political faith; the Russians were unable to accept a free election throughout Germany, which would obviously lead to the defeat of the puppet regime in the Soviet Zone. It followed that the Soviet Government also could not allow an all-German government to be in a position to choose freely between a Western and an Eastern alliance.

There was a sterile discussion on the relation between European security and the unification of Germany, in which the Western representatives did not gain the upper hand. Their main point was that European security could not be built on the foundation of a divided Germany. But neither could it be built on Soviet guarantees. If there were a chance that Russia would leave the Germans to themselves, it would have been perfectly possible to work out a system of guarantees for a peaceful Germany (or to keep Germany peaceful), whether united or divided. But such was not the case. Beginning with Potsdam, every Soviet move had been aimed at pulling the whole of Germany into the Communist orbit. Molotov had no intention of desisting from this policy. He hailed the formation of the Communist state in the Soviet Zone as "a turning point in the history of Germany as well as in the history of Europe as a whole." He went on to say that the German workers "found their real homeland for the first time in the form of the German Democratic Republic."[10] But Dulles reminded the conference that more than 2.7 million Germans had fled their ideal homeland and were continuing to escape to the West by the thousands.

This discussion could lead nowhere. Similarly, on disarmament, it did not matter that, as Secretary Dulles pointed out, there was a considerable similarity between Western and Eastern proposals. What did matter was that the foreign ministers were unable to solve the vital question of control. A revised Soviet text on disarmament, submitted on November 10, vaguely stated that "an effective international control shall be established."[11] The French Foreign Minister tried to find a way out of the deadlock by proposing agreement "on certain preliminary measures which could be combined to form an initial plan and put into force quickly."[12] This would have been possible if the problem were primarily technical, not political. On the one hand, the Soviet insistence on quick disarmament without control aroused the gravest suspicion. On the other, practical but slow measures, as proposed by the French, were of no interest to the Russians. Molotov therefore threw the responsibility for failure on the Western powers, charging that their proposal "does not contain a single word on terminating the armaments race."[13]

With this, the fate of the conference was sealed. But it was the third item on the agenda, the East-West contacts, which caused the most caustic discussion. More than any other subject, it exposed the gulf separating the Soviet regime from the West on matters of human relations, trade, art, and culture. It was as if emissaries of two alien civilizations took part in a debate without understanding each other's language. After a committee of experts had examined mutual suggestions, it appeared that the Soviet delegates kept only four or five of the seventeen Western proposals for consideration. To the Russians, the main item of interest was the lifting of controls on export of strategic goods, which Molotov called "discriminatory measures practiced by some countries vis-à-vis the U.S.S.R."[14] Macmillan said that "the only barriers which the Soviet Government could suggest as important to remove were the strategic controls."[15]

Dulles' general impression was that "the Soviet Union is not disposed at present . . . to promote the free circulation of information and ideas and to facilitate trade in peaceful goods. . . . The Soviet bloc system is based upon artificial conditions which cannot withstand free contact with the outer world."[16]

The conference was not a conspicuous success for the Soviet Union. Russia was publicly exposed as being against free elections, disarmament control, and freedom of thought. The reasons for the failure lay in the very structure of the Soviet state. Secretary Dulles hit the nail on the head when he remarked that it would have been easy to make "some apparent agreements with the Soviet Union [which] would have given an illusion of a meeting of minds."[17] Most probably that was what the Russians tried to achieve. One finds it difficult to believe that they seriously expected NATO to be dissolved (as they proposed at the first Geneva conference). After the second Geneva Conference, Foreign Secretary Macmillan said: "What worries me is that the Soviet delegation does not seem to mind our failure."[18] It thus seems possible that from the Soviet viewpoint, the setback was only relative. The Russians may have believed that, owing to the atmosphere generated by East-West negotiations since February, 1955, they had gained time in

their efforts to catch up with the United States in nuclear armaments. Possibly therefore in the opinion of the Kremlin, the setback was limited to the sphere of propaganda, and geographically
limited to America and England, while not seriously affecting Soviet interests in Asia, where the next act of the offensive was to
be staged.

On November 18, barely two days after the end of the Geneva
talks, Bulganin and Khrushchev arrived in New Delhi for a six-
week tour of India, Burma, and Afghanistan. During their extensive journey, Bulganin and Khrushchev made a number of speeches
attacking Western colonialism and presented themselves to the
Asian crowds almost as fellow Asians who, by their own efforts and
thanks to the Bolshevik Revolution, had made their country a
great power. Invectives against the West were paralleled with offers of "disinterested" economic assistance. Russia was then only
beginning to enter the field of foreign aid, but the move was well
timed to play up to the desire of the Asian nations for economic
growth and independence from the former colonial powers. In all
three countries they visited, Bulganin and Khrushchev negotiated
economic agreements. Their main points—as published in official
communiques—were as follows:

India. One million tons of Soviet steel as well as oil and mining
equipment, to be delivered during the following three years. During
the same period, Russia would purchase raw materials and manu-
factured goods in India. It was hoped that these purchases would
equal the value of Soviet deliveries and of the cost of maintaining
official Soviet organizations in India.

Burma. Russia was to provide materials and services for a program of agricultural development, irrigation works, and the establishment of industrial plants. This was either to be paid in deliveries of Burmese rice or credited for an unspecified number of years.

Afghanistan. A Soviet long-term credit of $100 million "for the
fulfillment of an agreed program of works for the development of
the Afghan economy."

The fact that these offers coincided with attacks on the West
made it clear enough that the Soviet Union was not handing out
economic assistance altruistically. In upbraiding the West, Khrushchev surpassed Bulganin in invectives. During a speech in Bom-
bay, he charged Britain and France with the responsibility for
unleashing Hitler's war and provoking the German attack on the
Soviet Union. In Kashmir, the Soviet leaders turned on Pakistan

and took India's side in the territorial dispute. In Afghanistan, Bulganin backed his hosts in the controversial question of Push-tunistan—the concept of an independent state of Pathans at the expense of Pakistan. Attacks on the West were repeated and even elaborated on in the reports Bulganin and Khrushchev submitted on their return to Moscow to the Supreme Soviet on December 29, 1955.[19] Khrushchev's speech again was unusually virulent. Both scored "British imperialists," "British colonialists" (calling them "gangsters"), "Portuguese usurpers," and also managed to include the United States.

It would be useless to speculate whether the tone would have been any different had agreement been reached in Geneva. The tour had been in preparation at least since June; no doubt the general content of Bulganin's and Khrushchev's public declarations was based on carefully established intelligence reports. The Russians also counted on the apparently inexhaustible patience of Western, and particularly British, opinion, for the next important trip was to England.

The invitation for an official visit to Britain had been extended to Bulganin and Khrushchev by Sir Anthony Eden at the time of the first Summit Conference in the wake of the "Geneva spirit." Shortly before the agreed date of the visit, Tass published a statement expressing the Soviet Government's regret that the program prepared by the Foreign Office would prevent the visitors from meeting "ordinary people working in factories."[20] The statement accused "some forces in Britain" of wishing to prevent such contacts. The British Foreign Office denied the Tass charges. The Soviet visit (April 18–27, 1956) was marked by impeccable courtesy on the part of the British Government, a mixed reception by Parliament and the general public, and considerable arrogance on the part of the guests, particularly Khrushchev. In public speeches Khrushchev again insisted on the lifting of bans on strategic goods, spoke of the first air delivery of a Soviet hydrogen bomb, and of "guided missiles with a hydrogen head that can fall anywhere in the world."[21]

An incident occurred at a reception in the House of Commons given by the Labour Party Executive. The Soviet guests refused to accept a list of about 200 names of Social Democrats imprisoned in Soviet Russia and other Communist-ruled states from Hugh Gaitskell, the Labour Party's leader. Gaitskell asked Bulganin and Khrushchev to intercede on behalf of these prisoners and also asked them to help curb anti-Semitism. Some sharp exchanges took place after Khrushchev reportedly answered in an offensive manner. Despite a conciliatory statement issued by the Labour Party after a second meeting, Khrushchev later described Social Democrats as "enemies of the working class."[22] He accused the members of the Labour Party of having raised their questions "to curry favor with reactionary circles."[23]

The discussions with the British Government concerned disarmament, the Middle East, and economic, scientific, and cultural relations. The communiqué published on April 26 was lengthy and insignificant. It contained the Soviet-favored formula of "relaxation of tension" but, with the exception of cultural, scientific, and technical contacts, registered no practical results.[24] The next day, at a news conference, the Soviet leaders evaded questions on disarmament control, demanded an "ultimate prohibition of nuclear weapons," attacked the Baghdad Pact, and again implied that they were prevented from meeting "any average British people."[25] Eden's radio and television broadcast that same day furnished additional proof that no political results were achieved in the Soviet-British conversations.[26] But he spoke hopefully of trade, cultural, and other exchanges, which indeed made some progress in the ensuing years.

The Soviet Government was also determined to revive the Geneva spirit in bilateral relations with the United States. On January 23, 1956, only a few months after the Geneva Conference, Bulganin in a letter to President Eisenhower proposed a twenty-year Soviet-American treaty of friendship and cooperation.[27] Eisenhower was quick to point out that the three substantive articles of the annexed draft treaty were already covered by obligations accepted by both countries as signatories of the United Nations Charter. Since the words of the Charter did not prevent international tension, the President asked, "How can we hope that the present situation would be cured merely by repeating those words in bilateral form?"[28]

In November, 1956, Russia did its best, not without some success, to push itself to the forefront as the defender of Egypt, while Soviet tanks suppressed the Hungarian Revolution. Bulganin threatened England and France with armed intervention, and at the same time addressed a letter to Eisenhower suggesting that the United States join forces with Russia for a military action in the Middle East: "The United States has a strong navy in the Mediterranean. The Soviet Union has a strong navy and a powerful air force. The joint and immediate use of these means by the U.S.A. and the Soviet Union, backed by a United Nations decision, would be a sure guarantee of ending the aggression against the Egyptian people."[29] It is improbable that Russia really expected America to embark on a common expedition with the Soviet Army against Britain and France. The maneuver was intended for the benefit of Arab public opinion. Yet the Suez campaign was the only instance since the war when Moscow perhaps could have made a successful bid for a *rapprochement* with the United States. But Russia's war against the Hungarian people prevented it from playing a more subtle game. In an official statement, the White House on November 5 pointed out that the U.N. had already called for a cease-fire and the withdrawal of foreign troops from Egypt. The statement said that by the action of its troops in Hungary, the Soviet Union itself was in defiance of a decision of the United Nations.

During 1957, Bulganin continued to bombard the governments of the United States, Britain, France, West Germany, Norway, Denmark and Turkey with notes proposing negotiations on various issues, but also threatening the Continental members of the Atlantic alliance. Bulganin's letters to the three Western powers on the Middle East attacked the Baghdad Pact and the Eisenhower Doctrine and proposed a four-power declaration for the maintenance of peace, which was contradicted by massive Communist arms shipments to the area. In September, Moscow whipped up a wholly artificial crisis over the alleged Turkish menace to Syria. Although the atmosphere of indignation over Russia's treatment of Hungary was not propitious to the revival of the Geneva spirit, Khrushchev, then still only First Party Secretary, in May again spoke of a summit meeting. But more pressing arguments were in preparation. On October 4, Russia put the first artificial satellite into orbit and a month later quit the U.N. Disarmament Committee. Finally, between December 10 and 14, Bulganin launched a massive diplomatic drive, with notes addressed to eighty-two members of the United Nations, fifteen members of NATO, as well as Switzerland and Spain. The Kremlin obviously counted on the effect of the first Sputnik. The Soviet notes denounced "military blocs," and by proposing a summit meeting they were designed to offer an alternative to the new defense measures up for adoption by the NATO heads-of-governments conference convening in Paris on December 16. More specifically, the purpose of the pressure was to frighten NATO members into barring American military bases, nuclear warheads and missile launching-sites on their territories. This Soviet

move did not succeed. On the other hand, it did set in motion negotiations that eventually brought about Western agreement on the
much-desired summit meeting.

But the road was still long and arduous. After a further exchange
of letters, Eisenhower wrote to Bulganin on February 27, 1958: "I
begin to wonder whether we shall get anywhere by writing speeches
to each other."[30] The method imposed by Russia in these negotiations was indeed sterile. The Geneva Summit Conference of 1955
was introduced by a show of Soviet "give and take" on Austria. But
by 1958, after the failure of the second Geneva Conference, and
particularly after the Hungarian Revolution, the Soviet international position had deteriorated greatly. The Kremlin must have
realized that a summit conference would now be possible only if the
Western powers could be induced to participate either by threats
or the force of circumstances. Such seems to have been Khrushchev's frame of mind when he replaced Bulganin as Prime Minister in March, 1958 (for reasons apparently not connected with foreign affairs). There was no manifest change of policy. One of Bulganin's last official acts was to demand a summit conference; one
of the first steps Khrushchev took was to repeat the demand on
April 4 in a letter to Macmillan. It was answered with a joint communication of the three Western powers, stating in essence that
a summit meeting would not be fruitful unless the ground was
prepared in advance. But Moscow wished to avoid diplomatic
spadework so as to be free to reject any undesirable substantive
agreement. As a result, there followed a series of further exchanges
with the Soviet Government on the defensive, because the demand
for an unprepared summit meeting was logically untenable. Khrushchev followed several other lines simultaneously, writing unceas-
ingly to the Western governments about disarmament, nuclear
tests, the avoidance of surprise attacks, and alleged American "provocative flights" in the Arctic. To complete this list, there was also
a Soviet proposal, contained in a note to Britain of July 15, of a
treaty of "friendship and cooperation among the states of Europe."
All this activity brought no practical results. But the opportunity
came after a *coup d'état* in Iraq in mid-July, when, at the demand
of the local governments, small American and British detachments
were landed in Jordan and Lebanon. The presence of these few
Western soldiers proved sufficient to preserve the independence of
the two countries and to forestall further difficulties on which Soviet Russia possibly was counting. But these landings also presented
Moscow with the opportunity to magnify the incident out of all

proportion, pretending to see in it the makings of a major international crisis. In letters to Eisenhower and the Prime Ministers of Britain and France, dated July 19, Khrushchev accused the United States and Britain of an armed intervention in Lebanon and Jordan. He called them colonialists and aggressors and charged that they were bringing the world "to the brink of a catastrophe."[31] He demanded a summit meeting in Geneva within four days. On July 23, Khrushchev accepted an Anglo-American suggestion for a summit meeting of the Security Council instead of a conference of the heads of governments of the big powers. Before the date of the meeting could be agreed upon (America and Britain proposed August 12), Khrushchev backed out, accused the Security Council of being "a kind of committee dominated by the member-countries of NATO, the Baghdad Pact, and SEATO"[32] and instead demanded that the Middle East situation be discussed at an emergency session of the General Assembly. This *volte-face* came on August 5, two days after Khrushchev's departure from Peking, where he had held secret talks with Mao Tse-tung. It is generally assumed that he yielded to Chinese pressure.

There the matter of a summit meeting rested for a while. A crisis arose in September, when the Chinese Communist forces tried to occupy the offshore islands of Matsu and Quemoy, but were defeated in air battles by the Nationalist Chinese from Formosa (Taiwan) equipped by America. This led Khrushchev to send accusing letters to Eisenhower, in which he maintained that the United States had forcibly occupied Formosa and the other islands ruled by Chang Kai-shek's government and was preventing their "liberation." Eisenhower pointed out that the Communist bombardment of the offshore islands had started on August 23, barely three weeks after Khrushchev's trip to Peking. The exchange became so sharp that Eisenhower returned the Soviet note of September 19, which the White House termed "abusive and intemperate" and which contained "inadmissible threats."[33]

The Soviet Government finally succeeded in its campaign for a summit meeting by threatening to provoke a dangerous crisis over Berlin. The action began in a speech by Khrushchev on November 10, 1958, and in a note dated November 27;[34] the Western powers were presented with a demand to withdraw, within six months, their detachments from West Berlin, which—according to Khrushchev—would become a demilitarized "free city." The Soviet demand set in motion a chain reaction of diplomatic moves, which eighteen months later culminated in the abortive Big Four Conference held in Paris in May, 1960. That the Western powers permitted Soviet pressure on Berlin to drag them to a virtually unprepared summit meeting does no credit to their political stamina or spirit of enterprise. The situation also is a logical consequence of the policy of containment, which gives Soviet Russia all the advantages of taking the initiative. In threatening to push the Allies out of West Berlin, the Soviet Government is able to negotiate from a position of strength, an advantage Khrushchev has put to good use several times since 1958. One can only wonder why Soviet diplomacy did not play this profitable game earlier, since the situation created by the 1944 agreements on Berlin was an open invitation to this kind of pressure.

The maneuver initiated by Khrushchev's November 10 speech—the occasion was a Moscow reception for a Polish delegation headed by Gomulka—was infinitely more sophisticated than the 1949 blockade. In essence it consisted of the following points:

1. The Western powers had violated the Potsdam agreements on which their rights in West Berlin rested. Therefore they had lost all claims to retain their "occupation regimes" in Berlin.

2. The Soviet Union considered the agreements of September 12, 1944, on the occupation zones of Germany and the administration of Greater Berlin as null and void.

3. Pending the reunification of Germany, West Berlin should become a free, demilitarized city.

4. If the Western powers do not reach an understanding with the Soviet Union on the free city within six months, the Soviet Government would relinquish formally to the German Democratic Republic all the rights it exercises on its behalf over the approaches to West Berlin. Simultaneously, Russia would interrupt all contacts with the Western representatives, military and civilian, on matters pertaining to Berlin.

5. Should the Western powers fail to recognize the Soviet arrangements with East Germany and try to open their way to West Berlin by force, the Soviet Union would defend its ally and cosignatory of the Warsaw Pact against any agression on its frontiers.

Thus, it seemed that, short of war, the Western powers had only two choices: to agree to the free-city concept and come to an understanding with East Germany at the probable price of diplomatic recognition, or walk out of West Berlin. As it turned out, a third choice became possible, because Khrushchev preferred diplomatic negotiations leading to a summit meeting to risking a war over Berlin. Further developments also showed that he could, and would, make short shrift of the interests and prestige of his East German satellite. This, however, was not known at the time, and Khrushchev pushed the issue very hard, so as to impress the West with his "final" decision to get what he wanted in Berlin at any price. But the Western powers also reacted strongly, rejected the project of a free city (which West Berlin really is and would cease to be if Russia had its way), and refused to relinquish their rights of access to, and presence in, West Berlin. They also rejected the unilateral abrogation of the agreements on Berlin and refused to deal with the East Germans. On January 10, 1959, the Soviet Government sent a note to all the countries that had been at war with Germany, together with a draft of a peace treaty with "the two existing German states."[35] Article 25 provided for making West Berlin a free city, pending the reunification of Germany. Russia also proposed a peace conference within two months. After that, events moved swiftly: On February 16, the West suggested that a four-power conference of foreign ministers take up the German question "in all its aspects." On February 21, at the initiative of the British Government, Prime Minister Macmillan and Foreign Secretary Selwyn Lloyd arrived in Moscow for a ten-day visit. They were still in Moscow when, on March 2, the Soviet Government sent out new notes proposing a summit meeting in April. In the same communications, Russia agreed to a four-power conference of foreign ministers before the summit meeting. The mechanism was thereupon set in motion, although somewhat more slowly than Moscow had demanded.

The conference of the four foreign ministers (with representatives of West and East Germany in attendance) was held in Geneva from May 11 to August 5, 1959, with a three-week interruption in midsummer. It failed to yield any results on the immediate question of Berlin and the wider problems of German unification and a peace treaty. In particular, the Western representatives were unable to reach agreement with Gromyko on their governments' rights in Berlin. Both sides strove for an interim arrangement, but on conflicting grounds. The Western powers proposed the unification of Greater Berlin as a self-governing area on the basis of free elections. The Russians would not hear of free elections in East Berlin. They again contended that Berlin was the capital of the German Democratic Republic and "as a concession" proposed the free-city status for the three Western sectors. Gromyko tried hard to negotiate a time limit for the presence of Western detachments in West Berlin, after which—failing agreement—Russia would sign a separate peace treaty with East Germany. But he clearly was under orders not to push the matter to the breaking point. He also suggested that American, British, and French troops in West Berlin be replaced by neutral soldiers, or by token detachments of the four powers. (This would have meant introducing Soviet troops into the Western sectors of the city.) In answer to a direct question from the British Foreign Secretary, Gromyko issued a statement assuring that Russia would not take unilateral action "while an interim arrangement on West Berlin is in force, as well as in the course of the negotiations to be held at a conference of states . . . to consider again the question of West Berlin."[36] In other words, the threat posed in November, 1958, still existed, and only was suspended while the negotiations were going on. The Western governments certainly so understood the situation, since despite the complete failure of the conference, two days before its inglorious end it was announced that Khrushchev had accepted Eisenhower's invitation to visit the United States in September. The President in turn was to visit Russia later in the year.

Eisenhower's invitation was a handsome reward for the Berlin squeeze. No Soviet Premier had ever visited the United States. Furthermore, the trip was a decisive step toward a summit meeting. Both the American journey and the summit conference opened to the Russians great scope for diplomatic maneuver and for probing the Western alliance. Also, they raised the hope of concrete concessions, which were urgently needed to prove the validity of the coexistence theory. In retrospect, it is apparent that the Soviet Government several times attempted to force a summit meeting by raising a war scare: In September, 1957, they invented a Turkish threat to Syria; in January, 1958, it was the ballistic missiles and the first Sputnik; in July, Jordan and Lebanon; and in August, the Formosa Straits. Three times the attempts misfired: In July, 1958, the meeting of the Security Council had to be called off because Peking did not like to see a "concert of powers" formed within the United Nations, which had branded Communist China as an aggressor. Some weeks later, a Communist victory in the Formosa Straits could have led to a summit conference with China's participation. But this was not to be, owing to the superior training and American equipment of Nationalist airmen. Berlin proved a suitable ground for diplomatic pressure because the Western powers were more sensitive to a war threat in the middle of Europe, and also because in this case it was probably easier for Russia to dispose of Chinese opposition.

Soviet behavior did not change radically after an agreement in principle was reached on the four-power meetings of foreign ministers and heads of governments. It continued to be aggressive and conciliatory in turn, which inclined some observers to compare Soviet methods to the experiments of the Russian physiologist Pavlov, who brought dogs to the point of hysteria and then to non-resistance by alternating, contradictory commands.[37] At any rate, the carrot-and-stick method was employed between February and September, 1959, when Khrushchev arrived in the United States. A few instances are of interest:

On January 10, Russia had proposed a peace conference on Germany and Berlin. But on February 17, Khrushchev made a bellicose speech in Tula complaining about rumors that the Western powers intended to shoot their way into Berlin. He said that the signing of a peace treaty would give East Germany sovereign rights over all its territory, "in the center of which Berlin is situated." If the frontiers of East Germany were violated, Russia could not stand by idly. "Those who attempt to violate these frontiers will . . . receive a shattering rebuff. . . . Our advice to those who are trying their hands at saber rattling is: If you are nervous, take a cold shower! Relax! Otherwise peace will be in danger."[38]

The Macmillan-Selwyn Lloyd visit to Russia was a conciliatory gesture of great importance. But Khrushchev made a harsh speech criticizing the Western powers as soon as the guests had left Moscow to visit a nearby town. Although he had not broached the subject before, he suddenly and publicly proposed that Britain sign a nonaggression pact with Russia; he again asked for a summit meeting and called the Western attitude toward Berlin "absurd." Two days later, Khrushchev failed to accompany his guests on a scheduled trip on the pretext that he had a toothache, which, however, did not prevent him from receiving an Iraqi delegation a few hours later. At one time Macmillan apparently considered breaking off the visit and returning to England.

As soon as Macmillan and Selwyn Lloyd left, Khrushchev rushed to East Germany, where on March 5, at Leipzig, he said that there was no Soviet ultimatum on West Berlin and that the date of May 27, 1959 (six months from the delivery of the Soviet note of November 27, 1958) was not irrevocable. This date, he said, could be moved to June or July.[39] But in other statements, notably in a speech on March 9 in East Berlin, Khrushchev again insisted on a unilateral peace treaty with East Germany.

During April, Russia sent strongly worded notes to Norway and Italy, threatening them with rockets for allowing NATO bases on their territory. In the last days of April, however, Field Marshal Montgomery visited Moscow and found the Russians more accommodating. After talking with Khrushchev, Marshal Malinovsky, and other military personalities, Montgomery wrote that the Soviet leaders were not planning to attack the West: "I do not believe this for a moment. They may use the threat of armed action, indeed of war, to gain their political aims—no more."[40] This diagnosis was most accurate. A particularly telling example occurred in the second half of June, when Averell Harriman had a long conversation with Khrushchev in the presence of Frol Kozlov, Mikoyan, Gromyko, and G. D. Zhukov. Joseph Alsop described Khrushchev's attitude during the conversation as "Hitler-like."[41] Harriman himself, in an article in *Life*, quoted Khrushchev as saying: "Your generals talk of maintaining your position in Berlin with force. . . . That is bluff. . . . If you send in tanks, they will burn, and make no mistake about it. If you want war, you can have it, but remember, it will be your war. Our rockets will fly automatically. . . ." Harriman's article was entitled: "My Alarming Interview with Khrushchev."[42] No doubt Khrushchev wanted it to be alarming; like Hitler before Munich, he intended to frighten Western public opinion into putting pressure on the governments, and thus gain concessions at the conference table.

When Vice President Nixon arrived in Moscow to open the American exhibition, Khrushchev involved him in a most unusual public debate in front of television cameras. The improvised discussion on July 24 in the American show-kitchen became world famous because Khrushchev treated Nixon (who, showing skill and composure, did not yield any points) to an unprecedented display of crude demagoguery. The topics of the debate were foreign bases, Germany, the merits of the two social systems, and particularly the Captive Nations' Week proclaimed by President Eisenhower. A few days later, in a speech at Dniepropetrovsk, Khrushchev brought up his debate with Nixon. He said that he had told Nixon: "If you want peace, why did you take such an unreasonable decision as to organize a week of the so-called captive nations? . . . So, you want to liberate our nations from Communist slavery? . . . Well, we consider you as slaves of capitalism."[43]

The special propaganda treatment accorded to Nixon was undoubtedly found necessary in view of America's prestige with the

Soviet people. And it was considered so important to downgrade the Vice President of the United States that Khrushchev personally took part. But it should be noted that Khrushchev's outburst was not merely a pretext; any allusion to Russia's precarious hold on Eastern Europe is treated in Moscow with near-hysteria.

In the period of preparations for Khrushchev's American trip, the Soviet Union also made proposals for military disengagement in Europe in the shape of "atom-free zones" or "zones of peace," broadly related to the Rapacki Plan of October, 1957. A southern atom-free zone was the subject of Khrushchev's speeches during a visit to Albania at the end of May and the beginning of June. On June 25, the Soviet Government formalized its proposals in notes to the United States, England, and France, as well as to Italy, Greece, and Turkey, the three countries Russia intended to include in the southern zone. A northern zone, comprising the Scandinavian Peninsula and the Baltic area, was suggested in Khrushchev's speech at Riga on June 11. Two additional recommendations come from the Soviet bloc: Romania wanted to call a conference of Balkan Prime Ministers; the East German Government asked for a non-aggression pact between the countries along the Baltic Sea. In a speech of June 6, Khrushchev declared that, should his proposals be rejected (the NATO countries did reject them), Russia and its allies would have to build rocket ramps "close to the aggressors' bases."[44]

The central target of all these exertions in diplomacy and propaganda was Germany, more specifically West Berlin, where the Soviet Government expected to gain the first concessions at a summit meeting with the Western powers. In view of the importance of the maneuver and the amount of effort and time involved, it is surprising how little imagination the Soviet apparatus used in the political argumentation, which remained commonplace and repetitious in the extreme.

However, the threat originally made in November, 1958, was repeated by Khrushchev: "If the state of affairs [in Germany and West Berlin] is allowed to remain as it is, this would mean always having a spark in the powder keg that might cause a sudden explosion."[45] A paucity of Soviet political argumentation characterized Khrushchev's entire American visit. He arrived in the United States on September 15, 1959, after a ten-month propaganda barrage and diplomatic preparations. The period of preparation also included the Twenty-first Congress of the Soviet Communist Party in January–February, the launching of a new Seven-Year Plan ac-

companied by fantastic predictions of economic growth,* as well
as spectacular achievements in planetary rocketry culminating in a
moon probe two days before Khrushchev's arrival in Washington.
Now, in America, he had the biggest stage on earth all to himself.
Yet, as far as it is possible to judge from the brief perspective of a
few years, he did not score lasting results either in politics or in
propaganda. Traveling around the country with a party of 100, followed by an army of reporters of all nationalities, Khrushchev failed
to strike a receptive chord with the American public, probably because the intellectual target he assigned himself was too low. This
may have been due to misinformation about the level of American
political sophistication, or simply to an inability to change his
habits. The more serious public or semipublic occasions (such as
the address to the National Press Club in Washington, the meeting
with trade-union leaders at San Francisco, or the farewell broadcast
from Washington) were spoiled by statements most Americans
knew to be distortions or untruths ("One must adhere strictly to
nonintervention of states in each other's internal affairs. . . . The
Constitution of our state is indeed a most democratic one."), or by
replies of unprecedented vulgarity: ("The question of Hungary has
stuck in some people's throat like a dead rat. He feels that it is un-
comfortable and yet he cannot spit it out. . . . This is a stupid question not worthy of discussion. . . . Why poke your nose into our
business? . . . I've never liked fleas when they jumped all over.
. . . Do you want a discussion or is this a bazaar?") [46]

As in England in 1956, the most dangerous encounters for Khrushchev were meetings with the representatives of organized labor.
Nothing was more damaging to him in America than the publication of a verbatim report of his discussion in San Francisco with
Walter Reuther, James Carey, Joseph Curran, O. A. Knight, Karl
Keller, and others. When asked questions he did not know how to
answer—on Hungary, Soviet dictatorship, the right of Soviet workers to strike, mass flights from Communist-ruled countries—Khrushchev called these labor leaders "capitalist lackeys." During this
discussion he also proclaimed the Soviet Government's right to
withhold information from the people: "As head of the working
class, I will protect the workers from capitalist propaganda." At
this point, *The New York Times* reported, Khrushchev "turned

* Khrushchev predicted that by 1965, the Communist bloc would be producing half of the world's industrial output, and that by 1970, or even earlier,
the Soviet Union would surpass the United States in total and per-capita
production.

his back to the table, bent downwards, flipped his coat up and gave an imitation of can-can," presumably to express his contempt for capitalist propaganda.[47]

On the political side, the only new major initiative was the proposal for "general and complete disarmament" in Khrushchev's speech to the General Assembly of the United Nations on September 18. To the expert, the move was not startlingly novel; in essence, it was a repetition of Litvinov's demagogic projects of the 1930's. Neither could it impress the general public. Too much had been told and written on the subject for many Americans to believe Khrushchev's assurance that general and complete disarmament would by itself, as if by magic, "ensure the complete security of all states."[48]

Not much is known of the Eisenhower-Khrushchev talks at Camp David on September 25–27. The official communiqué issued at the end of the meeting contained two important statements: that negotiations would be reopened on the Berlin question, and that Eisenhower's visit to Russia, planned for that year, would be delayed until spring.[49] On September 29, at the first news conference after Khrushchev's departure, Eisenhower declared that there would be no time limit on the negotiations on Berlin, although, he added, they should not be prolonged indefinitely. Khrushchev confirmed the President's statement in an interview with Tass on his return to Moscow. The President also stated that as far as he was concerned, many obstacles to a summit conference had been removed. This then was the political outcome of the visit: the ultimatum on Berlin was lifted but not entirely removed; a summit meeting, which had been a certainty since March, was confirmed. But some mystery surrounded the postponement of Eisenhower's visit to Russia. Some observers also believed that a shade of misunderstanding about a possible arrangement on West Berlin influenced the further course of events, culminating in the dramatic collapse of the May, 1960, Paris Summit Meeting.

One more hurdle had to be cleared by Khrushchev before the much-desired summit meeting. General de Gaulle stubbornly clung to the idea that a conference of the heads of governments should be well prepared on the diplomatic level. Washington and London seemed ready to give up this condition, and Khrushchev, on returning from the United States, again pressed for an early meeting. On October 23 it was announced that de Gaulle had invited Khrushchev to visit him first. A French Government declaration of October 27 stated that "a conference that finished without results or that would be the occasion of hasty decisions because it was insufficiently prepared would go directly against the aim we have in view." As usual when confronted with a strong stand, the Soviet Government gave in.

The Paris visit was fixed for March 15, but delayed until March 23, owing to an attack of influenza suffered by Khrushchev. This seemed to be a consequence of Khrushchev's strenuous February tour of India, Burma, and Indonesia, during which he made speeches with a definite anti-Western bias. At the beginning of March, he visited Afghanistan and again spoke out for an independent state of the Pathans. Still in February, the President of Italy, Giovanni Gronchi, and Foreign Minister Giuseppe Pella had paid a state visit to Moscow. At a reception in the Italian Embassy, Khrushchev behaved toward them with rare discourtesy. Since the argument involved the Western attitude toward Germany and Berlin, this was an indication of things to come.

But in France, where Khrushchev was intent upon winning de Gaulle's favor, he adopted a worldly-wise stance. He was genial and refrained from controversial remarks. No doubt little could be done in political matters. Khrushchev's stress of German militarism made little impression in a Paris allied to Bonn, nor did his allusions to the historic Franco-Russian ties evoke any nostalgic response. The visit passed without notable incidents; the large French Communist Party behaved in a most disciplined manner. Even his meeting with trade-union representatives passed without incident, though it should be stated that most persons present were members of the Communist-dominated Confédération Générale du Travail, the anti-Communist Force Ouvrière and the Christian trade unions having refused to meet him. Nor was there any public reaction on Khrushchev's part to the second French atomic bomb, exploded in the Sahara during his stay. According to reliable press reports, his conversations with President de Gaulle and the French Government consisted of mutual briefings and contained no new elements. The joint communiqué was of the usual banality. The visit ended with the signing of two agreements on scientific cooperation and peaceful use of atomic energy. But the one important result was that the way to the "summit" was now clear.

After the collapse of the 1955 summit negotiations, it took Soviet diplomacy nearly five years to prepare the ground for a new conference. The government heads met in Paris on Monday, May

16, 1960, for a preliminary session under de Gaulle's chairmanship. But literally within minutes it was all over. Khrushchev spoke first, and in a few moments destroyed the patient work of several years. He accused the United States of having committed "a provocative act" by the flight of the U-2 plane that had "invaded the Soviet Union." Therefore, Khrushchev declared, "the Soviet Government sees no possibility for productive negotiations with the United States Government at the summit conference" unless and until the United States does three things: (1) "denounce the impermissible provocative actions of the United States Air Force with regard to the Soviet Union"; (2) "refrain from continuing such actions and such a policy against the U.S.S.R. in the future"; (3) "call strictly to account those who are directly responsible for the deliberate violation of the state borders of the U.S.S.R. by American aircraft."[50]

The ultimatum, as President Eisenhower rightly called it in his answer, was obviously not delivered on the spur of the moment. It was the result of preparations that must have begun even before the U-2 plane was brought down on May 1 and concluded no later than May 9, when Khrushchev made a particularly violent speech against the United States during a reception at the Czechoslovak Embassy in Moscow. He said:

> This is a big disgrace for America, since everyone sees now how disgraced in the eyes of the world are those who committed such a shocking act of aggression. . . . This was done deliberately and deliberately timed for the summit meeting in Paris. . . . What kind of a state is this and what confidence can one have in the policy of such a state?[51]

But this was not the first warning. Ominous tones could have been heard in Khrushchev's speech at Baku on April 25, *before* the U-2 incident. In this address, Khrushchev bitterly complained about a recent speech by Under-Secretary of State Douglas Dillon, and called it "a collection of trite inventions about the Soviet Union." From Dillon's declarations Khrushchev drew the conclusion that "the United States Government will not be willing to reach an agreement on disarmament and on the ways of improving East-West relations unless its view on the Berlin question is accepted."[52] In other words, on April 25, the Kremlin was aware that America and its allies would not give in on West Berlin. We shall probably never know whether Khrushchev really believed that Eisenhower had made some kind of promise in regard to Berlin at

Camp David or whether he only pretended to believe it. The question should be projected against the background of the coexistence policy, to which Khrushchev was committed and which was supposed to yield some concrete gains. Since November, 1958, every Soviet move indicated that Russia expected West Berlin to be the first Western outpost to fall, and the first step toward this end was to be the proposed creation of a demilitarized free city endowed with any number of paper guarantees. But as the mid-May date approached, it became clear that no concessions would be gained at the summit conference; this therefore ceased to be a profitable proposition. The Baku speech thus appears to have been the first signal of the Kremlin's decision to wreck the conference, though the method may have been left open. A few days later came the U-2 incident. The extraordinary vehemence with which Khrushchev denounced it in a report to the Supreme Soviet on May 5 indicated that the Soviet Government was determined to make the most of it. Khrushchev called it an act of American aggression, compared it with "the madman Hitler's" flights over Russia before the German-Soviet war, and denounced the alleged impunity enjoyed by "American soldiery."[53] In these speeches—at Baku, in the Supreme Soviet, and in the Czechoslovak Embassy—Khrushchev insisted on the Soviet solution of the Berlin and German questions, upholding the threat of unilateral action backed by Russian arms. The most striking aspect, however, was the fact that in the report to the Supreme Soviet, Khrushchev openly related how another American plane had been spotted over Russia on April 9, and how, after a discussion in the government, it was decided not to protest to the United States but to lay in wait for the next opportunity. On May 1, early in the morning, Khrushchev said, when the government was informed that another plane had crossed the border, it gave the order to shoot it down.

Now came the second phase, the diplomatic exploitation of the incident. The Soviet Government had several choices. Normally the most drastic course of action would have been to refuse to participate in the summit meeting until satisfaction was given in the form of an apology, or even reparations. But the Kremlin had other plans. Despite a sharp note to the United States on May 10 threatening "retaliatory action," despite harsh words from Marshal Malinovsky about "bandit incursions,"[54] the pretense that Khrushchev would take part in the Paris meeting was kept up. "We are proceeding to the conference in Paris," he said to the Supreme Soviet on May 5, "with a pure heart and good intentions, and we shall shrink from no effort to reach an agreement acceptable to both sides." He even complained that President Eisenhower had informed him that he would be unable to stay in Paris after May 22. On May 9, Khrushchev sent a personal message to Macmillan stating that he still hoped for a successful Paris meeting. On arriving at Orly airport on May 14, he stressed the importance of the big four conference and said: "We all know each other fairly well as a result of our previous meetings, and I hope that this fact will contribute to the successful work of the conference. The Soviet Government will exert every effort to make the conference a success."[55]

It was only on the eve of the conference that Khrushchev told de Gaulle and Macmillan of the three conditions he was presenting to Eisenhower as the price for Soviet participation. Nothing could suit the Soviet plans better than Eisenhower's decision to attend the Monday meeting anyway and hear Khrushchev's declaration. This enabled Khrushchev to create an international scandal at the conference table, amid a flurry of abuse against the United States and accusations of alleged American aggression. His declaration was supplemented with *ad hominem* remarks not found in the text he had shown de Gaulle and Macmillan the day before. During the anxious hours that followed, when Macmillan vainly tried to salvage the conference, which de Gaulle already considered as irremediably lost, the Soviet tone increased in violence. At a press conference on May 18, Khrushchev outdid himself in vulgarity, shouting at journalists, calling them "provocateurs," and branding American policy as "thievish."[56]

There has been much speculation as to why Khrushchev acted in this way. Did he expect Eisenhower to bow to his conditions? Did he hope to break up the Western alliance? In part, the answers are contained in Khrushchev's declaration of May 16:

A conference at present would be a waste of time and deception of public opinion in all countries. . . . We are certain that reasonable agreements are possible, but, evidently, not now but at some other time. . . . The Soviet Government profoundly believes that if not the present Government of the United States, then the next one, and if not the next one, then the one after that, will understand that there is no other alternative but peaceful coexistence between the capitalist and the socialist systems. . . . Therefore we believe that some time should be allowed to elapse. . . . We would think that there is no better way out than to put off the heads of governments conference for about six to eight months. . . . We regret that this meeting has been torpedoed by the reactionary circles of the United

States of America, as a result of the provocative flights of American military aircraft over the Soviet Union.[57]

These excerpts make it clear that, in Eisenhower's words, Khrushchev "came all the way from Moscow to Paris with the sole intention of sabotaging this meeting." It also seems certain that the wrecking of the Conference was a premeditated Soviet move, devised around the second half of April (Baku speech), and probably prepared in all its detail in early May (address to the Supreme Soviet). All available information points to the conclusion that Khrushchev decided to wreck the conference rather than return from Paris empty-handed; the U-2 incident was the pretext, not the cause. It was easier to provoke an international scandal than to admit to the Communist activist, the Party apparatus, and the rivals for leadership, whether in Moscow or Peking, that five years of a "coexistence offensive" had brought no results.

The collapse of the Conference before it even got under way served another Soviet purpose: the cancelation of Eisenhower's visit to Russia, which had been fixed for June 10. As former commander-in-chief of the Allied forces during World War II and President of the United States, Eisenhower's prestige in Europe was then unequaled by any Western public figure. Nothing could better express America's desire for peace than this visit to Russia. But this would have been inconsistent with the new Soviet line of "American aggression." Khrushchev had already cashed in on his own visit to the United States, which, although so meager in results, was described to the Russian people as a triumph. The Soviet Union was flooded with propaganda on Khrushchev's great success. A film and book entitled *Face to Face with America* projected a distorted image of the United States while depicting Khrushchev with near-Stalinist adulation.* In this deformed picture of America, Eisenhower, however, was still shown as a man who genuinely desired peace. After the Paris episode, Eisenhower would have been a most embarrassing visitor for the Kremlin, unless his trip could

---

* *Face to Face with America* has been translated into English and is available in the United States. It is a classic example of distortion in Soviet propaganda. It shows how the good Communist Khrushchev at last told the amazed American people the truth about Communism and Russia. The book also exposes "capitalist maneuvers" to isolate Khrushchev from the ordinary people and relates how cleverly he outwitted them. The twelve authors of the book, among them Khrushchev's son-in-law Adzhubei, his translator O. Troyanovsky, and G. D. Zhukov, head of foreign cultural exchanges, were collectively awarded the Lenin Prize.

have been made to coincide with an important Soviet gain, for instance in Berlin. Since this was not the case, Eisenhower was not welcome, and Khrushchev said so in no uncertain terms.

It was typical of the Soviet method that after the Paris debacle the line of action in foreign policy did not show any substantial change. The wrecking of the conference by Khrushchev should be considered as proof that Russia does not insist on summit meetings solely for the sake of propaganda, but in the expectation of tangible gains. Similarly, the May, 1960, events can be taken as a confirmation that Khrushchev can create the most noisy uproar and shout terrible threats without really modifying his policy. Had Eisenhower submitted to his Paris ultimatum, Khrushchev would have pounded ahead to extort some concessions on Berlin. But since he was rebuked, and (despite some differences in attitude) faced with a united front, he reverted to a less aggressive stance. On his way from Paris to Moscow, Khrushchev stopped in East Berlin, the logical place to put the threat of a unilateral peace with the German Democratic Republic into effect. But his speeches on May 20 and 21 proved a political anticlimax. He again blamed America for having "torpedoed" the conference, accused Nixon, Dillon, and Herter of "arrogance," held forth against Adenauer and Willy Brandt, the Socialist Mayor of West Berlin; but he did not sign a treaty with the German Communists. The verbal excesses were intended, no doubt, to appease his German associates, but otherwise they had little political significance. Khrushchev declared that the Soviet Union and the other "peace-loving" nations now had the moral right to solve the Berlin question without delay by signing a peace treaty with East Germany. Had not the United States concluded "a unilateral peace treaty with Japan?" But, Khrushchev asked, was the time ripe for such a move? On May 20, he said:

> In present conditions it is worth while to wait a little longer and try to find, by the joint efforts of the four victor powers, a solution to the question of signing a peace treaty with the two German states—a question which has long been ripe for solution. That task won't run away. We shall do better to wait, and the question will become more mature.[58]

Despite this momentary moderation, uneasy months followed the breakup of the Paris Conference. On July 1, Soviet fighters shot down an American RB-47 reconnaissance plane over international waters of the Barents Sea. Four American airmen lost their lives. For twelve days, the Soviet Government refrained from informing

American authorities, who thought that the plane had met with an accident. But on July 12, Khrushchev frankly admitted that the Russians had tried to mislead the United States. Speaking at a news conference in Moscow, he said: "We trapped them on May 1, and we wanted to trap them again on July 1."[59] A White House statement made it clear that the RB-47 at no time flew over Soviet territory or territorial waters. It said: "The shooting down of the plane . . . can have only been a deliberate and reckless attempt to create an international incident."[60] Whether the downing of the plane was deliberate or simply exploited after the fact, it was used to surround the Soviet Union with an atmosphere of awe. Such apparently also was the aim of the continuous attacks against the West in general, and the United States in particular, in the Soviet press and by the traveling Soviet leaders. The results were rather meager. In June, Mikoyan was rebuked in Norway for assailing the United States while on an official visit. In July, Khrushchev was accorded a frigid reception in Austria, where his new interpretation of neutrality was found unacceptable and has not since reappeared in any Soviet statements. (On July 6, in a speech at Klagenfurt, Khrushchev warned the Austrians that Moscow would consider it a violation of Austrian neutrality if rockets fired from Italy passed over Austrian territory. The contention was politically absurd and inadmissible in international law. It was rejected three days later by Austrian Chancellor Julius Raab, who declared that "the interpretation and preservation of its neutrality is exclusively Austria's own affair.")

On June 27, the Soviet-bloc delegations broke up the Geneva disarmament negotiations. On August 1, the Soviet representative to the U.S. Disarmament Commission objected to its meeting in advance of the session of the General Assembly and asked that the heads of governments personally participate in the disarmament debate of the Assembly. The stage was thus set for a new major performance—Khrushchev's second trip to America and his participation in the proceedings of the Fifteenth Assembly, which he tried to transform into a mass summit meeting. Only a few heads of governments or states followed his example: Nehru, Tito, Nasser, Castro, Nkrumah. President Eisenhower made an important speech and returned to Washington. Of the Western leaders, only Prime Minister Macmillan was present,* and this did not do Khrushchev much good. Khrushchev was less than reasonable during Mac-

* The King of Denmark, on a visit to the United States, addressed the Assembly on October 17, after Khrushchev's departure.

millan's major policy speech before the Assembly. He interrupted, yelled, and pounded his desk, but was unable to ruffle the speaker. With the exception of a resolution on colonialism, all Soviet proposals were turned down. The Assembly rebuked Khrushchev for his suggestion that Dag Hammarskjold resign; it also rejected his demands to replace the Secretary General with a collective body, and that a special session of the General Assembly on disarmament be convened the following spring (in Geneva, Moscow, or Leningrad). Khrushchev's most serious setback, however, was his failure to have a meeting with President Eisenhower, probably the main object of his second trip to America. No confirmation of this assumption can of course be found in Soviet texts. But visitors to Russia reported that the news of the Paris upheaval and of the cancelation of Eisenhower's visit had made the people uneasy. Official Soviet propaganda explaining Khrushchev's role in these events apparently was not very successful, and there were rumors of war. Such information filtering out of Soviet Russia is obviously sketchy and has no concrete value. If correct, however, it would go a long way toward explaining Khrushchev's behavior in the General Assembly, where he made several unprecedented scenes, used rude language, took off and waved his shoe, and generally made himself ridiculous—but not in everybody's eyes, it seems. His tactics had some success with five "nonengaged" leaders (Nehru, Nasser, Tito, Sukarno, and Nkrumah), as well as with a number of other delegations, mostly Asian and African, to whom a Khrushchev-Eisenhower meeting appeared innocent enough, and "for the good of the cause." In fact, the appeal of the "five" that Eisenhower and Khrushchev meet, their draft resolution in the Assembly to the same effect, and the forty-odd votes it got, were an encouragement of the impermissible behavior Khrushchev had demonstrated both in Paris and in New York. Eventually, Khrushchev was frustrated by Eisenhower's rejection of the plea for a meeting. The President's answer pointed to the futility of a meeting with Khrushchev while the Soviet Union was engaged in a policy of the "increasing of tension throughout the world and in particular of damaging relations with the United States."[61] The "neutral" draft resolution failed to gain the necessary majority and was eventually withdrawn by its sponsors. Khrushchev left New York after a three-week exhibition that considerably harmed him in Western eyes, but at the same time showed the support that devious Soviet tactics could muster among some well-meaning delegations to the United Nations.

The Kennedy-Khrushchev meeting at Vienna in June, 1961, is too recent to be treated as anything but a postscript to this outline of top-level Soviet diplomacy. When Khrushchev, in May, 1960, spoke of another summit conference "in six or eight months' time," he was also giving notice that he wished to resume talks with the next President of the United States. Soviet impatience to test the new President was expressed, even before Inauguration Day, in informal suggestions for an early Kennedy-Khrushchev meeting. And there were other signs: a general change of tone with regard to the United States, which since the Paris conference had become the villain of Soviet propaganda; a warm telegram of congratulations from Khrushchev; the dropping of the U-2 case in the United Nations; the release of the two surviving RB-47 airmen. On the American side, there was the Moscow trip of two future members of the White House staff and their conversations with Deputy Foreign Minister Kuznetsov.[62] On February 22, Ambassador Llewellyn Thompson left Washington with a personal message from the President to Khrushchev. There is not enough documentary material on this period to permit an appraisal of the relative importance of these moves or for stating with any certainty whether there had been (as reported in the press) a change of attitude on Kennedy's part on the timing and preparation of a conference with the Soviet Premier. There is a general impression that, to begin with, both sides felt the need of probing and assessing the other's intentions. Also, not enough is known of the Laos negotiations to state with certainty whether the balance of power was suddenly upset there in January–February, 1961, because of increased Soviet military aid to the Communist Pathet Lao.* Was there, in the last days of March, a dramatic last-minute acceptance of the cease-fire demanded by America and England? Some facts point in that direction: Kennedy's strong statement on March 23 that America was faced "with a clear and one-sided threat of a change in the

---

* *Time* correspondent James Wise accompanied Prince Souvanna Phouma at the end of February to the Pathet Lao stronghold in the strategic Plaine des Jarres in Northern Laos. He wrote: "The entire Plaine des Jarres is bulging with Russian armaments and swarming with Vietnamese. The Ilyushins, which are lined up 18 deep at Hanoi airport, drone in by the hour, bringing 45 tons of equipment a day. About once a week, a convoy of 50 Gorki trucks rolls in. . . . The rebels have . . . Kalashnikov submachine guns, Simonov carbines, Degtiarev light machine guns, . . . Russian assault guns and 60- and 81-mm mortars. In the hills around the plain are new Russian 85-mm cannon manned by Viet Minh 'technicians.'" (*Time*, March 10, 1961, p. 26.)

internationally agreed position on Laos";[63] Dean Rusk's speech at a SEATO meeting in Bangkok on March 27, in which he reminded his audience of Korea and said that America's sense of responsibility in the defense of freedom had no geographical barriers; *Pravda*'s article of March 27 stating that a peaceful solution for Laos could be found, and Gromyko's sudden request a few hours later to be received by the President.[64] On the other hand there were reports, possibly inaccurate, that the White House took the first step toward a Kennedy-Khrushchev conference late in March.

The meeting in Vienna was officially announced on May 19 and took place on June 3 and 4, after a state visit by the President and Mrs. Kennedy to Paris. The joint communiqué called the conversations "useful," and specifically mentioned American-Soviet relations, disarmament, nuclear tests, and Germany among the topics discussed. The only point of agreement was the common support of "a neutral and independent Laos under a government chosen by the Laotians themselves."[65]

On June 6, in a radio and television address, Kennedy spoke of his talks with Khrushchev in a mood reminiscent of Churchill's war speeches. He said that their views contrasted sharply, and grimly reminded the nation of the dangers inherent in the Communist aims of subversion and revolution. The address made it evident that Khrushchev had taken pains to interpret for the President the theory of "wars of national liberation," which he had expounded in the report of January 6, 1961. The aim of such a performance on Khrushchev's part is not easy to fathom; if it was not merely a boast that the future belonged to Communism, one could interpret it as a warning to the United States not to interfere in areas that, according to Moscow, were fighting "wars of national liberation." If that was Khrushchev's purpose, then his psychological approach was wrong, for Kennedy's reaction was one of strength, not weakness. After Vienna, the United States defense budget rose to record peacetime heights, and preparations to meet the tactical and technical problems of infiltration, guerrillas, and local wars were accelerated.

During the Vienna meeting, Khrushchev handed Kennedy two memorandums of considerable importance. One dealt with a nuclear-test ban. It was a discouraging document for those who believed that Russia was ready to accept some form of international control. The Soviet Government repeated its well-known arguments and hedged any form of international inspection on its territory with conditions that would make it a dangerous illusion. Once more, the Soviet Union declared that the solution would be "universal and complete disarmament." The second memorandum concerned the peace treaty with Germany and the situation in Berlin. It asked for a peace conference "without any delay" and proposed that the four big powers appeal to the two German states to reach agreement between themselves "in any way acceptable to them." Should such agreement be reached, a peace treaty with a unified Germany would be concluded. Otherwise, two peace treaties, one with each of the two German states would be signed. The memorandum stressed, however, that these negotiations should not be allowed to drag out, and that the German states be given a six-month time limit for reaching an understanding. The peace treaty would specifically designate West Berlin as a demilitarized free city, which would also mean the liquidation of the "occupation regime," i.e., the withdrawal of the Allied garrisons, which could be replaced by token contingents of troops of the United States, the United Kingdom, France, and the Soviet Union, possibly also by neutral troops under U.N. auspices. The memorandum also proposed that lines of communications with West Berlin should be settled "through appropriate agreement with the German Democratic Republic." The alternative of a separate peace treaty between Russia and East Germany also reappeared: "If the United States does not show an understanding of the necessity for concluding a peace treaty, we shall regret this, since we would have to sign a peace treaty, which would be impossible and dangerous to delay further, not with all states, but only with those that want to sign it."[66]

It should be noted that the six-month time limit expressly referred to the termination of negotiations between the two German states, not to the signing of a peace treaty between Russia and East Germany; there also was a verbal concession on West Berlin, admitting an "interim solution" for an unspecified but "definite" period. The Soviet Government further stressed that it did not tie the conclusion of a peace treaty to the recognition of East Germany, and that it would allow the two German states to remain members of NATO and the Warsaw Pact, respectively, "for a certain time." The general tone of the memorandum was one of finality, but on closer analysis the Soviet Government reserved for itself room for maneuver.

On his return to Moscow, Khrushchev did not speak in public until June 15, waiting, no doubt, for Kennedy's address and other reactions. Apparently these were not satisfactory, for in his television and radio report of June 15, the Soviet Premier increased the pressure: "We ask everyone to understand us correctly: The question of a peace treaty with Germany cannot be postponed any longer: a peace settlement in Europe must be attained this year." Khrushchev went on to say (as he had several times before) that those who would seek to maintain "the occupation regime" in West Berlin despite a peace treaty between Russia and East Germany, and would try to cross the frontiers, "will assume full responsibility for the consequence of the aggression and will be properly rebuffed."

On Laos, Khrushchev kept to the known Soviet line, but on the whole he upheld the Vienna communiqué—that Laos should become an independent and neutral state. His most serious statement, however, concerned the universal application of the doctrine of which Soviet behavior in Laos was a local expression. Khrushchev said:

> It emerged from our talks with President Kennedy that we understand the peaceful coexistence of states differently. The President's idea is to build up something like a dam against the people's movement to establish in their countries social systems which the ruling circles of the Western powers consider unsuitable. . . . The representatives of imperialist states want to find a way to prevent liberation ideas, the ideas of Marxism-Leninism, from spreading further. When the people of a capitalist or colonial country, showing their discontent with the existing system, seek to change it . . . then the governments of the imperialist countries immediately announce that this is a Communist intrigue. . . . They are not averse to using such inventions as a pretext for interfering in the internal affairs of other countries.[67]

This was a direct reference to Khrushchev's exegesis of the coexistence policy, in particular to its application to civil wars and wars of national liberation. From Kennedy's address to the nation of June 6, we may infer that Khrushchev boasted of the efficacy of the new method. In summing up Khrushchev's declarations, the President said: "The revolution of rising peoples would eventually be a Communist revolution, and . . . the so-called wars of liberation supported by the Kremlin would replace the old methods of direct aggression and invasion."[68] In the broadcast of June 15, which was his public report on the Vienna meeting, Khrushchev stated that the Kremlin's resolve to further the expansion of Communism by this method was not negotiable:

Every people has the right to independence and a free national existence and no state should interfere in the internal affairs of other
countries.

A class struggle is under way in the capitalist countries. The people
are fighting against their oppressors, against reactionary regimes. It is
impossible to regulate these processes by agreement.[69]

As far as one can judge from this historically short perspective,
the Vienna meeting was one where nothing tangible was given
away by either side. Khrushchev was obviously interested in showing that he was again on speaking terms with the President of the
United States. This seems to have been his sole gain. On the other
hand, he may have lost more in political potential, for Kennedy
may have come to the conclusion, then and there, that a general
understanding with the present Soviet leadership was not possible.
Whatever ideas the President may have entertained on this subject before Vienna, afterward American policy ceased to stress the
hope of a global agreement with Russia, not even in the form of
agreeing to disagree. Local arrangements, in the sense of both substance and geography, are still being sought for, with an understanding that they can only be the results of a balance of power, global
or local, preferably both.

One more consideration comes to mind. When Khrushchev
talked to Kennedy in Vienna about disarmament and a nuclear-test
ban, the secret preparations for the massive Soviet test series begun
in September were in full swing. This is not likely to be forgotten
by American policy-makers.

Six years had elapsed between the Geneva Summit Conference
in 1955 and the Vienna meeting. In Europe, the only material
change brought about by Soviet action during this period was the
Berlin wall, closing the last gap in the Iron Curtain. This, however,
is also a symbol of Communist political defeat. The lack of any
other achievements in the fields of diplomacy and propaganda, not
to speak of more tangible areas, serves to explain the motivation behind Khrushchev's attitude in the Vienna talks. In effect, he seems
to have candidly told Kennedy that Communist frontal attacks on
"capitalist" positions were ineffective and that he was banking on
the indirect approach, the "coexistence" policy (which had already brought results in Cuba, Laos, and Vietnam).

17. DISARMAMENT

War against Germany and Austro-Hungary, civil war, and Communist terror—all these had drained Russia's military potential. In 1920, Tukhachevsky's troops, which were supposed to carry the revolution to Germany and other countries of western Europe, were defeated by the army of a Polish state resurrected a century and a quarter after the partitions. All the Communist revolutionary and military ventures had failed along the western border; the Soviets felt isolated and weak. In the early twenties, the Bolsheviks feared a possible French military intervention in Russia across Germany and Poland. Despite Lenin's oft-proclaimed antipacifism, these circumstances, as well as the hope of turning the universal longing for peace against the bourgeois governments, made Soviet Russia a persistent advocate of disarmament.

But from the outset, the Soviet approach to this problem was double-edged, the same as to "just" and "unjust" wars, to the right of nations to self-determination, and to the civil rights of the individual. Since the Genoa conference in 1922, when Chicherin announced that his delegation would propose "the general limitation of armaments," similar ideas had repeatedly been advocated by the Soviet Government. They clearly reveal Russia's intention to exploit the emotional appeal of disarmament and, at the same time, the constant attempt to maneuver others into disarming, without herself disarming. A telling proof of this attitude is the Kremlin's stubborn resistance to any international control of either armaments or disarmament. Both the 1946 Baruch Plan for atomic control and Eisenhower's 1955 "open-skies" system of mutual aerial inspection were branded as attempts to limit the sovereign rights of the Soviet state or a camouflage for espionage on Soviet territory. In a typical pronouncement, Khrushchev said: "If inspection is established without confidence, this will not be inspection. With spoiled relations between countries, such inspection becomes a form of military intelligence aimed at choosing the most favorable moment for either of the parties to commit aggression."[1]

Over the years, Soviet tactics on disarmament have varied little. There is not much difference between the "Declaration on General and Complete Disarmament"[2] presented by Khrushchev in the United Nations on September 18, 1959, and Litvinov's "Draft Convention for Immediate, Complete, and General Disarmament,"[3] submitted to the Preparatory Commission of the Disarmament Conference in 1928. Not only is the wording often similar, but in essence it is the same demagogical demand for total disarmament, occasionally accompanied by lip-service to the control and security arrangements that alone would allow the free nations to feel safe without arms.

In the twenties, the difficulties facing Russia's partners in disarmament negotiations were largely similar to those which have blocked progress in this field since the end of World War II. For example, at the conference held in Moscow in December, 1922, in which the Baltic states, Finland, and Poland participated, Litvinov proposed a reduction of military strength, but at the same time refused to conclude the nonaggression treaties demanded by the other delegations. In later years, the Soviet Government reversed its attitude toward such treaties. But in 1922, Litvinov stated that the "signing of merely formal declarations" could not create an atmosphere of confidence as long as Russia's western neighbors did not prove their good intentions by "adopting the only method which is really convincing, that is to show themselves ready to reduce their standing armies and to dissolve irregular military formations."[4]

This was reversing the situation. It was up to Russia to show some good will in meeting the legitimate misgivings of its smaller neighbors. Lenin's government had a bad record in discharging its international obligations. The 1922 Moscow conference foundered on Soviet evasive attitude in matters of security and control, and on Moscow's refusal to assume unequivocal obligations of nonaggression with regard to the western border states. Yet the Kremlin probably did not consider the conference a total loss.

It is doubtful whether the Soviet hierarchy really ever believed that a foreign state would voluntarily disarm without solid proof of simultaneous Russian disarmament. The appeals to disarm are in fact directed at the public opinion of the other countries, in the hope that while only specialists understand the intricacies of disarmament control, the masses believe that the Soviet Union really wishes to disarm and will press their own governments to do likewise.

Soon after the Genoa Conference, in May, 1922, the All-Russian Central Executive Committee asked for "universal and general disarmament." In an appeal to the peoples of the world, the same committee also announced a unilateral reduction of Soviet armed forces. A similar line was pursued by the Soviet delegation to the Preparatory Committee of the Disarmament Conference in Geneva. On February 15, 1928, Litvinov submitted a "Draft Convention for Immediate, Complete, and General Disarmament." It was rejected in March, since most delegations considered it unrealistic, if not purposely misleading. The plan was again submitted by the Soviet delegation to the Disarmament Conference in Geneva in 1932, and again it was rejected. Litvinov then suggested that the Conference "base its work on the *principle* of general and complete disarmament." In 1960, following a similar tactical pattern, Zorin made any further Soviet participation in the United Nations disarmament discussions dependent on the acceptance *in principle* of Russia's plan for "complete and universal disarmament."

Before Hitler's advent, Soviet maneuvering was not the only obstacle on the road to disarmament. Germany's demand for equality in armaments, presented as a matter of practical necessity as well as of national dignity and international justice, posed a thorny problem. While France, Poland, and Czechoslovakia viewed German rearmament with apprehension, the Soviet Government, in line with its secret collaboration with the Reichwehr, backed these demands.

The Western powers faced the difficult choice of either giving in to Soviet demagogic demands for "total disarmament" or agreeing to partial German rearming. They tried to placate Germany, but all such concessions became irrelevant once Hitler, in March, 1935, denounced the military clauses of the Versailles Treaty and embarked on a policy of large-scale armaments. This marked the end of any reasonable hope to reach an agreement on the limitation of armaments. When, on September 14, 1935, Litvinov spoke in the League of Nations Assembly of converting "the dying Disarmament Conference" into a "Permanent Peace Conference,"[5] this was in fact an appropriate epitaph to the disarmament efforts of the prewar period.

AFTER WORLD WAR II

Disarmament negotiations, within the framework of the United Nations or in various *ad hoc* bodies, were resumed in 1946. For the next seventeen years, their practical result was virtually nil. The first partial success was registered in August, 1963, when the limited-test-ban treaty was signed in Moscow. The main obstacle to agreement was again the Soviet Union's continuous rejection of international disarmament control within its boundaries. But the years of negotiating were used to good purpose by Soviet diplomacy, primarily to gain time for nuclear armaments. Indeed, since 1946, a remarkable reversion of power has occurred. When the war ended, the United States was the sole possessor of the new weapon of mass destruction that could obliterate the military superiority Soviet Russia had acquired due to rapid Western demobilization. Then, in June, 1946, the United States offered the Baruch Plan, under which all atomic power would be submitted to full international control. The Soviet Union rejected the plan, and instead engaged in an arms race that fifteen years later gave it nuclear strength second only to the U.S. By 1958, the "balance of terror" had been established. It was then that Khrushchev embarked on the drive to dislodge the Allied garrisons from West Berlin, expecting to obtain this important concession in a political settlement based on the new relation of power. It is doubtful, however, whether Khrushchev considered Berlin anything more than a transitory aim, intended also to divert Western attention. Even in Germany, Russia has wider ambitions. The main goal was revealed in September, 1961, when the Soviet Government broke a tacit moratorium agreement and performed the greatest series of nuclear tests to date. Had President Kennedy yielded to various pressures, instead of ordering new American tests, a Soviet breakthrough in nuclear weapons would now be a possibility to be reckoned with. On March 2, 1962, the President said:

> Further Soviet series, in the absence of further Western progress, could well provide the Soviet Union with a nuclear attack and defense capability so powerful as to encourage aggressive designs. Were we to stand still while the Soviets surpassed us . . . the free world's ability to deter, to survive and to respond to an all-out attack would be seriously weakened.[6]

Such, without doubt, was the Soviet goal. Its achievement would have put Russia in a situation of military superiority over the

Western powers similar to that of Hitler's over Europe in 1939. Moscow attempted once more to equal or surpass the U.S. in atomic strength in order to wring out political concessions, by secretly installing nuclear rockets in Cuba in 1962. There is no reason to think that this attempt will have been the last.

The Baruch Plan,[7] submitted to the United Nations Atomic Energy Commission in 1946, is the only proposal made thus far that might have averted the nuclear-arms race. Under the Plan, exclusive ownership rights of all sources of fissionable materials, exclusive rights of research in the field of atomic explosives, and full control of all stages of atomic production were vested with an international atomic-development authority. This would have permitted international inspectors to move freely on Soviet or satellite territory, and perhaps be stationed at uranium mines and in laboratories and factories engaged in atomic production. But a police state cannot afford such abdication of total authority. Gromyko said in the Security Council: "Only people who have lost their sense of reality can seriously believe in the possibility of creating such arrangements."[8] Furthermore, the Russian Communists were congenitally unable to trust the honesty of America's intentions, and they were fatally committed by doctrine to seek possession of the new weapons. At first, Russia countered the Baruch Plan with a draft convention simply prohibiting the use, production, and storing of atomic weapons. In March, 1947, Gromyko, speaking in the Security Council, subjected the Baruch Plan to scorching criticism, charging that its basic proposal of an international authority controlling atomic energy had reduced the idea of control to absurdity: "Unlimited control," he said, would mean "unlimited interference of the . . . controlling organ . . . in the economic life of the countries . . . and interference in their internal affairs."[9]

From then on the general pattern of the debate was set for years to come: The West tried to build a system of disarmament guaranteed by international control and on-the-spot inspection; the Soviet Union called for treaties proclaiming a ban on nuclear weapons and reductions in armaments, but evaded practical control measures on its own territory or in areas under its domination. In short, the Soviet Government tried to evolve a situation in which agreed prohibitions and reductions would in fact be checked only in the West. This could be achieved most easily by adjusting the agreements on control to the differences in the political and social systems. War preparations affecting thousands of people cannot be kept secret in open societies; without special arrangements they would remain uncontrollable in police states.

In 1946–47, when the disarmament negotiations began, the Soviet Union was interested primarily in a ban on the atomic weapons it did not possess. In conventional forces the situation was reversed, since Russia's superiority in this field was overwhelming. At the end of the war, the United States had about 12 million men under arms. A rapid demobilization reduced this number by 70 per cent during 1946; another reduction took place in 1947. By mid-1947, American armed forces did not number more than 1.5 million men, of whom less than 550,000 served overseas. Only a handful of divisions—American, British, French, one Polish (from the West), and some smaller Norwegian, Dutch, and Belgian units—were in West Germany. In 1950, after the outbreak of the Korean war, General Eisenhower, the NATO Commander-in-Chief, had under him fewer than 12 trained and equipped divisions, but not deployed for defense against an attack from the East. Facing this small force (after what Russia called its demobilization) were 175 first-line divisions, of which 22 were stationed in East Germany, and 60 in other East European countries. In addition, there were 145 Soviet reserve divisions to be ready within thirty days of mobilization. During a debate in the House of Commons in July, 1950, the British Minister of Defense stated that Russia had 2.8 million men under arms, 25,000 tanks, and 19,000 military aircraft. Churchill, then the leader of the Opposition, put the number of Soviet tanks at 40,000, "seven times that of the United States, and six times that of Britain."[10] According to a statement made by Khrushchev, the Soviet armed forces numbered nearly 2.9 million men in 1948. But in the period 1949–50, because of "the NATO threat and atomic blackmail," Soviet armed strength was again brought up to 5.8 million.[11]

Under these circumstances, the West would have been at Russia's mercy had America not been the sole possessor of the atomic weapons. Conversely, no conventional forces, however large, could be a match for American atomic bombs. Moscow, therefore, adopted the "humanitarian" line that atomic weapons should be destroyed and banned. But to demand only nuclear disarmament (as was the object of the Soviet draft convention submitted to the United Nations Atomic Energy Commission in June, 1946) would be an untenable negotiating position. Besides, Russia was interested in the withdrawal, or at least the maximum limitation, of American troops overseas. Therefore, the reduction of conventional forces was also introduced in Soviet proposals in various forms after August, 1946. However, the emphasis remained on atomic weapons. Many ingenious formulas were put forward to keep up the hope that the Soviet Government would eventually accept a working control system of disarmament, while Western representatives vainly strove to pin down Russian promises. In this protracted battle of wits, the Russians were mostly on the offensive, using simple ideas and catchwords. Over the years, they consistently pressed for radical solutions that would advance their aim of military superiority: immediate prohibition of atomic weapons, destruction of existing stocks, reduction by one third, and later one half, of conventional forces, liquidation of bases abroad.* To meet Western criticism that such measures might result in unilateral disarmament, the Soviet Government also proposed attractive-sounding control establishments. The catch was that all international inspection was made subject to the decision of the Security Council, in which Russia held the right of veto.

On May 10, 1955, during the period of *détente* preceding the Geneva Summit Conference, the Soviet Government introduced a comprehensive plan in the U.N. Disarmament Subcommittee, which was to be implemented as an international convention. It was to be completed in two stages, in 1956 and 1957. A world conference

---

* Following is a list of characteristic Soviet disarmament proposals made between 1948 and 1954: immediate prohibition of atomic weapons, and "as first step" the reduction by one third of armed forces within one year (1948); destruction of all existing stocks of atomic weapons within three months of the signing of a convention 1949); branding of the atomic weapons as weapons of aggression and the first government to use them as a war criminal (1950); atomic weapons to be prohibited, their production stopped, the use solely for civilian purposes of the atomic bombs already produced (1951); participation in "the aggressive Atlantic bloc and the creation by certain states, and primarily the United States of America" of military bases abroad to be declared incompatible with membership in the United Nations; a world conference to consider substantial reduction of armaments and armed forces and practical measures for prohibiting atomic weapons (1952); unconditional prohibition of atomic, hydrogen, and other types of weapons of mass destruction; reduction by one-third within one year of the armed forces of the five permanent members of the Security Council; recognizing that military bases on foreign territory increase "the threat of a new world war and . . . undermine the national sovereignty and independence of states" (1953); reduction of military appropriations and armed forces to the extent of 50 per cent of agreed levels from the actual expenditure during 1953, and the strength existing on December 31, 1953, respectively; complete prohibition of atomic, hydrogen and other weapons of mass destruction (1954).

on reduction of armaments and prohibition of atomic weapons was to be convened not later than the first half of 1956. In the course of that year, the major powers were to reduce the strength of their armed forces to agreed levels: 1 million to 1.5 million for the United States, Communist China, and Soviet Russia, and 650,000 for Britain and France. In the course of 1957, further reductions of conventional forces would take place; once they reached 75 per cent of the level indicated in the convention, a complete prohibition of the use of atomic, hydrogen, and other weapons of mass destruction would become effective. During both stages, an international control organ would exercise extensive rights of inspection on the territory of the states concerned, on a basis of reciprocity. The Soviet proposal contained one novel provision—i.e., that this international agency set up control posts at important road and railway junctions, in ports, and at aerodromes.

Despite its vagueness, the Soviet plan was well received. The American representative in the Disarmament Subcommittee said that the ideas advocated by the Western powers since 1947 were at last given serious consideration by the Soviet Union. At the Geneva Summit Conference in July, 1955, hopes rose to new heights. However, these expectations came to naught at the second conference, in November, 1955. Dissension on disarmament was not the main reason for its failure. However, an extensive discussion of the subject again made it clear that the Soviet Government was bent on making the most of its impressive propositions, but avoided the practical application of control measures. At this meeting, the Russians in substance repeated their May 10 plan, including the project for "effective international control." But the Soviet delegate refused to discuss the practical suggestions Eisenhower had made in June: to eliminate the fear of a surprise attack by permitting aerial photography (better known as the "open-skies" proposal) and by an exchange of military information ("to give each other a complete blueprint of our military establishment, from beginning to end, from one end of our country to the other").[12] The two projects had been politely rejected by Bulganin in August. In November, Molotov said in Geneva that such measures would further intensify mutual distrust. Later, Khrushchev called the open-skies proposal "preposterous" and a "spying proposition."[13] The confused situation with regard to disarmament control at the second Geneva Conference was well summarized by Foreign Secretary Macmillan, who asked: "But when will this international control be established? And what exactly will this control consist of? These are questions on which we have been trying to get the Soviet Union to clarify its position for years."[14]

At the time of the 1955 Geneva Conferences, Russia was undoubtedly nearing atomic warfare capability. The first atomic explosion in the Soviet Union was detected by Western instruments in September, 1949. A hydrogen bomb was exploded in August, 1953. Strategic bomber formations made their appearance at military parades in 1954–55. It was no coincidence that in 1954, Soviet proposals for reducing conventional forces shifted from one third to 50 per cent. In 1955, Russia agreed to consider these reductions not in terms of a percentage of the unknown quantity of Soviet land forces, but as a stated number. Furthermore, there was a shift in the timing of the proposed disarmament measures: The Soviet Government now agreed that a nuclear-weapons ban was possible after a considerable reduction in conventional forces had taken place. However, so long as there was no guarantee that the proposed measures could be checked on the spot, they remained merely paper concessions. For ten years, no reasonable assurance in this respect could be obtained from Soviet negotiators. Despite the mounting frustration, many illusions survived the 1955 crisis, and the Sisyphean labor of disarmament negotiations was resumed in 1956. Basically, the Russian tactics did not change. The Soviet Union had already gained a decade by noisy propaganda against the atomic weapons they themselves were secretly producing and testing, by proposing "strict" control systems and reduction of armed forces, and by well-sounding but meaningless declarations (like "a solemn and unconditional obligation not to employ atomic and hydrogen and other weapons of mass destruction,"[15] or "not to be the first"[16] to use them). In the same vein, Russia in 1954 had asked to join NATO. In 1955, the Soviet Government also claimed to have liquidated all bases abroad, ignoring the Soviet divisions stationed in Eastern Europe. In March, 1956, Moscow came up with a new idea—the creation in Central Europe of a "zone of limitation and inspection of armaments,"[17] the forerunner of the Rapacki Plan. In May, Russia announced a unilateral reduction of its armed forces by 1.2 million men, following a similar announcement of about 640,000 men in August, 1955. Secretary Dulles commented that there could be no verification of these reductions (from an estimated level of 4 million Soviet soldiers under arms). The Soviet moves did make some impact on world opinion, but they had no bearing on the progress of disarmament. In a statement published on October 23, 1956, President Eisenhower declared: "There is only one reason why no safe agreement has been effected to date: the refusal of the Soviet Union to accept any dependable system of mutual safeguards. In the past two years alone, the Soviet Union has rejected no less than fourteen American proposals on disarmament and control of nuclear weapons."[18]

Still negotiations continued. The Disarmament Subcommittee sat in London from March 18 to September 6, 1957. The Soviet delegation dragged the debate through the spring and summer, but in September suddenly refused to agree to Western suggestions that the talks be resumed on October 1, after a recess. On October 4, Russia launched the first earth satellite, and it soon became evident that it expected this technical achievement to influence East-West relations in all fields, particularly in disarmament negotiations. The orbiting of the Sputnik was the crowning feat of a period of intense space and nuclear activity that could be only partly observed from outside the Soviet Union. Secret Soviet tests of nuclear weapons were detected intermittently between August, 1956, and March, 1958. There were only two direct Russian announcements during this period: one in August, 1957, that a super long-distance intercontinental ballistic rocket had been successfully tried in the Soviet Union, and another in October, about the detonation of a powerful hydrogen warhead of a new type.

As a result of their progress in space and nuclear programs, the Soviet tone in international relations altered noticeably. Threats of atomic retaliation, particularly in regard to the smaller European NATO powers, became a recurrent theme of Soviet diplomacy. Moscow also made it clear that atomic disarmament now depended as much on its own decision as on the United States. This attitude found expression in Soviet demands to change the forum of disarmament discussions. In October, 1957, the Soviet Government took the view that the failure to reach agreement was due to the limited number of countries taking part in the debates of the Disarmament Commission and the Subcommittee. The Soviet delegation therefore demanded that the General Assembly dissolve the two bodies and replace them with a permanent disarmament commission consisting of all the member states of the United Nations. If discussion among the twelve members of the Disarmament Commission and the five members of its Subcommittee failed to bring results, then obviously it would be even more difficult, if not impossible, to reach agreement among all the eighty-one states then members of the United Nations. The proposition was an early indication of the new line in Soviet diplomacy: the drive for a summit meeting, and shifting away from general disarmament to a ban on nuclear tests. In November, 1957, the General Assembly decided to enlarge the Disarmament Commission by fourteen members. But this compromise move failed to placate the Soviet representative, who declared that his government would take no part in future disarmament proceedings of the United Nations. As a half-measure, Russia could agree to participate in a commission of thirty-two members, as proposed by Albania, if half of the membership would consist of Communist or "uncommitted" delegations. The Soviet delegate reserved the right to revive the eighty-one members proposition. The boycott of the U.N. disarmament proceedings was fully rewarded in November, 1958, when the Assembly voted to transform the Disarmament Commission into an all-member body. As Russia no doubt intended, this brought the disarmament activities in the United Nations virtually to a standstill. The Soviet Government then demanded that the all-important negotiations be reserved for the summit level. It was not until the summer of 1959, at the Geneva Foreign Ministers Conference (when Khrushchev's trip to the United States was already agreed upon), that agreement was reached to form a new ten-nations disarmament committee outside the U.N. machinery, its membership evenly divided between East and West: on the one side the United States, England, France, Italy, and Canada; on the other, Soviet Russia, Poland, Czechoslovakia, Romania, and Bulgaria. Thus, one more Soviet desire, parity in the negotiations, was satisfied—a matter of pure prestige, as none of these satellite governments could have an independent say in the matter.

Before the new committee met, international relations underwent a period of relaxation of tension marked by Khrushchev's visits to America and France, and the preparations for the ill-starred Paris Summit meeting. On September 18, 1959, Khrushchev, while in New York, introduced a "declaration on general and complete disarmament," Russia's most ambitious program in this field, in the General Assembly. In it, he proposed the abrogation within four years of all armed forces and armaments, with the exception of those needed for internal security. Not only were nuclear weapons to be banned, existing stocks destroyed, conventional forces disbanded, and military bases abolished, but the Soviet project also sought the abolition of war ministries, general staffs, and institutions of military education. The new plan was consistent with Russia's persistent efforts to bring about the disarmament of others, yet not herself disarming. Controls were foreseen, as complete and far-reaching as anyone might wish. But the Soviet text stated that "general and complete disarmament will remove also all difficulties connected with control. In such circumstances States will have nothing to hide from each other, and there will be every opportunity to carry out checks or inspection if there is any doubt about the good faith of any State in fulfilling its disarmament obligations."[19] But in fact, the establishment of international control over Soviet disarmament measures proved as elusive in subsequent negotiations as during the preceding thirteen years. But the idea of a disarmament utopia was attractive to world opinion, and no one could disagree with this ultimate aim. On November 20, 1959, the U.N. General Assembly registered the Soviet propaganda success by unanimously approving a resolution on universal and complete disarmament, sponsored by all member states. The Soviet proposals were referred for detailed examination to the new ten-nation disarmament committee.

The new body had a short and futile life. It met in Geneva from March 15 to June 27, 1960 (including a recess)—i.e., before and after the collapse of the May Paris Summit Conference. The debate centered on rival Western and Eastern plans, military bases abroad, and control. Even after the failure of the Paris meeting, there still seemed to be some hope of progress. But the Communist delegations walked out on the meeting on June 27, the very day a modified plan was to be presented by the United States. In a letter to President Eisenhower dated the same day, Khrushchev charged that the Western powers were seeking the adoption of "a plan of control without disarmament, i.e., of legalized military espionage."[20] Apart from wider political considerations, a point was obviously reached in Geneva when Russia preferred to break off negotiations rather than face the embarrassment of rejecting practical control measures. In its official report to the Secretary of State, the American delegation to the ten-nation committee stated: "The discussion showed that the Soviet delegation was unwilling to accept even in principle that international inspectors would have to determine if clandestine installations existed in excess of agreed amounts."[21]

The premeditated Communist walkout on June 27 was a particularly unpleasant performance. Zorin, the chief Soviet representative, had been informed beforehand that the American delegation would present new proposals. At the meeting, Zorin read a prepared statement in which he described the situation in the Committee as "abnormal and inadmissible," and declared that further debates could only confuse public opinion: "The Soviet Union cannot be an accessory to the deception of the peoples,"[22] he said. The other Communist delegates spoke in Zorin's support, but the Polish chairman, Marian Naszkowski, refused to give the floor to any of the Western representatives and declared the conference ended. There followed an extraordinary scene: The French delegate (Jules Moch) stood up and called out, "I wish to speak! I wish to speak!" Naszkowski hesitated a moment, looked at Zorin, then walked out of the room at the head of the Communist delegates, while Jules Moch shouted, "Hooliganism! Hooliganism!"[23]

Since 1957–58, public interest had veered from the general disarmament negotiations to the all-important projects of banning, or at least temporarily suspending, the nuclear-weapons tests. The ban was first suggested in April, 1954, by India's Prime Minister Nehru and later taken up by both Russia and the Western powers. But there was the perennial difficulty: While the West insisted on control, the Soviet Government pressed for prohibitions that in practice could not be checked on its territory. In June, 1957, the Soviet delegation to the Disarmament Subcommittee moved that tests be immediately stopped, "if only for a period of two or three years," contending that any shorter period would be meaningless as an effort to halt the arms race. But when, in August, the Western delegations agreed to a twenty-four month suspension of tests, renewable for further periods, the Russians backed out. They charged that the United States had made agreement impossible by linking it to other disarmament measures, like the cutoff in the production of fissionable materials for military purposes. The Western plan was complicated and difficult to understand for the general public, and thus helped the Soviet Government hide its motives behind a propaganda smokescreen. In fact its attitude could be easily explained: The West's proposal involved quick practical inspection measures; Russia was still carrying on a long series of nuclear test explosions, which did not end until November of the following year. On March 31, 1958, the Atomic Energy Commission disclosed that at least thirty-nine nuclear devices had been exploded in the Soviet Union since 1949. There were seven explosions in 1956, twelve in 1957, and nine between January and March, 1958. The Soviet Government made no announcements, but Prime Minister Macmillan told the House of Commons on March 27 that Russia had made at least fifty tests in the last few years. The last six explosions recorded by the Atomic Energy Commission took place between March 12 and March 22. Nine days later, on March

31, 1958, the Supreme Soviet passed a decree "unilaterally" ending the nuclear-weapons tests in the Soviet Union. On April 4, Khrushchev wrote to Eisenhower and Macmillan that his government had decided to implement the decree of the Supreme Soviet by discontinuing all atomic- and hydrogen-weapons tests after March 31, 1958. But Khrushchev warned that if the other nuclear powers did not follow its example, the Soviet Union would consider itself free to continue tests in the interest of its security. In his reply, Eisenhower reminded Khrushchev that the Soviet Union "has persistently rejected the substance" of his Atoms for Peace project, first proposed in 1953, had ignored Anglo-American suggestions on tests in 1957, refused to agree to a controlled reduction of the use of fissionable materials for production of weapons, as well as to the transfer of existing stocks for peaceful purposes. "It seems peculiar," wrote President Eisenhower, "that the Soviet Union, having just concluded a series of tests of unprecedented intensity, should now, in bold headlines, say that it will not test again, but add, in small type, that it may test again if the United States carries out its already long-announced and now imminent series of tests."[24] That was the crux of the matter. Russia had rejected all offers of a contractual and agreed-upon suspension. But in August, 1959, as soon as the Western powers decided to discontinue tests in order to further the conclusion of a written agreement, Moscow seized the opportunity to bring about an uncontrolled "voluntary" suspension. In view of later developments, one must conclude that from the first the Kremlin had maneuvered to make the Western powers suspend nuclear tests and stop preparations for further experiments while Russia could secretly ready herself for a massive series of explosions. After the failure of the 1955 four-power negotiations, the West made proposals to limit or stop testing or to conduct joint experiments with Russia repeatedly, particularly in March and April, 1956, in August, 1957, and in August, 1958. On October 10, 1958, American delegate Henry Cabot Lodge explained in the First Committee of the General Assembly that the offer to suspend testing did not even depend on any control agreement for the first year. After the first year, the suspension could be extended from year to year, if the parties were satisfied that an inspection system was working, and if reasonable progress were made in other disarmament fields. But on the same day, Soviet delegate Zorin declared that "the Western powers are doing everything in their power in order to barricade and block the way to agreement on the cessation of the testing of nuclear weapons."[25] Nevertheless, the three-power test-ban conference suggested by the United States and Britain in August began in Geneva on October 31, 1958. The United States and Britain did not test after that date; the Soviet Union (as far as is known) did not test after November 3. Thus began a tacit moratorium. It was transformed into a declared moratorium, based on unilateral statements—by Britain on July 30, 1959, the United States on August 26, 1959, and the Soviet Union on August 28, 1959. On that date, the Soviet Government announced that it had resolved "not to resume nuclear tests in the Soviet Union if the Western powers do not resume the testing of atomic and hydrogen weapons."[26]

The Soviet Union broke this pledge on September 1, 1961, by suddenly announcing its intention to resume nuclear testing the day before. The three-power Geneva negotiations had lasted thirty-four months, interrupted by several recesses. The delegations met in 338 sessions and agreed on a preamble, 17 articles, and 2 annexes of a draft treaty banning nuclear-weapons tests. But they failed to agree on the key issue: controlling the execution of the treaty. Once the Russians resumed testing on an unprecedented scale (in quantity and strength), the three years of negotiations seemed not only a waste of time but a period when the Soviet Union was allowed to make dangerous strides in developing weapons of mass destruction. For the Soviet Government, the Geneva talks meant three years of time gained, the same three years it was trying to obtain by its June, 1957, proposal on test suspension. Since in retrospect it is obvious that the Russians never intended to sign a treaty involving disarmament control on their territory, it would be futile to analyze the behavior of their representatives at the Geneva conference. The articles of the draft treaty which they temporarily accepted, or pretended to accept, give no useful insight into any hidden motives of Soviet policy, while it is perfectly clear why they hedged on or rejected the decisive control stipulations. It all boils down to a simple fact, consistent with the nature of the Communist regime: no foreign control on Soviet soil. In the statement published in Moscow on August 31, 1961, the Soviet Government tried to explain its decision by the "aggressiveness of the . . . NATO military bloc," the "threats" of the United States and its allies to take up arms in case of a peace treaty between Russia and East Germany, and the "feverish" war preparations by West Germany "and the present allies of German militarists."[27] Apart from these familiar slogans, the Soviet statement attached major importance to the four small-yield French tests in the Sahara and to the alleged

American preparations to develop a neutron bomb that, it said, would destroy life but not material objects: "Only aggressors dreaming of plunder, of capturing foreign lands and foreign property, can mobilize the efforts of scientists for the development of such weapons." The passage on the neutron bomb was the only one that showed real indignation, which perhaps meant that Russia was much behind in neutron-bomb research. As for the rest, the Soviet defense hardly deserves comment. The Berlin crisis was of Russia's own making, France was never part of the three-power Geneva negotiations, and its modest atomic tests were no valid excuse for a series of fifty explosions in two months, some of them in the 30–50 megaton range. There could be no explanation for the secret Soviet preparations for this series, conducted while Russian negotiators in Geneva pretended to discuss the details of a test-ban treaty. At the same time, Soviet diplomats in Geneva and elsewhere encouraged the Western governments in the logical belief that Russia hoped to rid itself of the terrible economic burden of nuclear armaments. The Russians never allowed the negotiations to go so far as to test their good will in matters of inspection. To obviate such danger, they gave a truly Byzantine performance of procrastination, deceptive tactics, and near-comical proposals, such as insisting that the international inspection posts in the Soviet Union be manned by Soviet nationals, and inventing a "national" system of international control, or inspection "by invitation." The Soviet Government also brought to the Geneva negotiations the concept of the "troika," a three-headed control organization (Western, neutralist, and Communist), and the demand of the right of veto over decisions reached. Although the circumstances were different, Soviet strategy at the test-ban conference was in essence similar to the negotiations Stalin and Molotov conducted with Britain and France in 1939, before they concluded the Molotov-Ribbentrop Pact: It aimed to reveal suddenly either a reversal of alliances or a military superiority of such magnitude that the other side would be thrown off balance without a chance to recover.

It is not necessary to enter into the details of further disarmament and test-ban negotiations between September, 1961, when the Soviet Union broke the moratorium, and the signing of a partial test-ban agreement in Moscow in August, 1963. The highlights of the period were: the resumption and collapse of the three-power test-ban conference in Geneva (November 21, 1961–January 29, 1962), the resumption, also in Geneva, of U.N. disarmament activities in a new Seventeen States Committee in March, 1962, and the Cuban crisis of October, 1962, which for a time put all disarmament talks under a shadow.* The Committee and a subcommittee of the three nuclear powers met on and off before the Moscow talks began in July 1963. The Geneva discussions brought no results as far as direct disarmament measures were concerned. Agreement was reached, however, on establishing a "hot line" of direct communications between Washington and Moscow, enabling the highest officials of both countries to get in touch without delay in case of a crisis endangering peace. The idea was developed from Paragraph F of the American "Outline of Basic Provisions" of a disarmament treaty submitted in Geneva on April 18, 1962, designed to reduce the risk of surprise attack or war by accident.[28] Although Soviet delegate Zorin accepted the proposal in July, 1962, as "an act of good will," the agreement could not be signed until June 20, 1963.

A partial ban on nuclear tests was proposed by the United States and Britain on August 27, 1962. It was part of a double offer to the Soviet Union, allowing it to choose between a total test ban and an agreement to cease tests in outer space, the atmosphere, and under water, but omitting underground tests. Only the latter could still not be policed by instruments placed at a distance, i.e., outside Soviet territory. The choice was offered on the correct assumption that the Soviet Government would not bring itself to accept any form of international control within its borders. Vassily Kuznetsov, who succeeded Zorin as head of the Soviet delegation, rejected both offers within twenty-four hours. He said that the Soviet Union was ready to negotiate only for a full test ban. Kuznetsov thought that a partial ban would "raise the nuclear temperature" and "legalize" underground testing;[29] he also repeated the charge that international on-the-spot inspection was tantamount to espionage. But new instructions must have come from Moscow, for the following day Kuznetsov offered to sign a full test-ban treaty without control on January 1, 1963; the difficulty about underground explosions was to be circumvented by a pledge on the part of all concerned not to test until a system of control acceptable to all parties had been worked out. This was the old moratorium idea in a new setting, to

* To meet the Soviet demand of "parity," the Committee was to be composed of an equal number of NATO and Warsaw Pact members, and of eight nonaligned states. But France refused to participate, feeling (not without reason) that only talks between nuclear powers could be of any use. Thus, the Committee became one of seventeen instead of eighteen nations.

which President Kennedy replied, not without irony, that "gentle-men's agreements and moratoria"[30] with the Soviet Union were unacceptable after what had happened in 1961.

Shortly after the Cuban crisis, in December, 1962, the Soviet delegation came up with a proposal for unmanned control stations that would register underground explosions. The West did not consider these "black boxes"—originally also an American idea—sufficiently perfected to replace on-site inspection. But their appearance in the negotiations suggested that the Russians wanted a test ban provided they could get it without control. Nevertheless, no progress was achieved at the conference until June 10, when it was announced that the three nuclear powers would conduct high-level test-ban talks in Moscow.

When and why did the Russians change their stand? In August, 1963, they signed a partial test-ban agreement, one which exactly a year earlier they had refused to discuss. According to a *Hongqi* and *Jenmin Jih Pao* article of September 6, 1963, Moscow had formally notified Peking as early as August, 1962, that the Soviet Union would conclude an agreement with the United States on the "prevention of nuclear proliferation." But negotiations with the West were then made to drag on for a whole year. The purpose of the delay seems to have been double: to press the Western powers still further in the hope of maneuvering them into a new moratorium, and to use the talks with the West as a lever in the dispute with China, and vice versa. Eventually (though for a short time) two Soviet teams of negotiators sat in Moscow carrying on simultaneous discussions with the United States and Britain and with the Chinese.

The decision to come to terms with the Allies was probably reached in Moscow in the spring. Until February, the Russians continued a fruitless discussion in Geneva on the number of yearly inspections of suspected underground tests on Soviet territory, controls they never intended to authorize. But in April and May, the exchange of letters among Kennedy, Macmillan, and Khrushchev (unpublished at the time of writing) must have given sufficient ground for optimism to allow the President to make the highly conciliatory speech at the American University in Washington on June 10, and the simultaneous announcement that the nuclear negotiations would be moved from Geneva to Moscow.

Khrushchev made the new Soviet attitude public in a speech at East Berlin on July 2, when he pretended to see no difference between a partial test ban with a moratorium for underground tests and one that would leave the underground tests entirely outside any contractual obligations. "We have made the proposal before," he said, contrary to evidence, and he blamed the Western powers, particularly the United States, for stalling and for advancing supplementary conditions.[31] This, however, was no more than a typical face-saving maneuver designed to mask the Soviet Government's retreat from its previous position. But there was no change in regard to the problem of control. "The imperialist gentlemen," Khrushchev warned, "should know that the Soviet Government will never abandon the security interests of its land, nor open the door to NATO spies."[32]

The Moscow negotiations began in July—with the Chinese on the fifth, and with the two Western powers on the fifteenth. But two important events had taken place in June. On the fourteenth, the Central Committee of the Chinese CP violently attacked Khrushchev's leadership in a letter to the CPSU; at the same time, the Soviet Union, long in deep trouble over its agricultural production (prices for meat and butter rose 30 per cent in June, 1962), suddenly faced a real catastrophe in the virgin lands of Kazakhstan and Siberia. Word reached the Western countries from various sources in summer and autumn that violent dust storms were burning and burying planted fields. This was confirmed by the Soviet press. *Pravda* of September 23, 1963, wrote that "in June dust storms began to blow on the steppes. And at the summer's end, when the time came to gather the harvest, torrential rains soaked the fields for many days." *Sovietskaya Rossiya* of September 6 described the terrible consequences of the dust storms in the Krasnoiarsk and Kha-Kass regions, in the Tuva and Buriat republics, "and in the whole of eastern Siberia." The article, signed by two high agricultural officials, spoke of "air erosion," of wind velocities of 40 meters per second: "For enormous distances the entire harvest was blown away." According to reliable information, the dust winds continued until October, reaching as far west as Volgograd (Stalingrad), where travelers at the airport saw "a black dust storm" that stopped traffic for twenty-four hours. These sand storms, which recur every three to four years, have a cumulative effect. In the winter of 1963–64, it looked as if Soviet agricultural production would be greatly impaired for several years.

The Soviet Union thus had two powerful reasons to generate a climate of good will toward the West: its festering dispute with China and its agricultural needs. Nothing could better serve that purpose than a test-ban treaty. Not that the Soviet motives to sign a partial test ban were only tactical. Other considerations may have played a role, for instance a need to reduce the high cost of nuclear atmospheric tests, or a belief that after the extensive testing in 1961–62, a saturation point had been reached, at least for a time. At any rate, the Kremlin's sudden urge to bring the talks with the West to a successful end was also demonstrated by the unusually amenable behavior of Soviet negotiators. They did not even insist on a nonaggression treaty between the Warsaw Pact governments and the NATO powers, although it would have considerably eased Moscow's position within the Communist camp.

The most important aspect of the Moscow Treaty, initialed on July 25 and signed on August 5, was political.[33] After seventeen years of barren negotiations, the Soviet Union for the first time formally agreed with the West on a matter directly related to disarmament. It is true that the scope of the treaty was more limited than that of the voluntary moratorium broken by the Soviet Union in 1961, since it expressly omitted underground tests. Also, the three signatories were no longer the only nuclear powers; France, which had already exploded several nuclear bombs, did not intend to accede to the Moscow Treaty. Characteristic of the treaty is the vagueness of Article IV, which provides for its unlimited duration but at the same time gives the signatories the right to withdraw on the basis of their unilateral decision, should any of them decide that "extraordinary events, related to the subject matter of this treaty, have jeopardized the supreme interests of its country." In practical terms this means that the Soviet Union can withdraw at any time with complete impunity, despite the three-month advance-notice requirement of the same article. While the vagueness of the treaty's provisions made it easier to secure the U.S. Senate's consent, it also compelled President Kennedy to state, in his message to the Senate, that the United States would maintain its nuclear arsenal through underground nuclear tests, and that it was ready to resume atmospheric testing "if the actions of others so require."[34]

Despite these shortcomings, the treaty also offered objective advantages, i.e., stopping the pollution of the atmosphere by radiation and inhibiting the production of nuclear weapons by nations that still do not have them. Among the few countries not signatories to the treaty, only China (apart from France) was considered capable of producing an atomic bomb on its own. But on October 28, 1963, China's Foreign Minister, Marshal Chen Yi, stated that his country would not be ready to explode an atomic bomb for several years.[35]

The initialing of the Moscow Treaty became a signal for a vigorous Soviet propaganda campaign presenting the partial test ban as the first step to solving still more important international problems, including those involving disarmament. But Moscow still had to fight on two fronts—to assure the Western powers that it seriously strove for further mutually acceptable agreements, and to refute the Chinese allegations of having "capitulated" to the United States; hence both the ambivalence of most Soviet texts and some differences in formulation, depending on their target. On the one hand, Moscow pointed to such component parts of the coexistence doctrine as the class struggle in capitalist countries and the national liberation movement, which "compel the governments of the Western powers to take concrete steps toward preventing the nuclear danger."[36] On the other hand, when speaking to the West, peaceful competition was stressed, "which completely rules out the use of force for asserting one's views."[37] Since both attitudes are completely consistent with the coexistence doctrine, there can be little doubt that the Soviet leadership considered the Moscow Treaty a major maneuver within the doctrine, and expected it to yield both short- and long-range advantages. Critics of the treaty were therefore branded as opponents of peaceful coexistence. They were "only a miserable, rabid group—the unrestrained imperialists of the United States, French President de Gaulle, who suffers from the atomic mania, and the revenge-seekers around Herr Adenauer."[38] Unfortunately, the governments of China and Albania,* which stubbornly refused to recognize the possible benefits to the Communist camp from the coexistence doctrine, were also among these opponents. The Kremlin's struggle on two fronts was also emphasized by its formal rejection of the "unlawful" signing of the Moscow Treaty in Washington and London by representatives of the Republic of China (Taiwan), and by its reservations on the West German signature. Some Soviet information media continued to censure the United States about NATO's alleged war preparations, about the Negro problem, and in particular about Latin America. While the mainstream of Soviet propaganda was directed toward a *détente*, this did not prevent Khrushchev himself from again demonstrating the Pavlovian technique of denying the Western powers any prolonged period of relaxation and of making their negotiators more amenable to Russian suggestions. In a conversa-

---

* North Vietnam and North Korea also did not sign the treaty. Cuba's signature was also missing, but significantly, Castro's regime was not scolded by Soviet propaganda on that account.

tion with a group of American businessmen on October 6, 1963, Khrushchev endorsed the latest incident provoked by Soviet troops against an American military convoy on the Autobahn to West Berlin. "We would not have retreated," he said, "and they would have had to pass over our dead bodies."[39] But in the same conversation, Khrushchev appealed for an extension of trade, stressing in particular Soviet need for fertilizers and capital equipment for the chemical industry.

When this conversation was taking place, the Soviet Government had already begun to make large purchases of wheat abroad. In September, it bought great quantities of grain from Canada, which previously had sold wheat to China and Poland. The Canadian sales of agricultural commodities to Communist-ruled countries in 1963 alone were estimated at nearly $1 billion; half of this sum pertained to the Soviet purchase announced on September 16. Previously the Soviet Union had bought $200 million worth of Australian wheat.[40] In October it was learned that Hungary, Bulgaria, and Czechoslovakia were also buying wheat in Canada and in the United States. Subsequently, the Soviet Government approached the United States for the purchase of 4 million tons of wheat valued at $250 million. Since it was known that Cuba received wheat from Russia, and Albania from China, one may conclude that the whole Communist camp (except Romania and possibly East Germany) was in the world market for massive wheat purchases.

Poor harvests, mismanagement, and above all a basically faulty agricultural system brought matters to a head: Moscow now looked for assistance to the "capitalists" and "imperialists" to restore its food reserves. Great quantities of food staples were readily being sold to the Russians, despite some isolated voices that trade with the Soviet Government should not be based on "business considerations."[41] Helping the Soviet and Chinese governments in their economic predicament regardless of their political aims of world domination seems as improvident as the assistance given Stalin during the war without taking into account the political aspects of the situation and its potential consequences in Europe and the Far East. Yet there is another similarity between the two situations: to deny food staples to the nations of Eastern Europe under imposed Communist rule would be as great a mistake as was applying the principle of unconditional surrender to Italy and Hitler's smaller reluctant allies—e.g., Hungary, Romania, and Bulgaria.

In order to appreciate how much the Soviet Government had at stake when it entered the new round of negotiations that led to the Moscow Treaty, one must bear in mind that the Kremlin is facing not just another agricultural difficulty. It is not only wheat that Russia is buying abroad. Its purchases of industrial equipment, steel, copper, and rubber exceeded $4.5 million in 1962. In 1962 and 1963, the Soviet Government sold $500 to $600 million of gold on the London market, the 1963 sales being almost double those of the previous year.[42] The Soviet economy is overextended. Its rate of growth declines.[43] All this was confirmed by the curtailment of foreign aid, an apparent slowing down of the space program, and the partial cessation of nuclear tests reflected in the Moscow Treaty. Faced with grave economic difficulties, the Russians will press desperately for an end to what they call "trade discriminations"—i.e., the limitations on exports of strategic goods to Communist-ruled countries—and will use any relaxation of political tensions to enter into favorable economic agreements. More than anything, the Soviet Union will want long-term industrial credits from capitalist countries, and the food grains it is lacking, together with the related facilities to produce chemical fertilizers. Just as Stalin, in the darkest hours of the war, sought and received unconditional Western assistance without deviating an inch from his political aims, so is Khrushchev, in an even more brilliant maneuver (for there is no war against a common enemy) trying to make the free world help him overcome a disastrous economic situation while unswervingly pursuing the goals of international Communism.

But the situation also presents unprecedented opportunities of far-reaching negotiations for the West, and particularly North America, which in 1960–61 accounted for 86 per cent of the world's grain exports, while the Soviet Union and China have become, and for a number of years will probably remain, grain-deficit areas.[44]

18. *NEW WORLDS TO CONQUER*

SOUTHEAST ASIA

Lenin himself outlined the course of action most likely to influence the nationalist movements in the colonial areas. In 1918, he spelled out the consecutive steps leading to Communist takeovers: "Support of democratic revolutions of all countries. Emancipation of the colonies. Federation, as a transition to voluntary amalgamation."[1]

Nowhere did this method seem more likely to succeed than in Southeast Asia. But, apart from some disturbances in Indonesia in the twenties, it was not until World War II that the Communists began to play an important role in the area—in the resistance movements against Japan. After Japan's defeat, the moment for implementing Lenin's advice seemed to have come. Whether Stalin was too impatient or whether he found it necessary to harass the colonial powers in Asia while a new phase of fighting Communism was beginning in Europe is impossible to say. It seems highly improbable, however, that the Communists would stage a series of armed insurrections—Burma (March, 1948), Malaya (May, 1948), Indonesia (September, 1948), the Philippines (October, 1948)—as well as a series of bloody riots in India without instructions from Moscow. With the exception of Vietnam, where a Communist-nationalist war against the French began in 1946, none of these armed ventures succeeded to the point of takeover. But neither can it be said that they ended in failure. Only in India and Indonesia were the mutinies quickly suppressed. In the other countries the rebellions lasted for years.

The Communist victory in the Chinese mainland dramatically changed the situation in Southeast Asia. Four years after Japan's defeat, the age-old imperialism of China re-emerged, but imbued with a new vigor born of Communist doctrine and revolutionary aims. Through China, the Soviet Union suddenly became a neigh-

bor of the Southeast Asian states. Aside from the Chinese attack on
India in October, 1962, which clearly embarrassed the Soviet Government, it was not easy to draw a distinct demarcation line between Soviet and Chinese goals even after 1960, when the Sino-
Soviet dispute came out into the open. Their quarrel, while deeply
affecting all Communist parties, seemed to leave untouched the
area of long-range Communist interests.

It may be an exaggeration to speak of a detailed Communist plan
for the conquest of Southeast Asia. But since 1954, there is a strong
indication of a recurring pattern of infiltration and subversion,
rather than bold military action. After the Korean experience, and
once the United States had extended its assistance to parts of Indochina, Moscow and Peking apparently understood that substantial
advances in Southeast Asia could be made only if, simultaneously,
other events paralyzed the West, at least locally. Consequently,
Communist forces at times are showing great restraint, to the point
of postponing a final offensive.

The Geneva Armistice Agreements of July 21, 1954, were a compromise; they created a provisional military demarcation line "from
the Song Ben Hat [Cua Tung River] to the Laotian frontier,"[2]
which cut the narrow Vietnam waist in two. North of this line a
new Communist state came into existence under the leadership of
Ho Chi Minh, one of the ablest Communists in Asia. South of the
line, a non-Communist government was allowed to subsist.

After the Geneva Conference of 1954, the Communists continued to press southward, in the general direction of the Malayan
Peninsula, across an area of vital strategic importance to any north-
south movement, whose occupation by a Communist power would
outflank India and Burma and open Indonesia and the Philippines
to Chinese-Soviet penetration. The main theater of Communist
operations was Indochina, specifically the small kingdom of Laos.
Malaya and Burma were then sideshows; Cambodia was left more
or less in peace. Chinese Communists kept up a guerrilla and terrorist warfare in the jungles and forests of the Malayan Peninsula for
twelve years. Although the Malayan authorities in July, 1960, proclaimed the end of the state of emergency existing since 1948, it
seemed that small hard-core Communist groups held out in remote,
inaccessible areas.

It seems certain that during the past decade neither China nor
the Soviet Union intended to precipitate the internal struggle in

Burma, where Communist guerrillas, as well as Karens and other minorities, battled against the central authorities. To Peking it was more important to make a show of good will by peacefully settling border disputes, thus leaving India as the sole target of China's territorial claims. A Chinese-Burmese treaty of friendship and non-aggression was signed on January 28, 1960, together with a frontier agreement resulting in an exchange of small border areas. But internal difficulties caused by various rebellions and disturbances continued. Although ruled by a nonaligned government and receiving economic aid from both sides, Burma proved unable to strengthen the fabric of its new state. The Communist problem was not really settled and could be revived in a dangerous form on orders from the north.

Only parts of Cambodia were occupied by Communist guerrillas during the Indochinese War. The Geneva cease-fire agreements of 1954 declared it an unaligned state that could not take part in any alliance. At the same time it received (together with neighboring Laos) a unilateral promise of assistance in the SEATO Treaty of September 8, 1954. For geographical reasons, and also because its head of state, Prince Norodom Sihanouk, put up strong resistance at Geneva, Cambodia was spared a Communist "assembly area." Prince Sihanouk made a show of friendship toward Communist governments, and as early as May, 1955, accepted a Chinese grant of $22.4 million. In the autumn of 1963, shortly after the overthrow of the Diem regime in South Vietnam, Sihanouk repudiated American economic and military aid—about $29 million in 1963, and a total $365 million since 1955, the year the country became independent.[3] A few days later, Cambodia received China's promise of military assistance in case of attack. The Cambodian head of state played a complicated game, taking advantage of renewed French interest in Indochina, and claiming that the only thing he wanted was neutrality for his country. This was probably true; Sihanouk, however, seemed to have made up his mind that Western assistance would not be adequate in case of danger, and that only Chinese "generosity" could help him achieve his aim. Cambodia's attitude, at a time when Laos' independence hung by a thread and Communist guerrilla warfare gained in intensity in the Mekong River Delta in South Vietnam, aggravated the general situation in Indochina.

It was in Laos, in the very center of the Indochinese Peninsula, that the Communists concentrated their main efforts. According to the 1954 Geneva cease-fire agreement for Laos, the Communist

Vietminh forces were to be grouped in provisional assembly areas and withdrawn from the country within a relatively short time. The Laotian Pathet Lao guerrillas were to concentrate in the two northeastern provinces of Sam Neua and Phong Saly, bordering both on North Vietnam and China. Despite provisions that the bringing of foreign troops, arms, and military equipment into Laos was prohibited, this northeast area became a Communist stronghold from which operations were launched against the rest of the country and later against South Vietnam.

During the seven years following the 1954 Geneva Conference, the Royal Laotian governments sought repeatedly understanding with the Communist leadership. But from the very first, the Pathet Lao, backed by Hanoi, Peking, and Moscow, attempted to organize a state within a state in the northeastern provinces. Negotiations between the two sides were interrupted and resumed time and again. Between September, 1954, and the summer of 1959, when a new Communist offensive began to take shape, the Pathet Lao agreed—and backed out—at least four times to integrate its armed forces and the administration of the two provinces under the central government's authority. In August, 1960, Captain Kong Le's coup against the central government which led to a civil war between the right-wing and Kong's "neutralist" forces, further complicated the situation. This resulted in a temporary alliance between Kong Le and Pathet Lao, with two rival "legal" governments, the "neutralist" being backed by the Communist powers. As a result of this alliance, the Pathet Lao made new gains. A comparison of the respective positions held by the Central Government and by Pathet Lao in 1954 and 1961 shows that the Communists were able to extend their areas of occupation to most of the country, with the royal forces reduced to a perimeter around Luang Prabang and disconnected areas along the Mekong River. North Vietnam, with Soviet and Chinese support, openly backed every claim of the Pathet Lao. At the beginning of 1961, Soviet arms and equipment were delivered in great quantities to the Communist forces in the strategic Plaine des Jarres.* The Soviet Union supported the Pathet Lao's claim to freedom of action in the northeastern provinces and their demands to have representatives in the Central Government and closer official relations with Communist governments. The Soviet Union and China also demanded the revival of the International Control Commission for Laos, which was suspended in

* Cf. Summit Diplomacy, p. 235n.

1958 on orders from neutralist Premier Prince Souvanna Phouma, half-brother of the Pathet Lao leader Souvanouvong; the Communist powers also favored a new international conference on Laos. In Laos, the central figure advocating a neutralist course and accommodation with the Communists was Souvanna Phouma. His sincere efforts were not always understood in the West, though there can be little doubt that he grossly underestimated the Communists' devious methods and ambitions.

With the Central Government's forces in a precarious position, Soviet diplomacy had its way; an international conference on Laos was convened in Geneva in May, 1961, with the participation of fourteen nations, including the United States, France, China, and the two Vietnam governments. The Conference was preceded by a Pathet Lao offensive violating the cease-fire, which led to a tense situation and a dispatch of some SEATO troops to Thailand. One more cease-fire was proclaimed, and Souvanna Phouma formed a coalition government that included representatives of right-wing parties and the Pathet Lao. The Geneva Conference lasted until July 21, 1962, when the participating powers signed two documents: the "Declaration" on Laos neutrality, and the "Protocol" dealing with the withdrawal of foreign troops and military personnel and the creation of an International Supervision and Control Commission, consisting (as had its 1954 forerunner) of representatives of India (chairman), Canada, and Poland. The Declaration amounted to an international guarantee of Laos' sovereignty, territorial integrity, and neutrality. An important provision endorsed Laos' repudiation of the 1954 unilateral SEATO promise of assistance.

The 1961–62 Geneva Conference did little to improve Laos' position. As in 1954, the Communist governments did not sign the agreements in good faith. Except for the withdrawal of American military advisers (some 800 men), the official check points at the borders registered fewer than 100 North Vietnamese soldiers leaving Laos, out of some 10,000 presumed to be in the country. An internal agreement reached in November, 1962, by the three groups of the coalition government to merge their military forces was never implemented, and they continued to occupy separate areas. At the end of 1962, Kong Le's neutralist troops began to split, some of them defecting to the Communists. The Pathet Lao resumed fighting in the spring of 1963 both against the neutralists and the right-wing forces. Kong Le, who had allied himself with the Communists in 1961, had to ask for help against them.

Despite a deterioration in Soviet-Chinese relations, no difference in their attitudes toward Laos could be detected at the 1961–1962 Geneva Conference. The following year, the Soviet Government paid lip service to the Geneva agreements, but at the same time helped to undermine them. During the spring and summer of 1963, the Soviet Government joined with the Pathet Lao, Hanoi, and Peking in preventing the International Control and Supervision Commission from holding an on-the-spot investigation of the fighting and the deliveries of arms and equipment in the Plaine des Jarres. Gromyko described a mission of the International Commission to the area as a violation of the Geneva agreements.[4] The Soviet Government also backed Communist claims that the International Commission should take its decisions unanimously, which would have amounted to veto power for its Polish Communist member, who for a while had successfully paralyzed the Commission's activities. On May 28, 1963, Warsaw issued a statement holding right-wing elements and the Western powers responsible for the deteriorating situation in Laos, and defended the calculated chicaneries of its representative on the International Commission.[5] The stand of the Warsaw government undoubtedly reflected the Kremlin's wishes. Moscow seemed to attach a great deal of importance to keeping any objective observers from investigating whose equipment was being delivered to the Pathet Lao and whether North Vietnamese troops were fighting in Laos. On June 6, 1963, Souvanna Phouma asked in an official communiqué: "Whence come these supplies? The Pathet Lao might perhaps furnish details of truck convoys of several hundred units which since the month of April, 1963, have been crawling from North Vietnam toward Khang Kay [Pathet Lao headquarters in the Plaine des Jarres] . . . similarly the Pathet Lao might inform the co-chairmen of the indisputable presence of North Vietnamese troops in the territory controlled by Pathet Lao."*[6]

Although an independent neutral Laos had been the only point of agreement between Khrushchev and Kennedy at their Vienna meeting, and despite repeated American and British diplomatic efforts in Moscow during 1962 and 1963, Communist activities in Laos continued. In 1954, 1961, and in 1963, the Soviet Union (and possibly China) threw large amounts of arms and equipment into Laos, while North Vietnam supplied the Pathet Lao with troops, instructors, and advisers. Thanks to these efforts, Communist guerrilla and terrorist activities between 1954 and 1964 shifted from

---

* Britain and the Soviet Union are co-chairmen of the conference on Laos.

northeast Laos and the Red River Delta in North Vietnam to south Laos and the Mekong River Delta in South Vietnam—some 600 to 800 miles farther south. But at the same time, whoever gave the final orders on the Communist side showed great restraint in avoiding possible international complications, such as could have developed if harsher conditions had been imposed on the French in 1954, or in case of a complete takeover in Laos in 1961, when the royal troops were clinging to a few strongholds along the Siamese border. Instead, the weight of the guerrilla warfare shifted to South Vietnam, where, since 1959, it has continued to increase in intensity. In January, 1962, the formation of a South Vietnam People's Revolutionary Party was announced in Hanoi. The strongly anti-Communist Ngo Dinh Diem government was unable to suppress the terrorist and guerrilla action despite technical American assistance. Initially, South Vietnam owed much to Diem, but in its last years his regime degenerated, its efficiency became impaired, and in November, 1963, it was toppled by a military junta.[7]

In their patient, long-term efforts in Southeast Asia, the Communists benefited from many factors: the unsettled political and economic conditions of Indochina, Burma, and Indonesia after the rapid withdrawal of the French, British, and Dutch colonial administrations, the low standard of living, the 15-million strong Chinese minorities spread over the area, etc. The two international conferences—on Indochina in 1954, and on Laos in 1961—both promoted by Communist powers at a time unfavorable for the West, turned to the Communist's advantage. There has been considerable criticism in the West of the way the French and later the Americans tried to stop Communist advances in Southeast Asia. But the critics generally failed to realize that the main reason for difficulties and failures was not the methods applied but the defensive attitude of the West in trying to contain the danger, instead of eradicating it at its source. As a result, established Communist states are able to support local Communist offensive actions. Such was the case in Indochina in 1949–54, in Korea in 1950–52, and such was still the case in Laos and South Vietnam in 1964. In the history of modern independence movements there is no instance of a successful insurrection against a strong power without active support from abroad. The Polish insurrections of 1830–31 and 1863–64, the German upheaval of 1953, and the Hungarian Revolution of 1956, despite overwhelming support of the population, could all be suppressed because they lacked outside assistance. The Balkan independence movements in the nineteenth century and, more recently, the Algerian rebellion succeeded largely because they were aided from abroad. It would be an exaggeration to form pat theories on these matters, for imponderables play a tremendous role. But such has been the general trend of events in the great majority of cases for more than a century.

The West's defensive attitude gives the Communists another important advantage. It enables them to use so-called national liberation movements and the threat of local wars as bargaining points. Thus, Moscow does not hesitate to give considerable arms support to Egypt and other Middle East states, which may upset the local balance of power and provoke Arab-Israeli conflicts. Similarly, the Soviet Union delivered arms to Indonesia (whom no one threatened). Although the Communist rebellion was suppressed in Indonesia in 1948, it did not prevent the Communist Party from gaining considerable influence in the country. Consequently, President Sukarno plays a dangerous balancing act between the Moslems, the Army, and the Communists. The satisfaction given him over Dutch New Guinea did not prevent him from threatening the new Federation of Malaysia. With a population of 100 million, a low standard of living, and a near bankrupt economy, Indonesia remains one of the danger spots in Southeast Asia in which subversive action could easily expand should Indochina fall into Communist hands. While Khrushchev showed that he opposed the Chinese aggression against India in 1962, Soviet behavior in Laos and toward Indonesia indicates that Moscow is not divided from Peking in favoring a slower movement to the south, which would extend Communist influence to Malaya and the Sunda Islands. This attitude was confirmed by an official statement published by Tass on February 25, 1964, in which the Soviet Government emphatically backed the "just revindications of the Vietnamese nation," i.e., that the U.S. cease to interfere in the affairs of South Vietnam, recall its military personnel and evacuate its military equipment, thus allowing the South Vietnamese nation to decide its own fate.

BLACK AFRICA

In the past, Communist interest in the revolutionary potential of the African Negro was at best perfunctory. Lenin and Stalin thought primarily in terms of Europe and Asia. As late as 1916, Lenin mentioned only Russia and Eastern Asia as the two world areas where "capitalism is not strongly developed,"[8] forgetting Africa altogether. In Stalin's classic collection of speeches and articles published under the title *Marxism and the National and Colonial Question,* neither the word "Negro" nor "Africa" appears; one finds only occasional references to Egypt and Morocco.

The task of rousing the Negro masses to revolution was clearly left to the Communist International, though even there an understanding of the problem was slow to mature.

Although the appeals and resolutions of the early years were meant to include the African peoples, the actual interest was directed mainly at the United States and South Africa, i.e., the two countries with a Negro industrial proletariat. It was understood, however, that the Communist parties of the West should work in the colonies of their respective countries. One of the conditions for admission to the Third International adopted at the Second Comintern Congress in 1920 asked that every party wishing to join support "not in words only but practically a movement of liberation in the colonies."[9] In the "Theses" of its Fourth Congress (1922), the Comintern stated that the Russian Revolution as well as the revolts among the Asiatic and Moslem peoples "have awakened the race consciousness of millions of Negroes."[10]

But the examples cited in the Theses referred only to Negroes in the Americas. Not until two years later did the Comintern show any real understanding that the core of the Negro problem lay in Africa. In 1924, its Executive Committee set up a standing Negro Commission with the participation of the Belgian, British, and French parties. Four years later, the Sixth Congress, one of the most momentous meetings of the Comintern, stated in its Theses: "The Negro problem has become a vital question of the world revolution . . . essential for the proletarian revolution and the destruction of capitalism."[11] Yet the overriding interest with the American Negro was not over, as was shown by Otto Kuusinen's proposal (at the Sixth Congress) to offer the American Negroes a separate state in the American South. The Sixth Congress also attacked Marcus A. Garvey's American Negro movement, accusing it of being a sort of "Negro Zionism," which, "instead of fighting American imperialism" advanced the slogan "Back to Africa."[12] The Negro writer George Padmore felt that in attacking Garvey, white Communists committed their biggest error in America. He called Kuusinen's proposal "a glorified Native Reserve."[13]

There had been some Communist attempts at agitating among the Negroes in the twenties and thirties: a congress in Chicago in 1925, an Anti-Imperialist Conference in Brussels in 1927, the "League Against Imperialism," and other more or less camouflaged front organizations. Much of the momentum of these activities abated when the Soviet Union joined the League of Nations in 1934, associating itself with the countries possessing the largest African colonies. But, according to George Padmore (speaking of the Sixth Comintern Congress), the Communist parties of Belgium, Britain, France, Holland, and Portugal "had sadly neglected anti-imperialist work since their formation."[14]

The lack of practical preparation by the Communist parties of the large colonial states thus seems to have been one of the reasons why little organized Communist activity existed in Black Africa after 1945, the time of the great changes. When the spirit of independence swept over Black Africa, bringing the most spectacular surge of newborn states history has known, not a single Communist regime came legally into existence south of the Sahara.

This is not to say that there was no Communism at all. Reliable sources list small groups or organizations under Communist influence in the forties and fifties in British and French African dependencies, though none of much importance. But Moscow and Peking began to pay increasing attention to the African Negroes, inviting students to attend Communist universities and training leaders for the future. Communist front organizations, like the World Federation of Trade Unions and the World Federation of Democratic Youth, considerably expanded their African contacts. Many Soviet radio programs were broadcast to Africa in English, French, Portuguese, and Swahili (a total of nearly fifty hours per week in 1961, not counting an equal number of hours in Arabic). The Chinese radio propaganda effort was even more intensive, both in English and in Cantonese, for Chinese were settled in South Africa, Madagascar, and Mauritius.[15]

In the years following statehood, the Communist position improved somewhat, though it remained strikingly out of proportion to the magnitude of the opportunity these historical changes seemed to offer. On the whole, in spite of justified grievances against the white man, the African Negro proved resistant to doctrines and counsels that could have served as welcome shortcuts to many forms of revenge. Tribal loyalties, religious feelings, nationalism in the more advanced communities, and illiteracy in more backward ones often combined to frustrate the efforts of the Western Communist parties, even such powerful ones as the French.

In consequence, the Kremlin's best chance to gain a foothold south of the Sahara appeared to rest on individual African leaders and non-Communist parties in positions of power in their respective countries.

In theory at least, the prevailing conditions seem to favor this method. Some African politicians may be attracted to the Communist version of Marxism for purely practical reasons, because they think that an authoritarian regime and a one-party system will yield quicker results in modernizing their countries. They also need economic assistance badly and may feel that they will never get enough. They ponder over the examples offered by Egypt and Indonesia where, so they believe, Soviet aid prompted more assistance from the West. The Russians, on the other hand, are not tight-fisted. Until the middle of 1962, five of the new states south of the Sahara (Ghana, Guinea, Mali, Sudan, Somali Republic) received $304.1 million in Soviet credits and smaller sums from other Communist governments.[16]

It is too early to measure the effectiveness of these new tactics, the more so as in several instances the patient, long-term policy was interrupted by incidents that were interpreted as rash attempts to gain power for Communist stooges by less cautious methods. In the Congo, Guinea, Ivory Coast, Liberia, and Cameroun, such occurrences, even if the result of local initiative, were blamed on Communist governments and jeopardized Soviet, Chinese, and Czechoslovak diplomatic and economic activities.

The most telling example of Soviet behavior in Black Africa was furnished in the Congo. There, within days after independence, mutinies in the army (Force Publique), wild political struggle, and tribal warfare threw the country wide open to foreign infiltration and subversion.

The Soviet Union was among the powers extending immediate diplomatic recognition to the first Congolese government of Patrice Lumumba on Independence Day, June 30, 1960. Russia also voted for the Security Council resolution of July 13, 1960, authorizing the dispatch of a U.N. military force, after the Congo Government had appealed for help. But on the same day, in Moscow, Foreign Minister Gromyko handed several ambassadors a note presenting the Congo situation in a completely distorted way. According to the Soviet note, Belgian officials, assisted by American, British, and French representatives, were plotting the liquidation of the new state. The mutinies in the Force Publique were supposed to have been "provoked" by Belgian officers; the panic that seized the European population was "organized." Further, the American Ambassador was accused of conspiring to expand Western intervention under the U.N. aegis, in connivance with Ralph Bunche, the U.N. Undersecretary General. At the Security Council meeting in New York, Soviet Delegate Arkadi Sobolev maintained that Belgium had committed armed aggression against the Congo with the support of the Western powers, including Western Germany; he asked for immediate U.N. action.

This initial Soviet stand seems to have been dictated, on the spur of the moment, out of fear that some Belgian troops would remain in the Congo permanently, or, even worse, that the Western powers would take it upon themselves to ensure peace, as was indeed suggested by President de Gaulle. U.N. action therefore appeared preferable to the Kremlin. But it was only a temporary deviation from a major tactical aim—to create a power vacuum in the Congo—which the Soviet Union persistently pursued: first by condoning the mutinies of the Force Publique and demanding that all Belgian troops leave the Congo, later by pressing for the withdrawal of non-African U.N. troops, and finally by moving that the U.N. operation be discontinued altogether.

For the time being, however, Khrushchev praised the Security Council. On July 15, in an exchange of letters with President Kasavubu and Premier Lumumba, he stated that the U.N. had done a good deed by asking the Belgian Government to withdraw its troops from the Congo. But should "aggression" continue, the need for more effective measures, both by the United Nations and "the peace-loving states," would arise. In a further statement on July 30, the Soviet Government contended that "Belgian aggression" had not ended and that Moscow "will not hesitate to take resolute measures to rebuff the aggressors, who . . . are acting with the encouragement of all the colonialist NATO powers."[17]

During this first period of the Congo crisis, political infiltration and propaganda were carried by several hundred Russian and Czechoslovak diplomats, technicians, and other agents. In a dispatch from the Congo on September 4, 1960, the London *Times* estimated their number as "at least 200," but probably much higher.* Much of this kind of Communist activity was temporarily hampered in September, 1960, when General Mobutu expelled the Soviet and Czechoslovak embassies from Léopoldville at forty-

* When the Soviet and Czechoslovak embassies left Léopoldville later in September, their total personnel, including technicians, was estimated at 450. (*New York Times,* September 18, 1963.)

eight–hours' notice. A five-man Chinese "good-will mission" left at the same time.

On the material side, deliveries of supplies from Soviet and other Communist governments did not match their high-sounding promises and must have disappointed those Congolese who had banked on them. The known amount of these deliveries to the Lumumba government was not striking, its value being estimated at $1.5 million. It was known at the time from official Soviet sources that in July, 1960, three Ilyushin aircraft bringing food supplies had arrived, or were scheduled to. According to a Tass announcement, the planes were then to go to Accra to assist in the transport of Ghanaian troops to the Congo. Two other aircraft were scheduled to arrive in Accra for the same purpose.* Also in August, a Soviet cargo ship brought 100 trucks and a workshop to Matadi. On September 2, an Ilyushin aircraft landed in Léopoldville. It was to be the first of fifteen such planes with Russian crews supplied to Lumumba's government; the others were scheduled to go to Stanleyville. Almost immediately, the planes began airlifting Congolese troops to Kasai, allegedly to repress tribal fighting. According to Hammarskjold's report to the Security Council on September 9, the troops massacred hundreds of Balubas "simply on the ground that they were Balubas." The Secretary General called this a "crime of genocide" directed at the extermination of a specific ethnic group. It seems that all the Ilyushin aircraft (including two donated by the Czechoslovak Government) were flown away when the Soviet Embassy had to leave Léopoldville. Further, a Soviet medical unit arrived in the Congo and was directed to Stanleyville. On September 8, a few days after Lumumba's dismissal, Foreign Minister Justin Bomboko, in a bitter controversy with the former Premier, accused him of keeping the receipt of the fifteen Ilyushin planes and the 100 Soviet trucks from the Cabinet. But he did not mention any other Soviet supplies, nor did any new information on the subject come out during a Security Council debate on September 14–17 (when Soviet Russia and some other delegations still considered Lumumba the legitimate Prime Minister, while the majority recognized his dismissal by President Kasavubu as lawful).

The true nature of Lumumba's relation to Moscow is still not entirely clear. This is due as much to the usual Russian secretive methods as to Lumumba's complex personality. Although one

---

* On August 11, the Soviet Government gave Lumumba an Ilyushin aircraft as a gift.

university and several streets in Communist-ruled countries were named for him after his tragic death, there is no indication that Lumumba had links to Communism before his Premiership. He had twice been condemned to prison, once for embezzlement and once for incitement to political violence; however, before Congolese independence he was not accused of plotting with the Communists. During his short term of office (from June 24 to September 5, 1960), Lumumba displayed feverish activity and traveled widely abroad. But he did not go to any Communist capital. His public statements were often erratic or patently false. On Independence Day, within the short span of a few hours, he both censured and praised Belgian achievements in the Congo. At a press conference in Montreal he maintained that no white woman had ever been raped in the Congo, while a detailed Belgian official report registered 291 rape cases. Lumumba also had a considerable gift for persuasion, a facility for public speaking, a talent for political demagogy, and a propensity to racial propaganda. In short—he was made to order as a potential tool of the Kremlin.

A few days after taking office, Lumumba was faced with mutinies and chaos in most of the country. He not only proved unable to bring the explosive situation under control, but complicated it by irresponsible statements, unreasonable demands, accusations against practically everybody (with the exception of the Russians), and requests for Soviet intervention. The first known message from Lumumba and Kasavubu to Khrushchev was dated July 14. Khrushchev answered with his "Hands off the Congo" statement, which later was distributed to Congolese soldiers in pamphlet form. The Soviet Premier charged that the Congo was the victim of "a collective imperialist aggression . . . a *fait accompli* of robbery and plunder of a peace-loving African state." The message hinted at possible Soviet intervention, asserting that this "aggression" was much more than a local conflict and "of tremendous significance to the whole world."[18]

It was hardly a coincidence that from then on Lumumba's activities, if any logic could be detected in them, paralleled the Soviet line. For a few more days he seemed to work with President Kasavubu; then he took a separate course. On July 15, Lumumba said in the Chamber of Representatives that the country's relation with Belgium was "similar to war" and that Belgian troops had to leave within twelve hours.* The first U.N. detachments began to arrive

* Contradictory Congolese statements regarding the return of Belgian troops after mutinies began in the Force Publique were noted on July 10, when

the same day; less than two weeks later, 10,000 men had come. Brussels was pressed to let these troops replace the Belgian soldiers sent in to protect the white population. Consequently, Belgian troops left the Léopoldville area on July 23; on September 2, it was announced that all Belgian combat troops had left the Congo. Whatever errors it may have committed later, in these first weeks the U.N. acted with extraordinary speed, military precision, and diplomatic adroitness. But Lumumba started a quarrel with Secretary General Hammarskjold, whom he reproached for not intervening in Katanga on behalf of the Central Government, as well as for meddling in the Congo's internal affairs. On August 13, *Izvestia* sharply attacked Hammarskjold for his Congo policy. Two days later, Lumumba wrote to Hammarskjold that he had lost confidence in him. Lumumba also demanded that Congolese troops be put in charge of all airfields; this request was backed by the Soviet Union in a note to the United Nations, which again could be interpreted as preparing the ground for some form of military intervention. The main subject of the quarrel now was Katanga. The Soviet Union threatened "other steps to curb aggression" and declared that the relations between Katanga and the Central Government could not be viewed as an internal problem of the Congo, "even after the withdrawal of the Belgian troops from Katanga."[19] Lumumba continued to press for U.N. troops to subdue "the rebel Katanga Government."

Finally, Lumumba repeatedly threatened to turn to the Soviet Union for military and other assistance. In fact, both he and his deputy, Antoine Gizenga, did ask for Communist help. On September 28, the Congolese College of Commissioners published photographic copies of Lumumba's letter to the Soviet Government dated August 15, in which he asked for arms, transport aircraft, and other equipment. A letter from Gizenga of September 8 asked Peking for tanks, aircraft, money, food, and personnel. Chou En-lai answered on September 12, informing him that the dispatch of volunteers was inappropriate and that the other questions would be studied. The authenticity of the letters was not seriously challenged. They confirm the strong circumstantial evidence that Lumumba and Gizenga were secretly in contact with Moscow and Peking, possibly as early as the first half of July, 1960. On July 4, Lumumba proclaimed a policy of "positive neutrality" for the Congo, but almost within hours was faced with an upheaval that

Foreign Minister Bomboko said that he had requested them to come, while Lumumba contended that they arrived in violation of Congolese sovereignty.

even more experienced politicians could not have dealt with. Bewildered by domestic chaos, Belgium's wrath, and the complex machinery of the United Nations, Lumumba may have thought of using the Communist governments to balance both Western and U.N. influence. This still seems to be the most plausible explanation for his behavior. But if such was indeed the case, the odds against Lumumba were overwhelming, for he became a tool in Communist hands. They used and manipulated him with the help of experienced agents, such as his press secretary, Serge Michel, and Mme. Andrée Blouin, a former French citizen, who played the role of close adviser to both Lumumba and Gizenga. Bomboko accused her of publishing inflammatory speeches in Lumumba's name in his absence. Serge Michel, a former French resident said to be of Eastern European origin, first gained public notice during the Algerian war, where he may have acted as a Communist contact man. In the Congo he belonged to Lumumba's inner circle of advisers. In at least one instance he issued a statement on his own couched in unmistakably Communist jargon.

Moscow continued to back Lumumba as the head of the "legitimate government" even after his dismissal by Kasavubu on September 5. Although all Communist and some African governments officially recognized Lumumba, the Soviet Union quickly lost its bid to force his comeback as Prime Minister. Because of a Soviet veto in the Security Council, a special session of the Assembly was convened despite Communist opposition. By seventy votes to none, with eleven abstentions, it adopted an Afro-Asian draft resolution fully supporting Hammarskjold's action in the Congo. The Soviet delegate withdrew his amendments referring, among other things, to the "legitimate" Congo government, and did not even vote against a resolution which, in effect, rejected his government's policy. On November 22, the Assembly seated President Kasavubu's delegation, thereby rejecting Lumumba's claims.

In the Congo itself, despite declarations that Soviet aid would continue to go directly to Lumumba, and despite turbulent agitation on his part, his role was played out. The Russians reacted very strongly to his arrest in December, 1960, and in February, 1961, to the news of his murder, but their policy did not go beyond protests and threats. A Soviet draft resolution, defeated in the Security Council on February 14, 1961, called for the dismissal of the Secretary General and for the cessation of U.N. operations in the Congo within a month. The following day, Valerian Zorin accused Hammarskjold of being an accomplice of colonialists whose hands were covered with the blood of Patrice Lumumba.[20] The violence of the Soviet attitude was meant to serve two aims: to obscure the paucity of its assistance to Lumumba and to introduce the next episode, in which Gizenga was cast in the role of Lumumba's "legal successor."

Perhaps this was the closest that any part of the Congo came to being ruled by a Communist or near-Communist regime. Gizenga assumed power in Stanleyville, the capital of Oriental Province, as Lumumba's deputy early in November, 1960, when his chief was still struggling for recognition in Léopoldville. After Lumumba's arrest he announced, on December 13, that he was the head of the legitimate government. When Lumumba's murder was revealed, the Soviet statement of February 14, 1961, gave Gizenga formal recognition: "The Prime Ministry of the Congo Republic, headed by his [Lumumba's] deputy, Antoine Gizenga, continues to discharge its functions. Having its seat in the temporary capital of the Republic at Stanleyville, it now exercises control almost over half the territory of the Congo and enjoys nationwide support."[21] Several other Communist and African governments, including the U.A.R., recognized Gizenga's claim. This situation lasted until August, 1961, when Gizenga accepted the post of Vice-Premier in Cyrille Adoula's Central Government. Then, slowly, his power over Oriental Province began to decline. His leading followers deserted him; General Lundula, the head of his troops, went over to the Central Government; embassies returned from Stanleyville to Léopoldville. A last-minute attempt, on January 14, 1962, to regain power by force in the capital of Oriental Province with the help of gendarmes was suppressed by Lundula's soldiers. Gizenga was dismissed as Vice-Premier, deprived of parliamentary immunity, and put under arrest. The episode had lasted for more than a year. While it seems probable that Moscow furnished Gizenga with funds, there is little evidence of arms deliveries or supplies of military equipment that might have turned Oriental Province into a rival to the Central Government. According to a press report, six trucks with Soviet-bloc arms reached Stanleyville via the United Arab Republic early in 1961.[22] One may assume that after that, the Kremlin preferred to wait and see. (After all, it took them well over two years to decide that Castro's Cuba should receive massive military assistance.) Gizenga is not a forceful personality. He did not show any tactical ability during the relatively long period when he had a territorial base of his own and a strong political position. Having lost the much abler Lumumba, the Russians may have felt that with this flaccid successor it was too dangerous to risk valuable military equipment as well as a loss of face in case of failure.

In retrospect, Soviet policy in the Congo is not too difficult to assess. Less than two months after Khrushchev wrecked the Paris Summit Conference, and on the eve of the November meeting of the Communist parties in Moscow, where a short-lived compromise was to be worked out with Peking, the Congo upheaval was a providential diversion for the Kremlin. It soon became more than that, furnishing the opportunity to gain a foothold in a strategic central African area. Did Moscow ever contemplate the use of some form of military force, for instance of well-armed "volunteers," to install a Communist regime in the Congo? All evidence seems to point to a different plan. Any Soviet military intervention, however camouflaged, would have clashed with the U.N. operations and possibly precipitated a major conflict with the Western powers. On the other hand, were a Communist or near Communist regime to win the upper hand in Léopoldville by its own efforts, Soviet assistance, even on a large scale, could not easily be objected to. The backing of Lumumba and Gizenga, the sabotage of the U.N. action, the censure of its military command and the Secretary General, the pressure to get the Belgians and later the white U.N. troops out of the Congo and to keep the airfields open by handing them over to Congolese control, all seem to point to the existence of an over-all Soviet plan. When it became clear that the basic requirement—a "friendly" Congolese government—could not be achieved, the Russians withdrew behind a smokescreen of virulent propaganda. But this became clear only after Gizenga faded out of the picture. After Lumumba's murder, the Soviet Government still seemed ready for a major adventure in Africa. President Kennedy's strong warning of February 16, 1961, that the United States would oppose any attempt by any government to intervene unilaterally in the Congo must have had a cooling effect on the Kremlin. Nevertheless, this was not the end of the story, for during the Tananarive Conference in March, 1961, and the Coquillatville Conference in April, as well as during the negotiations for the convening of the all-Congolese Parliament in May, Gizenga's position still appeared strong. Adoula and Tshombe tried to win his help, and Gizenga seemed able to dictate conditions. He was recognized by the Communist governments, including Yugoslavia, by several African states, and by Ceylon. Yet Gizenga's territorial base in Oriental Province could be nothing more than a temporary station. His value to the Soviet bloc was only as a potential Prime Minister of the

Congo. He tried to achieve that by accepting the Vice-Premiership in Adoula's government in August, 1961. But the situation had changed; the former Lumumbist forces were scattered and could no longer form a solid bloc to lay claim to the Premiership.

Thus the Russians lost the political contest in the Congo. Yet, despite their noisy propaganda, they acted with considerable restraint. They returned to Léopoldville in August, 1962, quietly recognizing the Adoula Government and resuming their efforts by offers of economic and technical assistance. In the meantime, however, Soviet equipment had proved deficient in a number of cases in Guinea and Ghana. In 1961, the Soviet bloc accounted for only 5 per cent of Africa's trade, although their exchange of goods with Egypt was still considerable. In May, 1963, Guinea signed several agreements with France, after having practically broken off financial and trade relations in 1958. In the same month, the African Summit Conference in Addis Ababa refused to admit observers from Communist governments. The rival groupings of African states—the Monrovia and Casablanca groups (the latter at one time subject to some Communist influence)—had become sufficiently compatible to make a conference possible. Even at the Afro-Asian Solidarity Conference (hitherto a tool of pro-Communist policy) in Tanganyika, critical words were heard for the first time. If these signs were interpreted correctly in Moscow, they could only be understood as mounting obstacles in the indirect penetration of Black Africa.

On the other hand, the unstable situation in many parts of Black Africa seems to invite further Soviet efforts. A case in point is Somalia's territorial claims on Ethiopia and Kenya, which led Somalia, in November, 1963, to reject American and other Western offers of economic assistance and to accept Soviet arms. The significance of the deal was not clear at the time of writing, but a look at the map shows Somalia's strategic importance, at the southern outlet of the Red Sea and facing Yemen, where Soviet and Chinese influences have been at work for several years.

It also is too early to evaluate the events in Zanzibar, where in January, 1964, an armed uprising overthrew the government barely weeks after the country had been granted independence. The political nature of the uprising was not clear at first, although some pro-Communists assumed leading positions. It has been confirmed, however, by Secretary of State Rusk and several press sources that guerrillas trained in Cuba had a part in the coup. According to one press report, the guerrillas had been training in Cuba since 1961. On January 18, Zanzibar was declared Africa's first people's republic. The new regime gained quick diplomatic recognition from Peking, Moscow, and other Communist governments. While most reports pointed to a Cuban role in the coup, and at least to Chinese foreknowledge of it (Chinese correspondents suddenly arrived on the island two days before the events), it was the Soviet Ministry of Foreign Affairs which, on January 26, issued a warning, presumably directed at Britain, that force should not be used against the new republic.[23]

LATIN AMERICA

Communism spread quickly throughout Latin America. Communist parties were formed in Argentina in 1918, in Mexico in 1919, in Brazil and Chile in 1921–22. In the 1930's, not one country from Tierra del Fuego to the Rio Grande was without overt or secret representatives of the Communist International. Conditions for revolutionary activities were particularly favorable: Unjust distribution of national income, low wages, and exploitation of the urban and agricultural worker prevailed throughout the area. Even in the late fifties, Latin America's average per-capita income was less than one-tenth that of the United States. Furthermore, a number of the countries have unsolved racial problems. Stable political conditions have therefore been the exception rather than the rule. Dictatorial regimes were natural targets for local revolutionary or reform movements, some of which were attracted to Communism and absorbed by Communist parties. Until the early sixties, Latin American Communists were as subservient to Moscow as their European counterparts. The local parties followed the zigzags of the Comintern and Cominform policies, in turn attacking the left-wing and reform movements or calling on them to participate in united or popular fronts. At the time of the Molotov-Ribbentrop Pact, the Latin American parties backed Stalin's alliance with Hitler but quickly somersaulted into the Allied camp when the Nazis attacked "the Fatherland of the proletariat." Similar Party discipline prevailed during and after World War II, when newly acquired Soviet prestige helped the Communist parties make unprecedented strides in Latin America. But since about 1960, Communist discipline has been impaired by the Soviet-Chinese rift. "Chinese wings" have shaken the unity of most Communist parties of Latin America; in some countries dissident pro-Chinese groups have begun to emerge.

It is interesting that in nearly five decades, and despite many opportunities, there were only two Communist attempts to seize power by force in the twenty republics. A Communist-led military conspiracy was frustrated in El Salvador in January, 1932. The uprising of some Brazilian garrisons in October, 1935, was instigated by a Communist-front organization. The El Salvador affair may have been a local experiment, with or without express Moscow permission. It is more difficult to find an explanation for the Brazilian uprising, for in 1935, the popular-front policy was already in full swing. The leader of the Brazilian Communist Party, Luiz Carlos Prestes, was a well-known military figure. He had returned to Brazil only the previous year after several years in Moscow, and undoubtedly was in touch with the Comintern. Nevertheless, it is not established whether the coup was a blunder of the local leadership or of the Comintern, or both. At any rate, these were the only two attempts of this kind in the history of Latin American Communism. Both instances of Communism in power—in Guatemala and Cuba—resulted from the betrayal of local revolutionaries and reformers by a crypto-Communist leadership.

Guatemala. Guatemalan developments between 1944 and 1954 present a typical picture of the difficulties and dangers of genuine reform programs in a Latin American country menaced from two sides—by narrow-minded right-wing dictatorships and by Communist subversion.

After fourteen years in power, the dictatorial regime of General Ubico was overthrown in 1944. Another would-be dictator had to be deposed a few months later. The young officers, intellectuals, and businessmen who led the revolution strove for political democracy, social reforms, and relief for the downtrodden Indian population. But they were outmaneuvered by a small, well-knit group of Communists who identified themselves with the nationalistic and social aims of the revolution. Juan José Arévalo, a professor living in exile, was elected President in 1945. He called himself a "spiritual socialist" and, whatever his true feelings, he threw the doors wide open for Communist penetration. Communists were placed in charge of many governmental activities, infiltrated other political parties, the trade unions, and practically every segment of organized political and social life in the country. Opposition was suppressed; in 1949, a serious contender for the Presidency, Colonel Arana, was murdered. In 1951, Arévalo was succeeded by Colonel Jacobo Arbenz, who went even further in collaborating with the Communists and following the line laid down by Moscow. His government seriously alarmed the other Central American states by its subversive activities, by sending undercover agents across the borders, instigating social and political strikes in the neighboring countries, and training Communist agents. In March, 1954, at the Conference of American States in Caracas, the Guatemalan delegation was the only one to oppose a declaration against Communist intervention proposed by the United States. In May of the same year, the Arbenz government received a shipment of arms from Czechoslovakia. According to testimony by the former Ambassador to Guatemala, John E. Peurifoy, the steamship "Alfhem" brought 2,000 tons of modern Czechoslovak arms from the Polish port Szczecin (Stettin) after having crossed the Atlantic by a zigzag course and having given false destinations three times.[24] Thus well armed, Guatemala brought charges of aggression against its neighbors. In the Security Council, the Soviet delegate vetoed a Brazilian and Colombian proposal to refer the Guatemalan situation to the Organization of American States. The Arbenz regime was overthrown in July, when Colonel Castilla Armas crossed the border from Honduras with a small group of followers.* Most of the Guatemalan Army went over to the insurgents. Arbenz fled and is supposedly living in Czechoslovakia.

The method of subversion from within used by the Communists in Guatemala has been called the "Guatemalan way." In testimony before a House of Representatives subcommittee, Raymond G. Leddy, in charge of Central American Affairs in the State Department, described it as the long-standing Bolshevik technique "whereby a determined, disciplined minority can get aboard a national movement and use the aspirations and energies of a vast majority of people . . . to lift itself into power."[25]

Until the downfall of Arbenz, Guatemala was a Soviet beachhead in the Western Hemisphere. But the related events seem to indicate that Moscow wanted Guatemala to remain an "unofficial" beachhead until action plans for the other Central American re-

---

* In his memoirs (*The White House Years: Mandate for Change*), President Eisenhower writes that he agreed for the U.S. to replace, through the intermediary of another country, two P-51 fighter-bombers Armas had lost in the struggle. Eisenhower felt that he was acting in the letter and spirit of the anti-Communist Caracas resolution of the OAS.

publics had matured, and possibly even after they had succeeded. Matters were coming to a head in the spring of 1954, hence the trip of the "Alfhem"; 2,000 tons of modern weapons were not necessary for Guatemala's defense.

Cuba. How long has Fidel Castro been following the "Guatemalan way"? In a speech on December 1, 1961, he said: "Do I believe in Marxism? I believe in it absolutely. Did I believe in it on January 1? Yes, I did. Did I believe in it on July 26? Yes, I believed in it on July 26." (The dates he mentioned refer to two major events in the Castro epos: January 1, 1959, when he seized power from Fulgencia Batista; July 26, 1953, when he led an attack on the Moncada military barracks in Santiago de Cuba.[26]) Although the speech contained some tactical reservations, nevertheless Castro publicly admitted in it that he had been a Marxist throughout the five-and-a-half-year struggle that carried him to power in Havana. Part of this time he spend in Mexico, from where he came to the United States to speak at anti-Batista rallies. On these occasions, as well as during his two years as guerrilla leader in the Sierra Maestra in Cuba, Castro passed for a liberal revolutionist fighting for the liberation of his country from dictatorship. On December 20, 1961, he explained that if he and his companions admitted they had been Communists at the time they were fighting and hiding in the Sierra Maestra, "it is possible that we would never have been able to descend to the lowlands from Turquino Peak."[27] Formally, Castro kept up the pretense of liberalism until May 1, 1961; then he proclaimed that Cuba was a "Socialist" state and would hold no more elections. The day before, Ernesto "Ché" Guevara, Castro's principal Communist collaborator, stated that Cuba's was the "first Socialist revolution in America." He said that all means of production would be nationalized. However, long before these declarations, it had become clear that Cuba was "Socialist" only in the Communist sense of the word. After a brief interlude of freedom following Batista's downfall, Castro ruled as the head of a totalitarian power machine run by an increasing number of known Communists. On December 2, 1961, he put the final touches to the system by announcing that there would be only one political party, and by making public his political credo: "I am a Marxist-Leninist and will be one until the day I die."[28]

When Castro assumed power, Cuba was a relatively prosperous country, with the fourth-highest per-capita income among the Latin American states and an annual export value of $700–800 million.[29] Thirty per cent of the gross national product came from the produce of export, 80 per cent of the export value from sugar; 80 per cent of the foreign trade was with the United States, which paid a premium on Cuban sugar in relation to world-market prices. Despite the unsatisfactory political situation under Batista, the economy expanded and the national income grew; although far from well-off by U.S. standards, and sometimes very poor owing to unjust social conditions, the Cuban people nevertheless were on the average the third best-fed Latin American nation, after Argentina and Uruguay.[30] In April, 1959, Fidel Castro unofficially visited the United States. He got a hero's welcome, spoke at public rallies and press meetings, met Secretary Christian Herter and members of foreign-relations committees of both houses of Congress. In public statements, Castro voiced opposition to Communism, promised to observe the obligations of the inter-American defense pact, and rejected all ideas of confiscating foreign property. Speaking in New York, he said: "The rich nation of the north has understood our just cause."[31] Despite some warnings and misgivings, Castro was accepted in the United States as a liberal and democratic leader who had replaced a disreputable dictatorship. An American embargo on arms deliveries to Batista in April, 1958, had played no small part in Castro's victory. American political and business circles were ready to help the new Cuban government and the Cuban economy. At the same time, Fidel Castro enjoyed the spontaneous backing of a large majority of the Cuban people. No struggle for power, no political or economic necessity forced him to embark on the road to Communism. He was the accepted leader of a free nation, with a unique opportunity to lead it to unprecedented prosperity. He chose the road to totalitarianism of his own free will, and there can be no other explanation than that Fidel Castro believed in Communism, as he stated in December, 1961.

The Soviet attitude toward Fidel Castro before he gained power is full of impenetrable shadows. Later events (as well as his own statements) support the assumption that Castro was in touch with Soviet agents when he established the Mexican training center. Once in power, he became a major problem, to be dealt with at the highest level of the Soviet hierarchy. But the accent was on caution. The Cuban revolution became a subject of Soviet propaganda, but for more than a year there was no overt political move. On January 3, 1959, *Pravda* used Castro's victory as an opportunity to castigate American "imperialists" and "ruling circles," which, according to the Soviet paper, were dismayed at Batista's defeat.

Pravda acknowledged that as leader of a "rebel movement" and of "Cuba's young people," Castro had the support of the Popular Socialist (i.e., Communist) Party of Cuba, "fighting staunchly for the unity and solidarity of all patriotic forces and for a real popular liberation movement."[32] The article set the tone for Communist propaganda, defending the Cuban revolution against American imperialism. In April, *Izvestia* sounded the alarm that a "new Guatemala" was in the making against the Cuban patriots headed by Fidel Castro.[33] The Soviet press also supported the mass executions of alleged Batista followers and the expropriation of foreign capital, and did not hide its sympathy for the new regime's role as a "contagious example" for other Latin American countries.

It was not until a year later (February, 1960), that Mikoyan arrived in Cuba to sign the trade agreement tying Cuba's economy to that of the Communist camp. The Soviet Government agreed to buy 4.425 million tons of sugar during 1960–64, granted Cuba a $100 million loan for machinery purchases in the Soviet Union, and offered technical assistance for plant construction. Soviet-Cuban diplomatic relations were not established until May 8, 1960, when Khrushchev obviously knew how he was going to act at the Paris Summit Conference a week later.* After the collapse of the conference, Soviet behavior with regard to Cuba became less reticent, but no political link was admitted. Trade agreements between Cuba and China and the European satellite governments were concluded during the following summer and autumn, when Antonio Nuñéz Jiménez, head of the Agrarian Reform Institute, visited Eastern Europe, Russia, and the Far East. It was then announced that Khrushchev had accepted an invitation to visit Cuba, a promise that did not materialize in the course of the following three years. In December, 1960, Ché Guevara, at the time the most prominent Communist in Castro's entourage and head of the Cuban National Bank, went to Moscow, where he signed further economic agreements. The communiqué published at the end of the visit referred to a statement by Khrushchev "to give all-out support in defending Cuba's independence from aggression."[34]

The promise to support the Castro regime, a much diluted version of a previous pledge, caused a sensation. On July 9, 1960, in the

* Sergei M. Kudryavtsev, the first Soviet Ambassador to Cuba, was appointed in July, 1960. As Counselor at the Paris Embassy, he had assisted Khrushchev during the hectic May days. In 1946, Kudryavtsev was mentioned in the Report of the Canadian Royal Commission on the Guzenko affair as probably heading a Soviet spy organization in Canada.

heat of the anti-Western campaign that followed the abortive
Paris Summit meeting, Khrushchev said: "The United States now
is not in such an unattainable distance from the Soviet Union as
formerly. Figuratively speaking, Soviet artillery forces if need be
can support the Cuban people with their rocket fire should the
aggressive forces in the Pentagon dare to start an attack against
Cuba."[35] In October, Khrushchev was interviewed by the director
of the Havana newspaper *Revolución*. Summarizing the conversation, Tass stated that Khrushchev wanted his statements on Soviet
assistance to Cuba to be regarded as "really symbolic." The Tass
summary was published by its English-language service but not in
Moscow. The interview was evasive in the extreme. The full text
revealed that although Khrushchev wanted the West to know that
his rocket threat to the United States had been withdrawn, he did
not want to admit this to the Cuban readers of *Revolución*.[36]

During and after the unsuccessful attempt of Cuban exiles to
establish a beachhead on the coast in April, 1961, the Soviet Government and Communist propaganda took the shrillest possible
line in defense of the "Republic of Cuba." But in reply to Kennedy's sharp warning against any outside military intervention,
Khrushchev abstained from pressing his contention that the Mon-
roe Doctrine was dead. On July 12, 1960, he had stated that "the
remains of this doctrine should be buried . . . so that it does not
poison the air with its decay."[37] This time Khrushchev complained
rather meekly that countries bordering on the Soviet Union have
concluded military treaties with the United States and accepted
American bases on their territory.[38]

Soviet political reticence with regard to Cuba was not matched
by a similar stance in the economic field. Here Moscow pledged
full support against the "American blockade." Khrushchev did so
personally on several occasions, notably in his July 9, 1960, speech.[39]
After 1961, the Communist-ruled countries accounted for 75 per
cent of Cuba's foreign trade. But despite the promises and the
far-reaching trade agreements with Soviet Russia, Communist
China, and the European satellite governments, Cuba's economy
was in a state of crisis. As a result of internal chaos, nationalization,
and insufficient imports, consumer goods practically disappeared
in the spring of 1962. Average daily food consumption fell below
minimal requirements, from 2,870 calories in 1958, to 2,400 calories
in 1962. Food rationing was instituted in July, 1961. In March,
1962, monthly rations of beans and rice, the basic local food
staples, were set at 1.5 lbs. of beans and 6 lbs. of rice. The full

extent of the Cuban economic crisis became apparent when Soviet Russia and Communist China found themselves beset by grave agricultural difficulties.

One other aspect of the Cuban tragedy deserves mention. The Communist governments have shown themselves incapable of keeping this small nation on its feet economically. But they seem to be able to send plenty of arms. It has been estimated that in April, 1962, military assistance by the Soviet bloc and China for the Castro regime amounted to $100 million. Arms already delivered to Cuba were reported to include 50–75 Soviet MIG fighter planes, 150–250 heavy and medium tanks, and a considerable number of assault guns, field artillery, and anti-aircraft artillery.[40]

But this was only a beginning. Sometime during the winter or spring of 1962, Moscow reached the decision to use the Castro regime for a major offensive move against the United States. We shall probably never know whether this represented a sharp change in the Kremlin's attitude or a logical evolution of Soviet-Cuban relations since 1960. It seems, however, that the new plan took shape before May 14, 1962, when a supplementary protocol was signed in Moscow for the supply of Soviet goods to Cuba during 1962. It raised the trade between the two countries by 40 per cent over the previous year.[41] Apart from other reasons, the protocol was clearly designed to explain the sudden increase of Soviet shipments that began to be noticed in July and aroused considerable attention during August. A Tass dispatch of August 28 stated that 100 Soviet ships were on the way to Cuba with cargoes of automobiles, agricultural equipment, canned goods, and timber. But according to American sources, the shipments included electronic gear, various arms, and ground-to-air guided missiles. Soviet military technicians, though not in uniform, were also said to have landed. It was only on September 2 that a Soviet-Cuban communiqué on the talks with a Cuban delegation in Moscow admitted that the Soviet Government had agreed to furnish Cuba with armaments and instructors "in connection with threats of aggressive imperialist quarters."[42]

Two days later, President Kennedy issued a warning that Cuba must not become a base for aggressive purposes. He said that to date there was no evidence that organized Soviet combat forces or missiles of an offensive capability were on the island. But he stated bluntly that "were it to be otherwise, the gravest issues would arise."[43] On September 7, the President requested authority from

Congress to call up 150,000 reservists during the Congressional recess. An official Tass statement of September 11 brought the Soviet answer. It was couched in aggressive, self-confident, and derisive terms. The Soviet Government denounced "the Witches' Sabbath staged in Congress and the American press about Cuba," the "bellicose-minded reactionary elements in the United States," the "vile" American propaganda, and described the President's request to Congress for the call-up of reservists as an act of provocation. Addressing itself to all "these people," the statement declared that what Soviet ships carried to Cuba was none of their business and advised them not to "poke your noses in where you shouldn't." Admittedly, apart from nonmilitary equipment, a certain amount of arms was being shipped to Cuba at its request, but they were "designed exclusively for defensive purposes." The Soviet Government stated explicitly that it need not place its rockets in Cuba in order to come to the assistance of any state that if attacked would ask for Soviet help. But while keeping its armed forces "at the peak of preparedness," the Soviet Government, unlike the United States, would not call up any reservists and would take only precautionary measures. Invoking the peaceful-coexistence policy, the Kremlin declared that it was willing to offer friendship to all countries and appealed to the United States to show kindness toward Cuba by restoring normal diplomatic relations. It was significant that the statement was not limited to the Cuban question but also touched upon other matters such as NATO, SEATO, CENTO, and particularly West Berlin. A curious device was applied in this respect: The Soviet Government offered not to press for a settlement of the German and Berlin problems until after the American elections in November.[44]

With that, the stage was set for the Soviet tactics employed during the following six weeks, until, on October 22, President Kennedy revealed the true nature of Russia's preparations in Cuba. During that period, there was no marked departure from the familiar mixture of menacing postures and appeals to peaceful coexistence. What stands out in retrospect is the consistent effort to divert American attention from Cuba by creating the impression that a crisis over Berlin was imminent. The Berlin problem was given prominence by Khrushchev, Gromyko, and the Soviet propaganda media. On August 22, in a gesture meant to imply that they were nearing the point of no return, the Russians, by abolishing their military headquarters in East Berlin, broke up the four-power control of the city. In mid-October, when the showdown was approaching, Soviet U.N. delegates spread rumors that Moscow was ready to follow a more moderate course with regard to Cuba if the United States became more accommodating on Berlin.[45]

These Soviet tactics succeeded up to a point in making Americans particularly sensitive to the Berlin situation, but not in distracting them from Cuba. Whatever the Russians may have contemplated in Berlin, it was contingent on the Cuban operation. It seems certain that at least in the initial stage of the Kremlin's "grand design," the tension centered on West Berlin was intended to increase the Cuban surprise.

The great deception was carried to its highest point in mid-October, when presumably the installation of the Soviet rockets at the Cuban launching pads was nearly completed. On October 16, Khrushchev told the new American Ambassador, Foy Kohler, that he expected to come to New York between Thanksgiving and Christmas to attend the General Assembly, and afterward hoped to visit the President. Two days later, at his own request, Gromyko was received at the White House and also had a long session with Dean Rusk. The purpose of these conversations was twofold: to divert American attention from Cuba to Berlin, and still more important, to stress the exclusively defensive character of Soviet weapons delivered to Cuba. As we learned four days later from the President himself, he already knew the truth on Thursday, October 18, when Gromyko sat in his office for over two hours and repeated, on his government's instructions, the assurance "that Soviet assistance . . . pursued solely the purpose of contributing to the defensive capabilities of Cuba."[46] In his speech of October 22, the President said that on Tuesday morning (October 16) he had received the first "preliminary hard information" regarding the Soviet installations in Cuba, which included medium-range ballistic missiles capable of carrying a nuclear warhead over a distance of more than 1,000 nautical miles. Preparations were observed for accommodating IBCM's of twice that range. The President therefore labeled the official Soviet declaration of September 12 and Gromyko's statements to him on October 18 as false.

What would have happened had American intelligence not been able to detect the nature of the Soviet nuclear build-up in Cuba in time? It has been stated that bad weather between the end of September and October 14 (Hurricane Ella) made impossible the aerial checking of Cuban refugee reports.[47] Had another hurricane formed around Cuba in mid-October, it might possibly have been too late to stop the work at the Soviet installations in time. The strange offer to refrain from pressuring for a Berlin settlement before the Congressional elections may have meant that the Cuban nuclear batteries pointing at the United States and the Panama Canal were to be ready about November 6. Whether Khrushchev would have revealed the fact in a dramatic gesture in the U.N. Assembly later in November or played a cat-and-mouse game is now immaterial. The aim of this "secret, swift, extraordinary build-up of Communist missiles" was described by President Kennedy as "a deliberately provocative and unjustified change in the *status quo* which cannot be accepted by this country."[48] What the Soviet Government had hoped to extort in terms of political concessions, what Khrushchev's initial demands backed by atomic blackmail would have been, is also unknown. But one thing seems certain: The Kremlin meant this to be a strategic breakthrough in the world balance of power, procuring for the Soviet Union a permanent advantage, one it intended to exploit to the hilt.

Then, the unexpected happened. The United States imposed a quarantine on all ships carrying offensive weapons to Cuba, demanded the removal of all such weapons already in Cuba, and warned that it would "regard any nuclear missile launched from Cuba against any nation in the Western Hemisphere as an attack by the Soviet Union on the United States requiring a full retaliatory response upon the Soviet Union."[49] The *casus belli* was thus defined with precision. Russia was taken by surprise before the Cuban atomic pistol could be brought into the contest. The Kremlin would not face a showdown and therefore had to retreat. An analysis of the first Soviet reaction to Kennedy's speech—the appeal of October 23 to "all governments and peoples to raise their voices in protest against aggressive action of the U.S.A."—suggests that the decision to retreat was taken in Moscow almost immediately after Kennedy's speech.[50] The Soviet appeal was strong in words but weak in substance. It called the quarantine a naval blockade (and rightly so), raged against "arrogant actions of American imperialism," accused President Kennedy of "recklessly playing with fire," and weakly repeated the falsehood that arms had been sent to Cuba only to increase its defensive potential. But the statement did not repeat the threat of September 11 to give assistance to Cuba or any other state that would ask for it. The most striking feature of the Soviet text was the omission of Kennedy's warning that any missile launched from Cuba against the Western Hemisphere would trigger American retaliation "upon the Soviet Union." The relevant passage was doctored to mean, rather vaguely,

American retaliation for an attack on U.S. territory. By thus twisting the President's strongest statement, the Soviet Government showed the crisis to its own public in a softer light. This also was the first indication of the masterly retreat Soviet diplomacy was to effect from the dangerous position into which it had placed itself. It may be assumed that from that moment on, the Kremlin set itself one major aim: to do everything possible short of war to save the Cuban Communist regime.

The dramatic week—from Monday, October 22, when President Kennedy gave the Soviet leadership their greatest surprise since World War II, until Sunday, October 28, when Khrushchev announced that orders had been given to dismantle and return to Russia the offensive weapons sent to Cuba—is still not an open book ready for exhaustive analysis. The known elements—the official statements; the exchange of messages and letters between Kennedy and Khrushchev, Khrushchev and U Thant, and Khrushchev and Bertrand Russell; and the voluminous press reports—fail to reveal all of what went on in the Kremlin. Despite the impression that the decision to retreat was made within hours after Kennedy's speech, there are strong indications of dissension in the Kremlin, at least over tactics, and possibly of moments of near panic. Some of the tergiversations in the Soviet course of action may have simply reflected the usual practice designed to confuse the other side. Khrushchev's letter to Bertrand Russell of October 24, much sharper in substance than the appeal of the previous day and hinting at a world war, but also suggesting a summit meeting, may fall under that heading. In search of expedients, Khrushchev, on the twenty-fifth, eagerly accepted U Thant's suggestion of a temporary "suspension of arms shipments to Cuba" and of the American blockade, which manifestly would have been to Russia's advantage. On the same day, *Krasnaya Zvezda*, the Soviet Army newspaper, published a speech by Marshal Malinovsky boasting that the Soviet armed forces were in a state of highest readiness. This was a turning point, for the quarantine had become effective on October 24, and twenty-five Soviet cargo vessels were now nearing Cuban waters. But during the night of the twenty-fifth and the following morning it became known that half of them had changed course. Moscow was giving in, or at least delaying a showdown, which was confirmed in Khrushchev's letters to U Thant and to Kennedy dated October 26. This unpublished letter to the President remains one of the intriguing components of the crisis. It has been described as highly emotional, "rambling, disjointed, and confused."[51]

However, what is known is that it contained an offer to remove
Soviet weapons considered as "offensive" from Cuba, under U.N.
supervision, in return for Washington's pledge to lift the blockade
and refrain from invading Cuba. But on the twenty-seventh it was
followed by yet another letter from Khrushchev couched in rather
different terms and proposing a deal: Soviet atomic installations
would be removed from Cuba in exchange for the removal of similar American facilities from Turkey. President Kennedy ignored
Khrushchev's second letter and the proposed deal on Turkey, but
answered the unpublished letter of October 26, accepting the gist
of its proposal. In a public statement, the White House also drew
attention to "inconsistent and conflicting proposals from the Soviet
Union."[52]

Thus, on Saturday, October 27, a new climax was reached. President Kennedy was reported to have remarked that evening that the
situation was touch and go. Failing a prompt Soviet agreement,
the United States would have had to prepare for further action.
The most restrained next step would have been the protection of
the reconnaissance flights over Cuba, and Air Force reservists were
called up.

On Sunday, October 28, Radio Moscow with remarkable haste
first announced and then broadcast the Soviet answer. Khrushchev
accepted the solution he had submitted himself without any new
conditions. Turkey was not mentioned.

This basic agreement satisfied the Kremlin's main concern, i.e.,
the preservation of the Communist regime in Cuba. Since 1961, a
large part of the population had turned against Castro, and he
could hardly have survived an American expedition to destroy the
nuclear installations. Once the Soviet Union agreed to their dis-
mantling under international supervision this was no longer necessary, and Moscow paid the price in loss of prestige. What went on
subsequently in Moscow and Havana—whether the Soviet Government had really been unable to make Castro accept U.N. control,
to what extent Mikoyan's efforts had been genuine, and what role
was played by the Chinese—has to be left to future historians. A
comic-opera episode in March, 1963, when Castro told a *Le Monde*
reporter that he would have boxed Khrushchev's ears had he come
to Havana instead of sending Mikoyan (a statement he later denied
vehemently), seems to confirm that during the crisis the Cuban
dictator had not been an easily controllable tool in the hands of
the Russians.[53]

But there is also little doubt that the Soviet Government itself wanted to evade the obligations incurred by the October agreement. According to a press report, a virtual ultimatum was needed on November 19, 1962, to make Khrushchev promise the removal within thirty days of the Ilyushin-28 bombers, as part of the offensive weapons.[54] In his statement of November 20, the day he ordered the naval quarantine of Cuba lifted, President Kennedy stressed that important parts of the October agreement had not been carried out. The major Soviet default was the fact that the promised U.N. supervision on Cuban soil never materialized. Without it, the United States had to rely on much less effective sea inspection, and to continue its air surveillance of Cuba. The President specifically stated that a number of Soviet ground-combat units had been identified in Cuba, and that he had been informed "that these and other Soviet units were associated with the protection of offensive weapons systems and will also be withdrawn in due course."[55] During the following months, it became known that this promise had not been kept. In May, 1963, the U.S. Senate Preparedness Subcommittee stated that according to available intelligence data, at least 17,500 Soviet military personnel had remained in or returned to Cuba, and other (possibly less reliable) sources put the figure as high as 40,000. The Subcommittee also emphasized that "there is no evidence that any of the combat ground units associated with the four mobile armored groups have been withdrawn."[56] The Subcommittee further reported that in the absence of reliable on-site inspection there was "reason for grave concern" lest some strategic missiles or other offensive weapons had been concealed on the island.

Thus it can be estimated that what the Soviet Government was able to salvage in Cuba from the October crisis was by no means negligible. The Communist regime was still in the saddle, and Cuba continued to play its role of advance base for subversive activities in Latin America. Finally, Soviet combat troops in organized units remained in Cuba, leaving the door open to possible future needs.

On the other hand, the price of the October understanding with the United States had been a loss of prestige the like of which the Soviet Union had not suffered since World War II. The Security Council debate of October 23–25 between Adlai Stevenson and Valerian Zorin ended in a resounding defeat for the Soviet delegate. To the intelligent public behind the Iron Curtain the net result was simple: the Soviet Union had matched its nuclear potential in a diplomatic showdown with the United States and had been forced to back down. Therefore, the Kremlin's much-vaunted nuclear superiority was a bluff.

But as they had done more than once before, the Soviet leadership preferred to incur a serious, though temporary, propaganda setback in order to hold on to a concrete asset, i.e., the Communist regime in Cuba. They beat a slow retreat from the painful October defeat, little by little distorting the true significance of the events. In his December, 1962, report to the Supreme Soviet, Khrushchev explained how Soviet action in the Caribbean had prevented an American invasion of Cuba and thereby saved world peace. "This," he said, "is precisely the policy of peaceful coexistence in action."[57] In a speech in East Berlin on January 16, 1963, Khrushchev said that by installing rockets in Cuba, the Soviet Union had compelled "the aggressive circles of U.S. imperialism" to retreat and to renounce the invasion of the island. Since "revolutionary Cuba is still there and is growing stronger," it was obvious, according to Khrushchev, "who really retreated and who benefited from the conflict."[58] Were it not for the public dispute with Red China and Albania, no one in the Communist camp could have openly challenged Moscow's claim that the evacuation of intermediate-range ballistic rockets and Ilyushin-28 bombers from Cuba under American pressure had in fact been a "major victory" of Soviet military might and diplomatic sagacity.[59]

FIVE

RENTS IN THE MONOLITH

THE DIVISIVE FORCES

It would be convenient to assume that nationalism is the common denominator in the difficulties the Soviet leadership encounters in maintaining cohesion, if not unity, in the Communist camp. But although nationalism does play a role in most of the revolts against Moscow, from East Germany to China, its influence varies. Rejection of Russian domination was the most powerful motive behind the Hungarian Revolution and the Polish "October" of 1956. Yet nationalism was only one of several factors in the Yugoslav heresy, the dispute with China, or the East German revolt of 1953. It plays practically no part in the revolt of the Albanian Communist Party. On the other hand, the rebel Hungarian and Polish workers and students and the East Berlin workers also and unmistakably rejected Communism as a system and a political regime, whereas the Yugoslav, Chinese, and Albanian quarrels with Moscow were, or are, primarily a falling-out between Communists. Although Khrushchev's regime holds nationalism to be as dangerous as dogmatism, adventurism, and revisionism, the troubles of the Communist camp cannot be ascribed to any single ailment.

How much nationalism is still left in the Ukraine or in Georgia after several decades of Soviet rule? Will the three small Baltic nations survive the pressure, and for how long? How great is the weariness of the intelligentsia in Eastern Europe and their disenchantment with the West? None of these questions lend themselves to easy answers. Yet the fact cannot be overlooked that during the last decade, Communist power and prestige have suffered a number of significant setbacks. In June, 1953, the workers of the Skoda works in Plzen (Pilsen) in Czechoslovakia revolted against a "currency reform," and occupied the town's administrative building for a few hours. On June 17 of the same year, the workers of East Berlin and other East German towns rebelled; they demonstrated in the streets and burned public buildings and Communist banners. Two motorized Soviet divisions drove into East

Berlin to quell the rebellion, killing many. On June 28–29, 1956, the workers of Poznan, Poland, triggered an uprising of most of the town's population. Several hundred people died or were injured in the street fighting against the police and security forces. There followed, also in 1956, the bloodless Polish revolution and the armed conquest of Hungary by Soviet forces. In 1948, the Yugoslav Communists were pushed out of the Communist bloc and then took their own Communist path. Finally, the rift between Moscow and China came out into the open, disclosing the magnitude of the Communist camp's "constitutional" problem. After China, the Albanian Party defied Moscow, Romanian Communists opposed Soviet economic plans, and Castro at first refused to sign the 1963 limited test-ban treaty. In all these cases Moscow tried, by means ranging from outright war to inter-Party diplomacy, to restore its primacy. But the monolith keeps cracking.

19. *THE YUGOSLAV HERESY*

Until 1948, Tito was the most devoted follower of Moscow's orthodox line among the non-Russian Communist leaders. Then, almost overnight, his party was called wayward, contaminated by Trotskyite and "imperialist" influences, and guilty of willful anti-Soviet policies. These and similar accusations were hurled at Tito and his followers, at first in private (in three letters from the Central Committee of the Soviet Communist Party of March 27, May 4, and May 22, 1948) and then publicly (in the Cominform communiqué of June 28, 1948, announcing the expulsion of the Yugoslav Communist Party). Ironically, Tito's Party became "heretical" only after its expulsion from the Cominform. Prior to this "excommunication," the Yugoslav Communists did not pursue policies distinct from the Soviet line. Between 1946 and 1948, totalitarian legislative measures nationalized virtually all industry, mines, communications, finance, and most of private trade. Contrary to Soviet charges, the Yugoslav Communists energetically pushed the "socialization" of agriculture, confiscating estates and large peasant holdings and rapidly extending the area run by various state organizations and kolkhoz-type cooperatives. From 1946 to 1950, the private sector of arable land declined from 98.8 per cent to 73.3 per cent, while the state and cooperative (kolkhoz) sectors increased from 0.8 per cent and 0.4 per cent, respectively, to a joint total of 26.7 per cent. Although full collectivization on the Soviet model was not introduced, the peasants were pressured by the Communist bureaucracy to abandon private holdings and join the kolkhozes.

Objective analysis shows beyond any doubt that the Soviet accusations of 1948 were not based on differences in doctrine or practice, but that the true reason for the dispute was Belgrade's resistance to Russia's colonial methods. The exchange of letters between the two Communist Parties revealed that the Yugoslavs had had the audacity to complain about the highhanded attitude of the Soviet Ambassador, the behavior and expense of the Russian mili-

tary advisers (they were paid four times as much as generals com-
manding Yugoslav armies, and three times as much as members of
the Yugoslav Government), the recruiting of agents for the Soviet
secret service in Yugoslavia, and the attempted economic exploitation. In his *Conversations with Stalin*, Milovan Djilas (formerly
one of the top four Yugoslav Communists) confirmed that the
Kremlin demanded complete submission of its satellites and brutally rejected even the slightest criticism. Tito's cautious complaint
in a confidential talk with the Soviet Ambassador in 1944, about
the looting, raping, and killing by Red Army officers and men in
northeastern Yugoslavia was never forgiven in Moscow (the issue
was revived in the 1948 correspondence). Djilas also described
official conversations in Moscow in February, 1948, with Yugoslav
and Bulgarian delegates whom Stalin treated like naughty children.
Stalin seems to have backed the plans of a Yugoslav-Bulgarian
federation since 1945 (if not earlier); in January, 1948, he told
Djilas that Russia also agreed to "Yugoslavia swallowing Albania."[1]
But a sudden change in the Kremlin's attitude occurred at the end
of that month, when *Pravda* rebuked the Bulgarian Communist
leader Georgi Dimitrov for announcing an East European federation and proposing a customs union between Bulgaria and Romania. Soviet policy with regard to the European satellite governments
in this period was most ambiguous; Djilas even suspected the
Kremlin of preparing the ground for a vast reorganization of the
Communist bloc with the aim of incorporating the people's democracies into a greater Soviet state. This also seems to have been
Dimitrov's interpretation of the situation at the time. It is certain
that in February, 1948, Stalin sharply opposed Yugoslav plans to
take over Albania, while the dispute between Moscow and Belgrade, which erupted soon afterward, upset the preparations for a
Yugoslav-Bulgarian federation. Tito and Dimitrov had already
signed a number of important protocols in Bled on August 3, 1947,
and a treaty of alliance on November 27. They had spoken in public of the fulfillment of "age-old dreams" and of a "new epoch" in
their countries' relations.[2] Two Yugoslav divisions were readied to
enter Albania. All this came to naught when Moscow's policy
changed. Stalin may have supported a Yugoslav-Bulgarian-Albanian
federation while toying with the idea of incorporating, one way or
another, the people's democracies into the Soviet Union. But at the
end of 1947, such plans appeared too hazardous, in view of the
general stiffening of Western policies, and particularly the appearance of Americans on the Greek scene after the proclamation of

the Truman Doctrine. As in Persia the previous year, Stalin was anxious to avoid a head-on clash with the United States; at the meeting with the Yugoslav and Bulgarian delegations described by Djilas, Stalin insisted that "the uprising in Greece has to fold up."[3] If at that time Stalin still planned to incorporate the people's democracies into the Soviet Union, the conflict with the Yugoslav Communists dealt such plans a body blow. Consequently, Moscow reverted to its more usual stand of opposing any groupings of states in which Russia was not a direct participant. Georgi Dimitrov, the hero of the Reichstag fire trial and a former secretary of the Comintern, could easily be brought to heel. He was an obedient tool of the Kremlin. Tito's situation was different. For geographical and local reasons, he could become troublesome and therefore had to be demoted and replaced by a more docile leader.

The exchange of letters between the Central Committee of the Soviet and Yugoslav parties in the spring of 1948 marked the beginning of a campaign of intimidation and pressure calculated to break Belgrade's resistance. It was this pressure that eventually caused the Yugoslav Communists to evolve a policy line of their own. But at first they tried hard to placate the Kremlin and continued to demonstrate their unrequited love for the Soviet Union and Stalin. The letters of their Central Committee contained a number of explanations and halfhearted admissions of possible errors. On July 21, 1948, three weeks after the publication of the scorching Cominform communiqué, Tito closed his speech at the Fifth Congress of the Yugoslav Communist Party with the invocation: "Long live the Soviet Union, long live Stalin."[4] The Yugoslav press, while defending Belgrade's position against Moscow, continued to denounce the Marshall Plan, NATO, and U.S. policy. It also backed the Soviet line on China and Greece and extolled the progress toward Communism in Yugoslav economic and social life. In August, 1949, Tito declared in Skoplje that the Communist Party held "all our industry, all our commerce and trade . . . we are advancing toward a full liquidation of capitalism in agriculture."[5] At the end of the year it was officially reported that the number of peasant "working cooperatives" had increased fivefold since 1948 (from 1,318 to 6,492).[6] All this indicates that, had Stalin wished to compromise, he could have done so at no great political cost for more than a year after the 1948 break.

The change of policy came during 1950. A "Basic Law" of June 27, 1950,[7] established workers' councils in industry. In autumn, the Yugoslav Government applied for American economic aid. In January, 1951, the kolkhozes were put on a voluntary basis; in May, compulsory deliveries of meat, milk, potatoes, and fodder were abolished. Collectivization was officially abandoned at the end of 1952. The practical consequences of these measures were soon felt. Figures for the total agricultural area by sectors show that the kolkhoz type of cooperative regressed from 17.8 per cent in May, 1950, to 1.3 per cent in December, 1953. Conversely, private holdings increased in the same period from 66.3 per cent to 79.5 per cent.[8] As in Poland after October, 1956, the peasants flocked back to private holdings from kolkhozes as soon as administrative pressure ceased.

Theoretical explanations did not precede these pragmatic changes; they took shape concurrently or in their wake. In January, 1951, Tito stated in an interview that a Socialist (i.e., state or kolkhoz) agricultural sector should compete freely with an independent sector. However, he stressed the need for planning, both in agriculture and in trade. In the autumn of 1951, Tito's deputy, Edvard Kardelj, declared that a "Socialist planned economy . . . in no case means . . . that the entire activity of society should be subordinated to the state apparatus."[9] According to Kardelj, "an overall progress of Socialist economy is only possible as a result of a free soaring of Socialist economic forces as they proceed to develop on the basis of communal ownership of the means of production." In less florid language, this meant that for practical reasons the totalitarian government had restored a limited amount of freedom in some sectors of the economy. The relaxation was greater in agriculture than in industry. The much advertised workers' councils did not fundamentally change the Communist structure of Yugoslav industry. True, workers and employees elected councils in factories and other state-owned businesses and were widely represented in administrative boards; but these bodies could not appoint or change the director through whom (as well as through the Party cells) the government remained in charge of industry. On the positive side (in a vague reference to Marx's surplus-value theory), the workers' councils received the valued patronage role of fixing and distributing bonuses. In a general way, the workers' councils fitted into a new system of administrative decentralization and a partly free marketing of products that made the Yugoslav economy a curious mixture of government planning, Communist Party control, and half-free enterprise. The new system, as outlined at the Sixth Congress of the Yugoslav Communist Party in November, 1952, and developed during the following year, was more adaptable to circumstances than the former rigid order on the Soviet model.

Whatever the merits of the reforms, it is doubtful that the Yugoslav economy would have survived without massive American economic assistance. When Soviet and satellite trade and credits abruptly ceased in mid-1948, Yugoslavia faced economic disaster. The country had been cruelly devastated by war, capital was lacking, inflation soared, trade was disorganized; 60–80 per cent of the main imports, most of the coal, pig iron, petroleum products, machinery, and fertilizers came from the Soviet-bloc countries. In these circumstances, Western support became indispensable. American aid, in particular, assumed proportions that in Yugoslavia must have appeared as an undreamed-of miracle. Total American grants and economic loans between 1950 and 1962, and military aid until 1959, given to Communist Yugoslavia during her estrangement from Soviet Russia amounted to nearly $2.5 billion.

The fact that Tito's government applied for and received Western economic aid made its challenge to Soviet domination particularly serious. Moscow rejected all offers of compromise and increased its pressure on the Yugoslav Communists. The intensity of this action was shown by the Yugoslav White Book of 1951, *On Aggressive Activities by the Governments of the U.S.S.R., Poland and the Other Satellite States*. It listed 1,067 border incidents with Yugoslavia's Communist-ruled neighbors from June, 1948, to October, 1950, as well as 46 treaties, agreements, and conventions broken by the other Communist governments.[10]

While it would be superfluous to speculate on what would have happened in Yugoslavia had the United States not come to Belgrade's aid, it is probable that, left to his own devices, Tito could not have maintained himself in power. Actually, the Soviet-bloc boycott, Western loans, grants and arms deliveries, and dire economic necessity contributed to the three main features of Tito's regime: a partly free but state-owned and state-controlled economy, a profitable neutralist stance in international relations, and doctrinal attitudes that Tito and his followers came to consider the true incarnation of Marxism-Leninism. However, this seemingly ideological separation from Moscow resulted from necessity; its contribution to Communist doctrine was rather slim. It is difficult to accept Tito's 1952 contention that "our Socialist revolution and proletarian dictatorship are different from their Russian counterparts in all their aspects"; even less well founded were the assertions that his rule is not based on a one-party system or that "in Yugoslavia the state is withering away."[11] Later, the much-lauded "Socialist decentralization" was little more (or less) than an opportunistic step toward free enterprise. The resolution of the Sixth Congress of the Yugoslav Communist Party (November, 1952) on the "Tasks of the Union of Communists of Yugoslavia,"[12] which marked the official beginning of the Yugoslav Communists' doctrinal independence, was mostly a mixture of internal and external policy slogans confirming the diagnosis that contemporary Communism is primarily a power machine and "has become a technique for power rather than an ideal for life."[13]

On the other hand, Tito never ceased to regard himself as a true Communist. As a practical politician he saw the danger of proclaiming a new doctrine. "Titoism as a separate ideological line does not exist," he said in 1952. Modestly and shrewdly Tito stated that the Yugoslavs "have added nothing to Marxist-Leninist doctrine." From this there was only one step to charging that Stalin was the apostate. "Stalin is the revisionist," he declared.[14] Whereas the Yugoslav doctrinal variations on Communist themes are of comparatively little interest, the practical importance of a Communist regime proclaiming its independence from Moscow was considerable. Possibly (though it cannot be proved), Tito's rebellion saved some of the European satellite states from becoming incorporated into the Soviet Union. It became an additional reason for Stalin's wish to end the Communist-instigated civil war in Greece. The very assertion that various roads may lead to Socialism provided a powerful disintegrating element within the Communist bloc.

We may never learn how Tito envisaged his future relations with Moscow during the years of rupture. The invasion of Yugoslavia, which he said Stalin was preparing, never materialized. He was also proved wrong on the contention that the conflict was a final break. It is not impossible that such public declarations were made for the benefit of the West. Suspicions that the quarrel between Moscow and Belgrade was nothing but a Communist conspiracy could not be substantiated, yet the undisguised relief of the Yugoslav press over Stalin's death and Tito's remarks on a possible change of Soviet policy suggest that he did not relinquish hope of coming to an understanding with the successors. Contacts were resumed as soon as Stalin was gone. Less than four months later, in June, 1953, the two governments agreed to appoint ambassadors again, a first step toward Tito's rehabilitation. Little is known of the preparatory negotiations;[15] both sides moved with great caution and secrecy, for much was at stake. The manifold difficulties were not resolved as long as Malenkov was Prime Minister and while Molotov still wielded a position of great power. But for someone preparing to undermine Stalin's posthumous authority while keeping the Communist empire intact, the understanding with Tito presented many advantages. Logically, Khrushchev became the moving spirit of the new policy expressed in his dramatic declaration of May 26, 1955, upon his arrival at the Belgrade airport at the head of an important Soviet delegation. In this text, the Soviet side admitted the responsibility for the seven-year rift between the two Communist regimes. The guilt, however, was put on the dead; according to Khrushchev, the conflict had resulted from the "provocation engineered . . . by the unmasked enemies of the people—Beria, Abakumov, and others." And he offered an abject apology: "We sincerely regret and resolutely reject all that happened and accumulated during that period."[16] A few days later, on June 2, in a joint statement Moscow officially accepted the theory of "different roads to Socialism": "Since questions of internal organization, of differences of social systems, and of different forms of Socialist development, are exclusively a matter for the peoples of the different countries."[17]

A year later, Tito's official visit to the Soviet Union led to far-reaching declarations of friendship and common policy aims. On arriving in Moscow, on June 2, 1956, Tito said that there would never again be such a misunderstanding. On another occasion he spoke of Yugoslavia as being part of the "family of Socialism." Two statements, by Tito and Marshal Zhukov, respectively, seemed to imply that the political alliance between the two states had been or was to be restored. In a public speech at Stalingrad, Tito said on June 11: "In peace as in war, Yugoslavia must march shoulder to shoulder with the Soviet people toward the same goal, the goal of the victory of Socialism."[18] According to press reports, Marshal Zhukov went a step further, implying the restoration of mutual assistance. On June 20, speaking in Tito's presence, he said that Yugoslavia and Russia would fight shoulder to shoulder in any future war.[19]

The way to this apparently total reconciliation was paved by the dissolution of the Cominform on April 18, 1956, and Molotov's dismissal as Foreign Minister on June 1, 1956. Although Stalin's name was not publicly mentioned among the guilty, this was a great victory for Tito. As events of the following years were to show, however, the reconciliation was based partly on a misunderstanding, if not on an intentional misinterpretation. The joint Belgrade statement specifically stressed the freedom of choice on the road to Socialism in the internal affairs of the countries concerned, but it was vague in regard to international affairs. It omitted the all-important matter of unity in the foreign policy of the "Socialist camp." Yet, during the following two years, until the next dispute came into the open, Moscow neither expressly objected to Tito's many international activities nor to his proclaimed neutralist policy line, and it condoned (at least by default) Yugoslavia's acceptance of Western economic and military aid. In the same period, the Soviet Union and the satellite governments resumed their economic assistance to and trade relations with Yugoslavia. Yugoslavia's $90 million debt to the Soviet Union was written off; a $30 million Soviet gold loan was promised; credit and loan agreements totaling $325 million were concluded with the Soviet Union, East Germany, and Czechoslovakia. But only a small part of these arrangements had been implemented when the new quarrel began.

That serious trouble had been brewing all through the summer and early autumn of 1956 was underlined by visits of Mikoyan and Khrushchev to Belgrade and a sudden trip of Yugoslav leaders to the Crimea. There were rumors of a letter by the Central Committee of the Soviet Communist Party criticizing anew the Yugoslav Communists. Despite formal denials, the Yugoslav official press admitted that "important conflicts and differences of views" appeared between Belgrade and Moscow, and it seems clear that Tito's position on the relative independence of Communist parties and governments had again come under Russian pressure.

The Hungarian Revolution put Tito in a quandary. Soviet military intervention in a Communist-ruled state was in itself too suggestive to be accepted lightly. But the abolition of Communist rule in a neighboring country by an angry populace also raised frightening prospects. The dishonorable violation by the Soviet authorities of the safe conduct granted Prime Minister Nagy after leaving the Yugoslav Legation was most embarrassing to Tito personally, as head of state. His changing attitude during the Hungarian crisis is probably best explained, or rationalized, by the danger he first saw in the Soviet military intervention and later in the anti-Communist popular uprising. His analysis of the Hungarian Revolution, contained in a speech at Pula on November 11, was a sort of Solomon's judgment: at first the Russians were at fault for intervening against a whole nation dissatisfied with the wrong kind of Communist leadership; but later Imre Nagy erred in calling the people to arms against the Soviet Army and in appealing to the West.* Tito said: "The justified revolt against a clique turned into an uprising of the entire nation against Socialism and against the Soviet Union." He further gave his personal blessing to the new Kadar regime imposed by the Soviet Army: "I know these people in the new government, and in my opinion they represent all that is most honest in Hungary."[20] But even this endorsement failed to satisfy Moscow, and as late as March 28, 1957, Prime Minister Bulganin said in a public declaration that Tito's attitude in the Hungarian question did not "in essence differ from that of the imperialists."[21]

Later that spring, Belgrade took the initiative on a new *rapprochement*. It was marked by an extensive visit to the Soviet Union by the Yugoslav Defense Minister, General Gosnjak, and by a secret meeting in Romania of Khrushchev, Tito, and high-ranking officials. If these conversations brought some measure of agreement, it did not survive the fortieth anniversary of the Bolshevik Revolution in November, 1957, when representatives of sixty-four Communist parties met in Moscow. The main task Khrushchev assigned to the meeting was the restoration of the Soviet political and ideological leadership and the doctrinal unity of the Communist camp. The Communist leaders attending the meeting included Mao Tse-tung (China), Ho Chi Minh (North Vietnam), Kim Il Sung (North Korea), Janos Kadar (Hungary), Wladyslaw Gomulka (Poland), Walter Ulbricht (East Germany), Enver Hoxha (Albania). But Tito did not come; the Yugoslav Party was represented by Vice President Kardelj. The reason for Tito's absence became evident when the Yugoslav delegation refused to sign a strongly worded declaration by the ruling Communist parties restating the Communist cold-war policies. American, British, French, "and other imperialists" were charged with conducting aggressive wars in many countries. "Certain aggressive groups in the United States" were described as "the center of world reaction, the sworn enemies of the people."[22] Obviously the signing of this declaration would have impaired Tito's relations with the West and severely limited his freedom of action in foreign policy. This no doubt was Khrushchev's aim.

Although the Yugoslav delegation in Moscow signed a more innocuous Peace Manifesto together with the other sixty-three Communist parties, a new dispute with the Russians erupted a few

---

* In fact, Imre Nagy at no time appealed to the West, but to the United Nations, asking that the Great Powers (including the Soviet Union) recognize Hungary's neutrality.

months later. It was triggered off by the draft program prepared for the Seventh Congress of the Yugoslav League of Communists to be held at Ljubljana in the second half of April, 1958. The draft was sent to the other Communist parties and last-minute efforts were made in Belgrade to appease Soviet critics; important changes were introduced into the draft after its publication by *Borba* on March 15. But in April, the Soviet Party theoretical magazine *Kommunist* came out strongly against the draft, charging the Yugoslavs with petty-bourgeois nationalism, ignorance of the basic tenets of Lenin's teachings, and mistaken attitudes in the struggle between "Socialism" and "imperialism." Consequently, the Yugoslav Congress was boycotted by all the ruling Communist parties; in May, an official visit to Belgrade by the Chairman of the Presidium of the Supreme Soviet, Marshal Klimenti Voroshilov, was postponed at the last moment; Tito also postponed a visit to Warsaw that was to have taken place on June 8; the relations further deteriorated when, at the end of May, the Soviet Union unilaterally decided to postpone the fulfillment of the January and August, 1956, agreements under which Yugoslavia was to receive $285 million in credits and industrial equipment; in a speech at a congress of the Bulgarian Communist Party at Sofia on June 3, Khrushchev stated that the 1948 condemnation of the Yugoslavs by the Cominform had been "basically correct."[23]

It seems unnecessary to trace in detail the Byzantine charges of doctrinal deviation that both sides exchanged again during the next year or so. In a speech on June 15, 1958, Tito pinpointed the underlying reason for the new Soviet onslaught as being the Yugoslav refusal to sign the Moscow declaration of November, 1957, designed to re-establish discipline and unity in the Communist camp, and referred to in later years as binding on the Communist parties. There was no logical reason why Tito should have submitted to the renewed Soviet political and economic pressure more easily in 1958 than in 1948. Did Khrushchev and Mao Tse-tung think that by renouncing American military assistance at the end of 1957, by recognizing the East German Communist regime, and by supporting Soviet Russia in some controversial foreign policy matters the Belgrade regime had burned its bridges to the West? If so, it was one of the major miscalculations Moscow and Peking committed during 1958, a year of "hard" attitudes and attempted "tough" solutions in Communist policies. It saw Khrushchev's ascendancy to the Premiership, the execution of Imre Nagy, the first Soviet ultimatum on West Berlin, vain Russian recriminations over

American and British troops preserving peace in Jordan and Lebanon, and the hapless attempt to conquer the Quemoy and Matsu Islands by blockade and artillery bombardment. At the time, Khrushchev and Mao apparently still agreed on the meaning of "peaceful coexistence." But the Chinese took the lead in accusing the League of Yugoslav Communists of various doctrinal deviations and of assisting "American imperialists." The *Jenmin Jih Pao* of May 5, 1958, stated that the Cominform had been "basically correct" in its 1948 censure of the Yugoslav Communists, a formula repeated a month later in Khrushchev's Sofia speech. The next day, *Pravda* reprinted the Chinese editorial and pointed out the harm that deviations from Marxism-Leninism could do to the foreign policy of the Communist camp. On May 11, *Pravda* contributed one more indication that the real reason for the new quarrel lay in Belgrade's independence in foreign relations: "Every Communist is justified in wondering why the United States imperialists, the worst enemies of Socialism, consider it profitable to help Yugoslavia. For what services? Is it not because the Yugoslav leaders are trying to weaken the unity of the international Communist and working class movement?"[24]

While Yugoslavia's relations with China continued to deteriorate after 1958, the new dispute with Soviet Russia never reached the intensity of the earlier quarrel. Ambassadors were not recalled; trade continued and even increased in volume. Even before the first cracks appeared on the façade of Soviet-Chinese amity, the Russians showed a tendency toward a second (or in fact a third) reconciliation with Belgrade. After Khrushchev's 1959 U.S. visit, which marked the real beginning of the quarrel between Moscow and Peking, a distinct correlation developed between the Soviet-Yugoslav and Soviet-Chinese relations: Yugoslavia and China became like the scalepans on a balance—when one went up in Moscow, the other came down. Despite some important (but temporary) fluctuations, the Yugoslav side of the balance definitely went up. In September, 1960, Tito was one of the five neutralist heads of government who attended the U.N. General Assembly at Khrushchev's suggestion, and Tito further assisted Khrushchev's policy by co-sponsoring a resolution asking President Eisenhower to meet with the Soviet Premier (who only a few months before had brutally scuttled the Summit Conference in Paris). In July, 1961, Yugoslav Foreign Minister Kocha Popovich visited Moscow; in April, 1962, Soviet Foreign Minister Andrei Gromyko came to Belgrade. Five months later, the Chairman of the Presidium of the

Supreme Soviet, Leonid Brezhnev, was met at the Belgrade airport by Tito.

This evolution was by no means steady; time and again mutual recriminations interrupted the process; most serious charges were contained in the Moscow Statement of eighty-one Communist parties in November, 1960, branding Yugoslav Communism as "international opportunism," "modern revisionism," and "betrayers of Marxism-Leninism."[25] Nevertheless, Brezhnev's visit to Yugoslavia in September–October, 1962, could be regarded by both sides as a limited success. It demonstrated an agreement on a number of foreign-policy matters, without pushing it to a point where it would hamper Tito's relations with the West. The joint communiqué issued at the end of Brezhnev's visit described this situation as "identity or proximity of . . . views." A characteristic example can be seen in German affairs: The communiqué stressed the need "to normalize the situation in West Berlin" (a code phrase for Soviet demands) but the formula of "ending the occupation regime" was not used; a peace treaty recognizing the two German states was found necessary, but the communiqué omitted the oft-repeated Soviet threat of a separate peace treaty with East Germany. Still, in a general way, the understanding registered Tito's siding with the Russian position on such important questions as "general and complete disarmament," an unpoliced moratorium on underground nuclear tests, atom-free zones in many areas, and "artificial barriers" in world trade. Despite the quarrel with Peking, the two governments considered it "intolerable that the People's Republic of China to this day does not occupy its lawful seat in this world organization [the U.N.]." The text also contained a significant reference to the 1955 Belgrade declaration—"a good basis for fruitful cooperation."[26] This showed a mutual desire to return to the idyl of the first reconciliation.

Brezhnev visited Yugoslavia officially as the formal Soviet head of state, in return for Tito's 1956 trip. Early in October it was announced in Belgrade that Tito would go to Soviet Russia "for a vacation." The journey took place in December and lasted eighteen days, culminating in an unprecedented compliment to a foreign head of state—Tito's speech in the Supreme Soviet.

Against the background of increasing propaganda warfare between Moscow and Peking, Tito and his party were warmly received in the Soviet Union. The pretense that their discussions with the Soviet leaders were limited to state relations, as distinct from Party ties, soon proved to be mere sophistry. But the net result of the visit did not go far beyond the Brezhnev-Tito talks. The most important difference lay in Khrushchev's open admission, in a speech to the Supreme Soviet on December 13, that doctrinal dissensions had not been fully ironed out: "There have been, and still remain, serious differences on a number of ideological questions. . . . But we, for our part, are ready to do everything in our power to overcome these differences."[27] This led the Soviet Premier once again to admit the possibility of "various roads to Socialism." He said: "A different interpretation of concrete questions of Socialist construction, a different approach to this or that question cannot be ruled out. . . . It would be a mistake to brand as renegades all who do not conform to the pattern." On the other hand, Khrushchev could boast that Moscow and Belgrade had "a common understanding, common views" on many international problems and in economic relations. The next day Tito said in the Supreme Soviet that "in the main" he agreed with Khrushchev's statements on Yugoslav-Soviet relations.[28] He also stressed that on major international questions, Yugoslav and Soviet viewpoints were "identical or similar." But on the whole, Tito did not depart from the cautious line adopted in the October communiqué with Brezhnev, and amid many compliments to Soviet foreign policy and Khrushchev himself (particularly on the settlement of the Cuban crisis) he described Yugoslavia as one of the "nonaligned, peaceful countries."[29]

It thus appears that not only did differences remain between the Russian and Yugoslav positions, but that they were differently interpreted in Moscow and Belgrade. For Khrushchev, Tito in 1962 was a sort of candidate-member of the Socialist camp; Tito seemed to see himself as no more than an associate member, retaining his freedom of action. He demonstrated his attachment to Communism by renewing his close ties with the Kremlin three times in seven years. But at no time during this period did Tito show any inclination to abandon the independent position of "positive neutralism," which circumstances had bestowed upon the Communist regime in Yugoslavia.

Tito obviously feels more at home in Moscow than in the Western capitals he visited. He may still believe in the ultimate victory of Communism, though possibly not in his own lifetime. He would be fearful of any attempt to achieve this victory by war, and therefore finds Khrushchev's peaceful-coexistence theory a convenient platform of collaboration with Moscow. However, should the balance of power suddenly be upset in Russia's favor, it would be difficult to imagine Tito as the last defender of the ramparts of neutralism. Signs of wavering were noticeable in Belgrade at the height of the Cuban crisis, when Yugoslav information media closely followed the Soviet line.

In 1962, Moscow confirmed once more the validity of Tito's theory of the "different roads to Socialism," a theory rejected by Stalin, accepted by Khrushchev in 1955, and then repudiated by him in 1958. The inducement to appease Tito at the price of toler- ance of doctrinal differences (but in return for declarations of solidarity in foreign policy) has become very strong in view of the greater danger of a schism with Peking. It would be rash, however, to consider Khrushchev's 1962 attitude toward the Yugoslav Com- munists as final, and to think that the Soviet leadership has once and for all renounced the tenet of Russian-Soviet supremacy in a united and disciplined Communist camp.

20. *THE DISPUTE WITH CHINA*

In the January 6, 1961, report to the ideological organizations of the Party, Khrushchev drew a comparison between the "struggle for Communism" and the "struggle for peace." The first, he said, was a class question; the latter, on the other hand, may be served by forces that, by implication, are opposed to Communism, such as the peasantry, the petty bourgeoisie, etc. But Khrushchev denied the obvious conflict of interest and concluded that: "the slogan of the struggle for peace by no means contradicts the slogan of the struggle for Communism. . . . The slogan of the struggle for peace is, as it were, a sputnik of the slogan of the struggle for Communism."[1]

The coexistence doctrine not only aims at subjecting free nations to Communism without war, it also makes it permissible to wage war if other means to impose their rule fail. On the other hand, the purpose of peace propaganda is to prevent the non-Communists from taking up arms to defend themselves. Therefore, from Khrushchev's point of view, his claim that to fight for peaceful coexistence is to fight for Communism is quite logical. To the West he says: "The call to peaceful coexistence scares those who do not want peace."[2] The formula is reshaped when put to opponents within the Communist camp: "If you are not for peaceful coexistence, you are not for Communism."

Within the Communist camp, the most serious objections to Khrushchev's ideas have been raised by the Chinese, who obviously could not be brushed aside with a slogan or a dialectical trick. Soviet-Chinese relations pose the most important problem in the Communist world, full of impenetrable shadows and mysteries. The material available for analysis consists almost exclusively of what is released for the public by the Parties in the various countries under Communist rule. In Russia and China, control and censorship are particularly strict. Under these conditions, the slow and devious dispute developing between Moscow and Peking could be followed only in general lines. Yet, it is certain that there was no public adverse reaction from Peking after the Twentieth Party Congress, when Khrushchev first outlined the new interpretation of the co-existence doctrine. For all practical purposes, the two countries continued their political collaboration until Khrushchev went to the United States in 1959.

At the end of July, 1958, Khrushchev and Mao Tse-tung met secretly in Peking. They were accompanied by Defense Minister Marshal Malinovsky, Deputy Foreign Minister Kuznetsov, and the Chinese Foreign and Defense Ministers. After the deliberations, the joint communiqué issued sharply attacked "aggressive imperialist circles, headed by monopolist groups in the United States." But the same communiqué also stressed that "countries with different social systems must coexist peacefully."[3]

Three weeks after this manifestation of Communist solidarity, China began a massive and almost daily bombardment of Quemoy. Troops were massed on the mainland facing Quemoy and Matsu. The Peking Government demanded the "liberation" of Taiwan and the offshore islands, as well as the withdrawal of American forces from the Formosa Straits. It is reasonable to assume that Russia was party to the Chinese military preparations leading to this display of force. On September 5, 1958, *Pravda* wrote that an attack on China would result in Russian assistance "by all available means." Khrushchev came out in support of Peking in a letter to President Eisenhower, dated September 8.

The close collaboration between the two Communist allies was further demonstrated by Khrushchev's refusal to participate in a heads of governments meeting of the U.N. Security Council, which he had previously agreed to attend. The sudden *volte-face*, on August 5, 1958, a few days after the Peking meeting, must have resulted from Chinese pressure.

Without going into the details of Soviet-Chinese relations during this period, it is well to remember that as late as February, 1960, at the Moscow meeting of the Warsaw Treaty powers, the Chinese observer K'ang Sheng continued to approve of the "Leninist principle of peaceful coexistence"; however, he sharply censured the United States, warned that "its imperialist nature will not change," and asked for vigilance against "U.S. double-dealing." He also voiced a strong reservation concerning the validity of any disarmament agreements arrived at without his Government's participation. While tersely remarking that "Comrade Khrushchev made a successful visit to the United States," K'ang Sheng omitted mentioning the East-West summit meeting scheduled to be held in May in Paris.[4]

The dispute then became public, with a number of articles on the subject appearing in the Chinese and Soviet press, and continued through the spring and summer. It began to abate before the November, 1960, meeting of the Communist parties in Moscow. In essence, the dispute revolved around the questions of violence and war. Can violence be avoided in the transition to "Socialism," and is war with the capitalist countries inevitable? In a major article, "Long Live Leninism," published in *Hongqi* (*Red Flag*) in connection with the ninetieth anniversary of Lenin's birth on April 22, 1960, Khrushchev, although not mentioned by name, was derided as one of those "well-intentioned persons who . . . get confused" and believe in the "end of violence." The Chinese theoretical journal invoked Lenin's authority to prove that "it would be impossible to wipe out counterrevolutionary violence without revolutionary violence." The article emphatically stated that "until the imperialist system and the exploiting classes come to an end, wars of one kind or another will always occur. . . . Marxism-Leninism absolutely must not sink into the mire of bourgeois pacifism." Further, *Hongqi* explained that to counteract imperialist double-dealing, the proletariat and the peoples of all countries must also have two tactics, one of exposing the imperialist peace fraud and the other "of preparing for a just war to end the imperialist unjust war when and if the imperialists should unleash it."[5]

To place the debate in its proper setting, it is well to remember that a Chinese delegation headed by Vice President Marshal Chu Teh participated in the Twentieth Soviet Party Congress, when Khrushchev said that "there is no fatal inevitability of war"; Mao Tse-tung himself was in Moscow in November, 1957, when the Chinese Party signed the Declaration stating that "there is a real possibility of averting war"; Chou En-lai was present at the Twenty-first Soviet Party Congress in January, 1959, when the Soviet Premier again emphasized that "war is not fatally inevitable" and spoke of "a real possibility of eliminating war as a means of solving international issues." The Chinese Premier then read a message from Mao Tse-tung praising "Khrushchev's correct leadership."[6] Altogether four years passed before any Chinese criticism was made public. It appeared only after the Soviet Premier returned from his visit to the United States, at a time when he was engaged in preparations for the May, 1960, Paris summit meeting. The chronology indicates that Peking did not object to Khrushchev's interpretation of coexistence until it was applied to the United States. Thus the Chinese objections were practical rather than doctrinal. Khrushchev's participation in a summit meeting would have left the Mao government out in the cold, disregarding its great-power ambitions. It would be adding insult to injury to hold such a meeting (as was contemplated in 1958) within the framework of the United Nations, which had branded Communist China as the aggressor in the Korean war. In 1959, the Chinese were no doubt shocked and possibly frightened by the manifestations of the "Spirit of Camp David." Yet, for the Mao government to begin an open quarrel with Moscow was no light matter. When Khrushchev arrived in Peking on September 30, 1959, on his return from the United States, after only a brief stop in Moscow, Chou En-lai congratulated him on his successful journey to America and commended the communiqué on his talks with Eisenhower. In reply, Khrushchev acknowledged Eisenhower's understanding of the need to relax international tension, again praised peaceful coexistence, and warned against the temptation to "test the stability of the capitalist systems by force." Khrushchev was accompanied by Foreign Minister Gromyko and Mikhail Suslov, a member of the Presidium. They held a number of conferences with Mao Tse-tung, President Liu Shao-shi, and Chou En-lai; but, contrary to the practice of official inter-Communist meetings, no communiqué was issued when the Soviet group left. One can only infer that in the private talks Khrushchev failed to convince the Chinese leaders that they could still safely accept his practical application of a coexistence policy. The slogan of external danger, of threatening aggression, was indispensable to a regime that was ruthlessly driving the entire population to communal labor. Khrushchev's evasions and escape clauses were too subtle for the tough Chinese situation, the fiasco of the communes, and the terrible food shortages. If there is no danger of war, why drive the people so hard? If the transition to "Socialism" can be peaceful, why so much oppression in a country that is already supposed to be Socialist? The Chinese leaders wanted the true Leninist doctrine of revolutionary violence maintained, not only in fact, as in Khrushchev's interpretation, but also in words: "We must not hide our principles before the masses," *Hongqi* wrote at the height of the dispute.[7]

There also were strong indications of a latent quarrel about the scantiness of Soviet economic aid. The Chinese, no doubt, felt that Russia was overextending its industrial and financial resources (not to speak of food) by helping various underdeveloped countries, while they—the largest nation under a Communist government—risked the most serious difficulties with a hungry population and had to buy grain from capitalists. A sore subject of major importance was the inadequate Soviet assistance to China in modern armaments, particularly the reluctance to provide the Peking Government with atomic weapons. Possibly the climax of this first stage of the dispute was reached at the congress of the Romanian Communist Party at the end of June, 1960. Then, shortly before the meeting of the eighty-one Communist parties in Moscow in November, 1960, a compromise began to take shape. It found expression in the unanimously adopted Statement, which upheld the general line of peaceful coexistence as the only correct and reasonable principle of international relations.[8] Concessions on interpretation were made by both sides. The main Soviet point of view was reflected in the affirmation that "a real possibility will have arisen to exclude world war from the life of society even before Socialism achieves complete victory on earth, with capitalism still existing in part of the world." The Chinese objections were met in part by sharp attacks on the United States and a reminder that "the peoples of all countries know that the danger of a new world war still persists. U.S. imperialism is the main force of aggression and war." Peking must also have been pleased with the renewed branding of the Yugoslav heresy and the dissociation of peaceful coexistence from revisionist views: "Peaceful coexistence of states does not imply renunciation of the class struggle, as the revisionists claim. The coexistence of states with different social systems is a form of class struggle between Socialism and capitalism." Both Russians and Chinese could accept the blending of their ideas in a short formula: "The aggressive nature of imperialism has not changed. But real forces have appeared that are capable of foiling its plans of aggression. War is not fatally inevitable."

A few weeks later, Khrushchev made additional contributions to the doctrine in the January 6, 1961, report to the ideological organizations of the Party. His theory of three kinds of war was calculated to placate the Chinese on the point that was of the greatest concern to them: violence and war. It is not without significance that the idea of "just wars," which was the upshot of Khrushchev's exposition, is also one of Mao Tse-tung's favorite theories. He developed it as early as 1935:

As the ancients put it, "there were no just wars in the Era of Spring and Autumn." This is even more true of imperialism today, and it is only the oppressed nations and the oppressed classes that can wage just wars. The February and October Revolutions in Russia were just wars. The revolutions of the peoples in various countries after the First World War were just wars. In China, the Anti-Opium war, the war of the Taiping Heavenly Kingdom, the Boxer War, the Revolutionary War of 1911, the Northern Expedition of 1926–27, the Agrarian Revolutionary war from 1927 up to the present, and the present war against Japan and the traitors are all just wars.[9]

Mao drew his idea of "just wars" from an old Chinese source, namely the Book of Mencius, written probably at the turn of the fourth and third centuries B.C. The "Era of Spring and Autumn" refers to a period of Chinese history between the eighth and fifth centuries B.C.

The condensation of Khrushchev's theory of three kinds of war into the succinct formula of "two wars" in the 1961 program of the CPSU* suggested a further point of ideological compromise. It was consistent with Lenin's views, to whom it did not matter whether a war was offensive or defensive, but only *which class* waged it. The two-war idea had also been expounded in the Stalinist *History of the CPSU (B), Short Course*, which drew a distinction between "unjust wars" waged to conquer and enslave foreign nations, and "just wars" waged "to defend the people from foreign attack and from attempts to enslave them, or to liberate the people from capitalist slavery, or . . . to liberate colonies and dependent countries from the yoke of imperialism."[10] Most of all, the condensed formulation of the 1961 program exactly matches Mao's lapidary definition of December, 1936: "There are only two kinds of war in history, just and unjust. We support just wars and oppose unjust wars. All counterrevolutionary wars are unjust; all revolutionary wars are just."[11]

Had the Soviet-Chinese dispute over peaceful coexistence been only a matter of doctrine, it would have been solved by the compromise reached in Moscow in November, 1960, and the additional concession on the nature of wars contained in Khrushchev's report of January, 1961, and the new Party program. As it was, both sides showed signs of dissatisfaction. China was in the midst of a grave crisis and badly needed more effective economic assistance; Soviet political help (as for instance in China's border dispute with India) was often less than lukewarm. Moscow and Peking were in a latent rivalry in Sinkiang, North Korea, Outer Mongolia, and the Indo-

* See pp. 23–25.

chinese Peninsula. Improving Soviet-Yugoslav relations could only increase Chinese suspicions. For Khrushchev it was essential to push the compromise to the point where the leading position of the Soviet Communist Party (and consequently his own) would be recognized in Peking, if not to the extent it had been in Stalin's lifetime, then at least as it had been until 1959. After several months of contradictory moves, the conflict flared up again at the Twenty-second Congress of the CPSU in October, 1961. Khrushchev took the offensive in a well-prepared, oblique attack on the Albanian Labor (Communist) Party, the only one that had openly supported Peking. The attack on the Albanians may not have been entirely unexpected, for they were not present at the Congress. The fact that Peking had chosen Chou En-lai to head the delegation indicated a tendency to find an accommodation with the Russians. If such was the intention, it obviously failed. It is not known if the Chinese had been informed beforehand of the impending draft resolution to remove Stalin's body from the Lenin-Stalin Mausoleum in Red Square. At any rate, Chou En-lai took a public stand on both the Stalin and the Albanian questions. On October 19, in a speech at the Congress, he defended the Albanian Communist Party by stating that "our Socialist camp, comprising twelve fraternal countries, is a single entity" from Korea to Albania. Chou stressed that public disputes among these fraternal countries and parties "in the face of the enemy" were not "a serious Marxist-Leninist attitude," thus implicitly censoring Khrushchev for bringing the quarrel into the open. On October 21, Chou En-lai left two wreaths at the Lenin-Stalin Mausoleum. The one for Stalin bore the inscription "To the great Marxist-Leninist."[12] The Chinese Premier left Moscow two days later, while the Congress was still in session. At the Peking airport, he was met by Mao Tse-tung personally.

Despite these demonstrations, the Chinese did not display the same belligerent mood as in the spring of the previous year. From the plane that took him to Peking, Chou En-lai cabled Khrushchev: "May the friendship of the Soviet and Chinese peoples blossom eternally." The tug of war proceeded indirectly, with Albanian Communists the target of Soviet attacks and the Chinese supporting the "correct leadership" of Enver Hoxha, First Secretary of the Albanian Party. On October 20, even before Chou En-lai's departure from Moscow, Hoxha described Khrushchev's attack as "anti-Marxist lies."[13] In December, Soviet Russia broke off diplomatic relations with Albania. That same month, the Albanian

Communists failed to participate in the session of COMECON (Council for Mutual Economic Assistance) in Warsaw. It also was reported that Chinese technicians had replaced Soviet advisers in Albania. A submarine base on the Albanian coast was apparently evacuated by Soviet personnel. Press reports also spoke of a "Free Albanian Committee" set up in Sofia with the aim of "liberating" the country from its anti-Soviet Communist leadership.

Soviet-Chinese relations fluctuated between euphemistic criticism and standoffish assurances of friendship. Neither side wished to admit in plain words that the central issue at stake was the leadership of the Communist camp. Having achieved a personal rule in the Soviet Union under the guise of "collective leadership," Khrushchev attacked the Albanians (i.e., the Chinese) for rejecting "collective leadership" and retaining an individual dictatorship. The real meaning of Khrushchev's reproof of the Albanian Party was that the decisions of the Soviet Party congresses were binding on all Communist parties. The Twentieth Congress, the first of the Khrushchev era, condemned Stalin and adopted the peaceful co-existence doctrine; other Communist parties, including the Chinese, had to follow suit. This challenged the assumption that there could be a degree of dual leadership of the bloc, as Mao probably believed after Stalin's death. For some time, Khrushchev evaded the issue, but in 1961 it became clear that he had temporarily accepted ambiguous situations to avoid a simultaneous struggle on two political fronts. Once his rivals in the Soviet Union were eliminated, he again asserted the unity of political command in the bloc. A derivative question was, Who is allowed to have satellites? Only Moscow, or Peking as well? In attacking the Albanian Party, Khrushchev in effect informed Mao Tse-tung that his support of Enver Hoxha against the Kremlin's wishes was out of order. The timing of Khrushchev's offensive was linked to China's internal difficulties. Gross economic errors, mismanagement and drought combined to bring about a catastrophe in agriculture that spilled over into the industrial sector of the economy. In the absence of reliable Chinese statistics, one should mention two unmistakable indications: the mass flight of refugees to Hong Kong and Macao in May–June, 1962, and the purchase of food in the free world. In 1961, Mao's government bought about 6 million metric tons of grain abroad, mostly from Australia and Canada. This gigantic food transaction was financed by the export of sorely needed silver and gold. During the same year, China shipped 43.4 million ounces of silver and about $1.2 million in gold bars to the London market.[14]

The extent of Soviet economic pressure on the Peking regime during this period has come to light only gradually. One of its first indications appeared in the summer of 1960, when it was reported that most of the Soviet technicians had left China. But agreements on trade and economic, scientific, and technical cooperation still seemed operative to some extent. New trade agreements were signed on April 7, 1961, June 19, 1961, and April 20, 1962. The trade protocol of April, 1962, showed that during 1960, China had incurred a substantial trade debt, which the Soviet Government agreed to defer without interest, to payments over five years. At the same time, all reliable information indicates that on the whole, Chinese foreign trade in 1959–61 declined. The most striking drop in 1961 was in trade relations with the Soviet Union and other East European countries. According to the U.N.'s *Statistical Yearbook for 1962*, Chinese exports to that area dropped to $925 million, below the 1955 level ($965 million), and imports dropped to $810 million, below the 1952 level ($860 million). The excess of exports over imports seems to indicate that China was still paying its trade debts to the Soviet Union.

Early in 1962, the intensity of the dispute slackened for a time. In February, the anniversary of the Soviet-Chinese 1950 treaty was marked by an exchange of civilities. *Pravda* and *Jenmin Jih Pao* published friendly editorials. The Soviet Ambassador in Peking, Stepan Charvenenko, spoke of the eternal and indestructible friendship between the two countries, and Madame Soong Ching-ling, Sun Yat-sen's widow, stated that the Soviet-Chinese alliance was a sacred duty. Similar compliments were exchanged on April 20, 1962, at the signing of a trade agreement. It was also in April that China first proposed a world-wide Communist conference for the solving of controversial problems. On July 2, Khrushchev warned that anyone who dares to attack China "will meet with a crushing rebuff from the great Chinese people, the people of the Soviet Union, and the whole Socialist camp."[15] He spoke—perhaps a little late—several days after President Kennedy had restated U.S. opposition to an armed conflict between the rival Chinese governments. In October, the Soviet Union once more vainly tried to have the Peking regime replace Nationalist China in the United Nations. A similar attempt by the Soviet delegation at the twelfth general UNESCO conference in November also failed.

But this conciliatory atmosphere, which probably reflected some private discussions, did not survive the summer. Leonid Brezhnev's official visit to Yugoslavia in September was regarded with great displeasure in Peking. A speech by Chou En-lai on September 30 showed the Chinese Premier in a fighting mood. He said, in essence, that China would neither submit to pressure nor change its just stand in international affairs. The two partners were probably still talking, but had difficulties in reaching agreement. The moment was ominous, for the Chinese were about to attack India, while the Russians were preparing their most adventurous undertaking since World War II—the Cuban missile base.

It is, of course, too early to attempt a historical appraisal of the 1962 Cuban crisis. Yet, in view of subsequent events, it does seem highly improbable that pure coincidence accounts for the launching of the Chinese offensive against India on October 20, shortly before the Soviet launching pads in Cuba were to be ready. Let us imagine for a moment what might have happened had American Intelligence not learned of the threat in time. Khrushchev (as he told several visitors) would have come to the U.N. General Assembly in New York, probably in November. Once there, he could have confronted the United States with an atomic pistol directed at its cities and vital defenses from Cuba. He would then have asked for a number of major concessions with the aim of upsetting the world balance of power in Russia's favor. If, as seems highly improbable, the United States submitted to the blackmail, Red China would have had a free hand in India. If the United States answered with a counterthreat and invaded Cuba to destroy the launching sites and the atomic warheads, American energies and forces would have been tied up for many months. By the time the Cuban operation would have ended (and who can say how long it may have lasted in the circumstances projected here), Chinese divisions would have smashed their way to the Bay of Bengal and dealt India a blow of incalculable consequence. Without some Chinese knowledge of what the Russians were preparing in Cuba, the Chinese offensive of October 20, after years of a smoldering border conflict, does not make sense. It would be even more difficult to find an explanation for the sudden unilateral cease-fire of November 21, when the Chinese forces were victorious on all sectors of the fronts. The reason for this extraordinary move could only be a complete change in the situation. Instead of having a free hand, China found America and Britain airlifting weapons to India. Should the Chinese offensive threaten India with major disaster, a Western military intervention would become a distinct possibility.

When the Cuban master plan failed and the Soviet Government

bowed to Kennedy's demands (with some hidden reservations, which were to appear later), the Chinese found themselves frustrated and isolated. They did their best to stir up Castro, but eventually had to resign themselves to the situation. More grievances were added to their account with the Soviet Union: The Russians did not support them diplomatically in the war with India; they had lost their nerve when confronted with Kennedy's strong reaction on Cuba; Tito's Moscow visit further increased Peking's resentment.

Kennedy's October 22 speech was the signal in Peking for a violent pro-Cuban, anti-American campaign, which soon also turned against the Russians, though still in an indirect way. The overt targets of Chinese criticism were "modern revisionists" and the "Tito group," to whom Palmiro Togliatti was added in December. Most painful for Moscow were no doubt the charges that the Russians had been intimidated by "American imperialism" to the point of begging for peace and sacrificing the vital interests of the Cuban people and their revolution. Chinese criticism of Soviet conduct in Cuba and allusions to Moscow's ambiguous stand in the Sino-Indian conflict were supported by doctrinal statements explaining that the difference between true Marxist-Leninists and modern revisionists lay precisely in their attitudes toward imperialism and their ability to distinguish between "progressive" and "reactionary" nationalism (i.e., Nehru's government).

Moscow's defense was also indirect. The November, 1962, issue of the *World Marxist Review* (the English-language edition of *Problems of Peace and Socialism*) answered the Chinese charges by stating that the "dogmatists" had no sound alternative to the policy of peaceful coexistence, and were even unable to attack the principle of this policy. "But the moment it comes to concrete action . . . the dogmatists begin to shout about 'departing' from the principles, and hurl all kinds of charges from 'fear' of imperialism well-nigh to 'rejection' of the revolution." The identity of those toward whom this was directed—the Chinese—was unmistakable. The Albanians were denounced by name as the authors of "a vicious smear campaign against the Communist Party of the Soviet Union, which, according to the resolution of the eighty-one Communist parties has been, and remains, the universally recognized vanguard of the world Communist movement, being its most experienced and steeled contingent."[16]

While some subtle undertones of conciliation with China could be read between the lines, the article was unequivocal on two points: Soviet Russia must remain the undisputed leader, and the method of implementing the world Communist aims must be that indicated by Khrushchev. "Imperialism is being eroded," the *World Marxist Review* stated emphatically, and it predicted the defeat of any attempt, "whatever its source," to split the "working-class movement."

On December 12, Khrushchev refuted his critics in a report to the Supreme Soviet. He used two different tactics in addressing himself to the Chinese Communists: He made the Albanians the target of his invective against left-wing opportunism, dogmatism, and sectarianism, while naming the Chinese only when he did not expressly disagree with them. This devious method allowed Khrushchev to keep up the pretense that there was no quarrel between Russia and China and at the same time to use very strong language in upholding his position. He likened the Albanians to "aggressive adventurist forces of imperialism," to "madmen" who want a thermonuclear war out of fear of the "inevitable historical prospect of the defeat of capitalism in peaceful competition with Socialism." Although calling themselves Marxist-Leninists, the Albanians were actually "dogmatists" who did not believe in the peaceful victory of Socialism and Communism.[17]

So as to leave no doubt that though speaking to proxies he was in fact addressing himself to the Chinese, Khrushchev compared the Albanians to a small boy whom someone had taught dirty words and given a few kopeks to shout them at adults. In the same sarcastic vein he reminded the unnamed critics that the "paper tiger" of imperialism had atomic teeth and asked them if they reproached China for not expelling the Portuguese and British from Macao and Hong Kong, respectively.* Khrushchev also defended Yugoslavia as a "Socialist country," and with obvious embarrassment spoke of the Sino-Indian conflict, praising the Chinese comrades only for having ceased military operations. But he seemed to imply that they did so out of fear of American and British intervention.

Peking's answer came in a particularly sharp editorial in *Jenmin Jih Pao* of December 31, 1962. This time the role of whipping-boy fell to Togliatti, who at the beginning of the month had attacked the Chinese position on war and peace at the Tenth Congress of the Italian Communist Party. Thereupon the dispute took on un-

---

* It should be noted that Khrushchev promised Soviet backing to the Chinese when they decided to tell the Portuguese and British to get out: "We shall welcome that step," he said. (*Soviet News*, No. 4783, p. 167, December 13, 1963.)

precedented vehemence; *Hongqi* even went so far as to label Togliatti's policy "parliamentary cretinism."[18] *Jenmin Jih Pao* accused Togliatti "and the other comrades" of willfully distorting the Chinese position in a number of cases, particularly on the subject of the inevitability of war. The editorial charged that "some people in the international Communist movement" do not like exposing imperialism and the United States; they believe that world peace can be ensured by negotiations alone; they beg the imperialists for peace and oppose revolutions of the oppressed peoples. Togliatti "and certain others" think that since the emergence of nuclear weapons, "war is no longer the continuation of politics, and that there is no longer any distinction between just and unjust wars." They in fact "submit to the U.S. imperialist policy of nuclear threats and blackmail," which leads to unconditional surrender and the abandonment of revolutionary ideals.[19]

For the correct assessment of the relations between the two warring partners it should again be noted that the journal reaffirmed China's acceptance of the policy of peaceful coexistence, but stated that it could not be achieved without class struggle and could not eliminate "the antagonism between the two systems, socialism and capitalism, and the antagonism between oppressed nations and oppressor nations." *Jenmin Jih Pao* also renewed the offer of a conference of the Communist and workers' parties of all countries to settle the current differences. Although this form of settling the issue seemed then unacceptable to the Russians, it was nevertheless an offer to negotiate. On January 18, at the Sixth Congress of the East German Communist Party in East Berlin, Khrushchev came out in favor of mutual toleration, patience, and restraint among the various Communist parties. Speaking in the name of the Soviet Central Committee, he proposed a truce in public polemics between Communist parties.

It is not known exactly when the Soviet-Chinese negotiations were resumed. It was probably some time toward the end of January or the beginning of February, 1963. Otherwise it is doubtful that Khrushchev would have made a public display of friendship at the Moscow reception for King Suvang Vathana on February 15. On this occasion, he seized the Chinese Ambassador's hand and told correspondents that Soviet-Chinese friendship would endure until they buried capitalism together.[20] Despite continued attacks in the Chinese and Albanian press, the Soviet Communist Party's Central Committee sent a formal message to its Chinese opposite number on February 21, requesting bilateral conversations. Two days later, Khrushchev received the Chinese Ambassador and Mao Tse-tung the Russian. But before accepting the Soviet proposal on March 9, Peking showed how it intended to prepare for the negotiations. The Chinese press published a number of Soviet statements, including Khrushchev's speeches and the polemical declarations by Togliatti and French Communist Party leader Maurice Thorez, thus establishing a dossier of the controversy. On March 4, *Hongqi* came out with a comprehensive indictment of Soviet foreign policy and of Russia's attitude toward China, which *Jenmin Jih Pao* ran in instalments for four days. Under the guise of answering Togliatti, the *Hongqi* article listed in detail a number of ideological and practical Soviet departures from what it considered the orthodox line. Since the Chinese opposition to a summit meeting in 1958, and in particular since the Camp David talks in 1959, the Communist movement led by Khrushchev was supposed to have sunk into an ideological quagmire; still without being mentioned by name, the Russians were accused of breaking agreements in such instances as the economic pressure against China in 1960, or even of betraying the Chinese in giving military assistance to India. Eventually, *Hongqi* charged, Russia led the Communist camp into defeat in the Cuban crisis of 1962.

This violent political barrage showed that Peking was not approaching the impending negotiations with the hope of reaching a quick understanding. The Chinese seemed to believe that they had the patience, the time, and the means to make gains in protracted negotiations.

The official letters exchanged between the two parties[21] were conciliatory in tone, though there was a good deal of juggling of controversial issues. Both parties invoked the Moscow Declaration of 1957 and the Statement of 1960 and agreed that their talks would prepare the ground for a general conference of Marxist-Leninist parties. But while the Russians perfunctorily explained "different approaches to the understanding of certain problems" by the different conditions in which the various Communist parties work, the Chinese squarely placed the reasons for divergent views on differences in the interpretation of basic doctrinal tenets, Marxism-Leninism in general, and the Declaration and Statement in particular.

Two more letters were exchanged before the negotiations began on July 5. The Soviet Communist Party wrote to Peking on March 30.[22] The Chinese answer came, after a significant delay, and was dated June 14.[23] Both messages confirmed the general position and the tactics adopted by the two sides since January; Moscow was anxious to end the public dispute and to talk in private at the conference table; Peking was reluctant to leave the public stage without repeating at length its grievances and reasserting its doctrinal orthodoxy.

The official message from Peking, another prolix document, purported to develop, in twenty-five points, "the general line of the international Communist movement," which the Chinese wished to discuss with the Soviet delegation one by one. But its chief significance was an all-out attack on Khrushchev himself in which his main concepts were refuted and ridiculed. Khrushchev, referred to as "certain persons," was accused of pretending to have discovered Lenin's policy of peaceful coexistence and of claiming a monopoly on its interpretation. He was said to have distorted Lenin's idea on the subject by wrongly applying it to the class struggle, to the struggle for national liberation and the transition from capitalism to socialism. Some of these accusations were contradictory or even obviously false in the light of Khrushchev's statements and behavior. But this is beside the point. What matters is that the Chinese Communist Party now declared that his interpretation of the coexistence policy was incorrect. He had wrongly made of it "the general line of the policy of the Socialist countries" instead of using it for "achieving peaceful international environment . . . for exposing the imperialist policies of aggression and war . . . and for isolating the imperialist forces." It will be remembered that an analysis of Khrushchev's doctrine of peaceful coexistence earlier in this volume pointed precisely to such deceptive tactical aims of Khrushchev's interpretation. But this was the beginning of a personal campaign with few holds barred. It challenged Khrushchev's Communist orthodoxy in the most important areas of doctrine and policy and questioned the value of his leadership as far back as the Twentieth Congress, in 1956.

In these circumstances, the Moscow negotiations between the delegations of the Soviet and Chinese Communist parties could lead nowhere, the more so since the Russians, in a move reminiscent of the 1939 double negotiations, timed them to coincide with the test-ban talks with Britain and the United States. It is not known what occurred during these Soviet-Chinese meetings, which lasted, on and off, from July 5 to July 20. The joint communiqué merely stated that both parties had agreed to a recess and had decided to resume the talks at some future date. The recess was proposed by the Chinese, who did not wish to accommodate the Russians by agreeing to negotiate in Moscow while the test-ban talks were being conducted.

The limited test-ban treaty initialed in Moscow between the United States, Britain, and the Soviet Union on July 25, and signed on August 5, unleashed a mass of frenzied Chinese accusations. The Peking Government's official statement of July 31 called the treaty "a big fraud to fool the people" by creating the illusion of a "fake peace." The Chinese Government took the propaganda line of calling for the total prohibition and destruction of atomic weapons and proposed that government heads of all countries of the world hold a conference to that effect. It charged that the treaty's central purpose was "to prevent all the threatened peace-loving countries, including China, from increasing their defense capability."[24] Simply stated, Peking drew the conclusion that Soviet assistance in producing an atomic bomb in China could no longer be expected. It was mostly for this reason that the Chinese grossly exaggerated the political significance of the agreement, pretending to believe that the Soviet Union had joined in a new "Holy Alliance" against revolution,[25] that it had "capitulated" to "U.S. imperialism," and that the interests of the Soviet and Chinese people, the people of the socialist camp and of "all the peace-loving peoples of the world have been sold out."[26]

There followed a flood of mutual accusations in official statements, press articles, and radio broadcasts. On both sides the tone became increasingly strident, with the use of words such as "slander," "abuse," "impudence," "insult," "betrayal," and "lies." In this exchange, the Chinese took the lead; at the same time, their statements were generally more to the point (although just as long). Moscow often took refuge in evading the issues and showed relatively more restraint; the Russians, embarrassed by possible Western reactions, for once could not speak two different languages at the same time. The Chinese had a simpler task, for they were addressing themselves mainly to the various Communist parties.

The new phase of the controversy, which had begun with the Chinese letter of June 14, 1963, revealed some unknown facts and stressed the importance of some partly concealed areas of conflict. Although both sides of the polemic contain discrepancies, half-truths, and possibly outright inventions, a number of the accusations are in the nature of political acts and should be treated as such. One of the most significant results of this battle of words was that it proved that supremacy within the Communist camp can only be attained by overwhelming pressure by the leading power. An article (the first of a series) published jointly by the editorial staffs of *Jenmin Jih Pao* and *Hongqi* on September 6, 1963, described the struggle of the Chinese delegation against the Khrushchev policy line at Communist Party meetings in 1957, 1960, and 1961. The article disclosed details of negotiations that preceded the short-lived 1960 compromise and charged that on the eve of the November, 1960, Moscow meeting of the eighty-one parties, the Soviet Party distributed a written accusation against the Chinese that "brought the meeting to the brink of rupture." According to the same source, the Chinese delegation enforced a compromise, thus changing "the previous highly abnormal situation in which not even the slightest criticism of the errors of the leadership of the Communist Party of the Soviet Union was tolerated and its word was final."[27]

A closer analysis of the voluminous Chinese texts seems to confirm that the 1957 Peace Manifesto and Declaration and the 1960 Statement were the result of mutual concessions. On the other hand, once the compromise had been reached, the Chinese found these agreements acceptable and demanded absolute adherence to the theses they contained. One may therefore assume that at the time they also accepted the principle of Khrushchev's coexistence policy. The only reservation that now seems objectively valid and not made after the fact is the one quoted above from the letter of June 14, 1963, to the effect that peaceful coexistence should not be regarded as "the general line" of Communist policy. Whether this means anything at all in practical policy is highly debatable. Chinese correspondence of 1957 and 1960, published by them in September, 1963,[28] shows that they objected vehemently to Stalin's posthumous demotion. They also warned repeatedly against the so-called "peaceful transition" (it will be remembered that both eventualities—peaceful and violent—were proffered in Khrushchev's speech at the Twentieth Congress in February, 1956). But criticism of Khrushchev's coexistence policy, which was stressed in their letter of June 14, 1963, and in subsequent statements, was only implied in the older texts. In other words, the Chinese have proved that in private they did in fact oppose Khrushchev's policy of denigrating Stalin's Communist achievements and the tendency to formulate new interpretations of some of Lenin's ideas, considering them dangerous and uncalled-for practices; they were concerned lest the concept of "peaceful transition" would drain the revolutionary fervor of the Communist rank and file; they wished to uphold, in theory and practice, the promise of assistance in "just wars" (as did Khrushchev). But, contrary to Soviet allegations, they did not advocate nuclear war. The polemic about Mao Tse-tung's statement in November, 1957, and a related passage in the *Hongqi* article "Long Live Leninism" of April, 1960, convey the impression that Peking wished to convince other Communists that despite the existence of atomic weapons, revolutionary and civil wars can be supported from the outside without provoking world wars.[29] This primarily was also the meaning they attached to the thesis that the United States is a "paper tiger."

Another highly significant fact came to light on August 15, 1963, in a statement by the spokesman of the Chinese Government.[30] He asserted that under the Soviet-Chinese agreement of October 15, 1957, on new technology in national defense, the Soviet Union undertook to provide China with a "sample" of an atomic bomb and technical data related to its manufacture. The Chinese spokesman said that on June 20, 1959, the Soviet Government repudiated the agreement. The joint article of *Jenmin Jih Pao* and *Hongqi* of September 6 provides additional information on the subject: "In 1958, the leadership of the Communist Party of the Soviet Union put forward unreasonable demands designed to bring China under Soviet military control."[31] One can gather from the context, as well as from Russia's reply of August 20, that Moscow never wanted to assist China unconditionally—if at all—to become an atomic power. Most probably, the 1957 promise was only intended as an inducement to bring China's military machine under Soviet sway. Next to the personal feud that seems to have developed between Mao and Khrushchev, this quarrel over the atomic bomb had a decisive bearing on the dispute. Without atomic weapons, China finds itself in a position of hopeless inferiority with regard to the Soviet Union and cannot back its claims to "fraternal equality" with a direct demonstration of force or a threat to provoke a nuclear war against the "imperialists."

This embarrassing weakness became apparent once more in September, 1963, when China's territorial grievances attracted worldwide attention. *Jenmin Jih Pao* had broached the subject on March 8, 1963, in an article that took exception to Khrushchev's remarks on Hong Kong and Macao in the speech of December 12, 1962. The Chinese daily reacted by reviewing the "unequal treaties" through which Japan and several European powers had deprived imperial China of vast territories since 1842.[32] Among these powers, Czarist Russia held a prominent place, having annexed part of the

Ili Valley in present Soviet Kazakhstan, as well as extensive regions between the Amur and Ussuri rivers and the Sea of Okhotsk, the Gulf of Tatary, and the Sea of Japan. The Maritime Province, Russia's most prized possession in the Far East, is part of these territories. Among the unequal treaties *Jenmin Jih Pao* mentioned the Russian-Chinese treaties of Aigun (1858), Peking (1860), and Ili (or St. Petersburg, 1881). But maps published in Communist China since the early nineteen-fifties claim even vaster expanses of Soviet territory, in particular the Sakhalin Island and large portions of the Kazakh, Kirghiz, Uzbek, and Tadzhik Soviet republics. The maps also include Burma, Thailand, Indochina and parts of the Philippines, i.e., any lands (inhabited by alien peoples) that at any time in history were subjected to Chinese suzerainty. *Jenmin Jih Pao* recalled that the Chinese Communist Government, since its formation, had given notice that it intended to revise or abrogate the unequal treaties: "When conditions are ripe, these outstanding issues should be settled peacefully through negotiations."[33]

Despite the chimerical character of most of the Chinese claims, the Soviet Government, in its statement of September 21, warned against "artificial creations in our time of any territorial problems, especially between Socialist countries." States would embark on a very dangerous path, it said further, should they make territorial claims "using as justification some ancient data and the graves of their forefathers." The statement also contained the astounding allegation that "the Soviet Union has no frontier conflicts with any of its neighbors. And we are proud of this."[34]

While the Moscow government would like all annexations of foreign lands by Czarist and Communist Russia to be forgotten, it is still on the offensive as far as Chinese territories are concerned. The Soviet regions of Central Asia and the Far East are sparsely populated, and it has been Khrushchev's policy to send large numbers of agricultural and industrial workers to the very areas regarded by the Chinese as possible settlements for their ever-increasing population. Chinese officials are known to have complained bitterly to foreigners about Soviet colonization of the "virgin lands" in Kazakhstan. Peking is also sensitive about Soviet pressure in Sinkiang, where Russian-Chinese rivalry dates back more than 100 years and where a virtual Soviet protectorate existed in the nineteen-thirties. The Soviet drive in this area abated during the German invasion in 1941–43, and again around 1950, when the Communists took over in Peking. But in 1959, simultaneously with the worsening of Sino-Soviet relations, Russian pressure was resumed.

This is the only area along the Soviet borders where Russian penetration is welcome, since the non-Chinese population of Sinkiang puts up strong resistance against the alien way of life and Sinicization Peking tries to impose, as it does in Tibet. Rumors of revolts among the Moslem Kazakhs, Uighurs, Uzbekhs, etc., have been circulating for several years. The Sino-Russian incident in the Ili Valley, in April, 1962, which the joint article of *Jenmin Jih Pao* and *Hongqi* revealed only on September 6, 1963 (a proof that the two countries are still quite closed to outside information), seems to have been the result of the food crisis and general mismanagement in China. The Sinkiang Kazakhs have long felt attracted to their more numerous cousins in Soviet Kazakhstan, where the living conditions, however rugged, are easier than under Chinese rule. It is certainly possible that officials of the Soviet Consulate in Kuldja encouraged the migration of several thousand Kazakh families over the border into Soviet Kazakhstan; on the other hand, this may have been a spontaneous movement in search of food and work. After this news, Moscow retaliated by charging that the Chinese were responsible for 5,000 border violations during 1962. For several years, there was some talk about disagreements concerning the islands on the Amur River and fisheries rights. A Sino-Soviet commission appointed to deal with these matters was apparently unable to make any headway. In 1963, however, Sinkiang seemed to be the most explosive issue. It is most valuable to China as a colonizing area, its main source of crude oil, and an important one of grain. It may also contain uranium. Peking is encouraging settlers from other provinces to move there, and the Chinese population of Sinkiang is said to have increased tenfold in the last decade.

A characteristic instance of mistrust in Soviet-Chinese relations in the Central-Asian border regions concerns the much advertised "short" railway link between Moscow and Peking through Aktogai, the Dzungar gap, the Sinkiang oilfields, Urumchi, and Lanchow. On the Soviet side, the line has apparently been completed up to the frontier station Druzhba (Friendship), but it seems that the Chinese have discontinued construction somewhere around Urumchi, and there is no news of further plans.

Public exchange of arguments did not shed much new light on the economic relations between the two Communist regimes beyond confirming that they had shrunk considerably since 1959. Both sides blamed each other as being responsible for this decline.

Chinese charges that Russia suddenly withdrew its experts in the summer of 1960 are substantiated by the logic of the situation. Faced with an open challenge of its general policy, the Soviet Union applied economic pressure. The Chinese accusation was not denied but justified by alleged humiliating situations to which the experts were submitted. The Soviet "Open Letter" of July 13, 1963, struck back with an accusation that it was China which took the initiative of reducing the volume of trade—by 67 per cent—with the Soviet Union, and by 50 per cent with "the countries of the Socialist community." It added that deliveries to industrial plants dropped to one-fortieth (it was not clear whose deliveries to whose plants). This part of the polemic confirmed Soviet criticism of the "great leap" and the peoples' communes in 1958, which the Chinese seem to have interpreted as an instance of "impermissible" interference in their internal affairs. The strong Soviet objections to Chinese suggestions that the Communist-camp countries should rely economically on their own resources clearly indicated that at the heart of the dispute in this sector was the extent and cost of Soviet economic assistance. And it was logical for China to counter Soviet pressure with an idea that would cut Moscow's influence in the dependent countries. In the Open Letter, the Soviet Party stated that "with the active assistance of the Soviet Union, China built 198 industrial enterprises, shops, and other projects," that it delivered to China 21,000 sets of scientific-technical documents, including 1,400 blueprints of big enterprises. The Open Letter also asserted that "now" (July, 1963) Russia was continuing to assist China in the construction of 88 industrial enterprises and projects. These data were intended to be impressive, but they remained vague and could not be considered an adequate answer to the Chinese charges that "Socialist countries" were subjected to unilateral demands, economic pressure, and "great-power chauvinism."[35] (There is no reason to believe that in its economic assistance to China, Soviet Russia abandoned the methods of exploitation and extortion it had practiced in Eastern Europe.) The Chinese letter of June 14 also bitterly opposed the "specialization," or international division of labor, used "to impose one's will on others, infringe on the independence and sovereignty of fraternal countries, or harm the interest of their people."[36]

All these harsh realities were shrouded in clouds of doctrinal dissensions, with the Chinese generally representing the traditional interpretation of Marxism-Leninism, while the Russians had to

make tactical concessions to the demands of their coexistence policy, the true meaning of which they were unable to disclose more
openly. Although both sides loudly claimed to be the heirs of
orthodox Leninism, neither could prove what the pragmatic and
cynical Lenin would have done in similar situations. One can sense
Khrushchev's exasperation at Chinese efforts to force him into the
open and defend his reputation as a true believer in Marxism-
Leninism, thereby dooming his plans for upsetting the capitalist
world by slow erosion. Chinese resentment was perhaps best displayed in their condemnation of the "Tito clique," contained in
another joint *Jenmin Jih Pao–Hongqi* article on September 26,
1963. Here (in Yugoslavia) was a Communist regime welcoming
economic and—for a number of years—military assistance from the
United States and other capitalist countries, introducing a hybrid,
halfway-house economic system, and getting away with it, staying
in power, and to some extent improving the lot of the population.
While it would be an error to accept China's indignant orthodoxy
at face value, there was a genuine concern about the consequences
of this policy, which surely could not be practiced in China without
endangering Communist rule.[37]

Once the Pandora box of Soviet-Chinese differences was opened
to public view, the various issues at stake could be reviewed one by
one in order of importance. The territorial conflict in Central Asia
and the Far East, reflecting national rivalries between Russia and
China, is older than modern Communism itself. Although its
importance should not be underestimated, it seems likely that in
different circumstances it could have smoldered for many more
years. The ideological controversy had existed, to some degree, since
1956. Chinese explanations why they hid it under a cloak of secrecy
—i.e., they submitted to the overriding interest of Communist
unity—are not convincing. This "sacred duty" was no less com-
pelling in 1960 and 1963 than in 1956. Since the dispute became
public, the ideological arguments gradually have grown thinner and
less able to conceal other, more pragmatic difficulties. The doctrinal quarrel—charged as it is with emotional resentment on both
sides—is of great importance. But it is not and never was a self-
contained problem, not even at the time of the Stalin-Trotsky
struggle. One cannot help feeling that in the course of years the
doctrine primarily has become the most convenient language to
convey arguments in a Communist environment.* By the process

---

* It might be useful to register President de Gaulle's opinion on the Sino-
Soviet ideological dispute. At his press conference on July 29, 1963, he said:

of elimination we thus come to the issues that could not be avoided or delayed and therefore triggered the public airing of the dispute. They are directly connected with political power: the primacy in the Communist camp, the possession of atomic weapons, and the division of wealth.

To Khrushchev, the 1960 compromise was not satisfactory, since it did not secure his position as the world's Communist leader. In 1961, he thought the moment opportune to resume the offensive against Peking. As a result, the Chinese Communists, and Mao in particular, must have reached the conclusion that their own safety was threatened as long as Khrushchev headed the Soviet Party. It is possible that Malenkov's ouster in February, 1955, was secretly encouraged by Mao when a Soviet delegation comprising Bulganin, Khrushchev, Mikoyan, Shepilov, and others visited Peking in September, 1954. Since June, 1963, the Chinese leadership acts as if it believed in the possibility of ousting Khrushchev. They have accused him (at first without mentioning his name, but nonetheless unmistakably) of betraying the interests of the international proletariat, of leading the people astray, of distorting Lenin's views and some basic tenets of Marxism-Leninism. These accusations became louder, until the official Chinese Communist press mentioned Khrushchev by name, stating that he had been "agitating for years" for the "new Holy Alliance," "aiding the Indian reactionaries," "fraternizing with the renegade Tito," and "joined an anti-China united front with the United States."[38] Khrushchev was also accused of serving the interests of "neocolonialist imperialism"[39] and of being an "out-and-out revisionist," and of having supported "anti-Party elements" in the Chinese Communist Party in 1959.[40] On the Soviet side, the most ominous accusation was that the Chinese intended to form a new international, discarding Marxism-Leninism in favor of "Maoism."[41]

In the Communist world, a man ousted from top office pays a heavy penalty—if no longer with his life, at least with isolation or transfer to remote provinces and menial jobs. A conspiracy by Mao to remove Khrushchev, or vice versa, would be an unforgivable sin

---

"The break? Over what ideology? During my lifetime, Communist ideology has been personified by many people. . . . I know as many holders of Communist ideology as there are fathers in Europe. . . . Each of these holders in his turn condemns, excommunicates, crushes, and at times kills the others. I refuse to enter into a valid discussion on the subject of the ideological quarrel between Peking and Moscow." (Official translation issued by the French Embassy in Washington.)

in Communist eyes, as are the public accusations the Chinese have hurled at Khrushchev. It therefore seems that a genuine reconciliation between Khrushchev and Mao is no longer possible, and even if practical considerations should compel them to work together, that would be only a temporary patching up of the feud. But since the long-range aims of Communism have not changed, future collaboration of the two parties and the two governments is by no means precluded.

In January, 1964, France's diplomatic recognition considerably strengthened Red China's position both within the Communist camp and on a wider international arena. It remains to be seen to what extent France will be able and willing to alleviate Mao's economic woes, and, conversely, whether the contact with one of the great nations of the West will soften his revolutionary foreign-policy line.

SELECTED BIBLIOGRAPHY

For the convenience of the reader not conversant with the Russian language, most of the documents and primary sources cited here are in English and other Western languages. Only a few essential documentary sources on Soviet policy in Russian are given, which, incidentally, are far from complete. On the other hand, there is a wealth of Soviet political and historical documentary material in English and other Western languages, as well as a large number of scholarly studies, and it is thus possible to gain a broad view of the subject.

ACHESON, DEAN. *Power and Diplomacy*. Cambridge, Mass.: Harvard University Press, 1958.
———. *Sketches from Life of Men I Have Known*. New York: Harper & Brothers, 1959.
ALLEN, W. E. D. *History of the Georgian People*. London: Kegan Paul, 1932.
———. *The Ukraine*. London and New York: Cambridge University Press, 1940.
American Foreign Policy, 1950–1955: Basic Documents. 2 vols. Washington, D.C.: Department of State, 1957–63. (Beginning with 1956, the foreign-policy documents have been issued separately for each year.)
ANDERS, WLADYSLAW. *An Army in Exile*. London: Macmillan & Co., 1949
———. *Hitler's Defeat in Russia*. Chicago: Henry Regnery Company, 1953.
———. *Katyn*. Paris: Editions France-Empire, 1948.
ANTONOV, K. V. (ed.). *Sborniki dokumentov po mezhdunarodnoi politike i mezhdunarodnomu pravu*. 9 vols. Moscow: Narodnyi Komissariat po inostrannym delam, 1932–34.
The Austrian State Treaty. Washington, D.C.: Department of State, 1957.
BECK, JOSEPH. *Dernier Rapport, Politique Polonaise, 1926–1941*. 2 vols. Neuchâtel: Editions de la Baconnière, 1951.
Beloff, Max. *The Foreign Policy of Soviet Russia, 1929–1941*. 2 vols. London and New York: Oxford University Press, 1947-49.

————. *Soviet Policy in the Far East, 1945–1951.* London and New York: Oxford University Press, 1953.

BERLINER, JOSEPH S. *Soviet Economic Aid.* New York: Frederick A. Praeger, 1958.

BILMANIS, ALFRED. *Latvian-Russian Relations: Documents.* Washington, D.C.: The Latvian Legation, 1944.

BOCHENSKI, J. M. *Der Sowjetrussische dialektische Materialismus (Diamat).* Bern, 1950.

————, and GERHART NIEMEYER (eds.). *Handbook on Communism.* New York: Frederick A. Praeger, 1962.

BORKENAU, FRANZ. *European Communism.* New York: Harper & Brothers, 1953.

BOR-KOMOROWSKI, T. *The Secret Army.* London: Victor Gollancz, 1950.

BRASCHICH, RANKO M. *Land Reform and Ownership in Yugoslavia, 1919–1953.* New York: Mid-European Studies Center, Free Europe Committee, 1954.

BROWDER, PAUL, and ALEXANDER KERENSKY. *The Russian Provisional Government: Documents.* Stanford, Calif.: Stanford University Press, 1961.

BRZEZINSKI, ZBIGNIEW K. *Ideology and Power in Soviet Politics.* New York: Frederick A. Praeger, 1962.

————. *The Soviet Bloc: Unity and Conflict.* Cambridge, Mass.: Harvard University Press, 1960.

BULLITT, WILLIAM C. *The Great Globe Itself.* New York: Charles Scribner's Sons, 1946.

BUNYAN, JAMES, and H. H. FISHER. *The Bolshevik Revolution, 1917–1918: Documents.* Stanford, Calif.: Stanford University Press, 1961.

BUSEK, VRATISLAV, and NICOLAS SPULBER (eds.). *Czechoslovakia.* New York: Frederick A. Praeger, 1957.

BYRNES, JAMES F. *Speaking Frankly.* New York: Harper & Brothers, 1947.

CATTELL, DAVID T. *Soviet Diplomacy and the Spanish Civil War.* Berkeley: University of California Press, 1957.

CHAMBERLIN, WILLIAM H. *The Russian Revolution, 1917–1921.* 2 vols. New York: The Macmillan Company, 1935.

———— (ed.). *Blueprint for World Conquest as Outlined by the Communist International.* Washington, D.C., Chicago: Human Events, 1946.

CHURCHILL, WINSTON S. *The Second World War.* 6 vols. Boston: Houghton Mifflin Company, 1948.

Communism: Its Plans and Techniques. Harrisburg, Pa.: Infantry Journal Press, 1949. (Publication in book form of The Strategy and Tactics of World Communism, Committee of Foreign Affairs, Washington, D.C.: Government Printing Office, 1948.)

Communist Occupation and Takeover. Special Reports Nos. 1–14,

H.R. Select Committee on Communist Aggression, 83d Cong., 2d sess. Washington, D.C.: Government Printing Office, 1954–55.

Correspondence Between the Chairman of the Council of Ministers of the U.S.S.R. and the Presidents of the U.S.A. and the Prime Ministers of Great Britain During the Great Patriotic War of 1941–1945. 2 vols. Moscow: Foreign Languages Publishing House, 1957. (A one-volume edition has been published by E. P. Dutton & Co., 1958.)

COULONDRE, ROBERT. *De Stalin à Hitler; Souvenirs de deux ambassades, 1936–1939.* Paris: Hachette, 1950.

CRANKSHAW, EDWARD. *Cracks in the Kremlin Wall.* New York: The Viking Press, 1951.

CRETZIANU, ALEXANDRE. *Captive Rumania: A Decade of Soviet Rule.* New York: Frederick A. Praeger, 1956.

CUSTINE, MARQUIS DE. *Journey for Our Time.* Chicago: Henry Regnery Company, 1951.

DALLIN, ALEXANDER. *The Soviet Union at the United Nations.* New York: Frederick A. Praeger, 1962.

————— (ed.). *Diversity in International Communism: Documents.* New York: Columbia University Press, 1963.

DALLIN, DAVID J. *The New Soviet Empire.* New Haven: Yale University Press, 1951.

—————. *The Rise of Russia in Asia.* New Haven: Yale University Press, 1949.

—————. *Soviet Russia and the Far East.* New Haven: Yale University Press, 1948.

—————. *Soviet Russia's Foreign Policy, 1939–1942.* New Haven: Yale University Press, 1942.

DANIEL, HAWTHORNE. *The Ordeal of the Captive Nations.* Garden City, N.Y.: Doubleday and Company, 1958.

DAVISON, W. PHILLIPS. *The Berlin Blockade.* Princeton, N.J.: Princeton University Press, 1958.

DEANE, JOHN R. *The Strange Alliance.* New York: The Viking Press, 1947.

DEBICKI, ROMAN. *Foreign Policy of Poland, 1919–1939.* New York: Frederick A. Praeger, 1962.

DEDIJER, VLADIMIR. *Tito.* New York: Simon and Schuster, 1953.

DEGRAS, JANE (ed.). *The Communist International, 1919–1934: Documents.* 2 vols. London and New York: Oxford University Press, 1956–60.

—————. *Soviet Documents on Foreign Policy, 1917–1941.* 3 vols. London and New York: Oxford University Press, 1951–53.

DELLIN, L. A. D. (ed.). *Bulgaria.* New York: Frederick A. Praeger, 1957.

DJILAS, MILOVAN. *Conversations with Stalin.* New York: Harcourt, Brace & World, 1962.

Documents on American Foreign Relations. Princeton, N.J.: Princeton

University Press, 1940–51; New York: Harper & Brothers, 1952–62.

Documents on British Foreign Policy. Series 3, vols. IV–VII. London: H. M. Stationery Office, 1951–54.

Documents on Disarmament, 1945–1959. 2 vols. Washington, D.C.: Department of State, 1960.

————, *1962.* Washington, D.C.: Department of State, 1963.

Documents on German Foreign Policy, 1918–1945. Series C, vols. I–IV (1957–62), Series B, vols. I-XII (1949–62). Washington, D.C.: Department of State.

Documents on Germany, 1944–1959. Senate Committee on Foreign Relations. Washington, D.C.: Government Printing Office, 1959.

Documents on Polish-Soviet Relations, 1939–1945. Vol. I, 1939–1943, edited by Sikorski Historical Institute. London: Heinemann, 1961.

Dokumenty Vneshnei politiki SSSR. 4 vols. Moscow: Ministerstvo inostrannych del SSSR, 1957–60.

DRAPER, THEODORE. *Castro's Revolution: Myths and Realities.* New York: Frederick A. Praeger, 1962.

DRUHE, DAVID N. *Soviet Russia and Indian Communism.* New York: Bookman Associates, 1959.

DZIEWANOWSKI, M. K. *The Communist Party of Poland: An Outline of History.* Cambridge, Mass.: Harvard University Press, 1959.

EBON, MARTIN. *World Communism Today.* New York: The McGraw-Hill Company, 1948.

FABRY, PHILIPP W. *Der Hitler-Stalin Pakt, 1939–1941.* Darmstadt: Fundus Verlag, 1962.

FALL, BERNARD B. *The Two Vietnams.* New York: Frederick A. Praeger, 1963.

Finland Reveals Her Secret Documents on Soviet Policy, March 1940–June 1941. Official Blue-White Book of Finland. New York: Wilfred Funk, 1941.

FISCHER, GEORGE. *Soviet Opposition to Stalin.* Cambridge, Mass.: Harvard University Press, 1952.

FISCHER, LOUIS. *The Soviets in World Affairs, 1917–1929.* 2 vols. Princeton, N.J.: Princeton University Press, 1951.

FISCHER, RUTH. *Stalin and the German Communists.* Cambridge, Mass.: Harvard University Press, 1948.

FISCHER-GALATI, STEPHEN (ed.). *Romania.* New York: Frederick A. Praeger, 1957.

FLOYD, DAVID. *Mao Against Khrushchev: A Short History of the Sino-Soviet Conflict.* New York: Frederick A. Praeger, 1964.

Foreign Relations of the United States, Diplomatic Papers: The Conference of Berlin (The Potsdam Conference), 1945; The Conferences at Cairo and Tehran, 1943; The Conferences at Malta and Yalta, 1945; The Soviet Union, 1933–1939; 1940; 1941. Washington, D.C.: Department of State, 1952–60.

GAFENCO, GRÉGOIRE. *Préliminaires de la guerre à l'est.* Fribourg: Editions de la Librairie de l'Université, n.d.

La Géorgie. Paris: Association Géorgienne pour la S.d.N., 1937.

GOODMAN, ELLIOT R. *The Soviet Design for a World State.* New York: Columbia University Press, 1960.

GROSS, FELIKS. *The Seizure of Political Power in a Century of Revolution.* New York: Philosophical Library, 1958.

HALECKI, OSKAR (ed.). *Poland.* New York: Frederick A. Praeger, 1957.

HALPERIN, ERNEST. *The Triumphant Heretic.* London: Heinemann, 1958.

HARRISON, THOMSON S. E. *Czechoslovakia in European History.* Princeton, N.J.: Princeton University Press, 1953.

HELMREICH, ERNST C. (ed.). *Hungary.* New York: Frederick A. Praeger, 1957.

HILGER, GUSTAV, and ALFRED G. MEYER. *The Incompatible Allies: German-Soviet Relations, 1918–1941.* New York: The Macmillan Company, 1953.

History of the Communist Party of the Soviet Union (Bolsheviks). Short Course. New York: International Publishers, 1939.

History of the Communist Party of the Soviet Union. Moscow: Foreign Languages Publishing House, 1960.

HULL, CORDELL. *The Memoirs of Cordell Hull.* 2 vols. New York: The Macmillan Company, 1948.

Hungary Under Soviet Rule: A Survey of Developments Since the Report of the U.N. Special Committee. New York: The American Friends of the Captive Nations and the Assembly of Captive Nations, 1957.

HUNT, CAREW R. N. *The Theory and Practice of Communism.* New York: The Macmillan Company, 1951.

JAMES, DANIEL. *Cuba: The First Soviet Satellite in the Americas.* New York: Avon Books, 1961.

———. *Red Design for the Americas: Guatemalan Prelude.* New York: The John Day Company, 1954.

KAAS, ALBERT, and FEDOR DE LAZAROVICS. *Bolshevism in Hungary: The Bela Kun Period.* London: G. Richards, 1931.

KANDELAKI, CONSTANTIN. *The Georgian Question Before the World (Acts, Documents, Evidence).* Paris, 1953.

The Katyn Forest Massacre. Final Report of the Select Committee to Conduct an Investigation. U.S. Cong., House Report No. 2505. Washington, D.C.: Government Printing Office, 1952.

KAZEMZADEH, F. *The Struggle for Transcaucasia, 1917–1921.* New York: Philosophical Library, 1951.

KENNAN, GEORGE F. *Russia and the West under Lenin and Stalin.* Boston: Little, Brown and Company, 1960.

———. *Soviet Foreign Policy, 1917–1941.* Princeton, N.J.: D. Van Nostrand Company, 1960.

KLYUCHNIKOV, YURII V., and A. SABANIN (eds.). 4 vols. *Mezhdunarodnaia politika noveishevo vremeni v dogovorakh, notakh i deklaratsiakh.* Moscow: Narodnyi Komissariat po inostrannym delam, 1925–28.

KOESTLER, ARTHUR. *Darkness at Noon*. New York: The Modern Library, 1946.

———. *The Yogi and the Commissar, and Other Essays*. New York: The Macmillan Company, 1955.

KOHN, HANS. *Pan-Slavism*. Notre Dame, Ind.: University of Notre Dame Press, 1953.

KOMARNICKI, TITUS. *The Rebirth of the Polish Republic*. London: Heinemann, 1957.

KORBEL, JOSEF. *The Communist Subversion of Czechoslovakia, 1938–1948*. Princeton, N.J.: Princeton University Press, 1959.

———. *Tito's Communism*. Denver, Colo.: The University Press of Denver, 1951.

KORBONSKI, STEFAN. *Fighting Warsaw*. New York: The Macmillan Company, 1956.

KULSKI, WLADYSLAW W. *Peaceful Co-Existence: An Analysis of Soviet Foreign Policy*. Chicago: Henry Regnery Company, 1959.

LAQUEUR, WALTER, and LEOPOLD LABEDZ. *Polycentrism*. New York: Frederick A. Praeger, 1962.

LENCZOWSKI, GEORGE. *The Middle East in World Affairs*. 2d ed. Ithaca, N.Y.: Cornell University Press, 1956.

———. *Russia and the West in Iran, 1918–1948: A Study in Big-Power Rivalry*. Ithaca, N.Y.: Cornell University Press, 1949.

LENIN, V. I. *Collected Works*. 7 vols. New York: International Publishers, 1939.

———.*Collected Works*. 17 vols. Moscow: Foreign Languages Publishing House, 1960–63; London: Lawrence & Wishart, 1960–63.

———. *Selected Works*. 12 vols. New York: International Publishers, 1943.

McNEILL, WILLIAM HARDY. *The Greek Dilemma*. London: Victor Gollancz, 1947.

MAO TSE-TUNG. *Selected Works*. 4 vols. New York: International Publishers, 1954.

MARX, KARL. *Selected Works*. 2 vols. New York: International Publishers, ca. 1933.

MEYER, A. G. *Marxism: The Unity of Theory and Practice—A Critical Essay*. Cambridge, Mass.: Harvard University Press, 1954.

MIKOLAJCZYK, STANISLAW. *The Rape of Poland: Pattern of Soviet Domination*. New York: Whittlesey House, 1948.

MILOSZ, CZESLAW. *The Captive Mind*. New York: Alfred A. Knopf, 1953.

MOLOTOV, V. M. *Problems of Foreign Policy: Speeches and Statements*. Moscow: Foreign Languages Publishing House, 1949.

MONTGOMERY, JOHN F. *Hungary, the Unwilling Satellite*. New York: The Devin-Adair Company, 1947.

MOSELY, PHILIP E. *The Kremlin and World Politics*. New York: Alfred A. Knopf, 1960.

MUNKMAN, C. A. *American Aid to Greece.* New York: Frederick A. Praeger, 1958.

Nazi-Soviet Relations, 1939–1941: Documents from the Archives of the German Foreign Office. Washington, D.C.: Department of State, 1948. (This volume incorporates the essential documents of the negotiations that led to the Molotov-Ribbentrop Pact. For the full documentation, see *Documents on German Foreign Policy, 1918–1945,* Series D, vols. VI and VII, published by the Department of State, 1956.)

ORWELL, GEORGE. *1984.* New York: Harcourt, Brace and Company, 1949.

PADMORE, GEORGE. *Pan-Africanism or Communism.* New York: Roy Publishers, 1956.

PILSUDSKI, JOSEPH. *L'année 1920.* Paris: La Renaissance du Livre, 1929.

Polish Documents Report. Select Committee on Communist Aggression. Appendix to *Communist Takeover and Occupation of Poland.* Washington, D.C.: Government Printing Office, 1955.

Polish-Soviet Relations, 1918–1943: Official Documents. Washington, D.C.: The Polish Embassy, n.d.

Polish-Soviet Relations, 1918–1943: Documents. New York: Polish Information Center, 1943.

Polish White Book: Official Documents Concerning Polish-German and Polish-Soviet Relations, 1933–1939. New York: Roy Publishers, n.d.

POSSONY, STEFAN T. *A Century of Conflict: Communist Techniques of World Revolution.* Chicago: Henry Regnery Company, 1953.

POTIEMKINE, VLADIMIR (ed.). *Histoire de la diplomatie.* 3 vols. Paris: Librairie de Medicis, 1946–53.

PROST, HENRI. *Le Destin de la Roumanie, 1918–1954.* Paris: Editions Berger-Levrault, 1954.

RADKEY, OLIVER H. *The Election to the Russian Constituent Assembly of 1917.* Cambridge, Mass.: Harvard University Press, 1950.

RAUCH, GEORG VON. *A History of Soviet Russia.* 3d rev. ed. New York: Frederick A. Praeger, 1962.

REI, AUGUST. *Nazi-Soviet Conspiracy and the Baltic States: Diplomatic Documents and Other Evidence.* London: Boreas Publishing Co., 1948.

Report of the Special Committee on the Problem of Hungary. New York: United Nations, General Assembly, XI Session, Supplement No. 18/A/3592/, 1957.

Revolt in June: Documents and Reports on the People's Uprising in East Berlin and in the Soviet Zone of Germany. Bonn: Federal Ministry for All-German Affairs, n.d.

The Revolt in Hungary: A Documentary Chronology of Events. New York: Free Europe Committee, 1957.

ROLLIN, HENRY. *La Révolution russe.* 2 vols. Paris: Librairie Delgrave, 1931.

ROOS, HANS. *Polen und Europa.* Tübingen: Mohr, 1957.

ROSSI, A. *The Russo-German Alliance, August 1939–June 1941.* Boston: The Beacon Press, 1951.

RUSSELL, BERTRAND. *The Practice and Theory of Bolshevism.* 2d ed. New York: The Macmillan Company, 1949.

Sbornik deistvuiushchikh dogovorov, soglashenii i konventsii zakliuchennykh RSFSR s inostrannymi gosudartsvami. Moscow: Narodnyi Komissariat po inostrannym delam, 1921–23; 8-vol. ed., 1925–35.

SCHAPIRO, LEONARD. *The Origin of the Communist Autocracy: Political Opposition in the Soviet State—First Phase, 1917–1922.* Cambridge, Mass.: Harvard University Press, 1955.

——— (ed.). *Soviet Treaty Series: A Collection of Bilateral Treaties, Agreements and Conventions, etc., Concluded Between the Soviet Union and Foreign Powers.* 2 vols. Washington, D.C.: Georgetown University Press, 1950.

SCHWARTZ, HARRY. *The Red Phoenix: Russia Since World War II.* New York: Frederick A. Praeger, 1961.

———. *Russia's Soviet Economy.* New York: Prentice-Hall, 1950.

———. *Tsars, Mandarins and Commissars: A History of Chinese-Russian Relations.* Philadelphia and New York: J. B. Lippincott Company, 1964.

SETON-WATSON, HUGH. *From Lenin to Khrushchev.* New York: Frederick A. Praeger, 1960.

———. *The Decline of Imperial Russia, 1855–1914.* New York: Frederick A. Praeger, 1952.

———. *The New Imperialism.* Chester Springs, Pa.: Dufour Editions, 1961.

The Sino-Soviet Economic Offensive in the Less-Developed Countries. Washington, D.C.: Department of State, 1958.

SMAL-STOCKI, ROMAN. *The Captive Nations: Nationalism of the Non-Russian Nations in the Soviet Union.* New York: Twayne Publishers, 1960.

Soviet Foreign Policy During the Patriotic War: Documents and Materials. 2 vols. London and New York: Hutchinson & Co., n. d.

Soviet Political Treaties and Violations. U.S. Sen. Staff Study, Committee on the Judiciary. Washington, D.C.: Government Printing Office, 1955.

The Soviet-Yugoslav Dispute. London and New York: Royal Institute of International Affairs, 1948.

STALIN, J. V. *Economic Problems of Socialism in the U.S.S.R.* New York: International Publishers, 1952.

———. *For Peaceful Coexistence.* New York: International Publishers, 1951.

———. *The Great Patriotic War of the Soviet Union.* New York: International Publishers, 1945.

————. *Marxism and Linguistics*. New York: International Publishers, 1950.

————. *Marxism and the National and Colonial Question*. New York: International Publishers, 1942.

————. *Problems of Leninism*. Moscow: Foreign Languages Publishing House, 1940.

————. *Works*. 13 vols. Moscow: Foreign Languages Publishing House, 1952–55.

Stalin. New York: Workers Library Publishers, 1940. (A *Festschrift* published on the occasion of Stalin's sixtieth birthday.)

STRAUSZ-HUPÉ, ROBERT, et al. *Protracted Conflict*. New York: Harper & Brothers, 1959.

SULLIVANT, ROBERT S. *Soviet Politics and the Ukraine, 1917–1957*. Cambridge, Mass.: Harvard University Press, 1962.

SWEET-ESCOTT, BICKHAM. *Greece: A Political and Economic Survey, 1939–1953*. London and New York: Royal Institute of International Affairs.

TABORSKY, EDWARD. *Communism in Czechoslovakia, 1948–1960*. Princeton, N.J.: Princeton University Press, 1961.

TARACOUZIO, T. A. *War and Peace in Soviet Diplomacy*. New York: The Macmillan Company, 1940.

Tensions Within the Soviet Captive Countries: Bulgaria, Rumania, Soviet Zone of Germany, Czechoslovakia, Poland, Hungary. U.S. Sen., Committee on Foreign Relations. Washington, D.C.: Government Printing Office, 1954.

THOMSON, S. H. *Czechoslovakia in European History*. 2d ed. Princeton, N.J.: Princeton University Press, 1953.

TROTSKY, LEON. *History of the Russian Revolution*. New York: Simon and Schuster, 1936.

————. *The Strategy of World Revolution*. New York: Communist League of America, 1930.

ULAM, ADAM B. *Titoism and the Cominform*. Cambridge, Mass.: Harvard University Press, 1952.

United States–Latin American Relations. U.S. Sen., Committee on Foreign Relations. Washington, D.C.: Government Printing Office, 1960.

VOIGT, F. A. *The Greek Sedition*. London: World Affairs Club, 1949.

VYSHINSKY, A. Y. *The Teachings of Lenin and Stalin on the Proletarian Revolution and the State*. London: Soviet News, 1948.

WANDYCZ, PIOTR. *France and Her Eastern Allies, 1919–1925*. Minneapolis, University of Minnesota Press, 1962.

WEINBERG, GERHARD L. *Germany and the Soviet Union, 1939–1941*. Leiden: E. J. Brill, 1954.

WEYL, NATHANIEL. *Red Star over Cuba*. New York: The Devin-Adair Company, 1960.

WHITNEY, THOMAS P. (ed.). *The Communist Blueprint for the Future*. New York: E. P. Dutton & Co., 1962.

WOODHOUSE, C. M. *Apple of Discord*. London: Hutchinson, 1948.

World Communism: A Selected, Annotated Bibliography. U.S. Senate, 88th Cong. 2d sess. Washington, D.C.: Government Printing Office, 1964.

WSZELAKI, JAN. *Communist Economic Strategy: The Role of East-Central Europe*. Washington, D.C.: National Planning Association, 1958.

ZELAR, CHARLES. *Yugoslav Communism: A Critical Study*. U.S. Sen., Committee on the Judiciary. Washington, D.C.: Government Printing Office, 1961.

ZEMAN, Z. A. B. (ed.). *Germany and the Revolution in Russia, 1915–1918: Documents from the Archives of the German Foreign Ministry*. London and New York: Oxford University Press, 1958.

ZINNER, P. E. (ed.). *National Communism and Popular Revolt in Eastern Europe*. New York: Columbia University Press, 1956.

NOTES

For the sake of brevity, the following abbreviations are used throughout the Notes: CPSU for Communist Party of the Soviet Union; *Keesing* for *Keesing's Contemporary Archives*; LNTS for *League of Nations Treaty Series*; NYT for *The New York Times*; SW for *Selected Works*; W for *Works*.

Introduction
(pp. 3–6)

1. V. I. Lenin, "General Description of Marxism," *SW* (New York: International Publishers, 1943), XI, 13.

2. J. V. Stalin, "Reply to Comrades," *Bolshevik*, No. 14 (1950).

3. Mao Tse-tung, "Reform Our Study," *SW* (New York: International Publishers, 1954), IV, 12.

4. Mao Tse-tung, "On Practice," *SW*, I, 293.

5. Stalin, "The Foundations of Leninism," *Problems of Leninism* (Moscow: Foreign Languages Publishing House, 1940), p. 2.

6. Arthur Koestler, *Darkness at Noon* (New York: The Modern Library, 1946), p. 27.

7. Georgi Malenkov's address to the Supreme Soviet, *Pravda*, August 9, 1953.

8. Nikita Khrushchev, *On the Communist Party Programme: Report on the Programme of the CPSU to the Twenty-second Congress of the Party*, October 18, 1961 (Moscow: Foreign Languages Publishing House), p. 26.

9. Program of the Communist Party of the Soviet Union, Tass release, reproduced in NYT, August 1, 1961.

10. Lenin, "General Description of Marxism," *SW*, XI, 3.

11. Program of the CPSU, *loc. cit.*

12. Cf. Bertram D. Wolfe's study of Lenin's behavior in regard to the Brussels-London Congress, in *Three Who Made a Revolution* (New York: The Dial Press, 1948), chaps. XIII–XV.

Chapter 1. Communist Doctrine and Soviet Foreign Policy
(pp. 9–18)

1. Karl Marx, "Manifesto of the Communist Party," *SW* (New York: International Publishers, ca. 1933), I, 205–6.

2. *Ibid.*, 219.

3. *Ibid.*, 241.

4. Marx, "Address to the Communist League," *SW*, II, 161.

5. Lenin, "The Tasks of the Proletariat in Our Revolution," *SW*, VI, 219.

6. Lenin, "Farewell Letter to Swiss Workers," *SW*, VI, 16.

7. *Ibid.*, 19.

8. Lenin, "The Socialist Revolution and the Right of Nations to Self-determination," *SW*, V, 270.

9. Stalin, *Marxism and the National and Colonial Question* (New York: International Publishers, 1942), p. 269.

10. Major-General Max Hoffmann, *War Diaries and Other Papers* (2 vols.; London: Martin Secker, 1929), II, 203.

11. Quoted by J. W. Wheeler-Bennett, in *Brest-Litovsk: The Forgotten Peace* (New York: St Martin's Press, 1939), pp. 185 ff., as confirmed to him personally by Trotsky in September, 1937.

12. Lenin, "Report to the Third All-Russian Congress of Soviets, January 24, 1918," *SW*, VII, 280.

13. *Ibid.*, 282.

14. Stalin, April 13, 1928, *Sochineniya* (1952 ed.), XI, 54.

15. Khrushchev interview with Tomoo Hirooka, in *Asahi Shimbun*, June 18, 1957, as reported by Tass, June 29, 1957.

16. *Pravda*, November 7, 1955.

17. Khrushchev's speech on Stalin, February 24–25, 1956, as released by the U.S. Department of State, *NYT*, June 5, 1956.

18. Stalin, "Political Report of the Central Committee, December 3, 1927," *W* (Moscow: Foreign Languages Publishing House, 1952–55), X, 296.

19. Lenin, "Report of the Central Committee at the Eighth Party Congress, March 18, 1919," *SW*, VIII, 33.

20. Lenin, "Military Program of the Proletarian Revolution," *Sochineniya*, XXIII, 67.

21. Lenin, "Collapse of the Second International," *SW*, V, 179.

22. Leon Trotsky, *My Life* (New York: Grosset & Dunlap, 1960), p. 383.

23. Lenin, "Military Program," *loc. cit.*

24. Lenin, "Left-Wing Communism, an Infantile Disorder," *SW*, X, 138.

25. Lenin, "War and Peace," *SW*, VII, 297.

26. Lenin, "Left-Wing Communism," *loc. cit.*

27. Malenkov's speech, *Pravda*, March 13, 1954.

28. Khrushchev's address to the Supreme Soviet, *Pravda*, April 27, 1954.

29. Khrushchev's report on the Party Program at the Twelfth Party Congress, *Pravda*, October 19, 1961. (This statement, with slight variations, recurs often.)

Chapter 2. PEACEFUL COEXISTENCE
(pp. 19–30)

1. Khrushchev's report to the Twentieth Party Congress, *NYT*, February 15, 1956, and *Pravda*, same date. A condensation of the report was published by *Soviet News* (London), No. 3357 (February 15, 1956).

2. *Ibid.*

3. "Peace Manifesto," *Soviet News*, No. 3732 (November 25, 1957).

4. "Declaration," *ibid.*, No. 3731 (November 22, 1957).

5. Khrushchev's report to the Twenty-first Party Congress, January 27, 1959, *ibid.*, No. 3994 (January 27, 1959).

6. Khrushchev's speech at the Third Romanian Communist Party Congress, *ibid.*, No. 4292, June 22, 1960.

7. *Kommunist*, No. 10 (July, 1960), p. 46.

8. Quotations from Khrushchev's report of January 6, 1961, are from *Soviet News*, Nos. 4410, 4411 (January 21 and 24, 1961).

9. *Kommunist*, No. 10 (1960), p. 49.

10. Program of the CPSU, Tass release, reported in NYT, August 1, 1961.
11. *Ibid.*
12. George Orwell, *1984* (New York: Harcourt, Brace and Company, 1949), p. 87.
13. Khrushchev's report to the Twentieth Party Congress, *loc. cit.*
14. *Foreign Affairs*, XXXVIII, No. 1 (1959).
15. Program of the CPSU, *loc. cit.*
16. *Pravda*, November 23, 1960; NYT, November 24, 1960.
17. "Statement of the Eighty-one Communist Parties," *World Marxist Review*, III, No. 12 (December, 1960).
18. *Pravda*, August 12, 1960.
19. *Le Monde*, October 5, 1960.
20. "Statement of the Eighty-one Communist Parties," *loc. cit.*
21. *Trybuna Ludu* (Warsaw), January 22, 1961.
22. *Ibid.*, June 6, 1960.
23. Lenin, "The Proletarian Revolution and the Renegade Kautsky," SW, VII, 125.
24. Lenin, "War and Peace," SW, VII, 296.
25. *Ibid.*, 299.
26. *Ibid.*, 300.
27. Lenin, "Speech in Reply to the Debate on War and Peace," SW, VII, 305.
28. Program of the CPSU, *loc. cit.* (This part of the sentence was expurgated from the same translation appearing in the *New Times*, No. 48, November 29, 1961, and in a pamphlet published by the Crosscurrents Press, New York, 1961.)
29. Marx, "Manifesto of the Communist Party," SW, I, 241.
30. Lenin, "Lectures on the 1905 Revolution," SW, III, 19.
31. Program of the CPSU, *loc. cit.*
32. Lenin, "The Proletarian Revolution," *loc. cit.*

Chapter 3. THE COMMUNIST INTERNATIONALS—COMINTERN
AND COMINFORM
(pp. 33–41)

1. Lenin, "Speech at the Opening of the First Congress of the Communist International," SW, X, 27.
2. *Ibid.*, 26.
3. *Ibid.*
4. NYT, April 18, 1956, from *Unità* (Rome).
5. Lenin, "Tasks of the Third International," SW, X, 45.
6. Lenin, "Conditions of Affiliation to the Communist International," SW, X, 202.
7. Lenin, "The Third International, Its Place in History," SW, X, 31.
8. Lenin, "The Second Congress of the Communist International," SW, X, 159.
9. Stalin, "On the Death of Lenin," *Sochineniya* (1952 ed.), VI, 51.
10. *Outline History of the Communist International* (Moscow: Society of Foreign Workers, 1934), p. 51.
11. Lenin, "Closing Speech at the First Congress of the Communist International," SW, X, 28.
12. "Program of the Communist International, September, 1928," in W. H. Chamberlin (ed.), *Blueprint for World Conquest* (Washington, 1946), p. 222.

13. P. E. Vishinsky, "Komunizm i Otchestvo," *Voprosy Filosofii,* No. 2, 1948.

14. *Blueprint for World Conquest,* pp. 41–72.

15. Lenin, "Theses on the Fundamental Tasks of the Second Congress of the Communist International," *SW,* X, 162–79; "Conditions of Affiliation to the Communist International," *ibid.,* 200–206.

16. *Blueprint for World Conquest,* pp. 149 ff., 249 ff.

17. Stalin, "Reply to Letter from Harold King," *The Great Patriotic War of the Soviet Union* (New York: International Publishers, 1945), p. 167.

18. *For a Lasting Peace, For a People's Democracy* (Belgrade), No. 1 (November 10, 1947).

19. *Meeting of the Information Bureau of the Communist Parties in Hungary, November, 1949* (pamphlet published by *For a Lasting Peace, For a People's Democracy,* 1950), pp. 8–9.

Chapter 4. REVOLUTION AND RESPECTABILITY—THE WESTERN BORDER
(pp. 42–48)

1. *Documents on Soviet Foreign Policy,* I, 201.

2. *Ibid.,* 203.

3. *Ibid.,* 218

4. Peace Treaty between the R.S.F.S.R. and Finland, October 14, 1920; *LNTS,* III, No. 1 (1921), pp. 6 ff.; also Helsingfors: Government Printing Office, 1921, pp. 5 ff.

5. *Documents on Soviet Foreign Policy,* I, 280.

6. *Ibid.,* 281.

7. *Ibid.,* 281, 398.

8. *Ibid.,* 40.

9. Cf. Henri Prost, *Le Destin de la Roumanie* (Paris: Editions Berger-Levrault, 1954), p. 91.

10. *Soviet Documents on Foreign Policy,* I, 435–36.

11. Vladimir Potiemkine (ed.), *Histoire de la Diplomatie.* (Paris: Librairie de Medicis, 1946–53), III, 171–72.

12. The text of this agreement may be found in *LNTS,* XI, No. 296, pp. 167 ff.

13. *Documents on Soviet Foreign Policy,* I, 372.

14. Soviet-Polish Peace Treaty, March 18, 1921, in *LNTS,* VI, No. 149 (1927), 52 ff.

15. *Documents on Soviet Foreign Policy,* I, 372.

16. *Ibid.,* 429.

Chapter 5. RAPALLO
(pp. 49–52)

1. Quoted by Gustav Hilger and Alfred G. Meyer, in *The Incompatible Allies* (New York: The Macmillan Company, 1953), p. 75.

2. Lenin, "The International and Internal Position of the Soviet Republic," *SW,* IX, 313–16.

3. Potiemkine, *Histoire de la Diplomatie,* III, 190–94; cf. Louis Fischer, *The Soviets in World Affairs, 1917–1929* (Princeton, N.J.: Princeton University Press, 1951), pp. 332 f., 340 f.

4. The text of the treaty may be found in Georg Cleinow, *Deutsche Wirtschaftsgesetze: Die Deutsch-Russischen Rechts- und Wirtschaftsverträge* (Berlin: Reimar Hobbing Verlag, 1926).

5. Potiemkine, *op. cit.*, III, 193.

6. Quoted by V. A. Yakhontov, in *U.S.S.R. Foreign Policy*, p. 7.

7. Jane Degras (ed.), *The Communist International, 1919–1943* (London and New York: Oxford University Press, 1956–60), I, 50.

8. Lenin, *Sochineniya*, XXVI, 14–16.

9. *The Communist International, Documents*, I, 347.

10. *Ibid.*, 343.

Chapter 6. THE YEAR OF RECOGNITION
(pp. 53–55)

1. *Documents on Soviet Foreign Policy*, I, 410–12.

2. *Ibid.*, 422.

3. *Ibid.*, 424.

4. Chicherin protested bitterly against this exclusion, although the United States acted in the interest of Russia's territorial integrity in the Far East. A delegation of the puppet Soviet Far Eastern Republic was unofficially admitted at the Conference.

Chapter 7. LOCARNO
(pp. 56–59)

1. *Documents on Soviet Foreign Policy*, II, 58.

2. *Ibid.*, 2.

3. *Ibid.*, 5.

4. *Ibid.*, 42.

5. Cf. Francis Delaisi, *Les deux Europes* (Paris: Payot, 1929).

6. *Documents on Soviet Foreign Policy*, II, 58.

7. Stalin, "Political Report of the Central Committee, Fourteenth Party Congress, December 18, 1925," W, VII, 280.

8. Stalin, "Report to the Eighteenth Congress of the C.P.S.U. (B)," *Problems of Leninism*, p. 627.

9. *Documents on Soviet Foreign Policy*, II, 58.

10. Potiemkine, *Histoire de la Diplomatie*, III, 329.

11. *Documents on Soviet Foreign Policy*, II, 80.

Chapter 8. SECURITY IN EASTERN EUROPE
(pp. 60–63)

1. *Documents on Soviet Foreign Policy*, II, 103.

2. *Ibid.*, 112.

3. *Ibid.*, 139.

4. *Ibid.*, 322.

5. Cf. Louis Fischer, *The Soviets in World Affairs*, p. 782.

6. The text may be found in *LNTS*, No. 2028 (1929), pp. 369 ff.

7. The text of the Soviet-Polish nonaggression treaty may be found in *LNTS*, CXXVI, No. 3124 (1933), pp. 41 ff.

8. The text of the Convention for the Definition of Aggression appears in the *Polish White Book* (New York: Roy Publishers), pp. 170–72 ff.

Chapter 9. HITLER'S IMPACT ON SOVIET POLICY
(pp. 64–70)

1. *Documents on Soviet Foreign Policy*, III, 122.

2. Hilger and Meyer, *The Incompatible Allies*, p. 256.

3. *Documents on Soviet Foreign Policy*, III, 55–56.

4. Joseph Beck, *Dernier Rapport: Politique Polonaise 1926–1939* (Neuchâtel: Editions de la Baconnière, 1951), p. 36n; also speech in Seym (Lower House), February 1, 1935, in *Przemowienia, Deklaracje, Wywiady, 1931–1937* (Warsaw: Gebethner i Wolff, 1938), p. 152.

5. *Documents on Soviet Foreign Policy*, III, 80.

6. *Ibid.*, 82.

7. Cf. Frederick L. Schuman, *Europe on the Eve: The Crisis of Diplomacy 1933–1939* (New York and London: Alfred A. Knopf, 1939), p. 99.

8. Georg von Rauch, *A History of Soviet Russia* (New York: Frederick A. Praeger, 1957), p. 263.

9. The text of the treaty may be found in *LNTS*, CLIV, No. 3540 (1934), pp. 93 ff.

10. *Documents on Soviet Foreign Policy*, III, 85.

11. Alfred Bilmanis, *Baltic Essays* (Washington, D.C.: Latvian Legation, 1945), p. 165.

12. Hilger and Meyer, *op. cit.*, p. 278.

13. *Documents on Soviet Foreign Policy*, III, 98.

14. *Ibid.*, 103.

15. *Ibid.*, 126.

Chapter 10. The New Policy
(pp. 71–76)

1. The text may be found in the *Polish White Book*, pp. 20–21.

2. The text of the Soviet-Polish Protocol, signed in Moscow on May 5, 1934, may be found in the *Polish White Book*, pp. 179–80; also in *Documents on Polish-Soviet Relations, 1939–1945* (London: Heinemann, 1961), I, 21–22.

3. *Documents on Soviet Foreign Policy*, III, 74.

4. The text of treaty with France of May 2, 1935, may be found in *LNTS*, CLXVII, No. 3881 (1936), pp. 395 ff.; of treaty with Czechoslovakia of May 16, 1935, *ibid.*, CLIX, No. 3677 (1935), pp. 347 ff.

5. *Documents on Soviet Foreign Policy*, III, 127.

6. Stalin, "The Party Before and After the Seizure of Power," *Sochineniya* (1947 ed.), V, 111.

Chapter 11. Spain
(pp. 77–78)

1. Salvador de Madariaga, *Spain: A Modern History* (New York: Frederick A. Praeger, 1958), p. 512.

2. *Documents on Soviet Foreign Policy*, III, 230 ff.

3. Madariaga, *op. cit.*, p. 483.

4. David Cattell, *Soviet Diplomacy and the Spanish Civil War* (Berkeley: University of California Press, 1957), p. 128.

Chapter 12. Hand in Hand with Hitler
(pp. 79–95)

1. U.S. Department of State, *Nazi-Soviet Relations, 1939–1941* (Washington, D.C.: Government Printing Office, 1948), p. 249.

2. Galeazzo Ciano, *The Ciano Diaries, 1939–1943* (Garden City, N.Y.: Doubleday and Company, 1946), p. 119.

3. Molotov speech of November 6, 1938, in *Documents on Soviet Foreign Policy*, III, 309.

4. Stalin, "Report to the Eighteenth Congress," *ibid.*, 315 ff.

5. *Nazi-Soviet Relations*, p. 76.

6. *Documents on Soviet Foreign Policy*, III, 324.

7. *Ibid.*, 328.

8. Peter Kleist, *Zwischen Hitler and Stalin, 1939–1945: Aufzeichnungen* (Bonn: Atheneum Verlag, 1950), pp. 28–29.

9. Kurt Assmann, *Deutsche Schicksalsjahre* (Wiesbaden: E. Brockhaus, 1950), pp. 93–94.

10. *Nazi-Soviet Relations*, p. 2.

11. Grigory Gafencu, *The Last Days of Europe* (New Haven, Conn.: Yale University Press, 1948), p. 146.

12. Robert Coulondre, Dispatch to Foreign Minister Georges Bonnet, in *Le livre jaune français: Documents diplomatiques 1938–1939* (Paris: Ministère des Affaires étrangères, 1939), p. 165.

13. *Nazi-Soviet Relations*, p. 6.

14. *Ibid.*, p. 7.

15. *Ibid.*, p. 15.

16. Georges E. Bonnet, *Fin d'une Europe* (Geneva: Les éditions du cheval ailé, 1948), p. 177.

17. Winston S. Churchill, *The Gathering Storm* (Boston: Houghton Mifflin Company, 1948), p. 362.

18. *Documents on British Foreign Policy*, Series 3, V, 222.

19. Churchill, *op. cit.*, p. 369.

20. *Documents on British Foreign Policy*, Series 3, V, 668.

21. *Ibid.*, 711.

22. *Ibid.*, 744.

23. Potiemkine, *Histoire de la Diplomatie*, III, 707.

24. *Documents on British Foreign Policy*, Series 3, VI, 89, 119.

25. *Ibid.*, 280. In a previous communication to the Ambassador, on June 21, Lord Halifax had stated that his government was prepared to give a general guarantee for the whole of Europe, as "we do not want to delay agreement on account of hypothetical cases which can never arise." (*Ibid.*, 128–29.)

26. *Documents on British Foreign Policy*, Series 3, VI, 422.

27. *Nazi-Soviet Relations*, p. 42n.

28. *Ibid.*, p. 9.

29. *Ibid.*, p. 21.

30. *Ibid.*, pp. 26–28.

31. *Ibid.*, pp. 38–39.

32. *Ibid.*, pp. 44–46.

33. *Documents on British Foreign Policy*, Series 3, VII, 4–5.

34. Churchill, *op. cit.*, p. 380.

35. Quoted by Bonnet, *op. cit.*, p. 281.

36. *Nazi-Soviet Relations*, pp. 71–72.

37. *Ibid.*, p. 75.

38. Bonnet, *op. cit.*, p. 291.

39. *Documents on British Foreign Policy*, Series 3, VII, 237.

40. Potiemkine, *op. cit.*, III, 711, 712.

41. *Ibid.*, 15.

42. *Nazi-Soviet Relations*, pp. 339–41.

43. Khrushchev's speech on Stalin, February 24–25, 1956, as released by U.S. Department of State, NYT, June 5, 1956.

44. Cf. Wladyslaw Anders, *Hitler's Defeat in Russia* (Chicago: Henry Regnery Company, 1953), p. 39.

Chapter 13. WAR AIMS
(pp. 99–137)

1. *Nazi-Soviet Relations*, p. 355.
2. Grégoire Gafenco, *Les préliminaires de la guerre à l'est* (Fribourg: Editions de la Librairie de l'Université), p. 247; also quoted by Churchill, in *The Grand Alliance* (Boston: Houghton Mifflin Company, 1950), p. 367, without indication of source.
3. Churchill, *op. cit.*, pp. 371–72.
4. Quoted by John A. Lukacs, *The Great Powers and Eastern Europe* (New York: American Book Company, 1953), p. 799.
5. Arthur Bryant, *Triumph in the West* (Garden City, N.Y.: Doubleday and Company, 1959), p. 108.
6. Stalin, *War Speeches: Orders of the Day and Answers to Foreign Press Correspondents During the Great Patriotic War, July 3, 1941–June 22, 1945* (London and New York: Hutchinson & Company, 1946), p. 139.
7. *Correspondence Between the Chairman of the Council of Ministers of the U.S.S.R. and the President of the U.S.A. and the Prime Minister of Great Britain During the Great Patriotic War of 1941–1945* (Moscow: Foreign Languages Publishing House, 1957), I, 21.
8. *Ibid.*, 24.
9. *Ibid.*, 13.
10. Churchill, *Closing the Ring* (Boston: Houghton Mifflin Company, 1951), p. 355.
11. *Ibid.*, p. 381.
12. W. H. McNeill, *America, Britain, and Russia* (London and New York: Oxford University Press, 1953), pp. 422, 495.
13. Churchill, *Closing the Ring*, p. 345.
14. *Foreign Relations of the U.S., Diplomatic Papers, The Conferences at Cairo and Tehran, 1943*, p. 493; cf. Robert E. Sherwood, *Roosevelt and Hopkins* (New York: Harper & Brothers, 1948), p. 780.
15. Churchill, *The Grand Alliance*, p. 380.
16. Sherwood, *op. cit.*, p. 341.
17. Churchill, *The Grand Alliance*, p. 395.
18. *Ibid.*, p. 457.
19. The text appears in *Documents on Polish-Soviet Relations, 1939–1945*, I, 259 (London: Sikorski Institute); also *Polish-Soviet Relations, 1918–1943* (Washington, D.C.: Polish Embassy), pp. 167–68.
20. Churchill, *Closing the Ring*, p. 362.
21. Churchill, *The Hinge of Fate* (Boston: Houghton Mifflin Company, 1950), p. 332.
22. *Ibid.*, p. 569.
23. Churchill, *The Grand Alliance*, p. 468.
24. Cordell Hull, *Memoirs* (New York: The Macmillan Company, 1948), II, 1247.
25. *Correspondence During the Great Patriotic War*, I, 72.
26. *Ibid.*, II, 37–38.
27. *Ibid.*, I, 105–6; II, 59.
28. Sherwood, *op. cit.*, p. 565.
29. *Correspondence During the Great Patriotic War*, II, 43–44.

30. *Ibid.*, 142.
31. Hull, *op. cit.*, II, 1266.
32. Churchill, *Closing the Ring*, pp. 293–94.
33. *Ibid.*, p. 288.
34. *Documents on American Foreign Relations*, 1943–1944, VI, 230.
35. *Correspondence During the Great Patriotic War*, II, 99.
36. Hull, *op. cit.*, II, 1309.
37. Churchill, *Closing the Ring*, p. 291.
38. *Ibid.*, p. 318.
39. Sherwood, *op. cit.*, p. 776.
40. Bryant, *op. cit.*, p. 63.
41. *The Conferences at Cairo and Tehran*, p. 510.
42. Churchill, *Closing the Ring*, p. 395.
43. *The Katyn Forest Massacre*, Final Report (H.R. Report No. 2505) of the Select Committee on the Katyn Forest Massacre, 82d Cong., 2d sess. (Washington, D.C.: Government Printing Office, 1952), *passim*.
44. Churchill, *Closing the Ring*, p. 395; cf. *The Conferences at Cairo and Tehran*, p. 599.
45. *Correspondence During the Great Patriotic War*, I, 196.
46. Sherwood, *op. cit.*, p. 778.
47. *Ibid.*, p. 793.
48. *Correspondence During the Great Patriotic War*, I, 207.
49. *Ibid.*, 211–13.
50. *Ibid.*, 249.
51. Hull, *op. cit.*, II, 1445.
52. McNeill, *op. cit.*, p. 433.
53. *Polish Documents Report*, H.R. Select Committee on Communist Aggression, 83d Cong., 2d sess. (Washington, D.C.: Government Printing Office, 1955), pp. 115–24; cf. Edward J. Rozek, *Allied Wartime Diplomacy: A Pattern in Poland* (New York: John Wiley & Sons, 1957), pp. 273–75.
54. *Correspondence During the Great Patriotic War*, II, 163.
55. Churchill, *Triumph and Tragedy* (Boston: Houghton Mifflin Company, 1953), p. 238.
56. *The Conferences at Malta and Yalta*, 1945 (Washington, D.C.: Government Printing Office, 1961), p. 972.
57. James Byrnes, *Speaking Frankly* (New York: Harper & Brothers, 1947), p. 25.
58. Sherwood, *op. cit.*, p. 860.
59. Byrnes, *op. cit.*, pp. 29–30; cf. *The Conferences at Yalta and Malta*, 1945, pp. 586, 595; Edward R. Stettinius, Jr., *Roosevelt and the Russians: The Yalta Conference* (Garden City, N.Y.: Doubleday & Company, 1949), pp. 154–55.
60. *The Conferences at Malta and Yalta*, 1945, pp. 973–74.
61. *Ibid.*, p. 979.
62. Cf. *The Strategy and Tactics of World Communism*, Supplement III, "Communism in China," pp. 27–30.
63. Sherwood, *op. cit.*, p. 902.
64. *The Conferences at Malta and Yalta*, 1945, p. 984.
65. Sherwood, *op. cit.*, p. 870.
66. *Polish Documents Report* (Washington, D.C.: Government Printing Office, 1955), pp. 163–64; *Poland and Great Britain Before and After the Crimea Conference* (London, 1945), p. 13.

67. McNeill, *op. cit.*, p. 563.
68. *Correspondence During the Great Patriotic War*, II, 198–213.
69. Byrnes, *op. cit.*, p. 58.
70. Harry S. Truman, *Memoirs* (Garden City, N.Y.: Doubleday and Company, 1958), I, 71.
71. Churchill, *Triumph and Tragedy*, p. 636.
72. For a report on the Hopkins-Stalin talks, see Sherwood, *op. cit.*, pp. 887–912.
73. *The Conference of Berlin (Potsdam Conference), 1945* (Washington, D.C.: Government Printing Office, 1961), II, 362.
74. Churchill, *Triumph and Tragedy*, p. 636.
75. *The Conference of Berlin*, II, 1588.

Chapter 14. THE TAKEOVERS
(pp. 138–67)

1. *Communist Takeover and Occupation of the Ukraine*, Special Report No. 4 of the Select Committee on Communist Aggression, H.R., 83d Cong., 2d sess. (Washington, D.C.: Government Printing Office, 1954), p. 8.
2. *Ukrainian Peace Treaty* (Washington, D.C.: Department of State, 1918), p. 9.
3. The text of the Polish-Ukrainian Treaty may be found in the Archives of the Josef Pilsudski Historical Institute of America.
4. *Communist Takeover and Occupation of Byelorussia*, Special Report No. 9, p. 7.
5. *Communist Takeover and Occupation of Georgia*, Special Report No. 6, p. 4.
6. For the text of the treaty, see *ibid.*, p. 8; cf. *Sbornik deistvuiushchikh dogovorov, soglashenii i konventsii zakliuchennykh RSFSR s inostrannymi gosudartsvami* (Moscow: Narodnyi Komissariat po inostrannym delam, 1921–23), Part 1, p. 27.
7. *Communist Takeover and Occupation of Georgia*, p. 11.
8. Lenin, "The Aims of the Revolution," *SW*, VI, 243.
9. Quoted from *Bulletin d'information de l'Azerbaïdjan*, No. 10 (March 1, 1920), in F. Kazamzadeh, *The Struggle for Transcaucasia 1917–1921* (New York: Philosophical Library, 1951), p. 279.
10. *Polish-Soviet Relations, 1918–1943, Documents* (New York: Polish Information Center, 1943), p. 23.
11. *Polish-Soviet Relations, 1918–1943* (Washington, D.C.: Polish Embassy), pp. 95–96; cf. "Final Report of the Polish Ambassador," *Documents on Polish-Soviet Relations, 1939–1945*, pp. 71 ff.
12. *Nazi-Soviet Relations*, p. 95.
13. Communist Takeover and Occupation of Poland, Special Report No. 1, p. 11; cf. Bronislaw Kusnierz (ed.), *Stalin and the Poles* (London: Hollis & Carter, 1949), chap. II, *passim*; Zdzislaw Stahl, *Polish Affairs* (London), No. 11–12 (December, 1963).
14. For texts of both agreements, see *Polish Documents Report*, Appendix to *Communist Takeover and Occupation of Poland*, pp. 6–7, 8–9; cf. *Documents on Polish-Soviet Relations*, pp. 141–42, 147–48.
15. *Stalin and the Poles*, pp. 152–53; cf. Wladyslaw Anders, *An Army in Exile* (London: Macmillan & Co., 1949), pp. 101–24.
16. *Dziennik Ustaw Polskiej Rzeczypospolitej Ludowej* (Warsaw), No. 35, April 26, 1947.

17. The text may be found in *Pravda*, December 18, 1956; *NYT*, December 18, 1956.

18. *Trybuna Ludu*, May 11, 1958.

19. Peace Treaty with Estonia, February 2, 1920, in *LNTS*, XI, No. 289 (1922), pp. 30 ff.

20. *Izvestia*, December 25, 1918. Quoted in *Communist Takeover and Occupation of Lithuania*, Special Report No. 14, p. 5.

21. *Ibid.*, p. 4.

22. *Nazi-Soviet Relations*, p. 107.

23. *Communist Takeover and Occupation of Lithuania*, p. 10.

24. *Communist Takeover and Occupation of Latvia*, Special Report No. 12, p. 7.

25. *Izvestia*, January 28, 1920. Quoted in *Communist Takeover and Occupation of Estonia*, Special Report No. 3, p. 3.

26. Testimony of A. Rei, Estonian Minister in Moscow, *ibid.*, p. 9.

27. *The Finnish Blue Book* (Philadelphia: Ministry of Foreign Affairs of Finland, 1940), p. 7.

28. The text may be found in *LNTS*, III, No. 1 (1921), pp. 6 ff.

29. League of Nations, *Official Journal*, XX (1939), p. 508.

30. Text in "The U.S.S.R. and Finland," *Soviet Russia Today* (New York, 1939), pp. 61–64.

31. *Ibid.*, p. 57.

32. Allied and Associated Powers, *Treaty of Peace with Finland*, in *Allied Peace Treaties*, 1947.

33. Robert J. Kerner (ed.), *Czechoslovakia* (Berkeley: University of California Press, 1949), p. 357.

34. McNeill, *America, Britain, and Russia*, p. 608.

35. *Communist Takeover and Occupation of Czechoslovakia*, Special Report No. 8, p. 15.

36. *Ibid.*, p. 23.

37. *Ibid.*

38. A. Kaas and F. Lazarovics, *Bolshevism in Hungary* (London, 1931), Appendix 5, pp. 324–26.

39. *Izvestia*, March 26, 1919. Quoted by Frederick L. Schuman, *Soviet Politics at Home and Abroad*, p. 172.

40. John Flourney Montgomery, *Hungary, the Unwilling Satellite* (New York: The Devin-Adair Company, 1947), p. 138. (The author is a former American Minister in Hungary.)

41. Cf. "Swiss Legation Report on the Soviet Invasion of Hungary," in Montgomery, *op. cit.*, pp. 239–45.

42. Allied and Associated Powers, *Treaties 1947*, *Treaty of Peace with Hungary*.

43. Radio Moscow, as reported in *NYT*, October 31, 1956.

44. Radio Free Kossuth, November 4, 04:20, in *The Revolt in Hungary, a Documentary Chronology of Events* (New York: Free Europe Committee, 1957), p. 82.

45. *Ibid.*, p. 83.

46. United Nations General Assembly, Res. 1131 (XI).

47. Cf. *Report of the Special Committee on the Problem of Hungary*, Official Records, United Nations General Assembly, Eleventh Session, Supplement No. 18 A/3592, p. 120.

48. *Ibid.*, p. 60.

49. *Ibid.*, p. 137.
50. *Nazi-Soviet Relations*, p. 155.
51. *Communist Takeover and Occupation of Rumania*, Special Report No. 11, pp. 5–6.
52. For figures of elections, see Henri Prost, *Le Destin de la Romanie* (Paris, 1954), pp. 188–215.
53. *Nazi-Soviet Relations*, p. 161.
54. *Ibid.*, p. 259.

Chapter 15. NEITHER WAR NOR PEACE
(pp. 171–205)

1. Abram Bergson, James Horton Blackman, and Alexander Erlich, "Postwar Economic Reconstruction and Development in the U.S.S.R.," *Annals of the American Academy of Political Science*, May, 1949, p. 53.
2. Cf. Anders, *Hitler's Defeat in Russia*, pp. 173 ff.; George Fischer, *Soviet Opposition to Stalin* (Cambridge, Mass.: Harvard University Press, 1952), pp. 45, 97, *passim.*
3. *Correspondence During the Great Patriotic War*, II, 266–68.
4. Lenin, "Left Wing Communism, an Infantile Disorder," *SW*, X, 140.
5. *Izvestia*, January 27, 1949.
6. *Documents on Germany, 1944–1959* (Washington, D.C.: Government Printing Office, 1959), p. 54.
7. *Ibid.*, p. 55.
8. Margaret Carlyle (ed.), *Documents on International Affairs, 1947–48* (London and New York: Oxford University Press, 1952), pp. 125–35.
9. *The Truth about Western Policy on the German Question* (Ministries of Foreign Affairs of the U.S.S.R. and the German Democratic Republic, 1959), p. 49.
10. *Ibid.*
11. Dean Acheson, *Sketches from Life of Men I Have Known* (New York: Harper & Brothers), p. 14.
12. *The Austrian State Treaty* (Washington, D.C.: Department of State, 1957), p. 94.
13. *Ibid.*, p. 47.
14. *Ibid.*, p. 77.
15. Churchill, *Triumph and Tragedy*, p. 285.
16. *Documents Regarding the Situation in Greece* (London: H. M. Stationery Office, 1945), Cmd. 6592.
17. *What We Saw in Greece* (London: Trade Union Council, 1945).
18. *Ibid.*
19. Churchill, *op. cit.*, p. 293.
20. Margaret Carlyle (ed.), "The Markos Letter," in *Documents on International Affairs, 1947–48* (London: Oxford University Press), pp. 318–20.
21. *Ibid.*
22. United Nations General Assembly, Third Session, Document A/574.
23. *Sbornik d.d.*, Part II, p. 73.
24. Department of State, *The Problem of the Turkish Straits* (Washington, D.C.: Government Printing Office, 1947), p. 49.
25. *Keesing*, 1953, p. 13101.
26. *Ibid.*, 1957, p. 15811.
27. Department of State *Bulletin*, XXXVII, No. 958 (October 16, 1957), 712.

28. Khrushchev speech, *NYT*, November 1, 1959; *Pravda*, same date.
29. *Keesing*, 1960, p. 17429; *Pravda*, May 14, 1960.
30. The text may be found in *Sbornik d.d.*, 1921, Part II, p. 36; *LNTS*, IX, No. 268 (1922), pp. 384 ff.
31. *White Paper: Persia No. 1* (1942) (London: H. M. Stationery Office, 1942).
32. *Documents on American Foreign Relations*, 1945–1946 (Princeton, N.J.: Princeton University Press, 1948), p. 858.
33. *Sbornik d.d.*, Part II, pp. 37–38; *LNTS*, IX, No. 268 (1922), pp. 384 ff.
34. *Soviet News*, No. 4006 (February 13, 1959).
35. Walter Lippmann, *New York Herald Tribune*, April 18, 1961.
36. *The Times* (London), November 12, 1956.
37. *Keesing*, 1956, p. 15218; *Pravda*, November 6, 1956.
38. *The Times*, September 12, 1956.
39. AP dispatch from Cairo, *NYT*, March 25, 1956.
40. *Economic Development in the Middle East*, 1958–1959, Supplement to *U.N. World Economic Survey*, 1959, pp. 93, 99.
41. Department of State, *Report to Congress on Mutual Security Program for Second Half of Fiscal Year 1959* (Washington, D.C.: Government Printing Office, 1960). Quoted by *Middle Eastern Affairs*, XI, No. 6–7, 208.
42. *Soviet News*, No. 3840 (May 19, 1958).
43. *Keesing*, 1959, p. 16794.
44. Roscoe Drummond, *New York Herald Tribune*, June 6, 1962.
45. *Current Digest of Soviet Press*, XIII, No. 7, 22–23. (The original Russian text appeared in *Trud*, January 6, 1961.)
46. Cf. Robert F. Zeidner, *Middle Eastern Affairs*, X, No. 1 (January 28, 1959).
47. *White Paper: Korea No. 1* (1950) (London: H. M. Stationery Office), p. 4.
48. Peter Calvocoressi, *Survey of International Affairs*, 1949–1950 (London: Oxford University Press, 1953), p. 479.
49. *Documents on American Foreign Relations*, 1950 (Princeton, N.J.: Princeton University Press, 1951), XII, 441.
50. *Current Digest of Soviet Press*, II, No. 23, p. ii. (The original Russian text appeared in *Pravda*, June 29, 1950.)
51. Calvocoressi, *op. cit.*, p. 473.
52. *Documents on American Foreign Relations*, 1950, XII, 442.
53. *Ibid.*, 1951, pp. 451–52.
54. Statement of Secretary of State John F. Dulles, July 26, 1953, quoted in Department of State *Bulletin*, XXIX, No. 763 (August 3, 1953).

Chapter 16. Summit Diplomacy
(pp. 206–39)

1. Stalin, *Economic Problems of Socialism in the U.S.S.R.* (New York: International Publishers, 1952), p. 30.
2. Bulganin speech, in *Documents Relating to the Meeting of the Heads of Government of France, the United Kingdom, the Soviet Union, and the United States, Geneva, July 18–23, 1955* (London: H. M. Stationery Office, 1955), pp. 18–25.
3. The text appears in *The Geneva Meeting of Foreign Ministers, October*

27–*November 16, 1955* (Washington, D.C.; Department of State, 1955), pp. 12–13.

4. *Keesing*, 1955, p. 14450; *Pravda*, October 2, 1955.

5. NYT, October 12, 1955.

6. *Documents on Disarmament, 1945–1959* (Washington, D.C.: Department of State, 1960–63), I, 496.

7. *Documents on American Foreign Relations, 1955* (New York: Harper & Brothers, 1956), pp. 311 ff.

8. The text appears in *Keesing*, 1955, p. 14451; *Pravda*, September 21, 1955.

9. *Geneva Meeting of Foreign Ministers*, p. 305.

10. *Ibid.*, p. 146.

11. *Documents on Disarmament*, I, 547.

12. *Geneva Meeting of Foreign Ministers*, p. 193.

13. *Ibid.*, p. 301.

14. *Ibid.*, p. 235.

15. *Ibid.*, p. 147.

16. *Ibid.*, p. 261.

17. *Ibid.*, pp. 5–6.

18. Joseph Harsch, *Christian Science Monitor*, November 19, 1955.

19. NYT, December 30, 1955; *Pravda*, same date.

20. *Keesing*, 1956, p. 14833; *Pravda*, April 9, 1956.

21. Drew Middleton, NYT, April 24, 1956.

22. *Ibid.*

23. *The Times* (London), May 1, 1956.

24. The text is found in *Keesing*, 1956, p. 14835.

25. NYT, April 28, 1956.

26. *Ibid.*

27. The text of the draft treaty is found in *Background of Heads of Government Conference, 1960* (Washington, D.C.: Department of State, 1960), pp. 61–62.

28. *Ibid.*, p. 63.

29. Bulganin to Eisenhower, *Keesing*, 1956, p. 15217; *Pravda*, November 6, 1956.

30. *Documents on American Foreign Relations, 1958* (New York: Harper & Brothers, 1959), p. 107.

31. *Soviet News*, No. 3891 (August 6, 1958).

32. *Pravda*, August 6, 1958; *Keesing*, 1958, p. 16346.

33. *Keesing*, 1958, p. 16473.

34. *Documents on Germany, 1944–1959*, pp. 308 ff.; cf. *The Soviet Note on Berlin, an Analysis* (Washington, D.C.: Department of State, 1959), *passim.*

35. Text of Draft Peace Treaty appears in *Documents on Germany, 1944–1959*, pp. 358 ff.

36. *Keesing*, 1959, p. 16947.

37. Cf. William Sargant, Department of Psychological Medicine, St. Thomas' Hospital, in a letter to the Editor of the London *Times*, May 18, 1960.

38. *Keesing*, 1959, p. 16711; *Pravda*, February 18, 1959.

39. *Soviet News*, No. 4018 (March 6, 1959).

40. NYT, May 17, 1959.

41. Joseph Alsop, *New York Herald Tribune*, July 2, 1959.

42. *Life*, July 13, 1959.

43. *Pravda*, July 30, 1959.

44. *Pravda*, June 7, 1959; *Keesing*, 1959, p. 16923.

45. *Soviet News*, No. 4091 (August 7, 1959).

46. Khrushchev, speaking at the National Press Club, NYT, September 17, 1959; meeting with labor leaders, NYT, September 22, 1959; for Soviet version, cf. Thomas P. Whitney, ed., *Khrushchev Speaks* (Ann Arbor, Mich.: The University of Michigan Press, 1963), pp. 330–60.

47. NYT, September 22, 1959.

48. Speech by Khrushchev in U.N. General Assembly, September 18, 1959, *Soviet News*, No. 4115 (September 21, 1959).

49. The text may be found in *Documents on American Foreign Relations*, 1959, pp. 193–94.

50. *Soviet News*, No. 4270 (May 17, 1960).

51. NYT, May 10, 1960; *Pravda*, same date.

52. NYT, April 26, 1960; *Pravda*, same date.

53. NYT, May 6, 1960; *Pravda*, same date.

54. *The Times* (London), May 5, 1960.

55. *Soviet News*, No. 4269 (May 16, 1960).

56. *Le Monde*, May 20, 1960; *NYT*, same date; *Soviet News*, No. 4272 (May 19, 1960); tape recordings broadcast by American radio stations.

57. *Soviet News*, No. 4270 (May 17, 1960).

58. *Ibid.*, No. 4274 (May 23, 1960).

59. NYT, July 13, 1960; *Pravda*, same date.

60. Department of State *Bulletin*, XLIII, No. 1101 (August 1, 1960), 1630.

61. *Keesing*, 1960, p. 17927.

62. According to David Wise, *New York Herald Tribune*, March 13 and 14, 1961, Walt W. Rostow and Jerome B. Wiesner, while in Moscow to attend the Sixth Annual Pugwash Conference of Scientists and Scholars, had important though unofficial political talks between November 27 and December 7, 1960, with Vasily Kuznetsov, First Deputy Foreign Minister; cf. AP dispatch in *NYT*, March 13, 1961.

63. NYT, March 24, 1961.

64. Joseph Alsop, *New York Herald Tribune*, March 29, 1961.

65. The text is found in the Department of State *Bulletin*, XLIV, No. 1148 (June 26, 1961), 999.

66. *Soviet News*, No. 4479 (June 13, 1961).

67. *Ibid.*, No. 4483 (June 17, 1961).

68. Department of State *Bulletin*, XLIV, No. 1148 (June 26, 1961), 994.

69. *Soviet News*, No. 4483 (June 17, 1961).

Chapter 17. DISARMAMENT
(pp. 240–62)

1. Khrushchev talk with Randolph Hearst, Jr., *Pravda*, November 29, 1957; cf. slightly different version published by Bob Considine in *New York Journal-American*, November 25, 1957.

2. The text is found in *Documents on Disarmament*, 1945–1959, II, 1460–1474.

3. M. M. Litvinov, "Report to Central Executive Committee, April 21, 1928," *Soviet Foreign Policy Documents*, II, 303–13.

4. *Ibid.*, I, 352–53.

5. Litvinov, *ibid.*, III, 143.

6. Speech by President John F. Kennedy, quoted in Department of State *Bulletin*, XLVI, No. 1186 (March 19, 1962), 445.

7. The text is found in *Documents on Disarmament, 1945–1959*, I, 7–16, 25–42.

8. *Ibid.*, 71.

9. *Ibid.*, 66–67, 69.

10. *Defence in the Cold War* (London and New York: Royal Institute of International Affairs, 1950), p. 66.

11. *Pravda*, January 15, 1960.

12. *Documents on Disarmament, 1945–1959*, I, 487.

13. *Pravda*, June 4, 1960.

14. *Documents on Geneva Foreign Ministers Meeting*, p. 130.

15. *Documents on Disarmament, 1945–1959*, I, 422.

16. *Ibid.*, 548.

17. *Ibid.*, 607.

18. *Ibid.*, 700.

19. *Ibid.*, II, 1467.

20. *Documents on Disarmament, 1960*, p. 133.

21. *Ibid.*, p. 193.

22. *Keesing*, 1960, p. 17602.

23. *Le Monde*, June 29, 1960. (The French term used by M. Jules Moch was "*voyoucratie.*")

24. *Documents on Disarmament, 1945–1959*, II, 983.

25. *Ibid.*, 1169.

26. *Ibid.*, 1441.

27. *Keesing*, 1961, pp. 18323–25; *Pravda*, August 31, 1961.

28. *Documents on American Foreign Policy, 1962*, p. 125.

29. *Keesing*, 1963, p. 19557.

30. *Ibid.*

31. *Pravda*, July 3, 1963; *Soviet News*, No. 4867 (July 3, 1963).

32. *Keesing*, 1963, p. 19530.

33. The text is found in Department of State *Bulletin*, XLIX, No. 1259 (August 12, 1963).

34. *Ibid.*, No. 1261 (August 26, 1963).

35. Emerson Chapin, NYT, October 29, 1963.

36. Radio Moscow, August 25, 1963.

37. Andrei Gromyko in U.N. General Assembly, *Pravda*, September 20, 1963.

38. Radio Moscow, August 25, 1963.

39. Khrushchev conversation with American businessmen, *Le Monde*, October 8, 1963.

40. William Blair, NYT, October 8, 1963; Raymond Daniel, *ibid.*, September 14, 1963.

41. A. A. Berle, Jr., "Dialogue? Yes—Concessions? Beware!," NYT *Magazine*, October 20, 1963.

42. Ray Vicker, *Wall Street Journal*, November 7, 1963.

43. CIA analysis, NYT, January 8, 1964.

44. *Man, Land & Food*, Department of Agriculture, Foreign Agricultural Economic Report No. 11 (Washington, D.C.: November, 1963), pp. 82, 131.

Chapter 18. NEW WORLDS TO CONQUER
(pp. 263–96)

1. Lenin, "Draft Program of the Communist Party," *SW*, VIII, 334.
2. Agreement on the cessation of hostilities in Vietnam, *Documents on American Foreign Relations, 1954,* Annex I (New York: Harper & Brothers, 1955), p. 300.
3. UPI dispatch from Phompenh, *NYT*, November 13, 1963.
4. Gromyko's message to Prince Souvanna Phouma, May 6, 1963, *Soviet News*, No. 4844 (May 13, 1963).
5. *Trybuna Ludu,* May 29, 1963.
6. UPI dispatch from Vientiane, June 6, 1963.
7. According to Noel F. Busch ("Behind the Buddhist Unrest in Southeast Asia," *Reader's Digest,* December, 1963), there is reason to suspect that the Buddhist disturbances which led to the downfall of Diem's regime were exploited, if not partly engineered, by Communists.
8. Lenin, "Imperialism, the Highest Stage of Capitalism," *SW*, V, 88.
9. Lenin, "The Conditions of Affiliation to the Communist International," *SW*, X, 203.
10. *The Communist International, 1919–1943,* I, 399.
11. *Ibid.,* 400, 401.
12. *Ibid.,* II, 513.
13. George Padmore, *Pan-Africanism or Communism* (New York: Roy Publishers, 1956), p. 307.
14. *Ibid.,* p. 319.
15. *The Times* (London), January 12, 1961.
16. *Dimensions of Soviet Economic Power* (Washington, D.C.: Government Printing Office, 1962), p. 474.
17. *Keesing,* 1960, p. 17754; *Pravda,* July 31, 1960.
18. *Pravda,* July 16, 1960; *NYT,* same date.
19. *Keesing,* 1960, p. 17780; *Pravda,* August 21, 1960.
20. *Keesing,* 1961, p. 18421.
21. *Soviet News,* No. 4424 (February 16, 1961).
22. Marguerite Higgins, *New York Herald Tribune,* February 17, 1961.
23. *Soviet News,* No. 4945 (January 27, 1964).
24. *Ninth Interim Report of Hearings Before the Subcommittee on Latin America,* Select Committee on Communist Aggression, H. R. (Washington, D.C.: Government Printing Office, 1954), p. 120.
25. *Ibid.,* p. 198; cf. Eudocio Ravines, *The Yennan Way* (New York: Charles Scribner's Sons, 1951), pp. 148–59.
26. Fidel Castro speech of December 1–2, 1961; tape recording, archives of The Truth About Cuba Committee, Inc.
27. *NYT,* December 23, 1961.
28. AP dispatch from Havana, *NYT,* December 3, 1961.
29. *U.S.–Latin American Relations,* p. 798.
30. *Agriculture and Food Situation in Cuba,* Department of Agriculture, Economic Research Service, ERS-Foreign-28 (Washington, D.C., May, 1962), p. 2. (The reference is to the daily per-capita intake of 2,870 calories.)
31. *Keesing,* 1959, p. 16901.
32. *Current Digest of Soviet Press,* XI, No. 1, 30. (The original Russian text appeared in *Pravda,* January 3, 1959.)
33. *Ibid.,* XI, No. 15, 30–31.

34. Soviet-Cuban communiqué, *Pravda*, December 20, 1960.
35. *NYT*, July 10, 1960; *Pravda*, same date.
36. Seymour Topping, *NYT*, October 29 and 30, 1960.
37. *Keesing*, 1960, p. 17590; *Pravda*, July 13, 1960.
38. *Statements by the USSR Government on the Invasion of Cuba*, April 18, 1961, p. 9.
39. *Pravda*, July 10, 1960.
40. Department of State *Bulletin*, XLVL, No. 1190 (April 16, 1962), 644–46.
41. *Soviet News*, No. 4673 (May 14, 1962).
42. *Pravda*, September 3, 1962; *NYT*, same date.
43. Kennedy statement, *NYT*, September 5, 1962.
44. The text appears in *Soviet News*, No. 4738 (September 12, 1962).
45. Thomas Hamilton, *NYT*, October 15, 1962.
46. Kennedy speech of October 22, 1962, Department of State *Bulletin*, XLVII, No. 1220 (November 12, 1962).
47. Joseph Alsop, *New York Herald Tribune*, November 2, 1962.
48. Kennedy speech of October 22, 1962, *loc. cit.*
49. *Ibid.*
50. The text appears in *Soviet News*, No. 4757 (October 24, 1962).
51. Rowland Evans, Jr., *New York Herald Tribune*, November 11, 1962.
52. White House Statement of October 27, 1962, Department of State *Bulletin*, XLVII, No. 1220.
53. *Le Monde*, March 22, 1963.
54. Pierre J. Huss, *New York Journal-American*, November 19, 1962.
55. Kennedy press conference, *NYT*, November 21, 1962.
56. Senate Preparedness Subcommittee Report, *ibid.*, May 10, 1963.
57. *Soviet News*, No. 4783 (December 13, 1962), p. 164.
58. *Ibid.*, No. 4796 (January 17, 1963), p. 39.
59. "Open Letter of the CPSU to Party organizations, July 13, 1963," *ibid.*, No. 4872 (July 16, 1963).

Chapter 19. THE YUGOSLAV HERESY
(pp. 301–14)

1. Milovan Djilas, *Conversations with Stalin* (New York: Harcourt, Brace, and World, 1963).
2. *Borba* (Belgrade), August 3, 1947.
3. Djilas, *op. cit.*, p. 181.
4. Vladimir Dedijer, *Tito* (New York: Simon and Schuster, 1953), p. 371.
5. Tito speech, *Borba*, August 16, 1949.
6. *Borba*, December 28, 1949.
7. *Sluzebni list* (*Official Gazette*), No. 43 (July 5, 1950).
8. Ranko M. Braschich, *Land Reform and Ownership in Yugoslavia 1919–1935* (New York: Mid-European Studies Center, Free Europe Committee, 1954), pp. 83, 119.
9. *New Yugoslav Law*, No. 4 (1951), pp. 35 ff.
10. *White Book* (Belgrade: Ministry of Foreign Affairs, 1951).
11. Dedijer, *op. cit.*, pp. 428–29.
12. *Borba*, November 8, 1952.
13. George Sokolsky, *New York Journal-American*, November 6, 1962.
14. Dedijer, *op. cit.*, p. 432.

15. Cf. Bohdan Raditsa, "Tito's Secret Alliance with Moscow," *Freeman* (New York), January 11, 1954.

16. *Pravda* (Khrushchev statement made at Belgrade Airport, May 27, 1955).

17. Soviet-Yugoslav declaration, *Pravda*, June 3, 1955; cf. *NYT*, June 3, 1955.

18. *Borba*, June 12, 1956.

19. *NYT*, June 12, 1956.

20. Tito speech delivered at Pula, November 11, 1956, *Keesing*, 1956, p. 15258.

21. *Ibid.*, p. 15731.

22. *Soviet News*, No. 3721 (November 22, 1957).

23. Khrushchev speech at the Seventh Congress of the Bulgarian Communist Party, *Soviet News*, No. 3850 (June 4, 1958).

24. *Pravda*, May 11, 1958.

25. *World Marxist Review*, III, No. 12 (December, 1960).

26. *Soviet News*, No. 4749 (October 5, 1962).

27. *Ibid.*, No. 4784.

28. *Ibid.*

29. *Borba*, December 14, 1962.

Chapter 20. THE DISPUTE WITH CHINA
(pp. 315–38)

1. *Soviet News*, No. 4411 (January 24, 1961).

2. Khrushchev, *Report on the Program of the CPSU* (Moscow: Foreign Languages Publishing House, October 18, 1961), p. 127.

3. *Keesing*, 1958, p. 16352; *Pravda*, August 4, 1958.

4. *Peking Review*, No. 6 (February 9, 1960).

5. "Long Live Leninism," *Peking Review*, No. 17 (April 26, 1960). (The original text appeared in *Hongqi*.)

6. *Keesing*, 1959, p. 16830.

7. Cf. Note No. 5, supra.

8. "Statement of the Eighty-one Communist Parties," *World Marxist Review*, III, No. 12 (December, 1960).

9. Mao, "Tactics on Fighting Japanese Imperialism," *SW*, I, 173–74.

10. *History of the Communist Party of the Soviet Union (Bolsheviks), Short Course* (New York: International Publishers, 1939), pp. 167–68.

11. Mao, "Problems of China's Revolutionary War," *SW*, I, 179.

12. Dispatch from Agence France-Presse, *Le Monde*, October 24, 1961.

13. Dispatches from Agence France-Presse, published in *Le Monde*, October 25, 1961.

14. David Spaeth, *Communist China, A Crucial Period for Its Agricultural Economy*, Department of Agriculture, Economic Research Service, ERS-Foreign-31 (Washington, D.C., May, 1962).

15. *Pravda*, July 3, 1962; *NYT*, July 3, 1962.

16. *World Marxist Review*, V, No. 11 (November, 1962), 36–38.

17. *Soviet News*, No. 4783 (December 13, 1962).

18. *Current Background* (Hong Kong), No. 706 (March 7, 1963). (The original text appeared in *Hongqi*, March 4, 1963. The expression is borrowed from Lenin, *CW*, X, 353.)

19. *Current Background*, No. 702 (January 3, 1963). (The original text appeared in *Jenmin Jih Pao*, December 31, 1962.)

20. Ernest Ferguson reporting from Moscow, *Baltimore Sun,* February 16, 1963.

21. The texts appear in *Soviet News,* No. 4820 (March 14, 1963).

22. Abstract of Soviet letter, *ibid.,* No. 4828 (April 3, 1963).

23. Chinese Communist Party message reported by Hsinhua (New China News Agency), *Survey of China Mainland Press,* No. 3003 (June 20, 1963).

24. Chinese Government statement, July 31, 1963, *Peking Review,* No. 31 (August 2, 1963).

25. *Selections from China Mainland Magazines,* No. 383 (September 23, 1963). (The original text appeared in *Hongqi,* September 9, 1963.)

26. Chinese Government statement, July 31, 1963, *loc. cit.*

27. "The Origin and Development of the Differences Between the Leadership of the CPSU and Ourselves" (joint article by *Jenmin Jih Pao* and *Hongqi,* September 6, 1963), *Peking Review,* No. 37 (September 13, 1963). (The *Peking Review* transliterates *Jenmin Jih Pao* as *Renmin Ribao.*)

28. *Ibid.,* Appendixes.

29. "Long Live Leninism," *loc. cit.*; open letter of the CPSU, July 13, 1963, *Soviet News,* No. 4872 (July 16, 1963); Soviet Government statement, August 21, 1963, *ibid.,* No. 4885 (August 21, 1963); statement by Chinese Government spokesman, September 1, 1963, *Peking Review,* No. 36 (September 6, 1963); Soviet Government statement, September 21, 1963, *Soviet News,* Nos. 4897, 4898 (September 23 and 24, 1963).

30. Statement by Chinese Government spokesman, August 15, 1963, *Peking Review,* No. 33 (August 16, 1963).

31. "The Origin and Development of the Differences," *loc. cit.*

32. "A Comment on the Statement of the Communist Party of the United States of America," *Survey of China Mainland Press,* No. 2936 (March 12, 1963). (The original text appeared in *Hongqi,* September 9, 1963.)

33. *Ibid.*

34. Soviet Government statement, September 21, 1963, *Soviet News,* No. 4896 (September 23, 1963).

35. Chinese Communist Party message, *Survey of China Mainland Press,* No. 3003 (June 20, 1963).

36. *Ibid.*

37. "Is Yugoslavia a Communist Country?" (joint article by *Jenmin Jih Pao* and *Hongqi,* September 26, 1963), *Peking Review,* No. 39 (September 27, 1963).

38. *Selections from China Mainland Magazines,* No. 383 (September 23, 1963).

39. "Apologists of Neo-colonialism" (joint article by *Jenmin Jih Pao* and *Hongqi,* October 21, 1963), *Peking Review,* No. 43 (October 25, 1963).

40. *Ibid.,* September 6, 1963; cf. "The Origin and Development of the Differences," *loc. cit.*

41. *Kommunist,* No. 15 (October, 1963), p. 40.

INDEX